THE POETICS OF EARLY RUSSIAN CRIME FICT
DECIPHERING STORIES OF DETECTION

# LEGENDA

LEGENDA is the Modern Humanities Research Association's book imprint for new research in the Humanities. Founded in 1995 by Malcolm Bowie and others within the University of Oxford, Legenda has always been a collaborative publishing enterprise, directly governed by scholars. The Modern Humanities Research Association (MHRA) joined this collaboration in 1998, became half-owner in 2004, in partnership with Maney Publishing and then Routledge, and has since 2016 been sole owner. Titles range from medieval texts to contemporary cinema and form a widely comparative view of the modern humanities, including works on Arabic, Catalan, English, French, German, Greek, Italian, Portuguese, Russian, Spanish, and Yiddish literature. Editorial boards and committees of more than 60 leading academic specialists work in collaboration with bodies such as the Society for French Studies, the British Comparative Literature Association and the Association of Hispanists of Great Britain & Ireland.

The MHRA encourages and promotes advanced study and research in the field of the modern humanities, especially modern European languages and literature, including English, and also cinema. It aims to break down the barriers between scholars working in different disciplines and to maintain the unity of humanistic scholarship. The Association fulfils this purpose through the publication of journals, bibliographies, monographs, critical editions, and the MHRA Style Guide, and by making grants in support of research. Membership is open to all who work in the Humanities, whether independent or in a University post, and the participation of younger colleagues entering the field is especially welcomed.

# The Poetics of
# Early Russian Crime Fiction
## 1860-1917

*Deciphering Stories of Detection*

CLAIRE WHITEHEAD

## LEGENDA

Modern Humanities Research Association
2018

Published by Legenda
an imprint of the Modern Humanities Research Association
Salisbury House, Station Road, Cambridge CB1 2LA

ISBN 978-1-78188-687-8 (HB)
ISBN 978-1-78188-688-5 (PB)

First published 2018

Copy-Editor: Dr Nigel Hope

# CONTENTS

*For Bettina, and the criminal masterminds in our midst,*
*Martha and Jean.*
*With all my love.*

# ACKNOWLEDGEMENTS

This book has been a long time in the researching and writing and I owe a debt of gratitude to a great many people and several institutions. Many of the less well-known primary texts that form the basis of the discussion here were collected during a trip to the National Library of Russia in St Petersburg in 2009 that was kindly funded by the Carnegie Trust for the Universities of Scotland. Other primary and secondary sources were retrieved by my colleagues in the Interlibrary Loans Department at the University of St Andrews, particularly Ian Martin. After years of research, much of this monograph was written during a period of leave made possible by the award of a Research Fellowship for the year 2015–16 by the Leverhulme Trust, to whom I am especially grateful. Other writing and revisions took place during institutional research leave kindly granted by the University of St Andrews.

Whilst academic research can sometimes, by its nature, be an isolating experience, I could not have written this book without the various invaluable interactions I have had with people over the years of its production. It has been a real pleasure to bring my research into the classroom at St Andrews, and I would like to thank the undergraduates who have been such enthusiastic and critical students on the course I have taught on 'Russian Crime Fiction' since 2011. They have allowed me to test out some of the ideas contained here and provided countless moments of inspiration. I was fortunate enough to spend one month as a visiting researcher at the Uppsala Centre for Russian Studies (now IRES, the Institute for Russian and Eurasian Studies) in autumn 2011 and colleagues there, especially Julie Hansen and Elena Namli, provided a stimulating intellectual atmosphere in which to think through various aspects of my research. Much closer to home, my colleagues, past and present, in the Department of Russian and the School of Modern Languages at the University of St Andrews have provided practical help, advice and criticism over a long period. My thanks go to Emily Finer, Roger Keys, Boris Dralyuk, Margarita Vaysman, Victoria Donovan, Katie Holt, Jesse Gardiner, Svetlana Booth, Lorna Milne, Margaret-Anne Hutton, Will Fowler, Derek Duncan and the late, and still much missed, Oliver Smith. I am indebted to Philip Bullock, Katherine Hodgson and Julie Hansen for their academic support and friendship over the period of this research. At Legenda, I would like to thank both Graham Nelson and Nigel Hope for their help and guidance. I would also like to thank the anonymous reader of the draft manuscript of this study for the insightful and constructive feedback that helped me to make this a much better book. And I am so grateful to my friend and former colleague, Carol Adlam, for the wonderful image that graces its front cover.

This book is for my wife, Bettina Bildhauer, without whom it could not have been written, and for our daughters, Martha and Jean.

★   ★   ★   ★   ★

Sections of this monograph have appeared in a different form in some of my previous publications:

Some of the details regarding the socio-historical context for the development of Russian crime fiction that appear in the Introduction were previously published in my article 'Debating Detectives: The Influence of *publitsistika* on Nineteenth-Century Russian Crime Fiction', *Modern Language Review*, 107.1 (2012), 230–58.

Sections of the discussion of the manipulation of time in Shkliarevskii and Dostoevskii that feature in Chapter 4 have previously been published in 'Shkliarevskii and Russian Detective Fiction: The Influence of Dostoevskii', in *Dostoevskii: Influence, Comparison and Transposition*, ed. by Joe Andrew and Robert Reid (Amsterdam: Rodopi, 2013), pp. 101–21.

A short section of Chapter 5 previously appeared as part of my article 'The Letter of the Law: Literacy and Orality in S. A. Panov's *Murder in Medveditsa Village*', *Slavonic and East European Review*, 89.1 (2011), 1–28.

Finally, Chapter 6 contains a section of substantially revised material on Chekhov's 'Shvedskaia spichka' that was previously published in 'Playing at Detectives: Parody in *The Swedish Match*', *Essays in Poetics*, 30 (2005), 229–46.

c.w., St Andrews, July 2018

# NOTE ON TRANSLATION AND TRANSLITERATION

Translations in the text are my own, unless otherwise stated. The vast majority of primary texts referred to in this study have not yet been translated into English. Nevertheless, for ease of reference for readers who do not know Russian, in the main body of the text, the titles of primary texts are given in the original on a first mention but are thereafter referred to in English. In footnotes and the bibliography, references to these works are given in the original Russian.

In transliterating Cyrillic, I have used the Library of Congress System (without diacritics). The only exception to this practice is the decision to use the widely accepted form, Gogol, and not Gogol'.

# INTRODUCTION

This book offers an in-depth study of early Russian crime fiction, and the various examples of the genre published between 1860 and 1917 that have been largely ignored until now. Scores of such works were written during this period and proved to be extremely popular with Russian readers. And for good reason: many of these are highly entertaining and sophisticated works that offer much to both the casual and the academic reader. Like many contemporary readers, in spite of being a fan of British and American crime fiction from a young age, I knew next to nothing about Russian detective stories. This situation did not change during my undergraduate Russian degree when, although Fedor Dostoevskii's *Prestuplenie i nakazanie* (*Crime and Punishment*) (1866) of course figured on the curriculum, we were not encouraged to consider it in terms of the genre of crime fiction. My journey into the Russian genre therefore began much later with a conference paper on Anton Chekhov's 'Shvedskaia spichka: ugolovnyi rasskaz' ('The Swedish Match: A Judicial Story'), first published in 1883, and the question of whom, amongst contemporary Russian writers, he might have been parodying. This inquiry has led me to uncover and appreciate numerous works by various authors who have been largely forgotten. So, in part, what this book seeks to do is to raise the profile of these little-known writers and of their underrated works that have given me so much pleasure over the last decade and more. It does so by focusing in particular upon the various storytelling structures that they employ and the manner in which these poetic devices affect the reader's interpretation. Most specifically, this study is preoccupied with understanding the role that these devices play in modulating the reader's experience of genre, authority, knowledge and 'truth', such as it is presented in crime fiction.

The popularity of crime fiction in contemporary culture is a recognized global phenomenon, with crime novels and thrillers frequently featuring in bestseller lists the world over. The reasons for this success are many and varied. The author of the Rebus series, Ian Rankin, enumerates just a few of these in his review of a work by fellow crime writer Kate Summerscale:

> Readers may flock to crime stories for the element of game-playing or puzzle, but such novels (and a lot of true crime, too) tell us more. They delineate culture, comment on class and society, and ask their readers big questions about morality and human nature.[1]

The vogue of crime fiction is no different in Russia where, since the fall of the Soviet Union in 1991, detective novels, police procedurals and thrillers have often dominated the literary marketplace. Although, because of the advent of market forces, there has been a dramatic drop in the total number of books printed in the post-Soviet era, publishing houses have been able to count on works of crime fiction selling in their millions to generate a reliable source of revenue.[2] The genre's rise to prominence during this period began with the relaxation of censorship laws and the liberalization of commercial conditions that accompanied the policy of *glasnost'* in the late 1980s. This more open society initially permitted an influx of crime thrillers and detective stories from the West: writers such as John le Carré, Tom Clancy and Martin Cruz Smith became freely and officially available in Russian translation for the first time and found an avid readership.[3] Soon afterwards, such works were joined and then overtaken by indigenous production: during that nearly thirty-year period, Russian readers have consumed the crime novels written by authors such as Aleksandra Marinina, Polina Dashkova, Daria Dontsova and Boris Akunin in huge numbers, making each into a wealthy celebrity.[4] Reflecting on the situation in 2004, Olga Sobolev claimed that: 'it is not an overstatement to say that today detective stories are, in fact, the only literature that many Russians read'.[5] Although this post-Soviet taste for crime fiction has attracted a good deal of media coverage and some academic interest, most commentators seem intent upon presenting it as a unique late twentieth-century phenomenon that is dependent upon the particular historical circumstances pertaining after 1991.

Crucially, for the purposes of this book, there is little or no recognition, even in academic circles, of the fact that Russian crime fiction can trace its roots back to the second half of the nineteenth century. Making a possible exception for Dostoevskii's *Crime and Punishment*, whose status as a work of crime fiction is still somewhat contested, many readers and academics are surprised to hear that there were crime novels and detective stories written in Russia before the turn of the twentieth century. In fact, the existence of Russian crime fiction in any era has frequently been omitted from the various literary histories of the country, although this is not an oversight unique to Russia.[6] The Academy of Sciences' 1945–54 *Istoriia russkoi literatury (History of Russian Literature)* makes no mention of either authors or works of crime fiction.[7] In the West, meanwhile, neither Victor Terras's *Handbook of Russian Literature* nor Neil Cornwell's *Reference Guide to Russian Literature* includes an entry for either detective or crime fiction.[8] Even studies specifically devoted to post-Soviet Russian crime fiction demonstrate an ignorance of, or disregard for, the genre's longer-term history. In his 2001 study, *Russian Pulp*, Anthony Olcott briefly mentions the 'pinkertony' (translations or adaptations of works featuring Sherlock Holmes, Nick Carter or Nat Pinkerton) of the early 1900s, but focuses primarily on the Soviet pre-history and works published since the 1960s. Similarly, Olga Sobolev's article on Boris Akunin casts the net back only as far as the 1940s to mention Iurii German's *One Year* (1940) and Lev Sheinin's *Diary of a Criminologist* (1945).[9] Such critical neglect is not surprising given that the process of canon formation in most, if not all, national traditions did not allow for a recognition of 'lowbrow' crime fiction until at least the latter half of the twentieth century. In Russia, the dominant narrative about the quality and importance of the great realist works of the 1850s–1880s left little room to acknowledge other literary genres in the same period.

Indeed, this lack of attention paid to Russian crime fiction is exhibited as much by nineteenth-century literary critics as it is by later commentators. Even though a number of the early works of Russian crime fiction were serialized in the culturally influential and well-regarded 'thick' journals of the 1860s and 1870s, none of them, with the exception of *Crime and Punishment*, were ever reviewed there. Whilst an 1865 volume of the journal *Russkoe slovo* (*Russian Word*) carried a review of an important generic precursor, V. V. Krestovskii's 1864 physiological-ethnographic novel *Peterburgskie trushchoby* (*St Petersburg Slums*), and praised it as 'решительный шаг вперед' ('a decisive step forward'), later works of crime fiction were seemingly deemed insufficiently literary to warrant comment.[10] Critical neglect did not (and does not), however, equate with public unpopularity because, as research undertaken by Avram Reitblat has demonstrated, numerous works of crime fiction in the second half of the nineteenth century figured amongst the most-widely read publications of their given year.[11] These include N. M. Sokolovskii's *Ostrog i zhizn': iz zapisok sledovatelia* (*Prison and Life: From the Notes of an Investigator*) in 1866, *Crime and Punishment*, N. P. Timofeev's *Zapiski sledovatelia* (*Notes of an Investigator*) in 1872, and A. A. Shkliarevskii's *Sobranie sochinenii* (*Collected Works*) in 1881.

So, a detailed examination of Russian crime fiction in the late Imperial era provides a more accurate picture of the Russian literary landscape of the time and of the public's reading tastes. However, harking back to Rankin's remark cited above, the practice of Russian crime fiction during this period also has much to reveal about socio-historical and ideological concerns: it reflects recent changes in the country's judicial system and, to some extent, explains the new legal landscape to the reader; it embodies optimism for the future of post-reform Russia in the figure of the detective; it participates in contemporary debates about the motivation(s) behind crime and the question of individual or collective criminal and moral responsibility for crime; and it mirrors various aspects of the modernization occurring at the time in the spheres of social organization, science, technology, religion and ethics. From a more purely literary-textual point of view, examples of early Russian crime fiction provide a wonderfully informative demonstration of the games that can be played with its narratives and the effects that this manipulation can have upon the reader. Reading Russian crime fiction allows us, for instance, to understand the potential that inheres in various narratological devices for legitimizing literary acts; it permits insight into the processes used to construct matrices of authority that encourage or discourage trust in a certain version of narrative events; it exploits various techniques to control the reader's access to knowledge and to the solution to the mystery; and it showcases the various means by which texts can playfully interact with others both within and outside the genre.

Crime fiction first made an appearance in Russia at a somewhat later date than in certain other national traditions. In Great Britain, for instance, Thomas Gaspey's *Richmond; or, Scenes in the Life of a Bow Street Officer, Drawn Up from His Private Memoranda*, published anonymously in 1827, was the first work to feature a police detective as its main protagonist. It was quickly followed in France by the memoirs published by the criminal turned detective, Eugène-François Vidocq, in 1828.[12] In the United States, the writer whom many critics consider to be the founder

of the genre, Edgar Allan Poe, published his trio of detective stories in the early
1840s.[13] During the same period, for both historical and literary reasons, there was
no home-grown crime fiction in Russia and readers had to rely on the translation
and importation of foreign works. Because the genesis of crime fiction in Russia
depended upon quite specific historical circumstances, and because many works
reference their particular historical and judicial context, it is worth outlining the
historical landscape in the middle of the nineteenth century in a little detail. Prior to
the 1861 Act of Emancipation, the country's social organization saw approximately
85 per cent of the population effectively 'owned' by the noble classes and therefore
subject to an *ad hoc* system of justice meted out by their proprietors. Moreover, the
country possessed an outmoded and unsatisfactory legal system that spoke volumes
about the injustices inherent in this patrimonial structure. Put simply, pre-1860s
Russia just did not possess a judicial system in which the individual detecting figure
frequently deemed to be a necessary precursor for crime fiction existed. Russia's
archaic legal system had remained virtually unchanged from the time of Catherine
the Great (1762–96) and so, by the early 1860s, there was little that was not wrong
with it. The main criticisms levelled at it included: the dizzying variety of different
courts in operation which exceeded that in any other European country at the
time;[14] the fact that there was no division between the executive and legislative
systems; the absence of the principle of the equality of all citizens before the law;
the continued existence of an inquisitorial legal process reliant on secret written
procedures in which the accused had no access to his/her accuser and no right
to a defence; the possibility of people accused of crimes being neither convicted
nor acquitted but left 'under suspicion' for an indefinite period; the snail's pace of
the legal process, which could see cases last for decades; and the persistence of the
recourse to capital punishment.[15]

Russia's defeat in the Crimean War in 1856 convinced the new Tsar, Aleksandr
II (1855–81), of the need for a series of Great Reforms to make the country
more modern and productive, and thus more likely to prevail in future military
conflicts. In the 1860s–1870s, Russia enacted wide-ranging reforms to its social
organization (with the freeing of the serfs), to education, the military, finance
and administration. The first in a series of significant changes to Russia's judicial
system came in June 1860 with the introduction of the new position of 'sudebnyi
sledovatel'' ('judicial investigator'). This new position, which resembled in many
respects the contemporary French 'juge d'instruction', is the closest approximation
in Russia at the time to the more Western concept of a police detective.[16] The
judicial investigator, who operated under the auspices of the local court system
and was answerable to the local procurator, assumed responsibility for the pre-trial
investigation into crimes that would previously have been conducted by the local
police. Indeed, dissatisfaction with the inefficacy of Russia's local police forces was
cited as being a chief motivating factor in the inauguration of the new position. As
the well-known criminologist I.Ia. Foinitskii noted in 1874:

> Недостатки проводимого полицией предварительного расследования
> были настолько очевидны, что передача следствия органам юстиции

могла быть осуществлена еще в условиях дореформенной судебной системы.[17]

[Inadequacies in the preliminary investigation conducted by the police were so obvious that transferral of the investigation to judicial organs could already be enacted in the pre-reform judicial system [that is before other reforms came into effect in 1864].]

The stated aim behind the introduction of the position of judicial investigator was to ensure 'greater professionalism, legality and objectivity in the investigatory stages of the case'.[18] However, promulgation of the 1860 Act was likely also to have been prompted, at least in part, by the desire to free up police time in order to deal with the civil unrest that was expected to be triggered by the Emancipation of the Serfs the following year. Under this Act, the judicial investigator enjoyed considerable authority including: the right to interrogate victims, suspects and witnesses either under oath or not; to collect material evidence and to search premises; and to place suspects under arrest. At the conclusion of his investigation, the judicial investigator had to present his written evidence to the procurator, who would make a decision about whether the case should come in front of a court. What is particularly noteworthy about the authority invested in, and the qualities expected of, this new role is how, in 1860, it was clearly intended to embody the values that would be further promoted by the more wide-ranging judicial reforms to be introduced four years later.

The publication on 20 November 1864 of 'Sudebnye ustavy' ('Court Statutes') represented the most significant act in the implementation of ambitious changes to Russia's inadequate judicial system. These statutes embodied Aleksandr II's efforts to provide Russia with a legal system that was, in his words:

swift, just and merciful [...], to give it the appropriate independence, and in general to strengthen in the people that respect for law, without which public prosperity is impossible and which should be the constant guide of each and everyone from the highest to the lowest.[19]

On the whole, the legal reforms were welcomed and are considered to be amongst the most successful and enduring of the various modernizing moves of the period. In the October 1862 edition of the journal edited by Dostoevskii, *Vremia* (*Time*), for example, one critic anticipates that they represent 'преобразование, которое по огромной важности своей равняется освобождению крестьян от крепостной зависимости' ('a transformation which, in terms of its immense importance, rivals the emancipation of the serfs').[20] David Keily describes the impact of these judicial reforms, which introduced into Russia elements taken from the English, French and German systems, in the following terms:

[they] completely transformed the jurisprudential discursive formation in Russia: judicial power became relatively independent from administrative power; an oral, adversarial legal procedure superseded a written, inquisitorial procedure; the concept of 'internal conviction' supplanted the doctrine of formal evidence; trial by jury replaced the machinations of chancellery clerks; courtrooms opened to the public and the press; and a new class of legal

professionals materialized. Legal discourse, formally the prerogative of the autocrat, was redistributed to new legal actors and was disseminated in new types of legal texts, to which new hermeneutic procedures were applied.[21]

As Keily acknowledges, these changes to the legal system in Russia prompted considerable discussion in the pages of the Russian press.

Beginning in 1860, journals such as *Vremia*, *Russkoe slovo*, *Sovremennik* (*The Contemporary*) and *Delo* (*Deed*) began to publish polemical articles — what is known in Russia as *publitsistika* — that debated various aspects of the judicial reforms. The crucial point about these articles, as I have argued elsewhere, is that they not only exerted an influence on politics and public opinion, but also played an undeniable role in shaping literary fictional treatments of crime and detectives in the nascent genre of Russian crime fiction.[22] In a similar fashion, the articles written by Dostoevskii for *Vremia* in the early 1860s, whilst ostensibly factual accounts of actual criminal trials in France, introduced various literary-fictional techniques designed to affect the reader.[23] Commenting on the attention prompted by the opening in 1866 of new legal courts in Russia, Keily observes:

> Like Gayot de Pitaval, Novikov, Schiller, and Dostoevskii before them, newspaper journalists found a treasure trove of topical, sensational, and instructive stories in legal narratives that were being generated every day in the new courts. In the late 1860s and early 1870s, therefore, they experimented with a variety of forms in which legal material could be communicated succinctly and dramatically. These forms had to complement the overall format and support the commercial exigencies of the newspaper medium, which prospered not only by informing, but also by entertaining its readers.[24]

And as Chapter 1 will outline in much greater detail below, just when journals were commenting on the judicial reforms, the year 1862 saw the appearance of the first works of Russian crime fiction: stories by N. M. Sokolovskii that would later be gathered together in the 1866 collection *Prison and Life: From the Notes of an Investigator*.

Sokolovskii's work sounded the starting pistol for a genre that quickly gathered momentum and popularity in Russia. During the 1860s, further early works of crime fiction were published by Dostoevskii and by a writer who, like many others discussed in this book, has been entirely forgotten by posterity: P. I. Stepanov. Like Sokolovskii, Stepanov published crime stories individually in journals before collecting more than a dozen together in a 1869 volume entitled, *Pravye i vinovatye: zapiski sledovatelia sorokovykh godov* (*The Innocent and the Guilty: Notes of an 1840s Investigator*). It was the 1870s that saw Russian crime fiction really reach maturity with a number of authors publishing numerous works in the genre that each garnered a significant readership. These include but are not limited to: K. Popov and N. P. Timofeev, whose works will be discussed in some detail in Chapter 1; S. A. Panov, whose five works were all published during this decade and are skilfully executed examples of the genre; N. D. Akhsharumov, P. I. Telepnev, and the prolific and entertaining writer, A. A. Shkliarevskii. Shkliarevskii wrote more than two dozen crime stories during the 1870s and 1880s and has quite rightly been the subject of a literary resurrection engineered by Reitblat, in the form of reissues of volumes of his stories in Russia since the 1990s. Timofeev continued to produce crime fiction during the 1880s and other writers publishing in this decade include A. P. Chekhov, with his parody 'The Swedish Match: A Judicial Story' that was mentioned above, as well as P. Letnev and D. A. Linev. The 1890s saw the emergence of one of the few female writers to figure in the genre in Russia during this early period: A. I. Sokolova, who was also known by her pseudonym, 'Blue Domino', and who published a series of crime fiction narratives, including *Bez sleda: ugolovnyi roman* (*Without a Trace: A Judicial Novel*) in 1890 and *Spetaia pesnia: iz zapisok starogo sledovatelia* (*The Song Has Been Sung: From the Notes of an Old Investigator*) in 1892.

The late nineteenth and early twentieth centuries were notable for the works written by A. E. Zarin that feature the recurring detective figure of Patmosov, who appears to share certain traits and techniques with Arthur Conan Doyle's Sherlock Holmes. In the first decade of the twentieth century, the great British detective was borrowed further into Russian crime fiction as Petr Orlovets published works such as *Pokhozhdenie Sherloka Kholmsa v Rossii* (*The Adventure of Sherlock Holmes in Russia*) in 1908 and *Prikliucheniia Sherloka Kholmsa protiv Nata Pinkertona v Rossii* (*The Adventures of Sherlock Holmes versus Nat Pinkerton in Russia*) in 1909. Simultaneously, R. L. Antropov cast a fictionalized version of Russia's first detective chief, I. D. Putilin, as the hero of his various crime stories that were published in the years before the revolution of 1917. As the appearance of Holmes and Pinkerton in Orlovets's stories suggests, although not a subject that is addressed directly in this book, the Russian reading public during this period was also treated to translations of various popular works of foreign crime fiction. So, for instance, between 1868 and 1874 more than ten works by the popular French crime novelist Émile Gaboriau were translated into Russian. Their popularity is attested to by the fact that, as outlined by Reitblat, these novels were often sold almost simultaneously by several different publishers and, unusually for the time, ran to two or three editions.[25] Wilkie Collins's *The Woman in White* (1859) and *The Moonstone* (1868) were also translated into Russian soon after their original publication date and exerted a certain influence. Conan Doyle's Sherlock Holmes stories first found their way into Russian translation in 1893–97 and were greeted not only by a receptive readership but by a number of authors, as indicated above, who were happy to display his influence overtly in their own works.[26]

The socio-historical factors that explain the relatively late appearance of crime fiction in Russia are complemented by a number of literary-aesthetic reasons. Prose did not succeed poetry as the dominant literary form in Russia until the 1830s, meaning that, even if the judicial context had been different, the country was arguably in no literary state to produce an equivalent to Edgar Allan Poe at a similar moment in its history. Moreover, until 1856, strict censorship was in place under the Buturlin committee to prevent the publication of critical material, and this level of oversight limited the extent to which crime could be depicted in literature. This system of control, coupled with Vissarion Belinskii's call for 'critical realism' and the dominant position occupied by the 'thick' journals, ensured that breaking through into Russia's inner literary circle was no mean feat for a writer. Without wishing to resurrect the now-outmoded distinction between 'highbrow' and 'lowbrow' forms of art, through the 1840s and 1850s Russian letters largely promoted an image of its canon as being populated by serious 'novels of ideas' that reflected not only upon the lot of the individual but also upon the fate of the nation. In such a context, just as in other countries, the appearance in Russia of what some critics label 'genre' literature — crime fiction, horror, adventure, science fiction, romance, etc. — had to bide its time before establishing itself in the reading consciousness.

However, as soon as it did first appear in Russia, crime fiction attracted a strong following amongst readers. To some degree, that popularity can be tied to improvements in Russian literacy levels and concomitant developments in the country's publishing industry resulting from the Great Reforms of the 1860s. The Emancipation of the Serfs Act in 1861 hailed the advent of significant improvements in literacy levels amongst the Russian population as it 'thrust the printed word into the villages'.[27] Furthermore, during the last decades of the nineteenth century, many former serfs left rural areas to find more varied types of work that often required the ability to read and write.[28] Increases in the percentage of the Russian population who were literate also prompted changes in the publishing landscape that proved favourable to the popularity of crime fiction during the late Imperial era. A number of crime writers at the vanguard of the genre in Russia had their work serialized and published in well-respected 'thick' journals, such as *Vremia*, *Otechestvennye zapiski* (*Notes of the Fatherland*) and *Biblioteka dlia chteniia* (*Library for Reading*).[29] However, in a development that mirrored the role that the penny dreadful had played in the dissemination of crime fiction and other forms of popular literature in Great Britain, the late nineteenth century in Russia witnessed the birth of a range of 'thin magazines' and boulevard newspapers. These cheaper and rather less serious-minded rivals to the tradition of the 'thick' journal were instrumental in providing a platform for various writers to find a reading public.[30] So, during this period, journals such as *Rodina* (*Motherland*), *Niva* (*Grainfield*) and *Ogonek* (*Spark*), and daily newspapers such as *Svet* (*Light*), *Peterburgskii listok* (*The Petersburg Gazette*) and *Moskovskii listok* (*The Moscow Gazette*), carried serializations of crime fiction that were relatively affordable for Russia's new readers. Certain of these publications also carried journalistic and court reports on actual crimes and criminal trials, alongside their fictional offerings, such as those about 'A Mysterious Case of Poisoning' that appeared in *Ogonek* in 1910.[31]

The boom in popular literature during the late Imperial era means that there are scores of works that could potentially have served as the basis for this study of Russian crime fiction. So, it is perhaps a good idea to outline which have been included, and why, and in so doing, to justify certain of the generic labels and terminology that are employed here. Throughout this book, reference is made to the corpus of texts under discussion using the terms 'crime fiction' and 'detective fiction'. This decision is informed not only by the fact that both are commonly encountered in critical work on the genre and thus easily recognizable by readers, but also by the fact that they are neither mutually exclusive nor contradictory.[32]

'Crime fiction' is the broader, umbrella term for all works that feature the depiction of a crime or criminal(s) and includes as one of its subsets 'detective fiction'. As a translation, 'crime fiction' functions as a more accurate equivalent of the labels 'ugolovnyi rasskaz' or 'ugolovnyi roman' that were frequently applied to these works in the original Russian.[33] However, the works discussed here are all, with the exception of Dostoevskii's *Brat'ia Karamazovy* (*The Brothers Karamazov*), ones that can also be referred to as 'detective fiction'. This is because they each feature some form of criminal investigation that is conducted by a detective, whether that figure be a professional or a more amateur investigator.[34] So, for example, many of the narratives have as their main protagonist (and sometimes also their narrator) either a 'sudebnyi sledovatel'' ('judicial investigator') or 'syshchik' ('detective'). However, reference is also made to works in which the investigation is conducted by an interested, but amateur, party, such as N. D. Akhsharumov's *Kontsy v vodu* (*And None Will Be The Wiser*).[35]

The preference shown here for works of 'detective fiction' derives from the fact that the main impetus driving this book is the desire to focus upon the role that narrative techniques play in guiding the reader's affective response to a sense of mystery about the 'truth' of a particular criminal case. Whether details are initially lacking about the identity of the culprit, or about the motivations that have resulted in the crime, detective fiction inevitably highlights the impact of devices that modulate the authority of particular voices in the text, that fragment the provision of information and that play with the reader's networks of pre-existing knowledge. It should be noted, at this stage, that the works analysed here rarely, if ever, fit the mould cast by Edgar Allan Poe in his three early stories featuring Chevalier Auguste Dupin: 'The Murders in the Rue Morgue' (1841), 'The Mystery of Marie Rogêt' (1842) and 'The Purloined Letter' (1844). Unlike, Dupin, the investigators encountered in the Russian genre are not armchair detectives primarily engaged in ratiocinative endeavours and feats of astounding, supposedly rational, interpretation. Rather, as we shall see, particularly in the early years of its existence in Russia, the detectives tend to be fairly ordinary, uncharismatic investigators, albeit displaying certain ideologically inflected characteristics and abilities, who follow procedure to solve relatively straightforward mysteries. Indeed, as Louise McReynolds has so valuably demonstrated, there is a vogue in early Russian crime fiction for works where the central question to be resolved by the investigator is not the more generically conventional 'whodunit', but 'whydunit'.[36] Examples of the Russian genre, particularly from the 1860s and 1870s, contradict the claim made by Marty Roth in *Foul and Fair Play* that 'one of the determining conventions of detective fiction is the absence of the criminal as criminal until the end of the work'.[37] In these early works, as will be demonstrated in the main body of this book, the identity of the culprit is often known from the outset of the narrative. As such, these works have more in common with the Dickensian crime story that, according to Dennis Porter, 'derives from a humanitarian's interest in social problems and a realist's concern to explore the circumstances and possibilities of less than average life'.[38] Even in such narrative circumstances, the detective nevertheless finds himself with a job to do, either because information relating to the circumstances around, or motive(s) for the crime, is missing or because the necessary confession has not been provided by the culprit. As such, the detective figure still finds himself engaged in a search for knowledge and, by extension, the reader finds him/herself encountering narrative devices that are used to obfuscate, delay or complicate the revelation of the essential details of the case.

From the starting point of Chekhov's 'The Swedish Match' mentioned above, this journey of inquiry into early Russian crime fiction has led me to discover many authors whose work has been largely forgotten since it was first published. Writers such as N. M. Sokolovskii (1835–19?), P. I. Stepanov (1812–76), N. P. Timofeev (1841–?), N. D. Akhsharumov (1819–93), S. A. Panov (?–?), A. A. Shkliarevskii (1837–83), A. I. Sokolova (1833–1914), A. E. Zarin (1862–1929) and R. L. Antropov (1876–1913) are all deserving of a higher profile than they currently enjoy. Thanks to the post-Soviet vogue for crime fiction, certain of these works have been reprinted in recent years, usually for the first time since their original publication in the late Imperial era.[39] At the time of writing, however, none of these works has yet been translated into English, meaning that knowledge of them outside Russia is necessarily limited. Whilst none of these works can rival Dostoevskii's *Crime and Punishment* for scope or quality, they each showcase the use of a range of narrative techniques that mediate the reader's access to full knowledge about not just the criminal act, but also the criminal investigation that results from it. It is the narrative construction of works of crime fiction, and the various ways in which it influences the reader's perception of issues such as authority, knowledge and textual play, that form the central focus of this study. In spite of the fact that the very first work of Russian crime fiction, Sokolovskii's *Prison and Life*, is considered in some detail in the first chapter, this book does not provide a chronological study of the development of the genre between 1860 and 1917. A teleological version of the story of the early years of Russian crime fiction, in which one work is considered to engender another in a neat sequence of literary influence, is not the most interesting or productive way to approach such a rich subject. Moreover, an emphasis on narrative poetics rather than historical circumstance provides the opportunity to highlight generic practice that is neither geographically nor historically specific. History, however, cannot be ignored and so the temporal span of this book is determined by the fact that 1860 marks the introduction of the figure of the judicial investigator into the Russian legal landscape, and an end date of 1917 recognizes that, as Harriet Murav argues, 'the revolution of 1917 destroyed the institutions and the legal culture created by the 1864 reform'.[40] After this date, the genre changed drastically, having been hijacked by socialist and communist ideology in the wake of the revolution.

The history of critical inquiry into crime and detective fiction has ably demonstrated that a range of approaches can be productively adopted towards the genre, including historical, sociological, psychoanalytical, generic, thematic and postcolonial, amongst others. However, as mentioned above, this book opts for a narratological approach to look at the various devices that are used to affect the reader's response to the text. Specifically, it is interested in how various aspects of story construction impact upon the reader's experience of the epistemic games played in crime fiction. Crime fiction is a genre that deals acutely in the modulation of knowledge and 'truth',[41] and where, in an exaggeration of the situation pertaining in every literary text, the reader is not granted access to the full story of the crime or the investigation into it at the outset. The act of reading a work of crime fiction involves the reader in a search for information regarding the true nature of the criminal act(s), the identity of the perpetrator(s), the motive(s) for the crime, the pre-history of the perpetrators and the victims, the course of the investigation and the detective's progress towards establishing the truth and offering a resolution to whatever is the central mystery of the text. Crime fiction narratives can thus be seen to function as paradigmatic examples of the various storytelling devices that are employed to reveal information in a piecemeal fashion or to construct competing or contradictory versions of the truth. As Carl Malmgren argues, detective fiction offers particularly fruitful subject matter for the investigation of the impact of poetic devices because:

> it highlights certain aspects of genre theory, such as the relation between fiction and reality, because it dramatizes certain plot functions, such as relationships between *fabula* and *sujet* or between hermeneutic and proairetic codes, and because it foregrounds and interrogates different forms of readerly investment in narrative.[42]

With regard to this book, specifically, the aspects of story construction to be analysed include: the blurring of generic lines between fact and fiction in the very earliest examples of the genre; the various techniques employed to create an image of the investigator and/or the narrator as a figure of authority in the discourse; the existence of multiple voices in a narrative and the negotiation of a hierarchy of authority between these voices; the harnessing of a range of devices related to the presentation of time in the text as a means of fragmenting storylines and knowledge; the role of intertextuality and metatextuality in simultaneously establishing authority and problematizing knowledge; and the mastery of conventional generic devices and structures that is required to enact successful and entertaining parodies of crime fiction. The examination of these questions makes reference to a range of structuralist and post-structuralist work, not all of which of course is itself focused upon the practice of crime fiction. From the field of general narratology, the work of Gérard Genette and Susan Lanser figures prominently because of its clear enunciation of the potential inherent in a variety of devices related principally to questions of narrator identity, narrative voice and level as well as temporal organization. In terms of theory related more closely to the example of crime fiction, this study makes use of the work by critics such as Tzvetan Todorov, Donna Bennett and Peter Hühn. However, the approach here is not exclusively narratological. Where appropriate, it not only considers how particular poetic structures might be seen to reflect socio-historical, cultural or literary concerns during the late Imperial era, but also introduces other analytical approaches, such as those related to the politics of listening or the practice of parody.

As Malmgren's enunciation of the potential inherent in a study of detective fiction clearly suggests, the focus upon textual features ought to include attention to the experience of the reader. In a similar vein, in his contribution to a collection on detective fiction and literary theory, George N. Dove argues that:

> By and large, critics' efforts to isolate the uniqueness of the detective story have fallen short, for the reason that they have been almost exclusively text-oriented; because it remains the most popular genre in popular fiction, a much more profitable line of investigation of the detective story would be an effort to determine what is different or special in the *reading* of it.[43]

The present book attempts to tread a mid-line between Dove's two methodologies, by paying close attention to textual devices whilst never losing sight of their effect upon the experience of the reader. Reference is repeatedly made here to the manner in which the reader is likely to interpret, or be affected by, the use of a particular device or structure. Arguably the two most essential questions in this regard are, first, how a particular device encourages or discourages the reader to place trust in a particular voice within the diegesis and the version of events it offers; and, second, how the device mediates the reader's access to knowledge about a particular event or state of affairs that is presented in the *siuzhet*. In so doing, this analysis has in mind an image of the reader that is somewhere between a real, extratextual reader (and probably a fan of crime fiction not dissimilar to myself) and the figure of the informed or implied reader that is posited by the text and identified by critics such as Stanley Fish and Wayne Booth.[44] Whilst discussion of the mediation of knowledge and 'truth' in the text has primarily in mind a figure closer to the implied reader, references to the effect of a particular device envisages more of a real reader. It is important to recognize that crime fiction enjoys a particularly avid readership, with enthusiasts frequently reading many different works by a variety of authors, as well as entire series of detective novels by individual writers. It is reasonable to posit, therefore, that many readers of crime fiction more closely resemble the image of the informed reader than might be the case in other genres.

This study of the poetics of early Russian crime fiction is divided into six chapters, organized into three parts. The first part, entitled 'Authority', examines in its first chapter how some of the earliest examples of the genre sought to establish their own legitimacy as literary works, as well as the authority of the accounts of crime and criminal investigations they gave, by means of a blurring of the lines that conventionally divide fictional and non-fictional modes. The chapter considers the various ways in which these works encourage the reader to view them as non-fictional accounts of actual lived experience, more akin to the practice of memoir than to literary fiction. Yet it also highlights the various examples of more conventional literary-fictional practice that they exhibit. Chapter 2 moves on to consider how these early works, as well as slightly later, more unambiguously fictional examples of the genre, construct the criminal investigator as a figure of both social and diegetic authority. It examines how this authority is established by means of the depiction of the investigator's own qualities and attributes; how it depends to some extent upon a comparative view of this figure vis-à-vis less powerful figures populating the fictional world; and finally, upon the fundamental question of whether the narrative voice in the text possesses autodiegetic, homodiegetic or heterodiegetic authority. That is, does the narrative voice belong to the investigator who is also the main protagonist in the fictional world; does the narrative voice belong to a figure other than the principal investigator in the fictional world; or does the narrative voice occupy a position apparently outside the realms of the fictional world?

Part II of the book concerns itself with a discussion of poetic techniques intended to modulate the reader's experience of 'Curiosity and Suspense'. Chapter 3 opens with an examination of the role of direct dialogue in works of crime fiction as a means of promoting a sense of verisimilitude and drama, whilst acknowledging the frequently 'coerced' nature of many of these speech acts. It then moves on to argue that the genre makes frequent use of multiple voices in the narrative not only as a metaphor for the fragmented clues that the criminal investigator needs to reconstruct to arrive at a full story of the crime, but also as an effective means of confronting the reader with a series of competing voices supplying piecemeal information. It considers one example of conventional practice before analysing an example from A. A. Shkliarevskii where the generic rules are turned on their head with original results. The fourth chapter considers how various manipulations of the chronological relationship between *fabula* and *siuzhet* in Russian detective fiction can be employed to highlight gaps in the reader's knowledge about the past of the crime as well as to generate a sense of suspense about the future outcome of the investigation.

Finally, Part III of the book addresses the relationship that has long been acknowledged to exist between the genre of crime fiction and the notion of play or textual games. Chapter 5 reveals how, from its inception, Russian crime fiction demonstrated an acute sense of its own 'literariness' by means of the practice of both intertextuality and metatextuality. Intertextuality is considered to be another means by which these texts earn authority for themselves in the particular context of the late Imperial era. Meanwhile, metatextuality sees them interrogating the notion of the investigator as both an author and a surrogate reader as well as reflecting upon the status of the written word both within and outside the confines of the literary text. The final chapter offers up a reading of two quite different parodies of crime fiction produced at a relatively early stage of the genre's history in Russia. S. A. Panov's *Iz zhizni uezdnogo gorodka: iz zapisok sudebnogo sledovatelia* (*From the Life of a Provincial Town: From the Notes of a Judicial Investigator*), published in 1876, sees many of the characteristics of crime fiction that even then had become conventional being inverted and debunked during the account of a corrupt investigation into a case of child abandonment. It is complemented by a reading of Chekhov's 'The Swedish Match', which enacts a series of subtle exaggerations or reversals of generic practice before revealing its brilliant sting in the tail/tale. What these two parodies demonstrate is that early Russian crime fiction was eminently aware of the structures and devices that best served the intentions of the genre (especially the modulation of authority, curiosity and suspense), and was able to invert and exaggerate them in original and skilful ways that enriched the scope of the genre.

## Notes to the Introduction

1. Ian Rankin, 'The Birth of the Detective', *The Guardian*, 12/ April 2008, <https://www.theguardian.com/books/2008/apr/12/history.ianrankin> [accessed 10 January 2017]. One might also include the readers' desire to find pure escapism within the pages of crime fiction.

2. Anthony Olcott, *Russian Pulp: The* Detektiv *and the Russian Way of Crime* (New York & Oxford: Rowman & Littlefield, 2001), pp. 1–3. Olcott notes that the popular Russian crime writer, Aleksandra Marinina, was said to have more than 9 million copies of her various novels in print in 1997.

3. Ibid., p. 3.

4. Aleksandra Marinina has written more than thirty novels and has been translated into over twenty languages. Many of her detective novels feature a female investigator, Anastasia Kamenskaia, and a number of these novels were adapted into the television series, *Kamenskaia*, that was aired in Russia from 1999 to 2011, with another series planned for 2017–18. Polina Dashkova published her first crime novel, *Krov' nerozhdennykh* (*Blood of the Unborn*), in 1999 and has since produced more than twenty others that are usually translated into English and German. Between 1995 and 2004, the publishing house *Eksmo* published more than 27 million copies of Daria Dontsova's crime novels featuring the private detective Dasha Vasil'eva. Boris Akunin's first historical detective novel, featuring Erast Fandorin, was published in 1998, since which time the author has written two other detective series, to a total of some twenty-one novels.

5. Olga Sobolev, 'Boris Akunin and the Rise of the Russian Detective Genre', *Australian Slavonic and East European Studies*, 18.1–2 (2004), 63–85 (p. 66).

6. 'Official' recognition in works of literary history of the existence of crime fiction did not begin in France, for instance, until sometime in the 1980s.

7. *Istoriia russkoi literatury*, 10 vols (Moscow: Akademiia nauk, 1945–54).

8. Victor Terras, *Handbook of Russian Literature* (New Haven, CT: Yale University Press, 1985); Neil Cornwell (ed.) *Reference Guide to Russian Literature* (London: Fitzroy Dearborn, 1998).

9. See Olcott, *Russian Pulp*, pp. 4–6, and Sobolev 'Boris Akunin', p. 66. The original title of German's work is *Odin god* and Sheinin's work is *Zapiski sledovatelia*. The most notable exception to this rule of general neglect is the Russian literary critic A. I. Reitblat, who is the author of several valuable studies of the nineteenth-century roots of Russian crime fiction.

10. *Russkoe slovo*, 1865: 7 (July), p. 68, of the section 'Literaturnoe obozrenie'.

11. A. I. Reitblat, In *Ot Bovy k Bal'montu i drugie raboty po istoricheskoi sotsiologii russkoi literatury* (Moscow: Novoe literaturnoe obozrenie, 2009), Reitblat lists the most widely read fictional publications for the years 1856–95.

12. The resemblance between these two works and the first works of crime fiction in Russia is discussed in some detail in Chapter 1 below.

13. The three stories are: 'The Murders in the Rue Morgue' (1841), 'The Mystery of Marie Rogêt' (1842) and 'The Purloined Letter' (1844).

14. See Samuel Kutscheroff, 'Administration of Justice under Nicholas I of Russia', *American Slavic and East European Review*, 7.2 (1948), 125–38: 'To the first instance as courts of original jurisdiction belonged district courts, city courts, guildhalls, aulic courts (restored by Catherine II), boundary offices, and commercial courts. In addition, there were *sovestnye sudy*, arbitrational courts, and special courts for every class of society. The peasants had their village and village district administration (*volostnye sudy*) with judicial functions. [...] The second instance was represented by the civil and criminal tribunals (*Palaty*), which in small towns were contracted into one court. [...] The third instance was the Ruling Senate, consisting of senators appointed by the government.' (ibid., p. 127)

15. V. A. Shuvalova, 'O sushchnosti sudebnoi reformy 1864g. v Rossii', *Sovetskoe gosudarstvo i pravo*, 10 (1964), 121–27 (p. 123). In her *Russia's Legal Fictions* (Ann Arbor, MI: University of Michigan Press, 1998), Harriet Murav sums up the pre-reform legal system in the following terms: 'That there is no rule of law, or even a professed ideology of the rule of law, in Russia in 1850 goes without saying. There is no equality before the law, no access to one's accuser, no right to a defense, no principle of innocent until proven guilty. [...] The judiciary institutions are

subordinated to the tsar's autocratic powers. [...] The police and the courts are one institution. Instead of 'procedural norms', which allow for flexibility and predictability in the exercise of the law, there is a forest of specific and particular regulations. [...] In the prereform inquisitorial court there is no contest about what happened, no evaluation of the individual circumstances of the case, no interpretation and no *story*, but a grid of matching crimes and punishments: "the act of the criminal compared with the laws".' (p. 19)

16. The position of 'syshchik' ('detective') was largely unofficial in late nineteenth-century Russia and is most commonly used to refer to the judicial investigator's sidekick. The position was formalized in 1908 by the creation in eighty-nine Russian cities of detective departments.

17. I. Ia. Foinitskii, 'Russkaia karatel'naia sistema', in *Sbornik gosudarstvennykh znanii*, ed. by V. P. Bezobrazov, 1 (St Petersburg: Kozanchikov, 1874), p. 15. In the 'Vnutrennye novosti' section of *Vremia* (*Time*) for March 1861, p. 9, the author recalled how the Moscow procurator outlined to the newly appointed judicial investigators 'горестное положение, в котором находилась до сих пор следственная часть, бывшая в руках наружной полиции' ('the pitiful state in which the investigative section had found itself until then, being as it was in the hands of the external police').

18. William Burnham, 'The Legal Context and Contributions of Dostoevsky's *Crime and Punishment*', *Michigan Law Review*, 100.6 (2002), 1227–48 (p. 1240).

19. Quoted in Richard Wortman, *The Development of a Russian Legal Consciousness* (Chicago, IL: Chicago University Press, 1976), pp. 261–62.

20. 'Nashi domashnie dela', *Vremia*, 10 (1862), p. 33.

21. David Keily, '*The Brothers Karamazov* and the Fate of Russian Truth: Shifts in the Construction and Interpretation of Narrative after the Judicial Reform of 1864', unpublished PhD thesis, Harvard University, 1996, p. 272.

22. See Claire Whitehead, 'Debating Detectives: The Influence of *publitsistika* on Nineteenth-Century Russian Crime Fiction', *Modern Language Review*, 107.1 (2012), 230–58.

23. Dostoevskii, 'Protsess Lasenera' ('The Lacenaire Trial'), *Vremia*, 2 (1861), 'Madam Lacost'' ('Madame Lacoste'), *Vremia*, 5 (1861), 'Tainstvennoe ubiistvo: iz ugolovnykh del Frantsii 1840 goda' ('A Mysterious Murder: From the Judicial Affairs of France in 1840'), *Vremia*, 1 (1862), 'Ubiitsy Peshara: Frantsuzskoe delo 1857–8 g.' ('Pechard's Murderers: A French Criminal Matter from 1857–58'), *Vremia*, 2 (1862).

24. Keily, '*The Brothers Karamazov*', p. 124.

25. A. I. Reitblat, 'Detektivnaia literatura i russkii chitatel'', *Knizhnoe delo v Rossii vo vtoroi polovine XIX–nachale XX veka*, no. 7 (1994), 126–40 (p. 126).

26. Reitblat (ibid., p. 133) notes that, although the first translations of Doyle appeared in the years 1893–97, many of these early stories passed unnoticed. The true popular reception of the Sherlock Holmes stories began in the years 1902–04, when they would appear one after another and often simultaneously with different publishers.

27. Jeffrey Brooks, *When Russia Learned to Read: Literacy and Popular Literature, 1861–1917* (Evanston, IL: Northwestern University Press, 2003), p. 5.

28. Brooks notes that, 'although literacy among the rural population was low — no more than perhaps 6 percent in the 1860s and 25 percent in the 1910s — male literacy was high throughout the industrialized provinces of central Russia' (ibid., p. 4).

29. The term 'thick' journals is applied to the range of serious, high-brow literary journals that were popular across much of the nineteenth century in Russia, and each volume of which ran to many pages.

30. In *When Russia Learned to Read*, Brooks explains: 'The pioneer in reaching a wide and diverse reading public in the nineteenth and early twentieth centuries was the so-called 'thin magazine', the illustrated weekly that was contrasted with the more serious and ideologically focused monthly 'thick journals' intended for the educated reader. The thin magazines flourished in the last quarter of the nineteenth century, and provided a source of light reading, serious fiction, and news for a diverse group of readers, including provincial gentry as well as village schoolteachers and parish clergy.' (ibid., p. 111)

31. In her 2013 study, *Murder Most Russian: True Crime and Punishment in Late Imperial Russia*, Louise McReynolds outlines some of the intriguing consequences of the co-existence of factual and

fictional accounts of crime in such publications. McReynolds, Louise, *Murder Most Russian: True Crime and Punishment in Late Imperial Russia* (Ithaca, NY: Cornell University Press, 2013).

32. Certain scholars dedicate a great deal of time to outlining the differences between different types of crime and detective fiction. See, for instance, David Keily's thesis, 'The Brothers Karamazov', in which he outlines the definition of four different types of crime narratives, based upon previous work by Edgar Marsch, where the distinctions between each depend upon whether the story of the crime and of the criminal investigation occur in the fabula or the siuzhet, and in chronological order or not (ibid., pp. 103–06). Such a complicated schema for distinguishing one supposed type of crime fiction from another is not necessarily helpful to the subsequent analysis of the works themselves.

33. In 'Detektivnaia literatura i russkii chitatel'', Reitblat clarifies that 'Термин «уголовный роман» охватывал все произведения (в том числе и исторические), где речь шла о преступлении, независимо от характера конфликта и типов персонажей' ('The term "crime novel" comprises all works (including historical works) in which the subject is crime, regardless of the nature of the conflict or the type of characters included') (p. 126).

34. Consequent upon this choice is the exclusion from this book of reference to works such as Krestovskii's *Peterburgskie trushchoby* and, later, Dostoevskii's *Krotkaia* (*The Meek One*) because, although these works deal with crime, they are not dedicated primarily to the investigation of those crimes.

35. In Akhsharumov's novel, the role of detective is played by Cherezov, a man with no professional investigative training or responsibility, but who is desperate to find out the circumstances of his female cousin's sudden death.

36. Louise McReynolds, ' "Who Cares Who Killed Ivan Ivanovich?": The Literary Detective in Tsarist Russia', *Russian History*, 36 (2009), 391–406.

37. Marty Roth, *Foul and Fair Play: Reading Genre in Classic Detective Fiction* (Athens, GA: University of Georgia Press, 1995), p. 162.

38. Dennis Porter, *The Pursuit of Crime: Art and Ideology in Detective Fiction* (New Haven, CT: Yale University Press, 1981), p. 25.

39. Works including K. Popov's *Vinovatye i pravye: rasskazy sudebnogo sledovatelia* (*The Guilty and the Innocent: Tales of a Judicial Investigator*) (1871), S. A. Panov's *Tri suda, ili ubiistvo vo vremia bala: rasskaz sudebnogo sledovatelia v dvukh chastiakh* (*Three Courts, or Murder During the Ball: Tale of a Judicial Investigator in Two Parts*) (1872), various of Shkliarevskii's stories, N. Ponomarev's *Peterburgskie pauki* (*Petersburg Spiders*) (1890), and Zarin's novel and stories have been republished in Russia since the fall of the Soviet Union, with more appearing all the time.

40. Murav, *Russia's Legal Fictions*, p. 11.

41. Albert D. Hutter contends that: 'detectives are [...] inevitably concerned with the problem of knowledge, a problem only intensified by the urban upheaval of the world in which they move, by the disorder, by the multiplicity of detail, the constant impinging presence of other people, other accounts, other viewpoints.' (Albert D. Hutter, 'Dreams, Transformations, and Literature: The Implications of Detective Fiction', in *The Poetics of Murder: Detective Fiction and Literary Theory*, ed. by Glenn W. Most and William M. Stowe (New York, NY: Harcourt Brace Jovanovich, 1983), pp. 230–51 (p. 235)

42. Carl D. Malmgren, 'Anatomy of Murder: Mystery, Detective and Crime Fiction', *Journal of Popular Culture*, 30.4 (1997), 115–35 (p. 116).

43. George N. Dove, 'The Detection Formula and the Act of Reading', in *The Cunning Craft: Original Essays on Detective Fiction and Literary Theory*, ed. by Ronald G. Walker and June M. Frazer (Macomb, IL: Western Illinois University Press, 1990), pp. 25–37 (p. 26; original italics).

44. Stanley Fish defines his concept of the 'informed reader' as being: 'neither an abstraction, nor an actual living reader, but a hybrid — a real reader (me) who does everything within his power to make himself informed'; see Fish, 'Literature in the Reader: Affective Stylistics', in *Reader Response Criticism: From Formalism to Post Structuralism*, ed. by Jane P. Tompkins (Baltimore, MD: John Hopkins University Press, 1980), pp. 70–100 (p. 87). Wayne Booth outlines his notion of the 'informed reader' in *The Rhetoric of Fiction* (Chicago, IL: University of Chicago Press, 1971).

PART I

# Authority

CHAPTER 1

# Blurring the Lines: Fact and Fiction in Early Russian Crime Writing

This opening chapter focuses on some of the earliest examples of crime writing in Russia and examines the ways in which they inhabit and exploit positions on generic borderlines.[1] In the ample attention paid to Dostoevskii's *Crime and Punishment* since its serialization in *Russkii vestnik* (*Russian Messenger*) in 1866, it is easy to forget that this novel was not, in fact, Russia's first example of indigenous crime fiction. So, in part, this chapter establishes with greater clarity the specific details of the birth of crime fiction in the Russian context by identifying the authors and the publication history of the works that inaugurated the genre. However, having done so, its central focus is then directed towards the style of these early works and, specifically, the ways in which, as McReynolds has accurately noted, they 'skirt the boundary between fact and fiction'.[2] Referring to the work of Edgar Allan Poe, Stephen Rachman argues that:

> The intersection of fact and fiction has [...] been central to detective stories from its inception, and as much as this might be relevant to the development, for example, in the 1960s of the true-crime novel, it also derives from the cultural preoccupations of the 1830s and 1840s. [...] As Neil Harris has shown, Poe's hoaxes and ratiocinative fictions were, like the humbugs of P. T. Barnum's American museum, part of a modern public interest in the line between truth and fiction.[3]

In the first decade or so of its existence (1862 onwards), notable examples of Russian crime writing were characterized by the way in which they combined elements of various different, though related, genres that themselves occupy different points on the fact/fiction continuum. These include: *publitsistika* (polemical journalism), court reports, physiological or ethnographical sketches, but most importantly memoir and literary fiction.[4] The central argument put forward in this chapter is that these early works invoke the model and display characteristics of memoir whilst simultaneously presenting themselves to the reader as literary fictions. It considers how such generic hybridity shapes the construction of the narrative voice and its relationship with the implied reader and how, in so doing, this hybridity establishes patterns for the subsequent development of the genre.

## The Birth of Russian Crime 'Fiction'

As stated in the Introduction, the very first example of crime 'fiction' in Russia is N. M. Sokolovskii's *Ostrog i zhizn': iz zapisok sledovatelia* (*Prison and Life: From the Notes of an Investigator*).[5] Although the full work under this title was only published in 1866, numerous parts of it had appeared separately in various journals over the preceding years. The first set of three stories appeared in the December 1862 volume of Dostoevskii's journal, *Vremia*. They were grouped together under the general title 'Iz zapisok sledovatelia v arestantskoi rote' ('From the Notes of an Investigator in the Penal Battalion') and the individual titles were: 'Foma, nepomniashchie rodstva' ('Foma, Ancestry Unknown'), 'Batka' and 'Chapurin' (the names of their eponymous protagonists). The January 1863 volume of the same journal included three further stories under the same collective heading and were: 'Kosushka vodki' ('The Bottle of Vodka'), 'Posledniaia stranitsa' ('The Final Page') and 'Samoubiitsa' ('The Suicide').[6] All of these stories then reappeared, in slightly modified form or under different titles, along with previously unpublished works, in the full 500-page volume of *Prison and Life* in 1866.[7] This complete version attracted a significant readership at the time and is cited by Reitblat as being one of the most widely read works of that year.[8] Keily characterizes Sokolovskii's work as 'a series of purportedly non-fictional ethnographic sketches, each of which is organized around a crime or a criminal'.[9] As the title of the volume suggests, the seventeen stories it comprises are all narrated by the figure of a narrator-investigator but are varied in their focus: some recount cases that he has worked; others describe scenes he has witnessed in prison; whilst yet others tell the back stories of the men incarcerated or their relatives outside the prison walls.

A second work of Russian crime fiction which predates *Crime and Punishment*, at least in some of its parts, is P. I. Stepanov's *Pravye i vinovatye: zapiski sledovatelia sorokovykh godov* (*The Innocent and the Guilty: Notes of an 1840s Investigator*). As with Sokolovskii, the eventual publication of the full two-volume work in 1869 was preceded by the appearance in various journals of a number of its ten constituent chapters. The first to appear was 'Rodimaia storonka' ('Dear Native Land') in *Biblioteka dlia chteniia* in March 1863, followed by 'Krovnaia obida' ('The Bloody Offence') in the May and June 1865 volumes of the same journal, and then 'Na p'edestale' ('On a Pedestal') which was published in *Otechestvennye zapiski* in February 1866. Again, not all of the ten stories can be readily classified as crime fiction, but the first volume does comprise six that feature criminal investigations conducted by the narrator, who is a governor's secretary charged with looking into possible miscarriages of justice. It is worth pointing out that, as its title indicates, Stepanov's collection is the only one to feature a pre-1860 investigator as the central protagonist. The third work to be discussed in this opening chapter is N. P. Timofeev's *Zapiski sledovatelia* (*Notes of an Investigator*), which comprises seven chapters or stories, was first published in St Petersburg in 1872 and, like Sokolovskii's, became one of the most popular works of the year.[10] Five of its chapters align themselves fairly neatly with the model of crime 'fiction', recounting as they do investigations conducted by the narrator-detective. The first chapter functions like an extended foreword and the fourth story, 'Tiuremnyi mir' ('The Prison World'), in a clear echo of Sokolovskii's volume as well as Dostoevskii's *Zapiski iz mertvogo doma* (*Notes from the House of the Dead*) (1862), describes the characters and traditions one meets inside a prison.[11] Unlike Sokolovskii and Stepanov's works, however, there is no evidence that any parts of Timofeev's *Notes of an Investigator* were published separately before this date; indeed, its foreword is dated January 1871, which suggests that the entire work was composed for publication only shortly before this date. Although Timofeev's work does not, therefore, predate the appearance of *Crime and Punishment*, the author's biography, as well as its exploitation of the fact/fiction generic border-zone, place it firmly in a group with Sokolovskii and Stepanov's earlier and ground-breaking works of Russian crime writing.

## Investigators Turned Authors and the Role of Titles/Subtitles

As McReynolds notes, Sokolovskii, Stepanov and Timofeev (as well as their contemporary, K. Popov, who published *Vinovatye i pravye: rasskazy sudebnogo sledovatelia* (*The Guilty and the Innocent: Tales of a Judicial Investigator*) in 1871) each spent part of their professional lives working as 'law enforcement officers'.[12] The entry for Sokolovskii in the *Brokhaus-Efron Encyclopaedic Dictionary* identifies him as a 'writer and lawyer' born in 1835 who graduated from Kazan University's law faculty. Although it gives no details for his employment as an investigator, it does say that he became a 'prisiazhnyi poverennyi' (barrister) in St Petersburg later in his career and that he was simultaneously the author of various *publitsistika* and more general articles devoted to legal and social questions. Stepanov (1812–76) appears to have been the best known of this trio of writers, at least during his lifetime, and enjoyed a varied career. Having graduated from Moscow University, he started work in the office of the city's Governor General, serving as an investigator during the 1840s, before becoming a judge. His active legal career ended in 1855 when he was called up to the army and served during the siege of Sevastopol, later writing and publishing accounts of his military experiences. Thereafter, he worked very successfully for the Society of Russian Railways until he joined the Ministry of Transport in 1868. However, alongside this civic career, Stepanov found time to write, penning both crime narratives seemingly drawn from his own experiences, as well as various dramatic works. Timofeev, who was born in 1841, started out as a judicial investigator before becoming an assistant procurator in the Moscow circuit court in the 1880s.[13] Both Stepanov and Timofeev, it should be noted, wrote other works informed by their professional legal experience, with the latter being particularly prolific.[14]

Contemporary readers may well have been unaware of the link between the respective biographies of Sokolovskii, Stepanov and Timofeev and the subject of their works. However, each author encourages speculation about the potentially factual nature of his work by using a variation, in either the main title or subtitle, of the label 'zapiski sledovatelia' ('notes of an investigator'). And it is the 'notes' part of these (sub)titles that is especially fascinating as a perspective from which to consider the birth of crime fiction in Russia. It is significant that three of the earliest works each employ this same term that then falls largely out of use in the subsequent development of the genre.[15] Amongst the various paratexts that mould the reader's expectations of a published work before s/he gets to the main text itself, it is the title and/or subtitle that are the most influential and that are most frequently employed to reveal information regarding its genre, mode or contents.[16] So, why should Sokolovskii, Stepanov and Timofeev all choose to designate their works as 'zapiski'? Reitblat attempts an explanation when he argues:

> Стремясь избежать ассоциаций с презираемым детективным романом, авторы книг о преступлениях, написанных в 1860-х–начале 1870-х гг., старались «подключиться» к другой литературной традиции, подчеркивая (даже в названии) документальный характер своих публикаций (и действительно, они, как правило, не «сочиняли» а пересказывали случаи из жизни). Сложилась даже устойчивая формула для обозначения подобных произведений — «записки следователя».[17]

> [In order to avoid associations with the despised detective novel, authors of works about crime written in the 1860s and early 1870s attempted to link themselves with a different literary tradition, underlining (even in their titles) the documentary nature of their publications (and in fact, as a rule, they were not 'composing' but recounting events from real life). A standard formulation for denoting such works even came into being: 'notes of an investigator'.]

Although Reitblat's claim in the first clause above is misleadingly anachronistic, the second gets closer to the truth of the matter, albeit in an overly simplified manner.[18] A more accurate and productive reading of the use of the term 'zapiski' is that it is one that possesses the potential to signal implicitly the borderline generic status of the three works. By the 1860s, 'zapiski' had enjoyed long-standing popularity amongst Russian authors. Even the most cursory glance at examples of its use demonstrates its capacity for generic fluidity and inclusiveness, encompassing, as it does, works located anywhere on a spectrum running between supposedly factual memoirs at the one end and purely literary fictional accounts at the other. Indeed, the sheer variety of English terms used by translators to render 'zapiski' (notes, memoirs, diary, sketches, papers) speaks to its inclusive, but also ambiguous, potential.[19] Examples of works closer to the 'factual' pole might include A. A. Bibikov's *Zapiski o sluzhbe Aleksandra Il'icha Bibikova* (*Memoirs on the Life and Service of Aleksandr Il'ich Bibikov* (1817) or I. V. Lopukhin's *Zapiski* (*Memoirs*) from 1870, where both accounts offer a 'documentary' insight into the lives of actual historical figures. On the literary fictional end of the scale, two examples that will be familiar to many readers are N. V. Gogol's 'Zapiski sumasshedshego' ('Notes of a Madman', but often translated as 'Diary of a Madman') from 1835 and I. S. Turgenev's *Zapiski okhotnika* (translated variously as *Notes of a Hunter* or *Sketches from a Huntsman's Album* or *A Sportsman's Sketches*) of 1852.[20] Of particular relevance to the literary context in which the works of Sokolovskii, Stepanov and Timofeev appeared, given its own generic hybridity, is the example of Dostoevskii's *Notes from the House of the Dead* that was serialized in *Vremia* in 1861–62. As Karla Oeler argues:

Dostoevskii cast into question the generic status of the text that emerged from his prison notes — is it a memoir or a novel? — introducing in the preface a fictional narrator, Aleksandr Petrovich Gorianchikov, who has little in common with the more autobiographical narrative voice that emerges in the subsequent memoir.[21]

It is the term 'zapiski' in the title, however, that foreshadows the generic hybridity and ambiguity of Dostoevskii's work, even before the fictional narrator is introduced. The question that Oeler asks of Dostoevskii's novella — is it a memoir or a novel? — is one that is key to an interpretation of the first works of Russian crime fiction.

## Fact or Fiction and the Role of Memoir

As both the terms of Reitblat's argument and the examples of Gogol, Turgenev and Dostoevskii demonstrate, the decision by Sokolovskii, Stepanov and Timofeev to each employ 'zapiski sledovatelia' ('notes of an investigator') in their (sub)titles represents the first move in claiming an 'authentic' or 'factual' referential status for their works. Distinguishing between fact and fiction in literary writing is a notoriously difficult issue that has preoccupied numerous critics.[22] Even though brief biographies of these investigators turned authors have been given above, it is not within the scope of this study to discuss whether the contents of the works derive from factual events in their lives. The focus here falls rather on the narrative aspects and poetic devices that are used to encourage the reader to consider them to be potentially factually informed. In *The Narrative Act*, Susan Lanser suggests that literary works can locate themselves along an axis of 'report/invention', where 'the mode closest to the axis of report is the fictional text that insists on its historical truth by claiming to be a factual document, a biography or an eyewitness account'.[23] The (sub)title 'zapiski sledovatelia' in these three works is the first step towards such a claim because it suggests to the reader that they are comprised of 'written notes' made by the investigators either during their careers, or at some point afterwards. As such, it is legitimate for the reader of Sokolovskii, Stepanov and Timofeev to expect that these works either belong to, or demonstrate some degree of kinship with, the genre of memoir. Such a claim is indirectly corroborated by the fact that, when the term 'zapiski' falls largely out of favour in the genre a little time later, it is replaced by labels which much more unambiguously denote fictionality. Beginning in the early 1870s, 'rasskaz' ('tale'), in particular, and then later 'istoriia' ('story') become far more popular epithets.[24] In spite of this shift in terminology, the impulse towards making headline claims of referentiality for works of crime fiction remains strong through the subsequent years of the genre's popularity, even when it is intended ironically. A. P. Chekhov's *Drama na okhote* (*The Shooting Party*), published in 1884–85, for example, is subtitled 'istinnoe proizshestvie' ('a true event'), and the initial framing narrative sees the editor-narrator attempting to establish the 'truthful' credentials of the 'povest'' ('tale') told by former judicial investigator, Ivan Kamyshev. The works of Sokolovskii, Stepanov and Timofeev are different, however, in the manner in which they employ the term 'zapiski' to signal their works as potentially 'authentic' and 'factually informed' works of memoir.

The fact that these first works of Russian crime writing present themselves as being akin to memoirs echoes the development of crime fiction in certain other national traditions, albeit with some distortion. Historians of the genre in France, for instance, point to the crucial initiating role played by the work of Eugène-François Vidocq who published his *Mémoires de Vidocq, Chef de la Police de Sûreté, jusqu'en 1827, aujourd'hui propriétaire et fabricant de papiers à Saint-Mandé* (*The Memoirs of Vidocq: Chief of Investigative Police until 1827, and now owner and producer of paper in Saint-Mandé*) in 1828. Vidocq was a well-known brigand in the late eighteenth and early nineteenth centuries who switched sides, becoming first a police informer and then a member of the detective police force. His memoirs, authored in part by a ghost writer, are full of accounts of his days as a criminal as well as equally lurid descriptions of his adventures as a policeman, and they became a bestseller in both France and England. Various critics argue that the origins of French crime fiction lie in Vidocq's memoirs, with Julian Symons claiming a significant role for him both within and beyond France's borders:

> The influence of Vidocq (1775–1857) on writers of crime fiction in his own lifetime, and on detective story writers after his death, was immense. [...] Balzac was a friend of Vidocq's and based upon him the character of Vautrin, who appears in *Le Père Goriot* and other books. Poe had read Vidocq, and it is right to say that if the *Mémoires* had never been published Poe would not have created his amateur detective.[25]

In Great Britain, although the vogue for factual memoirs written by police officers and detectives only gathered pace towards the end of the nineteenth century, notable examples of pseudo-factual memoirs were published long before this time. In 1827, for instance, *Richmond: or, Scenes in the Life of a Bow Street Officer, Drawn Up from His Private Memoranda* purported to provide an account of the work of one member of the country's earliest police force, although it is commonly considered to be a work of fiction.[26] Similarly, *Recollections of a Police-Officer*, which was serialized in *Chambers's Edinburgh Journal* between 1849 and 1853, before being published as a single work in 1856, provides an account, again most likely fictional, of the professional career of the narrator-detective, 'Waters'.[27] *Recollections* garnered significant success amongst the reading public, was issued in America, as well as being translated into French and German.[28]

Although the situation in the French, British and Russian contexts is slightly distinct, the appearance in each of works styling themselves as memoirs is surely significant. The lure of memoir for early Russian crime writing stems, in part, as Reitblat suggests, from the established reputation of the genre by the 1860s. Taking a broader perspective, Beth Holmgren argues that memoir plays an important role in 'the making and understanding of Russian culture and history'[29] and that it has long enjoyed a particular popularity with Russian writers and their audience:

> Promising to inscribe the memoirist's self among (often famous) others, with reference to and commentary about the real world, the memoir has powerfully attracted and obligated Russians who were eager to articulate their engagement

with their singular, developing society, yet also muted by political censorship in other forms of writing. For centuries, Russians have embraced the memoir as a form of autobiography with (depending on one's point of view) a conscience or an agenda.[30]

The reference to self-inscription here suggests another possible reason why these early works in the Russian genre styled themselves as quasi-memoirs. The form promotes a construction and orientation of the narrative voice that can often be complex, multi-perspectival and highly effective. In memoir, the narrative voice can provide insight into, and analysis of, people and situations; search for causes and connections in the human experience; express its subjectivity and personal experience, but simultaneously its objectivity and reliability; act as a guide for the reader into little-known worlds; and demonstrate the ability to self-mythologize as a role model whilst simultaneously promote itself as a 'representative individual'. For the early works of Russian crime writing that concern us here, what appears to be particularly valuable is the potential scope that memoir offers for providing purportedly truthful accounts of aspects of (criminal) life which are unfamiliar to readers, accompanied not only by analyses of human psychology but also by accounts of the narrator-investigator as a professional and just practitioner of the law. A consideration of the status and performance of the narrative voice in these early works therefore prepares the ground for the more in-depth analysis of narrative authority that is to come in Chapter 2. However, it is also essential to acknowledge that the status of the works by Sokolovskii, Stepanov and Timofeev as generically liminal, which is one of the most productive consequences of their presentation as quasi-memoirs, is itself a result of memoir's own generic hybridity. Holmgren believes that memoir's popularity with Russian readers across the years stems, at least in part, from its generic indeterminacy between the documentary/factual and imaginative/fictional and the fact that it combines 'individualised expression and reliable reportage'.[31] Along with other forms of documentary writing, memoir enacts what Lydia Ginzburg calls an 'orientation towards authenticity'[32] and exploits various techniques to establish its relationship to 'reality' and truthfulness, even if the text does not in fact relate an actually verifiable truth. And it is to an examination of the techniques used to create this sense of generic fluidity, this sense of a text presenting itself as simultaneously factually inspired and fictionally constructed, that the remaining sections of the present chapter devote themselves.

The differing degrees to which examples taken from Sokolovskii's *Prison and Life*, Stepanov's *The Innocent and the Guilty* and Timofeev's *Notes of an Investigator* inform that discussion can be explained by the fact that each work occupies a quite distinct position on Lanser's report/invention spectrum. In the case of Stepanov, for example, apart from the subtitle and a few other restricted instances, *The Innocent and the Guilty* functions relatively straightforwardly as a work of literary fiction, albeit one desirous of emphasizing its realist credentials. Indeed, an interesting, although ultimately unanswerable, question concerns how the reader's reception of Stepanov's work might have differed when its separate stories were published in journals prior to 1869 without the inclusion of the all-important subtitle. Standing at the mid-point of these three works, and considerably closer to the 'report' end of Lanser's axis than Stepanov, is Timofeev's *Notes of an Investigator*. Although the main body of the text, comprising the second to the seventh stories, again reads largely in the style of generically conformist imaginative literature, it is preceded by a 'predislovie' ('preface') and a first chapter that establish the text's possible status as memoir and in which the dividing line between fact and fiction is deliberately blurred. It is perhaps this blurring that explains Stephen P. Frank's interpretation of Timofeev's collection as an entirely factual account.[33] Finally, Sokolovskii's *Prison and Life* is the work in which features of factual and fictional writing are most closely intertwined. The focus of the discussion in this chapter will fall largely upon the first story in the collection because of its role in establishing the reader's generic expectations; however, many of the features identified therein are equally present throughout the remainder of his work. The analysis to follow examines the devices encountered in Sokolovskii, Stepanov and Timofeev's works that suggest their 'authentic' or 'factual' status, many of which are also to be found in memoir. Space is also devoted to a consideration of the compelling evidence these works provide of memoir's generic fluidity, given that they include passages characteristic of documentary writing, the professional manual or textbook, polemical journalism (*publitsistika*), philosophical tract, physiological or ethnographic sketch, the diary and confession. Albeit more briefly, the chapter then concludes with a discussion of those aspects of the works that promote a reading of them as aesthetically oriented examples of literary fiction.

## Inscription of the Self: The Dominant 'I' in Early Russian Crime Writing

The most significant consequence of the decision to style these three early works of crime writing as memoirs is the dominant position that this form ascribes to the voice of the first-person narrator. Just as in the earlier quasi-memoirs published in France and England, the works by Sokolovskii, Stepanov and Timofeev feature a highly visible narrator figure who is keen to place himself at the forefront of the discourse.[34] Memoirs are overwhelmingly, although not absolutely necessarily, works written in the first person and, as in autobiography, they emphasize the recording of the individual's experiences. Implicitly, it is this foregrounding of the narrating 'I' in his/her role as witness that persuades the reader of the factual and authentic status of the account being presented. However, in the genre of crime fiction as it is broadly conceived, and especially outside of the Russian context, such a first-person narrator-detective stance is somewhat unusual. The generic convention for narrators in crime fiction is either that they are heterodiegetic (i.e. not a figure present in the diegesis) or that, if they are homodiegetic, they are not the detective himself.[35] Examples of the former type include the novels of Émile Gaboriau, published in France in the 1860s and 1870s, whilst the latter mode is encountered in both Edgar Allan Poe's Dupin detective stories and Arthur Conan Doyle's stories featuring Sherlock Holmes, where Dr Watson acts as the narrator. The particular consequences of first-person narration in crime fiction will be

examined in greater depth in Chapter 2, but it is sufficient to note at this point that
the sense of suspense that is such a hallmark of the genre is considered to be more
easily generated in works that feature a narrator who is not himself the investigator.
Russian crime fiction, particularly in its earliest incarnations, but also for a longer
period than in other national traditions, therefore represents something of a case
apart in its taste for first-person narrator-investigators. And this nationally distinct
predilection can be traced, in large part, to the influence that these early examples
of quasi-memoir had upon the subsequent development of the genre.

The scope that memoir offers for allowing the narrative 'I' to dominate is exploited
to varying degrees in the works of Sokolovskii, Stepanov and Timofeev, largely in
line with the extent to which each wishes to emphasize its authentic, factual nature.
Where it appears frequently and is particularly underscored, the intentions are
manifold, but include the desire to convince the reader of the 'truth' of the account.
The status of the narrator-investigator as witness is reified and obliquely recalls the
role of the *flâneur* as informant in the feuilleton.[36] Amongst these three works, it
is in Sokolovskii's *Prison and Life* that the figure of the first-person narrator looms
largest, and most especially in the opening chapter 'Skvernye minuty' ('Unpleasant
Moments'). The importance of the narrator figure to this text is heralded by the
fact that he reveals his first-person stance as early as the second sentence. Moreover,
he does so in order to claim a special status for himself, differentiated from other
people because of the nature of his experience:

> На «скверные минуты» жизнь не скупится, всех и каждого оделяет она
> ими в изобилии, но я полагаю что незавидное преимущество в этом
> случае должно остаться за следователем.[37]

> [Life is not sparing in its 'unpleasant moments'; it gives more than enough
> of them to each and every one of us. But I believe that, in this regard, the
> unenviable position at the head of this list must belong to the investigator.]

Thereafter, and throughout the remainder of the stories in the collection, this
narrator-investigator figure remains resolutely centre stage, continually directing as
much of the spotlight onto his own self and experiences as onto the various other
characters with whom he interacts. His text is repeatedly adorned with phrases in
the first person that underscore the account as one informed by his reminiscences
('я помню', 'I remember' is used frequently), that record his personal opinions ('мне
так казалось' 'it seemed so to me'; 'для меня', 'for me'; 'я не знаю' 'I don't know';
'я понял' 'I understood', etc.), and that make clear his role as the principal actor in
numerous criminal investigations and encounters with prisoners already convicted
('Мне следовало сделать обыск у Драгунова; я объявил ему об этом', 'I had to
undertake a search of Dragunov's house so I informed him of this fact'; 'женщин
тоже приводилось мне лишать свободы' 'I have also had to deprive women
of their freedom').[38] The sheer number of statements made in the first person in
Sokolovskii's text results in a sense of this narrator as a quasi-fetishized figure, who
functions unmistakeably as the gravitational centre of the diegesis. Not only does
this repeated use of the first-person pronoun promote belief in the events described
as deriving from lived experience, and in the account as one that is faithful to the

reality of actual life, it also serves to establish the narrator as a figure of considerable authority, who functions as the reader's initiator into this probably unknown world of criminal activity and investigation.

Although the first-person 'I' of the detective figure is also in evidence throughout Timofeev's *Notes of an Investigator*, it creates a somewhat different effect. Indeed, its less dominant position here is hinted at by the fact that the pronoun 'я' ('I') does not appear until the very bottom of the second page, the narrator preferring before this point occasional uses of the more inclusive first-person plural pronoun 'мы' ('we'). Throughout the collection, Timofeev's narrator appears to be less inclined to thrust himself into the foreground of the stories and he makes considerably less play of emphasizing the individual and apparently unique position bestowed upon him by his work as a criminal investigator. That said, as suggested above, both the 'Preface' and the first chapter of the work, 'Pervye vpechatleniia' ('First Impressions'), are distinct in style from the remaining stories, and in these two sections the first-person narrator is unmistakeably present.[39] As will be discussed in greater detail below, in these first two sections of Timofeev's work, the figure of the narrator-investigator is very much to the fore, overtly reflecting in the preface on both his attitude to crime and his decision to write and then using the opening chapter to record his route into the job and his memories having been first appointed. The experience of reading the more straightforwardly 'fictional' stories that come later in the volume is profoundly modified by the prism constituted by the preface and first chapter, in which the first-person narrator is at pains to establish his credentials not just as a professional and empathetic criminal investigator, but also as a modest and altruistic writer of his memoirs.

Of these three early authors, it is Stepanov who places least emphasis on the first-person identity and experience of his narrator-investigator. Indeed, as the next chapter will discuss in greater detail, it is not until the third chapter of the first story in *The Innocent and the Guilty*, 'Uzdechka konokrada' ('The Horse-Rustler's Bridle'), that the narrator reveals himself to be the investigator depicted in the diegesis. At this point, the narrator briefly informs the reader that he is a secretary working for the regional Governor on special assignments before retreating largely into the background for the remainder of the chapter. It is only in the fourth chapter, which recounts the story of his investigation into the first in a series of apparent miscarriages of justice, that this narrator-investigator steps more deliberately out of the wings, although even then he is far less inclined than either Sokolovskii's or Timofeev's narrators to make himself the focal point of the story. The consequence of the less visible position of this first-person voice, who is supposedly the author of the 'notes', is that the status of the work as factually inspired memoir is downplayed. Moreover, perhaps in keeping with Stepanov's narrator's role not as a fully fledged judicial investigator, as is the case in Sokolovskii and Timofeev, but as a secretary with investigative responsibilities, the less frequent insertion of the narrative 'I' implicitly hints at the lesser authority possessed by this figure. Nevertheless, in each of the three works, the role of the first-person narrator remains central as the individual stories, and the various events recounted and characters described, are all united by the experiencing presence of this voice.[40]

## Characteristics of Memoir in Early Russian Crime Writing

As noted above, Timofeev's *Notes of an Investigator* is the only one of these three early works explicitly to include a foreword, and the author uses it, in part, to inform the reader of the intentions behind his writing. This explanation further aligns the work with the genre of detective-memoir in which, according to Haia Shpayer-Makov, such justifications are a relative commonplace:

> Almost invariably, the writers of detective memoirs felt a need to explain their motivation in approaching this task, an apologia that may have indicated a certain unease at venturing into a domain outside their natural habitat.[41]

Indeed, it was not just memoirists on the right side of the law who favoured the use of such pre-emptive self-justifications for their decision to write. In his memoirs, the renowned nineteenth-century French murderer (and poet), Pierre François Lacenaire, informs readers that his act of writing should be considered the equivalent of autopsying his own body and dissecting his own brain; and he insists on the importance of his role as the author of these acts as a means of preventing all the other supposed 'experts' who are waiting to pick over his post-execution corpse from drawing the wrong conclusions.[42] Timofeev provides a far less melodramatic justification than Lacenaire for writing his 'memoir', preferring to underline the inherent interest of its contents and its potential value to the field of Russian letters:

> Разнообразие испытанных мною среди преступного мира впечатлений и ощущений, и самый интерес многих уголовных происшествий, мною обследованных, навели меня на мысль, составить и издать в свете свои записки, по тем наброскам, которые я от времени до времени записывал для себя. Смею думать, что заключая в себе изложение уголовных происшествий, представляющих собою события из мира действительного, они не могут не быть интересны, и вероятно многие прочтутся не без удовольствия, тем более, что при вполне понятном и легко объясненном стремлении всякой образованной среды к чтениям подобного рода, отечественная наша литература в этом отношении представляет еще довольно значительный пробел. Принести с своей стороны посильную лепту на пополнение этого пробела — вот цель, которую я имею, издавая в свет свои записки.[43]

> [The variety of impressions and sensations that I have experienced in the criminal world, and the inherent interest of many of the criminal incidents that I have investigated gave me the idea of compiling and publishing my notes, based on the outlines that I sketched for myself from time to time. I dare to think that, comprising as they do criminal incidents, which are events taken from the real world, they might be not without interest, and that probably many people will read them not without pleasure; that, moreover, in spite of the completely understandable and easily explicable desire of any educated environment to read such things, our native literature in this respect still features a rather significant lacuna. Attempting to fill this gap by making the contribution of which I am capable is the aim I have in publishing these notes.]

This passage is quoted at some length here in order to highlight the various moves

Timofeev makes to persuade the reader of the factual source for his writing: the emphasis on his own experience; the fact that *Notes of an Investigator* elaborate upon sketches that he occasionally made for himself at the time; and that they are drawn from the 'real' world. Of course these claims do not establish beyond doubt the status of *Notes of an Investigator* as factual memoir; but they do indicate Timofeev's wish to convince the reader that they are something other than a work of fiction.[44] In a fascinating link back to Lacenaire, there is an unmistakeable resemblance between parts of Timofeev's apologia and the explanation that Dostoevskii gave to readers of *Vremia* in February 1861 for the inclusion of an account of the Frenchman's trial in the journal. In a footnote, Dostoevskii argues:

> Мы думаем угодить читателям, если от времени до времени будем помещать у себя знаменитые уголовные процессы. Не говоря уже о том, что они занимательнее всевозможных романов, потому что освещают такие темные стороны человеческой души, которых искусство не любит касаться, а если и касается, то мимоходом, в виде эпизода, — не говоря уже об этом, чтение таких процессов нам кажется будет не бесполезно для русских читателей.[45]

> [We think it might please readers if, from time to time, we devote space to famous criminal trials. Not only are they more exciting than any novel imaginable because of the way in which they illuminate those dark sides of the human soul that art does not like to treat, or if it does so, then only in passing, in the form of an episode; but it also seems to us that reading such trials will not be without use for Russian readers.]

No claim is being made here that Timofeev's justification is drawn directly from Dostoevskii, although some degree of influence is quite possible. It is rather the case that the authors of detective memoirs were broadly convinced, whether or not they make explicit claims to that effect, of the interest and potential usefulness of their recollections.[46] In the case of Sokolovskii's *Prison and Life*, any such claims are largely implied in the generalized comments that he makes about the criminal world. Whilst for Stepanov, in another indication of the more restricted claims this author makes about the referential status of his work, there is absolutely no commentary, either explicit or implicit, about why he has written his work. What Timofeev's preface demonstrates, however, is that, at its inception, Russian crime fiction felt the need to persuade its readership of its value and usefulness, at least in part, on the basis of its derivation from a form of actual lived experience that had thus far remained largely hidden from the Russian reading public. In fact, this informative function is one that Russian crime fiction continues to promote even after the first years of its development.

The intersection in these early works of crime 'fiction' between an individualized first-person narrator and the desire, announced explicitly in Timofeev, to make a broader contribution to Russian society is reflected on a diegetic level in their combination of generalized commentary with specific examples or references. In fact, the effect of this repeated recalibration of the focus between the general and the specific is a key facet of the reader's experience of Sokolovskii's text most markedly, but also of Timofeev's. Even in Stepanov, the individual stories are intended to appear representative of broader socio-historical and psychological forces and phenomena. The contention here is that this impulse towards a more universalizing extrapolation from the more specific is a feature often associated with non-fictional modes of writing.[47] In Timofeev's *Notes of an Investigator*, for example, the relatively delayed first appearance of the narrator's 'I' on page 2 is explained by the fact that, prior to this point, this voice has been speaking from a more general, less personal, perspective about crime and its triggers. In a tone much more in keeping with the type of social criticism encountered in *publitsistika* from the same period, the opening line of Timofeev's preface reads:

> Психологическая и нравственная сторона жизни каждого человеческого общества имеет всегда немало отпечатков в преступных ее проявлениях, говоря иначе, преступная сторона жизни каждого человека, есть по большей части непосредственное и прямое последствие психических настроений и движений его сердца, ума и воли. — Преступником никто не рождается, но преступников формирует сама жизнь.[48]

> [The psychological and moral side of life in each human society always leaves not inconsiderable imprints in its crimes; to put it another way, the criminal side of the life of every person is to a great extent an immediate and direct consequence of the psychological makeup and movement of his heart, his soul and his will. No one is born a criminal; criminals are moulded by life.]

This authoritative tone is maintained throughout most of the preface as the narrator argues that crime is the result of social factors, that it can never be eradicated, and that, with the exception of career criminals, all those who fall foul of the law do so not because they are morally deficient but because they are socially compelled. In terms of content, then, as well as tone, Timofeev's preface resembles closely the debates conducted in *publitsistika* in the early 1860s about the nature and causes of crime.[49] The opinions on crime voiced here also place Timofeev's narrator in an intriguing position vis-à-vis Dostoevskii and the views illustrated in *Crime and Punishment*. At first glance, it might appear that he shares the socially deterministic position advocated by such radical critics as N. V. Chernyshevskii and D. I. Pisarev that is so effectively ridiculed in the novel through Dostoevskii's portrayal of the utilitarian Lebeziatnikov. Yet, Timofeev's contention not only that the future eradication of crime is impossible but that it would speak not to the perfection but to the deformity of human society is quite distinct from the radical and socialist utopian position voiced by Lebeziatnikov. More pertinent to the purposes of this chapter, however, is the fact that the desire evidenced by Timofeev's narrator to engage in a debate about the causes of crime, through the prism of the question of progress, aligns his text with examples of contemporary polemical journalism. And the generic hybridity of his work stems in part from the fact that, even if Timofeev's narrator does not state it directly, what the reader is being invited to expect is that the 'fictional' stories that follow in the main body of the text provide more specific and concrete substantiation of the 'factual' and overarching contentions being made in the preface.

Generalized commentary employed as a framing device is a not uncommon feature of prefaces. However, its presence in the main body of Sokolovskii's *Prison and Life*, as well as its occasional appearance in the main body of Timofeev's volume, is rather more unusual.[50] The opening sentence of Sokolovskii's first chapter refers to a similarly collective experience as that outlined in Timofeev's preface: 'Воспоминания прошлого для каждого не легкая работа: у всех в итоге не велика сумма радостей, за то всем на долю досталось довольно страданий' ('Recollections of the past are not easy for anyone: in sum, everyone has not so very many joys, and more than their share of sufferings.')[51] The alternation between the general and the specific that becomes a distinctive feature of Sokolovskii's work as a whole is enacted in the very next sentence when the narrator, as we have noted above, singles out the investigator as the person who has experienced the greatest number of 'unpleasant moments'. Following more generalizing commentary in the opening pages, including comparisons between the investigator and both an anatomist and a dramatic actor, Sokolovskii's narrator then begins to recount the story of one particular criminal, the thief Dragunov, with whom he has to deal on three separate occasions.[52] The story of Dragunov's descent from opportunist and repentant thief at the time of his first arrest, to unapologetic recidivist because of social circumstance by the time of his third apprehension, lasts for some six pages before the more reflective tone reappears as the narrator offers an initial conclusion:

> Это один из эпизодов «следственной» деятельности. Скажите, можно ли относиться к ним хладнокровно, можно ли ближайшим свидетелям их, почти участником, не переживать очень много и очень тяжелых впечатлений? Бесстрастие достоинство ли тут?[53]

> [This is one episode from my 'investigative' work. Tell me, can one react to such episodes cold-bloodedly, can one, as the closest witness to, and almost a participant in them, not experience very many and very painful impressions? Is dispassion a virtue in such cases?]

The generalized commentary extends for a further eight pages until the narrator then outlines four more specific examples of cases in which he has witnessed the suffering of people whom he has been obliged to deprive of their freedom: Semyon Dedko, a thief who calls out his daughter's name at the fateful moment of his arrest; an unnamed Chuvash jewel thief whose lament as he is taken into custody touches the investigator deeply; a handsome homeless man, Ivan, whose comment 'my share is bitter' contains such suffering; and finally, the case of the prostitute, Lizaveta, who has robbed a young client and is the first woman that the narrator-investigator has to detain, who falls to her knees in a deep faint when informed of her fate. Sokolovskii's first chapter then comes full circle as its final paragraph adopts a broadly philosophical tone:

> Не всякая юридическая правда — человеческая правда. Мы видим только факт, выходящий из уровня обыденной жизни (чаще всего по внешней условленной форме, а не по внутреннему содержанию), называем его преступлением и казним совершителя его, — стало быть мы только требуем и наказуем: требуем неисполнения преступного, наказуем за исполнение; а чем уравновешиваются эти требования и наказания?[54]

[Not every judicial truth is a human truth. We see only the fact emerging from the level of trivial life (more often than not its external agreed form, and not its internal contents), call it a crime and punish its perpetrator. That is, we simply make demands and punish: we demand that crimes not be committed and punish their commission. But how do we balance out these demands and these punishments?]

In addition to the resemblance between the broader philosophizing sections of Sokolovskii's and Timofeev's work and *publitsistika* writing, readers might also associate the style encountered here with certain features of the feuilleton, another generically fluid genre popular at the time in Russia. Although Sokolovskii's tone is certainly not jocular or light-hearted as would befit the feuilleton, his inclusion of summaries of cases which can read like anecdotes, the suggestion that the events he encounters are part of everyday life, his inclination towards 'sociological generalisation' and his construction of a close relationship to the reader (which is to be discussed below) are all features shared with that genre.[55] Valuable work has already been done on the relationship between the feuilleton and crime fiction that does not need to be repeated here.[56] It is sufficient to note for the terms of this argument that the generic fluidity and the blurring of the line between the factual and fictional in the feuilleton are characteristics shared by these early works of Russian crime 'fiction'. In their inclusion of such reflective and generalizing sections, and their resemblance in this regard to *publitsistika*, these early works announce what will long remain a central preoccupation of Russian crime fiction: the provision of social commentary on crime and its causes. McReynolds has argued very effectively that the Russian genre's preoccupation with the 'whydunit' rather than the 'whodunit' speaks to its desire to ascribe guilt not to individual criminals but to the collective construction of nineteenth-century Russian society.[57] The initial attempts to understand crime, as the polemical journalist Popov had invited in *Vremia* in 1863, that are achieved through the combination in Sokolovskii and Timofeev of factually informed reflection and fictional-seeming anecdotes lay essential groundwork for the more purely fictional engagement with this question which comes later. Indeed, even in subsequent works of Russian crime fiction, where the type of generic hybridity being discussed here is absent, as in the stories of A. A. Shkliarevskii for instance, this more general and philosophizing tone is still to be found.[58]

In memoir, the narrative voice conventionally assumes authority thanks to its role as an initiator and guide into a previously little-known world, and this same characteristic is in evidence in these early Russian works. The degree of authority possessed by the narrator-investigators in Sokolovskii, Timofeev and Stepanov is enhanced not simply because of their specific professional status, but also because, due to the recent reforms to the judicial process, their professional landscapes were largely unknown territory to the reader. Although, as has been noted above, the narrators' foregrounding of their narrative 'I' emphasizes their status as an individual, all three are equally keen to highlight their more representative, institutional role as investigators. In this guise, these three narrators provide explanations of their role, their *modus operandi* and/or the functioning of the law that serve further to underscore the factual referential status of their works.

So, for example, at the beginning of the fourth chapter of the story 'The Horse-Rustler's Bridle' in Stepanov's volume, the narrator explains the difficulty he encounters in trying to exonerate the peasant Pakhom Karpov after the first police investigation has resulted in a miscarriage of justice and his wrongful incarceration for the murder of his cousin:

> Преследование несравненно труднее следствия. Нужно много твердости, чтоб не увлечься односторонностью взгляда, предупреждением. Это борьба между направлением первого следствия и целью нового, хотя цель раскрыть истину. Легко сказать «раскрыть истину», когда потеряно время, когда многие подробности изгладились из памяти очевидцев, сведущих людей, когда эти люди, давши раз показание, боятся сделать противоречие, проговорится и подпасть под ответ. Именно в этом положении находился я.[59]

> [A reinvestigation is incomparably more difficult than an investigation. It demands a considerable amount of resolve not to be distracted by a one-sided approach or by a preconviction. It is a battle between the direction of the first investigation and the aim of the new one, albeit that the aim of both is to uncover the truth. It is easy to say 'uncover the truth', when time has been lost, when many details have slipped out of the memory of witnesses, of people with knowledge of the case, when these people, having given evidence once, fear contradicting themselves, of letting something slip and of tripping themselves up with an answer. I found myself in exactly that position [of having to conduct a reinvestigation.]

This passage is notable in Stepanov's first story as one of the few moments at which the narrator steps out of his diegetic function to reflect with greater distance upon his role as investigator. In both Sokolovskii and Timofeev, however, this informative, almost educative, impulse is displayed more clearly and more frequently. In Timofeev's preface, for example, the narrator gives an explanation of the role of the judicial investigator, beginning with the obvious statement that it is his job to investigate the various motives behind a crime, before moving on to provide a more insightful description. He outlines how the investigator's obligation is just as much to uncover facts that might exonerate the accused as condemn him, and that the first of these duties is especially vital when dealing with the uneducated classes whose suspicions of the legal process are likely to make them conceal evidence that might actually extenuate their guilt. Subsequently, in the first chapter of the volume, 'First Impressions', the narrator, albeit in a less declarative fashion, offers factual-sounding descriptions of the various visits he must make and procedures he must complete before actually being able to begin his first investigation. Finally, the starkest examples of this instructive expositional impulse are again to be found in Sokolovskii's *Prison and Life*. Part of the generalizing passage in the midst of Sokolovskii's first chapter that has been mentioned above comprises a one-and-a-half-page section outlining for the reader the functioning of the reformed legal code regarding the arrest and detention of suspected criminals. It begins: 'До издания последнего наказа судебным следователям, подсудимых подвергали заключению в тюремном замке *без соблюдения формальностей*' ('Prior to the publication of the recent law related to judicial investigators, suspects were able to be imprisoned with very few formalities being observed'),[60] before moving on to inform the reader in some considerable detail about the various post-reform options for detention or surveillance and then to explain the procedural steps necessary for detention. In such passages, where the narrator assumes the guise of an expert ready to educate the reader, the text comes to resemble something closer to an explanatory pamphlet or even instruction booklet than a work of fiction, or even a memoir. Moreover, there is some echo here again of *publitsistika* and the articles in the early 1860s that precisely set out to explain to readers the way in which proposed judicial reforms would function, whilst simultaneously debating their relative merits. Such passages are notable not only for their generic hybridity and conflation of the factual and fictional impulses, but also for the authority that they bestow upon the narrative voice. As Chapter 2 will explore in much greater depth, the construction of narrative authority, and the specific question of education, is a key characteristic of all crime fiction.

Whereas such instructive passages serve to establish a marked experiential difference between the narrator and the reader, the works of Sokolovskii and Timofeev also make a concerted effort to draw the reader into the narrative by seeking to dissolve the boundary between the fictional and extrafictional worlds. The texts employ a range of means to do so, including the use of direct address to the reader and shifting pronouns to refer to the narrative voice that are intended to associate the reader and narrator more closely. In so doing, the texts implicitly underscore their status not as fictional works whose diegetic world is safely fenced off from the 'real' world of the reader, but as quasi-factual texts that implicate the reader in their existence almost as much as the narrator. They also give an early indication of the intriguing relationship that exists between the narrator and reader throughout the history of the development of crime fiction.

The most effective technique that Sokolovskii and Timofeev deploy to achieve this dissolving of the boundary is the effective and strategic use of personal pronouns and modes of address other than 'I'. Indeed, Sokolovskii's chapter 'Unpleasant Moments' offers a fascinating example of a text, in a manner reminiscent of both memoir and feuilleton, that is constructed around a number of shifting narrative positions that modulate the relationship between speaker and listener. Both his dominant 'I' and the more impersonal reference to himself as the 'investigator' have been noted above. Arguably, however, the key device used to draw the reader into the text and to confront him/her with the reality of the investigator's experience is the forceful, yet also occasionally fluid, use of the pronoun 'вы' ('you', in the plural and/or polite form).[61] Early on in 'Unpleasant Moments', the narrator outlines a second analogy (after that of the anatomist) to help the reader understand the position the criminal investigator finds himself in. He introduces it by saying that the investigator is not a bystander to the criminal drama that unfolds before him, but a participant in it, and he continues:

Если вас увлекает художественная игра актера, если под ее впечатлением вы переживаете все моменты драмы, усваиваете, как свои собственные, чужие радости и страдания, если вы свое участие вправе считать законным, то еще законнее участие следователя в проходящих пред ним явлениях, еще анормальнее тут его юпитерское бесстрастие. Пред вами — театр, подмостки, мишура, перед следователем — жизнь, неподдельные страдания, изуродованный, но не подкрашенный человек.[62]

[If you are distracted by the artificial game of the actor, if, under its impression, you experience all the moments of the drama, if you experience the joys and sufferings of another as if they were your own, if you consider your participation in them rightly justified, then the investigator's participation in the phenomena that occur in front of him is even more justified, and his floodlit impassivity in such cases is even more abnormal. Before you stand the theatre, the stage, the decor; before the investigator stand life, genuine sufferings and a disfigured, but not made-up (i.e. decorated) person.]

The early use of 'вы' (and its associated forms) in this passage points up the interpretive problems it poses. Whilst its presence in these lines is part of an attempt to give the reader a greater degree of understanding of the investigator's position, the semantic structure of the final sentence simultaneously establishes an equivalence between the two and underscores the fundamental and stark difference between their experiences. When watching a play, the reader, referred to here as 'вы', is responding to an artificial, constructed scenario, whilst the narrator is forced to confront real life: they stand on two different sides of a distinct boundary. A little later in the story, the same pronoun is used in an example where the reader is invited to cross this threshold and stand in the shoes of the investigator. The narrator introduces this example by imagining the hypothetical scenario in which the reader asks him whether all the criminals he has had to confront are really criminals. He outlines his hypothetical response thus:

вместо ответа, я заставил бы вас самих выслушать их мрачную исповедь [...] и потом посмотрел бы, чтобы вы сказали сами, посмотрел бы, — поднялась ли бы рука и у вас, чтобы бросить камень в изуродованное преступлением лицо злодей...[63]

[instead of answering, I would make you listen to their gloomy confessions yourself [...] and then see what you would say yourself, see whether you would raise your hand in order to throw a stone into the face, disfigured by crime, of the miscreant...]

Here, there is still clearly differentiation between the reader and the investigator, although there is an obvious move to reduce the distance between the two that is present in the theatre analogy. And in its physicality, the challenge to the reader to consider whether or not to cast a stone is an effective means of creating empathy not just between reader and investigator, but also between reader and criminal.[64]

Elsewhere in Sokolovskii, however, this use of 'вы' becomes more ambiguous as its referent slips from being clearly the reader to a position of greater self-referentiality and quasi-synonymity with the narrative 'I'. On page 4, for instance, the proximity of a form of 'вы' ('вам') and 'я' ('I') render them substitutes for one another:

'можно гораздо хладнокровнее относиться к явлениям, которые прошли уже
перед вами несколько раз, но я не знаю, что должны быть за чувства' ('it is
possible to respond much more dispassionately to phenomena that have appeared
before you several times, but I do not know what are supposed to be one's feelings').
Later on, the narrator opens one paragraph by saying: '"Кто виноват?" навязчиво
вертится в вашей голове, и бесконечный лабиринт открывается перед вами'
('"Who is guilty?" obsessively whirls around in your head, and an endless labyrinth
opens up before you').[65] Here, the use of 'вы' is much more akin to the English
'you' or the French impersonal pronoun, 'on', and seems to refer to the habitual
experience of the investigator rather than to the reader. However, the use of this
pronoun to refer unambiguously to the reader only a matter of lines earlier in the
same chapter undoubtedly blurs the lines of interpretation. So, the challenge for the
reader of Sokolovskii's work in the narrator's use of 'вы' and its related forms is to
decide when it refers only to the reader, when to the investigator, and when to both
simultaneously. Such slippage in the referential intention of the pronoun 'вы' is an
extremely effective means of drawing the reader into the diegesis and, crucially
for the future development of the genre, to invite the reader to imagine himself/
herself as the investigator, confronted with not just the epistemological, but also the
emotional challenges of the job.

As a bridge to the final section of this opening chapter, it is also worth briefly
considering the use and effect of the pronoun 'мы' ('we') in these works. In
Sokolovskii, the repeated use of 'you', as well as the dominant position accorded
to the narrative 'I', means that appearances of the more straightforwardly inclusive
first-person plural, 'we', are restricted. The reader has to wait until well into the
second half of the opening chapter to encounter the first use of 'наш' ('our'), when
it is employed to unite the reader and the investigator in their mutual distance from
the less educated common people. Discussing the difficulty frequently encountered
in persuading such people to put their names to written reports of testimony or
interrogation, the narrator notes: 'Известно, что наш народ вообще не охотник
ни до каких рукоприкладств' ('It is well known that our people are generally not
fans of signatures of any kind').[66] Crucially, however, the pronoun makes a striking
reappearance in the concluding paragraph of *Prison and Life*'s opening chapter
in the lines that have been quoted above about not every judicial truth being a
human truth. At this point, the repeated use of the pronoun 'мы' unambiguously
suggests the universality of the investigator's experience: it is not just he who has
an insufficient conceptualization of crime and its punishment, but all members of
society. Timofeev's *Notes of an Investigator* makes a much less sustained use of the
inclusive pronoun 'мы' than does Sokolovskii's work, although it still appears.
Following the more impersonal generalizing declarations on the first page and a
half of the first chapter, the narrator uses forms of this pronoun to make a point
about 'our' collective reaction to prisoners in chains:

> Кто будет спорить противу того, что громаднейшая масса разных
> каторжных и ссыльных, только потому возмущает и оскорбляет в
> нас наше нравственное чувство, что мы видим ее в кандалах, с

полувыбритыми головами, с бубновым тузом на спине, и обыкновенно при весьма неблаговидной обстановке[?][67]

[Who would disagree that the overwhelming mass of various prisoners and those sent into exile only discomfit and offend our moral feeling because we see them in irons, with half-shaved heads, with an ace of diamonds on their back and usually in the most unseemly situations?]

Thereafter, it is the 'I' pronoun that dominates the subsequent stories that make up the main body of Timofeev's collection as the investigator outlines his own experiences. Nevertheless, this singular pronoun is occasionally expanded to suggest a shared experience such as when the narrator concludes the fourth chapter, 'The Prison World', by saying: 'Вот каков, в общих видах, у нас есть и обретается по острогам тюремный мир' ('This is the type of prison world that exists in our jails').[68] Equally, in the fifth story 'Grabitel'skaia shaika' ('A Gang of Thieves'), the narrator uses the more conventional 'мы' to outline how the narrative will proceed: 'Удастся ли ему это намерение, или нет — увидим дальше, а теперь займемся рассматриванием записной книжечки' ('We will see later whether his plan succeeds or not; but not let's concern ourselves with an inspection of his written notebook').[69] The impulse behind, and the effect of, the use of the pronouns 'вы' and 'мы' are quite distinct in these early works of crime fiction. Whilst the former aims to emphasize the quasi-factual status of the writing by simultaneously collapsing the diegetic boundary separating reader from narrator and underscoring the narrator's direct experience of the situations he describes, the latter is a far more straightforward trope of all writing, including literary fiction. In this respect, therefore, the use of 'мы' can be taken as just one signal of the presence in these works of very many poetic devices that not only denote the literary pretensions of memoir writing but also fit squarely into the genre of literary fiction.

## The Pursuit of a Literary-Fictional Aesthetic

In the preface to *Notes of an Investigator,* Timofeev's narrator explicitly claims not to entertain any literary pretensions in the writing of his work. He states:

В заключение прошу читателя не ожидать и не требовать от меня блестящего литературного изложения, потому что я вовсе не имею поползновения стяжать себе своим трудом какую-нибудь литературную известность.[70]

[In conclusion, I would ask the reader not to expect or to demand a brilliant literary exposition from me because I have no pretensions whatsoever to any sort of literary fame by means of my work.]

Timofeev's disclaimer should, however, be treated sceptically. Although, as we have seen, these three early examples of Russian crime writing employ a range of techniques that encourage the reader to view them as quasi-factual memoirs, each of them reads equally well as a work of literary fiction. All three, but most notably Timofeev's *Notes of an Investigator* and Stepanov's *The Innocent and the Guilty,* feature stories that read no differently from the sort of straightforward crime *fiction* that will become the mainstay of the genre in Russia from the 1870s onwards.[71] Given the aesthetic aims evinced by the genre of memoir, the presence of such literary fictional touches does not, of course, serve to disprove the potentially factual status of the events that inspire the accounts. However, so as to underscore further the generic hybridity of the works by Sokolovskii, Stepanov and Timofeev, this final section of the chapter will briefly consider certain of their techniques that indicate either a preoccupation with the aesthetic, rather than the purely factual, or which are akin to devices often encountered in works of literary fiction.

The first of these concerns the shared use between memoir and literary fiction of techniques related to the creation of a sense of verisimilitude. As Holmgren argues with regard to an historical period that overlaps with the birth of Russian crime writing:

> the relationship between realist fiction and the memoir [...] proved reciprocal: while fiction 'digested' and transformed the memoir, the memoir absorbed and flaunted literary features [...] Russian fiction's dependence on and interaction with the memoir intensified over the second third of the nineteenth century, as Russian writers and critics avidly pursued a poetics of realism [...].[72]

There are, of course, numerous devices that contribute to the 'poetics of realism', but one that plays a significant role not only in these three works but in the effect created by all crime fiction (as will be discussed at greater length in Chapter 3), is the use of dialogue and direct speech. The collections by Sokolovskii, Timofeev and Stepanov all accentuate the mimetic presentation of conversations or interviews that are supposed to have taken place during the course of their investigations by incorporating a great deal of dialogue. There are two aspects of this use of dialogue that are worth noting at this stage. The first is the degree to which these early works include examples of local dialect and more popular or lower-class pronunciation to create the sense of a mimetic fictional world. In Timofeev's *Notes of an Investigator*, for instance, whilst descriptions provided by the narrator-investigator's voice are in standard Russian, the exchanges he has with characters he meets in the Western provinces of the country where he is first appointed are far more colloquial and marked with local colour. In the opening chapter, 'First Impressions', the speech of the character, Gershko, who is desperate to be taken on as the narrator's steward, is clearly differentiated from standard, educated Russian. As he tries to ingratiate himself with the narrator, he boasts: 'А знаете, сто я вам сказу, васе благородие, в целом свете нет таких паненок як у нас, хотите я вам показу' ('Know what, yer 'onour: round 'ere we 'ave the best girls in the world. You want me to show you?').[73] Moreover, and in a more ethically questionable display of verisimilitude, in a text that overtly displays the anti-Semitic sentiments of some of the characters, the pronunciation and speech patterns of the many Jewish characters are also captured: 'Послусайте, господин, вам сто надо? [...] Здесь, васе благородие, васа квартира' ('Listen, sir, what you need? [...] Here, yer 'onour, is yer apartment').[74] Such presentation of more colloquial styles of speech is not restricted to Timofeev's work. It is a prominent feature of the work of Sokolovskii as well as of Popov's collection, *The Guilty and the Innocent*. Indeed, for the non-native speaker of Russian, comprehension of these two collections presents something of a challenge given the degree to which slang and local dialect are employed to imbue the narrative with a sense of realism. The practice here recalls that enacted by Dostoevskii with regard to Shishkin and various of the other characters in *Notes from the House of the Dead*, a work informed by research undertaken for his ethnographic study, *Sibirskaia tetrad'* (*The Siberian Notebook*). Alexander Burry's explanation of the relationship between these two works by Dostoevskii serves to illuminate this aspect of our discussion of crime writing: '*The Siberian Notebook* contains 522 direct quotations of the lower-class prisoners' utterances — folk songs, convict songs, proverbs, slang, and other colloquial expressions — of which 306 appear in *Notes from the House of the Dead*.'[75] Whilst arguably not as emphatic as in Dostoevskii's work, the inclusion of a high degree of such vernacular and stylized speech in the collections by Sokolovskii and Timofeev is undoubtedly intended to persuade the reader of the verisimilitude of the fictional world. And it is a technique employed widely across various forms of literary fiction during the same period.

Stepanov's *The Innocent and the Guilty* provides examples of the second way in which dialogue is harnessed to promote a sense of realism in early Russian crime writing. On a number of occasions, Stepanov's work presents verbal exchanges between characters in a form that suggests a lack of narrative mediation: in the manner of a dramatic script or libretto, the name or title of the character is given at the start of the line and then his/her speech appears with no speech tags as the voice of the narrator withdraws entirely.[76] The removal of the voice of the narrator from such dialogues is a favoured technique for attempting to persuade the reader that the characters are 'speaking for themselves' in a manner that more closely replicates extrafictional reality. Interestingly, it is a device that successfully spans the aesthetic-realist/quasi-factual divide because this same form of untagged discourse is to be found in certain passages of court transcripts reproduced in newspaper or polemical articles. So, for example, it appears on a couple of occasions in Dostoevskii's article 'Protsess Lasenera' where it imitates the style of the original transcripts of the trial published in French newspapers of the time.[77] Whether in Dostoevskii's article or in the early works of Russian crime writing, this dramatic presentation of dialogue remains an element of literary-aesthetic stylization. It coexists in each case with other forms of speech presentation, including directly reported untagged speech, direct speech featuring tags from the narrator, and indirect speech paraphrased by the narrator. Whilst these various forms may occupy different points on a spectrum of mimetic presentation, they all remain, to some extent, constructs of literary fiction intended to produce a particular effect upon the reader. The emphasis placed on modes of direct speech in these early works of Russian crime writing responds, therefore, to the demands of a poetics of literary realism whilst also, as will be seen in Chapter 3, contributing to the texts' pursuit of suspense and a hierarchy of authority.

In spite of the emphasis that each of these three early works places on their utilitarian or educative intentions, each one also demonstrates an undeniable preoccupation with the aesthetic, as evidenced by their use of both artistically inspired analogies and literary symbolism. The inclusion in Sokolovskii's *Prison and Life* of analogies drawn between the criminal investigator and the anatomist, as well as to dramatic performance, have been referred to above. However, the importance of specifically artistic analogies to both the referential and aesthetic effect of Sokolovskii's work is revealed by his inclusion of at least two more comparisons in the opening two chapters of his volume. Each one reveals a more lyrical side to Sokolovskii's narrator as he reaches across to different aesthetic traditions. So, in the first chapter, the narrator embarks on an elaborate and mixed analogy in order to criticize the illogicality of condemning a man such as the recidivist thief, Dragunov, in whose fate social conditions play such a decisive role. The narrator explains:

> Но в том-то и беда, что гораздо легче написать слово «преступник», чем добросовестно произнести приговор над человеком, в том то и беда, что от худых семян, да от худой почвы могла только и вырасти, что одна худая трава, в том то и беда, что прилагать к худой траве закон возмездия за то что она не стала к обоюдному желанию хорошей, больше странно, чем тянуть к ответу человека, ни разу не бравшего в руки музыкального инструмента, за то, что он не может усладить вас симфонией Моцарта.[78]

> [But the trouble is that it is much easier to use the word 'criminal' than to conscientiously pronounce a sentence on someone; the trouble is that from poor seeds and from poor soil only a single poor blade of grass can grow; the trouble is that to take vengeance on this poor blade of grass for the fact that it has not, for the general good, turned out better is much stranger than holding to account a person who has never held a musical instrument in their hands for the fact that they are not able to please you with a Mozart symphony.]

Despite the earlier dramatic analogy, this mention of Mozart strikes the reader precisely because of the association it makes between elements of so-called 'low' and 'high' culture. Just as the analogy seeks to collapse the hierarchical divisions between an ex-serf forced into crime and a world-famous composer, so perhaps it also aims to bring writing about previously masked elements from lower social strata closer to examples of high culture. Equally, the repetition here of the construction 'but the trouble is' lends the text a more poetic and stylized appearance as the effect of the analogy builds.

Sokolovskii demonstrates a similar taste for cultural cross-reference in the extended description of the life of the criminal, Kariag, which is recounted as part of the third chapter, 'Nabolevshie' ('The Long-Suffering'). Kariag is used by Sokolovskii as an example of an individual whose fateful crime is the result of a single, seemingly inconsequential event, but one that acts to tip the scales in a lifetime full of suffering. Kariag is described as a lifelong barge hauler on the river Volga, a job that, even before Ilya Repin's famous 1872 painting, was taken to be broadly emblematic of the inhumanity of serfdom and the potential for suffering in the human condition. He works for twenty years without ever complaining until, at the end of one particularly harsh summer, Kariag goes into an inn with a new landlord and asks for some vodka. The inexperienced landlord serves Kariag before taking his money and, when he realizes that his customer has no money to pay, he seizes the barge-hauler by the neck. This act, the narrator says, is the straw that breaks the camel's back: Kariag punches the landowner so hard that he kills him on the spot. Alongside classical references to Kariag's 'геркулесовк[ая] силищ[а]' ('Herculean strength'),[79] the narrator also includes a couple of lines from a Russian folk song used by both peasants and barge haulers to regulate their working rhythm: 'Ох! Дубинушку охнем! | Ох! зеленую дерним! | Подерним!' ('Oh! Heave ho! | Oh! Pull the green! | Pull!'). The appearance of these song lines in the midst of Sokolovskii's narrative serves to remind the reader of its aesthetic intentions and credentials. It enhances the sense of poetry that has already been created by the terms of Sokolovskii's description of Kariag's stoicism and fortitude in the face of his inhumanely demanding working life. Its fleeting appearance also serves as an implicit *mise en abyme* of Sokolovskii's narrator's claim regarding the minute changes that have to occur in order to transform a law-abiding man into a criminal.

The collections of Sokolovskii, Stepanov and Timofeev offer up myriad other instances of such aesthetic reference and poetic stylization. However, we will content ourselves here with a couple of examples taken from Timofeev's *Notes of an Investigator* that are broadly representative of the phenomena being described. The opening chapter, 'First Impressions', sees the narrator describe how he comes to be appointed as a judicial investigator and how he travels to his first posting in the T★★★ region. What is significant here, not least because it is representative of a more broadly encountered trend, is the manner in which the narrator combines a description of his expectations about his future in a new job with a description of a train journey. Such an association between musings about the future and the image of the journey is a popular literary trope, and one that had been rehearsed in the Russian context by authors such as Aleksandr Radishchev in his 1790 work *Puteshestvie iz Peterburga v Moskvu* (*Journey from Petersburg to Moscow*) and Nikolai Gogol in *Mertvye dushi* (*Dead Souls*) from 1842. Timofeev's narrator begins by noting that: 'Открывающаяся передо мною новая жизнь, новые довольно серьезные обязанности, меня приятно радовали' ('The new life and new and rather serious obligations that were opening up in front of me pleased me').[80] The association drawn here between the sense of geographical movement into an unknown space and the embarkation on a new professional adventure is obvious. Moreover, the symbolic resonance of the narrator's description of how his initially hopeful expectations become more pessimistic and fearful as day turns to night on the train is difficult to miss. He confesses that, in the darkness, 'Я стал чего-то бояться, путался в своих соображениях, в попытке вразумить себя путем логики, что именно меня тревожит, чего я боюсь, и при всем желании этого не достигал' ('I began to be afraid of something, got lost in my musings, in my attempt to reason with myself, by means of logic, about what exactly was worrying me and what I was afraid of, but in spite of these desires, was not able to do so').[81] His fears only multiply as he nears his destination and the description of his progress becomes more urgent. Indeed, his fears are never definitively resolved but just replaced by actual practice as he arrives at his posting and begins to undertake his work. Timofeev's narrative reinforces the sense of symbolic interpretation later in this same chapter through the use of pathetic fallacy. In a description that features a further instance of journeying, as the narrator-investigator travels on to the town where he will finally be stationed, the elements appear to reflect his state of mind. In an echo of his earlier pessimism on the train, the narrator is filled with a sense of foreboding as he sets out in an uncomfortable carriage and he describes:

> Погода, когда я выехал из К__ц, была порядочная, но по мере приближения к С__кам она стала портиться, начался дождь, сначала слабый, а потом все сильнее и сильнее, подул порывистый ветер, и я был уже совершенно прозябшим от холода.[82]

> [When I set out from K__ts the weather was fine, but as I drew closer to S__k it began to deteriorate: it began to rain, at first lightly but then more and more heavily, and a gusting wind began to blow and I was already completely frozen from the cold.]

The description of these inhospitable weather conditions presages the foreboding appearance on the horizon of lights belonging to men who have formed an impromptu roadblock. The description of the combination of darkness and inclement weather poetically expresses the narrator's state of mind as he undertakes this journey into the unknown and is a feature encountered in various other literary-fictional genres.

The quotation above illustrating the Mozart analogy in Sokolovskii's *Prison and Life* contains evidence of a further element that promotes the perception of these works as literary-aesthetic texts. The rhythmic repetition of the phrase 'the trouble is' in that excerpt gestures towards a preoccupation with literary and poetic language that is shared by all three works and that contributes significantly to a sense of them as occupying a border zone between factual and fictional writing. In each, the desire to find appropriate linguistic terms for the description and reproduction of lived experience is constantly married with a concern for the aesthetic impact and emotionally persuasive power of language. Indeed, the preoccupation with language they share is clearly announced by Sokolovskii when he expresses a variation of the oft-voiced concern about the inadequacy of words to capture experience. In the opening chapter of the volume, Sokolovskii's narrator opines:

> Окончательное открытие следователя — только известная формула, выраженная дубого-канцелярским языком — но за нею скрыта вся жизненная суть, все те лихорадочно-страстные проявления борьбы, свидетель которых бывает один только следователь. Эти последние не укладываются на бумагу, их не уловишь, как не уловишь откуда-то донесшийся звук, откуда-то промелькнувший луч...[83]

> [The ultimate discovery of the investigator is just a well-known formulation, expressed in wooden judicial language; but behind it is concealed the whole web of life, all of the feverishly passionate displays of the struggle, to which the only witness is the investigator. These displays cannot be put down on paper, they cannot be captured, just as it is impossible to capture a sound being carried from far away, or a ray of light penetrating from somewhere...]

In spite of this dissatisfaction with the descriptive powers of language, each of these early Russian crime writers nevertheless attempts to harness it in order to promote the aesthetic qualities of their descriptions of reality and, in so doing, to provoke an emotional reaction in the reader. So, for instance, the description in *Prison and Life*'s first chapter of the narrator-investigator's visit to the thief Dragunov's family home is constructed in such a way as to create as stark a contrast as possible between the peace of the natural scene around the hut and the horrific picture of human suffering presented by Dragunov's wife in labour on the floor, surrounded by her bewildered and bedraggled children. The narrator describes how: 'на дворе был славный, осенний день; в разреженно-холодном воздухе стояла ничем не возмутимая тишина' ('it was a glorious, autumnal day in the yard; and an undisturbed silence hung in the sharply cold air').[84] However, in the very next sentence, this gentle pastoral scene is abruptly interrupted by the moans of Dragunov's wife and her husband's plea not to have to go into his house: 'на куски меня режьте [...] умирать мне легче' ('cut me into pieces [...] death would be easier than this').[85] The juxtaposition of such benign and such violent imagery is a powerful expression of the role of social circumstance in the commission of crime: over the course of the narrator's acquaintance with Dragunov, the thief comes to express no remorse for his various criminal transgressions, yet he is utterly broken by the suffering of his wife and children.

Elsewhere, and in quite different terms, in Stepanov's story 'The Horse-Rustler's Bridle', the narrator-investigator demonstrates his concern with the aesthetic impact of his account during a description of a visit he makes to the village of Churilovo. The narrator sets out to this relatively well-off settlement on the trail of the murderers of Filka the horse rustler and the account of his arrival shows a concern not just for realistic detail but also for aesthetic verbal expression. Given some of the more down-at-heel places he has visited as part of this and other investigations, the narrator is impressed by the investment into and workmanship of (if not the quality) of the village's houses and his attention is particularly caught by their shutters and canopies:

> Вот и живопись: на ставнях ярко раскрашены горшки с цветами неизвестной флоры доморощенного маляра! вот сапоги намазаны, а вот на фронтоне два охотника [...] между ними не то собака, не то лев, а вот и холщевой навес с своими баранками, хлебом, огурцами и разными разностями [...][86]

> [The image was thus: on the shutters in bright colours were painted pots with flowers of an unknown kind by a primitive painter! Here were daubed boots and here on the pediment two hunters [...] between them stood either a dog or a lion, and here was a canvas canopy featuring ring-shaped rolls, bread, cucumbers and different variations [...]]

This description succeeds in simultaneously providing the reader with a detailed account of the image on the shutter and, by means of its verbal structures, implying its rather original nature. The repetition of the 'вот' ('here') demonstrative imitates the movement of the narrator's eye across the image as it picks up the various constituent elements, whilst the 'не то' ('either') suggests his confusion as to the exact nature of certain parts. Whilst hardly lyrical, the description offers clear evidence of Stepanov's narrator's ability to incorporate more conventionally literary passages into his 'notes'. Similarly, the opening passages of the next story in the collection 'Podnevol'nyi brak' ('Forced Marriage'), skilfully depict a tranquil pastoral scene that is reminiscent of those described in Turgenev's *Notes of a Hunter*. Before the violent murder of the peasant, Andrei, is revealed (he is killed by a hammer and is then further disfigured by falling face first onto a tree stump), the focus is on his cousin, Ermolaich, patiently ploughing his field. As with the example above taken from Sokolovskii, the description of the benign natural world as the sun sets, the shadows lengthen and the air cools contrasts starkly with the violence of the murder that is committed at this very same moment in the forest close by.

Although Timofeev is keen to underline the utilitarian intention of his work and, as has been seen, the traces of quasi-memoir are manifold in it, *Notes of an Investigator* also provides ample evidence of his aesthetic and literary inclination. So, for example, the story 'Prestuplenie sueveriia' ('A Crime of Superstition'), that details a horrific case of the disinterment and mutilation of multiple corpses from a cemetery, owes a clear stylistic debt to the Gothic short stories and folk tales popular in Russia earlier in the nineteenth century. The catalyst behind the crime is an old female fortune teller who closely resembles the archetypal witch figure in both appearance and behaviour. Moreover, a significant thread in the narrator's investigation involves tracing the provenance of a black cat that has been buried with one of the bodies and that the villagers take to be an incarnation of the devil. Meanwhile, in the collection's final story 'Prostitutka' ('The Prostitute'), the narrator-investigator demonstrates his capacity for more lyrical description as he recounts the victim, Tereza Pavlovna's, fall into destitution and sex work. For a time before her death, Tereza is apparently a popular prostitute amongst the soldiers stationed in the town of Priazhsk, but:

> затем постоянное беспросыпное пьянство, бессонные ночи, проводимые в кутежах, бродячая жизнь, безысходная беда, безвыходность, беспомощность сокрушили ее до конца [...] И звезда первой величины, так не давно и так ярко сиявшая на кабацком горизонте, день ото дня все больше и больше меркнула и наконец погасла в воде под льдинами.[87]

> [then the constant and incessant drinking, the sleepless nights spent carousing, the itinerant life, the inescapable poverty, the hopelessness, the helplessness shattered her before the end [...] And this great star that had until so recently shone so brightly on the tavern horizon, faded more and more with each passing day and was finally extinguished in the water beneath the ice floe.]

The extended sentences here, combined with the repetition in the first of the alliterative 'без' prefix, succeed in capturing the sense of an inexorable descent towards death in Tereza's biography. The narrator-investigator's empathy for this woman, a characteristic visible not only elsewhere in Timofeev's volume but also in the work of Sokolovskii and Stepanov, is evident both in this more lyrical passage and in a slightly later one. A couple of pages later, the narrator is prompted to consider how easily and randomly a person's life can be changed beyond recognition. And this consideration leads him into a passage where he imagines Tereza not as she is in death but as a nineteen-year-old girl who is full of life and of beauty. Again, this idealized vision is described in poetic terms that are carefully constructed so as to produce a persuasive effect on the reader, and it is a passage that stands at odds with other of the more reportage- or documentary-style elements of Timofeev's work.

## Conclusion

The consideration of aesthetic reference and effect in these three works is not intended to suggest that the genre of memoir is uninterested in producing an aesthetic effect. Rather, the aim has been to demonstrate that these three examples of early Russian crime writing skilfully combine impulses and techniques that are broadly associated with both non-fictional and fictional genres. In their use, for instance, of (sub)titles, their construction of an authoritative narrative voice and their gestures towards the reader, the works of Sokolovskii, Stepanov and Timofeev seek to persuade the reader that the accounts they provide are authentic and based on factual reality. At the same time, however, each work is notable for what the editor of a 2013 electronic edition of Popov's *The Guilty and the Innocent* calls 'бесспорн[ое] литературн[ое] дарован[ие]' ('an unquestionable literary talent').[88] These three founding works of crime fiction in late Imperial Russia choose to inhabit generic border zones. Most strikingly, they employ stylistic devices associated with the genre of the quasi-factual memoir whilst also encouraging the reader to engage with them as more conventional literary fictions. As Gary Saul Morson argues in *The Boundaries of Genre*, with regards to Dostoevskii, the 'systematic defiance of generic norms is quite common in Russian literature'.[89] The generic hybridity present in the works of Sokolovskii, Stepanov and Timofeev suggests that they can be considered to be examples of the first category of what Morson goes on to call 'threshold literature'. He defines this type thus: 'the author of a threshold work may create an entire text of uncertain status and exploit the resonance between two kinds of reading'.[90] These three early Russian crime writers all successfully create and exploit the resonance between conventionally factual genres, such as documentary sketches, polemical journalism and memoir, and that of imaginative literary fiction. The tendency towards the factually inspired genres speaks to early Russian crime writing's preoccupation with the concepts of truth and authenticity. Implicit in this choice is a sense of the authors' awareness of the need to persuade the reader of the nascent genre's credentials by associating it with the real world of lived experience. Would readers respond more favourably to this new mode of writing, with its concentration on the seamier side of life, if its early exponents emphasized the material's factual nature and the value that might be drawn from that? Yet these are also writers who wish, even if they make claims to the contrary, to present their texts as works of art with aesthetic and literary preoccupations and aspirations. Arguably the most significant consequence of the generic fluidity of these works is the spotlight that it shines upon the figure of the narrator and, crucially, the various ways in which these narrator-investigators earn authority in the eyes of the reader. The intertwined notions of moral and judicial authority, and the search for truth, as embodied in the figure of the criminal investigator, will form the basis of much of the analysis offered in this book's subsequent chapters of works that belong more squarely in the category of Russian crime *fiction*.

## Notes to Chapter 1

1. Precisely because of their generic fluidity, I hesitate to use the term 'crime fiction' to refer to these works.
2. Louise McReynolds, *Murder Most Russian: True Crime and Punishment in Late Imperial Russia* (Ithaca, NY: Cornell University Press, 2013), p. 24.
3. Stephen Rachman, 'Poe and the Origins of Detective Fiction', in *The Cambridge Companion to American Crime Fiction*, ed. by Catherine Ross Nickerson (Cambridge: Cambridge University Press, 2010), pp. 17–28 (p. 22).
4. I have previously written about the intersections between Russian crime fiction and polemical journalism in 'Debating Detectives: The Influence of *publitsistika* on Nineteenth-Century Russian Crime Fiction', *Modern Language Review*, 107.1 (2012), 230–58.
5. There has previously been confusion about the publication details of *Ostrog i zhizn'*. McReynolds, who mentions the work in her *Murder Most Russian*, but does not discuss its contents in any detail, erroneously claims that it was serialized in *Vremia* in 1866, even though that journal had been closed in 1863 (p. 24). The Brokhaus-Efron encyclopedia entry for Sokolovskii states that *Ostrog i zhizn'* was published in 1863. Konstantine Klioutchkine claims in 'The Rise of *Crime and Punishment* from the Air of the Media', *Slavic Review*, 61.1 (2002), 88–108 (p. 97), that elements of the work appeared in the February 1863 volume of *Vremia*. Correct information about the publication of Sokolovskii's work is provided in David Keily's unpublished thesis '*The Brothers Karamazov* and the Fate of Russian Truth'.
6. Later in 1863, the October volume of *Sovremennik* carried three more stories: 'Skvernye minuty' ('Unpleasant Moments'), which is central to much of the discussion of Sokolovskii in this chapter, 'Zabavy' ('Amusements') and 'Myl'nye puzyri' ('Soap Bubbles'), under the slightly more concise main title 'Iz zapisok sledovatelia' ('From the Notes of an Investigator'). During 1864 and 1865, Dostoevskii's second journal, *Epokha* (*Epoch*), published various others of Sokolovskii's stories including 'Trushkov' and 'Shamsheev' (in March 1864), 'Za gorodskoi chertoi' ('Beyond the City Limit') (in November 1864) and then 'Ozorkov' in May 1865.
7. For example, 'Skvernye minuty' becomes the opening chapter of *Prison and Life* and includes in the later publication a couple of minor changes, including to the name of the protagonist and the excision of the closing sentence of the original story. The original version of 'Zabavy' is retitled 'Zabavy i naslazhdenie' ('Amusements and Pleasures') in the longer work and has a new second section added to it. 'Iz zapisok sledovatelia' is recast as 'Sadovod guliai' in the full version, the name of the protagonist is changed, and again the final sentence of the original is omitted in the later publication.
8. Reitblat, *Ot Bovy k Bal'montu*, p. 193.
9. Keily, p. 121.
10. Reitblat, *Ot Bovy k Bal'montu*, p. 196.
11. The significant distinction between the works of Sokolovskii and Stepanov on the one hand, and Dostoevskii on the other, is that, in the former works, the description of prison life is provided by an agent of the law, rather than by one of the other criminals.
12. McReynolds, p. 24. She does not, however, provide many details of their respective employment histories. K. Popov, *Vinovatye i pravye: rasskazy sudebnogo sledovatelia* (originally published Moscow: Mamontov, 1871; republished by Salamandra P.V.V., 2013, see <http://www.salamandrapvv.blogspot.co.uk/p/blog-page_87.html>).
13. Ibid., p. 79.
14. Most notable amongst Timofeev's other publications for the purposes of this monograph are *Iz vospominanii sudebnogo sledovatelia: ocherki i rasskazy* (*From the Reminiscences of a Judicial Investigator: Sketches and Tales*) from 1878, *Iz ugolovnoi khroniki* (*From the Criminal Chronicle*) of 1879 and *V*

*pogone: na poiskakh za pokhishchennym rebenkom* (*In Pursuit: The Search for an Abducted Child*), published in 1880. He also authored a number of works informed by his work as a procurator, rather than as an investigator, including *Po nabliudeniiam v ugolovnom sude* (*On Observations in the Criminal Court*) and *Sud prisiazhnykh v Rossii: sudebnye ocherki* (*Jury Courts in Russia: Judicial Sketches*), both of which were published in 1881. Stepanov also wrote 'Kto podzhigatel'?' ('Who is the Arsonist?'), which appeared in the journal *Vsemirnyi trud* (*Universal Work*) in January 1868 and 'Kabala' ('The Cabbal') which was serialized in several consecutive volumes of *Nedelia* (*The Week*) in 1869.

15. S. A. Panov uses 'iz zapisok sudebnogo sledovatelia' ('from the notes of a judicial investigator') as the subtitle to his 1876 novella *Iz zhizni uezdnogo gorodka* (*From the Life of a Provincial Town*). A. P. Chekhov uses the same formulation not for the entirety of the work but for the framed narrative in *Drama na okhote* (*The Shooting Party*) from 1884–85. A. I. Sokolova then uses it more prominently in her 1892 work *Spetaia pesnia: iz zapisok starogo sledovatelia*.

16. According to Gérard Genette in *Palimpsests: Literature in the Second Degree*, trans. by C. Newman and C. Doubinsky (Lincoln, NE: University of Nebraska Press, 1997) paratexts include: 'a title, a subtitle, intertitles; prefaces, postfaces, notices, forewords, etc.; marginal, infrapaginal, terminal notes; epigraphs; illustrations; blurbs, book covers, dust jackets, and many other kinds of secondary signals, whether allographic or autographic' (p. 3).

17. Reitblat, 'Detektivnaia literatura i russkii chitatel'', p. 128.

18. It is not the case that by the early 1860s in Russia, when Sokolovskii first used this subtitle, the detective novel was a 'despised' genre. Such a reputation was established rather later, as Reitblat implicitly acknowledges, when he refers to the translation of works by the French writer Émile Gaboriau and Wilkie Collins, for example.

19. The decision in this work uniformly to employ the term 'notes' in the translations of Sokolovskii, Stepanov and Timofeev's titles is intended to indicate the generic ambiguity they have in common.

20. It is also fascinating to consider that Charles Dickens's first novel, *The Pickwick Papers* (or, *The Posthumous Papers of the Pickwick Club*) of 1836, was published in Russian as *Posmertnye zapiski Pikvikskogo kluba* in the late 1840s. The novel also features a chapter in which the eponymous hero encounters prisoners in the Fleet in a manner not dissimilar to that encountered in places in Sokolovskii's *Prison and Life* in particular. In the Soviet period, as mentioned in the Introduction, Lev Romanovich Sheinin published the autobiographical cycle, *Zapiski sledovatelia*, having worked in the USSR Prosecutor's Office.

21. Karla Oeler, 'The Dead Wives in the Dead House: Narrative Inconsistency and Genre Confusion in Dostoevskii's Autobiographical Prison Novel', *Slavic Review*, 61:3 (2002), 519–34 (p. 519).

22. Monika Fludernik notes in *An Introduction to Narratology* (London: Routledge, 2009) that, 'the issue of fictionality in narrative is complex and highly controversial'; she argues that 'any decision as to whether a text reports real events or imagined ones needs to be taken by the reader or listener, and this decision will depend on the context' (pp. 58 and 60). See also Lennard J. Davis, *Factual Fictions: The Origins of the English Novel* (New York, NY: Columbia University Press, 1983) and Barbara Foley, *Telling the Truth: The Theory and Practice of Documentary Fiction* (Ithaca, NY: Cornell University Press, 1986).

23. Susan Lanser, *The Narrative Act* (Princeton, NJ: Princeton University Press, 1981), p. 163.

24. A. A. Shkliarevskii is the true champion of the term 'rasskaz', using it repeatedly in his stories, including 'Rasskaz sudebnogo sledovatelia' ('The Tale of a Judicial Investigator') of 1872, *Ubiistvo bez sledov: rasskaz iz ugolovnoi khroniki* (*A Murder Without Traces: A Tale from the Judicial Chronicle*), published in 1878, and 'Rokovaia sud'ba: rasskaz sledovatelia' ('Deathly Fate: The Tale of an Investigator') from 1880. Timofeev subtitles as 'rasskaz' the stories 'Katorga dushi' ('Servitude of the Soul') and 'Nezakonnarozhdennaia' ('Born out of Wedlock') in his 1878 collection *Iz vospominanii sudebnogo sledovatelia*. Several of A. E. Zarin's works in the early twentieth century employ 'istoriia', including 'Chetvertyi: istoriia odnogo syska' ('The Fourth Man: The Story of an Investigation') and 'Poteria chesti: tragicheskaia istoriia' ('Loss of Honour: A Tragic Story'), both from 1909. Zarin is primarily known as an historical novelist, but also wrote a number of interesting detective stories.

25. Julian Symons, *Bloody Murder: From the Detective Story to the Crime Novel: A History* (London: Pan Books, 1994; first published 1972), pp. 37–40. Sita A. Schütt also talks about the influence of Vidocq in her chapter 'French Crime Fiction', in *The Cambridge Companion to Crime Fiction*, ed. by Martin Priestman (Cambridge: Cambridge University Press, 2003), pp. 59–76 (p. 75).

26. Ian Ousby, in his *Bloodhounds of Heaven: The Detective in English Fiction from Godwin to Doyle* (Cambridge, MA: Harvard University Press, 1976) (p. 59 and p. 183 n. 24) attributes the work to Thomas Gaspey, although it was originally published anonymously. See Thomas Gaspey, *Richmond: or, Scenes in the Life of a Bow Street Officer, Drawn Up from His Private Memoranda* (London: Colburn, 1827)

27. Ousby (ibid., p. 66) labels *Recollections of a Police-Officer* 'fiction elaborately but ineffectively masquerading as fact' and identifies the author as the 'hack novelist' and journalist William Russell, who was known to use 'Waters' as a pseudonym.

28. Ibid., p. 72.

29. Beth Holmgren in the 'Introduction' to her edited collection *The Russian Memoir: History and Literature* (Evanston, IL: Northwestern University Press, 2003), pp. ix–xxxix (p. ix).

30. Ibid., p. x.

31. Ibid.

32. Lydia Ginzburg, *On Psychological Prose*, trans. and ed. by Judson Rosengrant (Princeton, NJ: Princeton University Press, 1991), p. 6.

33. See Stephen P. Frank, *Crime, Cultural Conflict and Justice in Rural Russia, 1856–1914* (Berkeley, CA: University of California Press, 1999), pp. 202–03.

34. In *Richmond: or, Scenes in the Life of a Bow Street Officer*, for example, this dominant position is signalled by the fact that the pronoun 'I' is the first word in the text and is then repeated fifteen times in the first four short paragraphs of the text. It is similarly to the fore in Waters's *Recollections of a Police Officer*.

35. The decision to use the terms 'heterodiegetic', 'homodiegetic' and later 'autodiegetic' with reference to narrative voices recognizes the valuable contribution made by Genette in demonstrating the inaccuracy of the terms 'first-person' and 'third-person'. In *Figures III* (Paris: Seuil, 1972), Genette defines a heterodiegetic narrator as one who is absent from the story he recounts, whereas a homodiegetic narrator is present as a character in his story (pp. 252–53). An autodiegetic voice is one that belongs to the main protagonist in the fictional world.

36. Further resemblances between these early works of Russian crime fiction and the feuilleton will be discussed below. However, the roaming eye of the *flâneur* in the feuilleton shares characteristics with the sense of the individual journey and related observations conveyed in memoir.

37. Sokolovskii, *Ostrog i zhizn'*, p. 3.

38. Ibid., p. 6 and p. 21.

39. Narratological theory would rightly insist on differentiating between the voice encountered in any preface and that used in the main body of the narrative. However, in the case of memoir, it is legitimate to assume that the 'extrafictional' voice of the preface and the narrative voice in the main body closely resemble one another.

40. In 'Explaining the Rise and Success of Detective Memoirs in Britain', Haia Shpayer-Makov argues that 'the disparate anecdotes of crime investigation on which each of the [works of memoir] is based are connected into a narrative with a beginning and an end. His life as a detective and his voice as a narrator provide a unifying structure to the book.' Haia Shpayer-Makov, 'Explaining the Rise and Success of Detective Memoirs in Britain', in *Police Detectives in History, 1750–1950*, ed. by Clive Emsley and Haia Shpayer-Makov (Aldershot: Ashgate, 2006), pp. 103–33 (p. 116).

41. Ibid., p. 115.

42. Pierre François Lacenaire, *Mémoires, poèmes et lettres* (Paris, Albin Michel: 1968; first published 1836), p. 26. The similarity between Lacenaire's autopsy analogy and certain comparisons in Russian crime fiction, and particularly their influence on authority, will be discussed in Chapter 2.

43. Timofeev, *Zapiski sledovatelia*, pp. 4–5.

44. The emphasis on the usefulness of the notes represents a further similarity with the genre of the feuilleton that claimed to discuss various cultural topics of interest to the general public.

45. Dostoevskii, 'Protsess Lasenera', p. 1.

46. The ironic preface to Waters' *Recollections of a Police-Officer*, which denies its own status as a preface, refers to the same issue of usefulness when it states that the work to follow describes 'incidents more or less interesting and instructive of the domestic warfare constantly waging between the agents and breakers of the law' (p. vi).

47. In *The Distinction of Fiction* (Baltimore, MD: Johns Hopkins University Press, 1999) Dorrit Cohn argues: 'History is more often concerned with humanity in the plural than in the singular, with events and changes affecting entire societies, than those affecting the lives of individual beings' (p. 18).

48. Timofeev, *Zapiski sledovatelia*, p. 1. Much later in the collection, in the story 'Prostitutka' ('The Prostitute'), the narrator indulges in an extended passage of reflection on the role of chance in human life that chimes with broader debates in the nineteenth century regarding determinism and human free will (pp. 341–42).

49. In an article entitled 'Vyderzhki iz russkogo zakonodatel'stva' ('Excerpts from Russian Legislation') in the February 1862 volume of *Vremia*, O. Filippov states: 'Ни одна отрасль законодательства не выражает так ярко, живо и отчетливо быт народа в каждый момент пройденной им жизни, как его уголовное право' ('No branch of legislation expresses in as clear, as lively and as distinct a manner the everyday life of the people in every lived moment as does its criminal law') (p. 558). In two long articles published in *Vremia* in March and April of 1863, V. P. Popov argues that, because criminals know in advance that killing and stealing are wrong, there must be a reason why they commit their crimes regardless. He proposes, as a consequence, that the principal preoccupation of Russia's new judicial system should be precisely the search for and eradication of this reason (p. 131). He contends that there can be only two explanations for crime: the physiological or psychological make-up of the perpetrator and/or social conditions.

50. P. I. Stepanov's *The Innocent and the Guilty* includes only very few moments of such generalized commentary. One example comes on p. 70 when the narrator reflects: 'Убийство — развязка только драмы, это катастрофа; но чтоб развить ее, нужен был пролог, первый разгар страстей, причины действия, вызвавшие такую развязку' ('Murder is only the denouement of the drama; it is a catastrophe. But in order to unravel it, there needs to be a prologue, the first flaming of passions, reasons for the action which have led to such a denouement'.)

51. Sokolovskii, *Ostrog i zhizn'*, p. 3.

52. In Sokolovskii's narrator's comparison between the role of the investigator and that of the anatomist, there are echoes back to Lacenaire's reference to conducting a post-mortem on his own body.

53. Sokolovskii, *Ostrog i zhizn'*, pp. 10–11.

54. Ibid., p. 27.

55. These characteristics of feuilleton are taken from Donald Fanger, 'Dostoevsky's Early Feuilletons: Approaches to a Myth of the City', *Slavic Review*, 22.3 (1963), 469–82. See also Raffaella Vassena, *Reawakening National Identity: Dostoevskii's Diary of a Writer and its Impact on Russian Society* (Bern: Peter Lang, 2007). Vassena notes that the feuilleton genre became popular in Russia between 1830 and 1840 and that Dostoevskii was 'fascinated with the possibilities of formal experimentation' it provided (p. 29).

56. See, for instance, Marc Lits, *Le Roman policier: introduction à la théorie et à l'histoire d'un genre littéraire* (Liège: Editions du CÉFAL, 1993), Todd Herzog, 'Crime Stories: Criminal, Society and the Modernist Case History', *Representations*, no. 80 (2002), 34–61; Carlo Salzani, 'The City as Crime Scene: Walter Benjamin and the Traces of the Detective', *New German Critique*, no. 100 (2007), 165–87.

57. Louise McReynolds, '"Who Cares who Killed Ivan Ivanovich?": The Literary Detective in Tsarist Russia', *Russian History*, 36 (2009), 391–406 (p. 393).

58. In Shkliarevskii's 'Kak liudi pogibaiut: rasskaz sledovatelia' ('How People Die: The Tale of an Investigator') from 1872, for instance, the narrator briefly steps back from describing action in

the fictional world to acknowledge that the new breed of judicial investigators often act more like the soon-to-be-introduced justices of the peace in their desire to exercise leniency towards criminals by acknowledging extenuating circumstances (see *Sochineniia A. Shkliarevskogo. Rasskazy sledovatelia*, p. 113).

59. Stepanov, *Pravye i vinovatye*, p. 23.
60. Sokolovskii, *Ostrog i zhizn'*, p. 14.
61. Both Fanger and Vassena note the feuilleton's 'typical device of appealing to the reader' (Vassena, p. 30) and treating him/her as an interlocutor that is undoubtedly picked up by Sokolovskii here.
62. Sokolovskii, *Ostrog i zhizn'*, p. 4.
63. Ibid., p. 11.
64. Timofeev's *Zapiski sledovatelia* features repeated direct addresses to the reader that not only orient his/her interpretation of the main stories but also serve to draw him/her closer into the fictional world.
65. Sokolovskii, *Ostrog i zhizn'*, p. 12.
66. Ibid., p. 16.
67. Timofeev, *Zapiski sledovatelia*, p. 2.
68. Ibid., p. 209.
69. Ibid., p. 237.
70. Ibid., p. 5.
71. Many of the 'literary' devices present in these three works will be discussed as part of the remaining chapters in this book, including: their construction of the narrative voice and characterization; the incorporation of a variety of competing and complementary voices; the exploitation of time to generate both curiosity and suspense; and the use of intertextuality and metatextuality.
72. Holmgren, *The Russian Memoir*, pp. xxvii and xxvi.
73. Timofeev, *Zapiski sledovatelia*, p. 19. In the original Russian, the vernacular speech is indicated by alterations in the spelling of standard Russian words, particularly to the use of consonants.
74. Ibid., p. 34.
75. Alexander Burry, *Multi-Mediated Dostoevsky: Transposing Novels into Opera, Film, and Drama* (Evanston, IL: Northwestern University Press, 2011), p. 76.
76. See, for instance, pp. 20–23 and 27–28 in 'The Horse-Rustler's Bridle' and pp. 71–79 and 83–85 in the following story, 'Podnevol'nyi brak' ('Forced Marriage').
77. Dostoevskii, 'Protsess Lasenera', pp. 24–25, 27, 28–29.
78. Sokolovskii, *Ostrog i zhizn'*, p. 11.
79. Ibid., p. 77.
80. Timofeev, *Zapiski sledovatelia*, p. 12.
81. Ibid., p. 13.
82. Ibid., p. 33.
83. Sokolovskii, *Ostrog i zhizn'*, p. 5.
84. Ibid., pp. 6–7.
85. Ibid., p. 7.
86. Stepanov, *Pravye i vinovatye*, p. 32.
87. Timofeev, *Zapiski sledovatelia*, p. 339.
88. Popov, *Vinovatye i pravye*.
89. Gary Saul Morson, *The Boundaries of Genre: Dostoevsky's Diary of a Writer and the Traditions of Literary Utopia* (Evanston, IL: Northwestern University Press, 1988), p. 4.
90. Ibid., p. 50.

# CHAPTER 2

# Legal Power:
# Authority and its Construction in
# Early Russian Crime Fiction

## The Various Guises of Authority in Crime Fiction

The previous chapter has recognized that the generic hybridity of early works of Russian crime fiction exerts an influence upon the authority enjoyed by the narrative voice. Their various quasi-factual characteristics promote a view of the narrator-investigator as a figure whose accounts of his criminal cases are highly realistic. However, although this aspect of narrator performance has a significant and undeniable part to play in the construction of authority in crime fiction, it is far from being the only one. This second chapter takes the question of authority as its central concern and examines, from a range of perspectives, how it is established and mediated.

The idea of authority, conceived in the broadest terms, is one that, unsurprisingly, lies at the very heart of all crime fiction. In its 'conventional' (that is, non-postmodern) form, crime fiction offers a depiction of the exercise of authority by the state over the transgressive individual, using the law as its instrument. This manifestation of authority in the genre has long been perceived both positively and negatively by critics. William O. Aydelotte, for example, argues that:

> the detective story introduces us to a secure universe. We find here an ordered world obedient to fixed laws. The outcome is certain and the criminal will without fail be beaten by the detective. In this world man has power to control his own affairs and the problems of life can be mastered by human agency.[1]

This characterization is not applicable to all instances of crime fiction, of course, but it does capture effectively the sense of the genre as an essentially conservative literary form in which concepts of good and evil are still clearly delineated and where the former prevails. Such sociological readings focus on crime as an act that disrupts the desired status quo which the exercise of authority seeks to reassert. Particularly with regard to western European practice, however, the nature of the genre's depiction of social and collective authority is often viewed more critically. Martin A. Kayman gives voice to such a reservation when he states that many scholars see detective fiction as:

a literary reflection of, if not propaganda for a new form of social administration and control based on state surveillance. [...] In this sense, detective stories are open to the charge of being fictional promotions of the values of the modern police discipline, defending bourgeois property values, sexual morality and bureaucratic rationalities.[2]

Albeit in more intertextual terms, Ronald R. Thomas expresses a similar view when he argues that:

> the elevation of detective fiction to the pitch of sensational popularity it enjoyed in 1890s England signals the emergence of a narrative of authoritarian containment to compete with and discipline the dominant nineteenth-century narrative of self-determination represented best by the period's fascination with autobiography.[3]

Not only in sentiment, but also in their choice of language, such views unmistakeably echo the work of Michel Foucault in *Discipline and Punish*. Foucault argues that over the course of the nineteenth century a new conception of the criminal emerged in which, as Todd Herzog summarizes, this figure 'becomes someone not just to be judged and punished but also to be known and disciplined'.[4] The significant differences that exist between the models of social organization in western Europe and Russia in the nineteenth century clearly problematize views of Russian crime fiction as a statement of bourgeois authority. Nevertheless, the sense of the genre as one that advances a notion of social administration and control remains highly pertinent in the Russian context. In light of the profound changes wrought to the social landscape in Russia by the 'Great Reforms' of the 1860s and 1870s, crime fiction can be seen to respond to the perceived need to demonstrate that systems of authority and social control continued to function. Although much of the country's social and civic fabric was being significantly remodelled during this period, crime fiction was able to provide reassurance to those who needed it that not only did order and authority as embodied in the judicial system still exist, but that they were now operating on improved terms.

The notion of authority does not exist simply in the abstract in crime fiction, however. Rather, it finds expression in individual characters, most notably in the criminal investigator.[5] In the most straightforward sense, as Peter Thoms points out, 'the investigator's authority inheres [...] in his official status as a representative of the law'.[6] However, just as crime fiction's engagement with the letter of the law can take various forms, so the figure of the detective becomes an embodiment of authority in much more than a strictly legal sense. For Peter Hühn, the detective 'acts as society's agent in order to [...] bind the criminal again to the constraining rules of society through arrest and punishment (imprisonment or execution)'; Kayman characterizes investigators as 'repositories of social power'; and Thomas sees in the literary detective 'a designated figure of social authority'.[7] Whatever the particular epithet applied, it is clear that, in this representative role, the investigator assumes considerable ideological significance. In the nineteenth-century Russian context, where the institution of the judicial investigator was the first step in broader judicial reforms, the status of this figure as a key ideological element in the representation of authority is even greater. By and large, the broadly held opinion, as expressed in *publitsistika* articles of the time, was that the hopes for the reformed legal system in Russia were to be personified in the new judicial investigator. This investigator's position atop a hierarchy of legal authority is made clear in a polemical article from 1860 written by A. Lokhvitskii:

> По действовавшему до сих пор закону все производство следствий лежало на полиции [...]; теперь роль полиции сделалась второстепенной, предварительной а главная передана новому юридическому агенту — судебному следователю.[8]

> [According to the previous legal situation, the entire conduct of investigations was the responsibility of the police [...]; now the role of the police has been made secondary and preparatory and the primary responsibility has been given to a new judicial agent — the judicial investigator.]

Later in the same article, he explains that, whilst police powers are now largely restricted to establishing the mere fact that a crime has taken place, 'власть и права следователя весьма обширны' ('the power and rights of the investigator are extremely wide-ranging').[9] Russian crime fiction in the 1860s and 1870s gave writers the opportunity to illustrate the execution of these new powers and the functioning of this new judicial arrangement in literary form. This depiction tended to be overwhelming conservative: judicial investigators act according to the statutes of law in order to solve a crime and bring the perpetrators to justice. In so doing, they provide not just reassurance that authority still exists in Russian society but also function as positive role models whom other members of society can aspire to emulate.[10] As will be demonstrated in the first main section of the chapter below, the behaviour of the judicial investigator in these works enacts the right type of authority: not a dry and cruel authority, but one which seeks to be more benevolent not just to the victims of crime but also to the perpetrators. By means of such a display of power, the investigator becomes the embodiment of the values considered desirable by the society that has produced him.

The role of metatextuality in crime fiction will be discussed in detail in Chapter 5, but it is worth noting briefly here that the genre's interrogation of authority frequently exploits the etymological link to 'authoring'. One prevalent view of the genre casts the criminal as an author who writes the story of a crime that is then read (and deciphered) by the investigator.[11] The criminal's act of authoring is thus seen to establish an authority that runs counter to that of society and that constitutes an expression of his freedom from constraint. However, it is equally possible to see the detective, whether he simultaneously occupies the position of narrator or not, as the author of the definitive account of the crime that, thanks to his work, becomes legible to the rest of society. His job consists in reading not only the story authored by the criminal, but also all of those recounted by the various witnesses, and of rewriting them into a new and convincing narrative that will be accepted by the judicial system as the truth. Thoms makes clear the relationship between authority and this function of the detective when he says:

> The detective's figurative writing emerges [...] out of a desire to exert control

over others and sometimes [...] over himself. In gratifying a desire to control others, detection often appears as an expression of egoism; here the writing or assembling of the case becomes a method of imposing power upon individuals, who are given characters and assigned places within the plot that the detective devises.[12]

Moreover, a degree of the investigator's authority derives from the fact that he takes the inadequate or undesired story authored by the criminal (inadequate because it is missing certain components that make it a mystery), and, by means of his investigation, remodels it into a more complete story. As such, the genre offers up an implicit interrogation of the power and authority claimed by those occupied in the art of arranging life into acceptable and desirable narratives, such as authors.

Whilst cognizant of the various ways in which authority might be figured in works of crime fiction, the present chapter chooses to address it in terms of how authority is embodied in the persona of the detective and how it is constructed in narrative terms. Informed by narratological theory, the discussion here considers the means used to portray the investigator as a character to be trusted more than any other in the fictional world. In the simplest terms, as Eyal Segal suggests, the question of authority is significant because it means that 'the detective is presented in a manner that establishes the reader's confidence in his ability to solve the mystery'.[13] In actuality, however, matrices of authority in detective fiction function in a more complex fashion. Consequently, this chapter analyses the construction of the investigator's authority from three different, but interrelated, angles. All three relate to Susan Lanser's category of 'diegetic authority' which, along with 'mimetic authority', make up the constituent elements of what she labels the 'status' of the narrative voice.[14] While 'mimetic authority' in Lanser's poetics refers to questions of honesty and reliability, 'diegetic authority' gets subdivided into questions of 'authorization' and 'social identity'. The discussion here takes the latter category first and, in its opening section, evaluates which aspects of social identity prove to be the most influential in establishing the detective's authority in Russian crime fiction. In so doing, it draws up an inventory of the personal and professional attributes that characterized the 'ideal' investigator figure in late Imperial Russian crime fiction. However, an investigator's authority does not derive simply from his possession of individual personal qualities; the perception of authority is largely relational and comparative. In the second section of the chapter, therefore, the attribution of authority to the detective is considered by means of a comparison (either positive or negative) between this figure and various other characters in the fictional world, still in terms of social identity. Initial steps in this direction have been taken in Chapter 1 by the references to the analogies drawn between the investigator and the anatomist and the actor in Sokolovskii's *Prison and Life*, but this second chapter will extend this analysis to include local policemen, doctors and priests. The third and final section of the present chapter moves on to discuss Lanser's category of 'authorization', and, specifically, the part that poetic devices play in the construction of authority in crime fiction. It is informed by a belief in the validity of Lanser's claim in her later work, *Fictions of Authority: Women Writers and Narrative Voice*, that, 'the authority of a given voice or text is produced from a conjunction of social and rhetorical properties'.[15] This part of the argument considers more closely questions of 'representation' and 'privilege'. Whereas the opening section of this chapter discusses the various attributes of investigators with little regard to whether they are also the narrators of the work, the final section explicitly acknowledges that this question is essential to the attribution of authority. It therefore debates the extent to which attribution of either autodiegetic/homodiegetic or heterodiegetic status (and the limited or omniscient privilege that flows from it) influences perceptions of the investigator's standing as the pre-eminent authority in the text. What this analysis uncovers is the penchant that certain examples of early Russian crime fiction display for deliberately blurring or suddenly shifting the essential characteristics of the narrative voice, and the consequences that these moves have upon the experience of authority.

## The Social Identity of Investigators

Although the poetics of point of view that Lanser elaborates in *The Narrative Act* is largely focussed on narrators, it can actually be applied to any speaking character in a given text. As voices within the diegesis capable of possessing a greater or lesser degree of authority, it is valid to consider the social identity of investigators, whether they are the primary narrators in their respective text or not. Lanser outlines the relationship that exists between social identity and authority in the following terms:

> The problem of the narrator's identity properly begins where it would begin with any person or persona: with social and personal information about the speaker against which we can (consciously or not) determine how much power to accord the narrative voice.[16]

According to Lanser, a narrator's social identity comprises the following aspects: profession, gender, nationality, marital situation, sexual preference, education, race and socio-economic class.[17] In the particular case of late Imperial Russian crime fiction, however, where all of the investigators are white males from the same profession, a similar social class and of the same religious denomination, I would argue that different characteristics are emphasized in order to persuade the reader of their authority and reliability. These include, but are by no means limited to: education, experience, expertise, professionalism, incorruptibility, rationalism and, finally, humanity and compassion. This first section of the chapter therefore considers various examples of how these traits are embodied by the investigators that populate early Russian crime fiction, before mentioning a couple of counter-examples. Throughout, the focus is on how the depiction of these attributes of social identity encourage the reader to consider their possessor as a figure of authority.

To a certain extent, and with only a few exceptions, the detectives in crime fiction are granted considerable authority simply thanks to their professional occu-pation. That is, even in the reform period of the early 1860s when the figure of the judicial investigator was a relative novelty, these characters automatically enjoy a degree of authority, without necessarily having to earn it. Investigators occupied a comparatively elevated position in Russia's regimented system of social stratification and, at least in the early years of crime fiction, they are frequently depicted interacting with characters of lesser social status, often in rural or semi-rural settings. So, for example, in the opening story in Popov's collection, *The Guilty and the Innocent*, where the investigator is serving in the western regions of rural Russia, the very first line sees a carriage driver addressing the narrator as 'ваше высокоблагородие' ('your Excellency'). In fact, the locals' respect for the newly arrived investigator is given rather humorous illustration in this story because, amongst the various characters who repeatedly refer to him using 'your Excellency' is a middle-aged woman working as a *desiatskii* (peasant police helper), who is upbraided for seemingly demoting him. In spite of repeated reminders of the correct epithet, she keeps referring to him as only 'ваше благородие' ('your Honour'), or, more clumsily, as 'большое благородие' ('big Honour')![18]

More striking than scenes where serfs or peasants show respect for the investigator are those instances where landowners, or other more established members of society, are reminded of this figure's authority. So, for example, in the story 'Khoteli predat' sudu i vole Bozhiei' ('They Wanted to Betray the Court and God's Will') in Stepanov's *The Innocent and the Guilty* volume, the governor's secretary conducts another reinvestigation, this time into the death of a peasant, Zadornyi, who has been beaten to death outside a tavern one night, and for which no culprits have originally been traced. Because the investigator in this collection is working in rural Russia before the Emancipation Act of 1861, he has to negotiate his dealings carefully with the local landowner, Gulianov, who is accustomed to being the most powerful figure in the area. Indeed, the investigator quickly comes to suspect that the original investigation into Zadornyi's death achieved no results precisely because of the landowner's meddling. However, when Gulianov wishes to object to the new investigator's arrest of men on his estate, he is informed by his associates that the hierarchy of power has altered because 'да он-то [следователь] по закону действует, ему власть дана' ('he [the investigator] is acting according to the law; he has the authority').[19] In a slightly later work, Panov's 1876 story, *Ubiistvo v Mukhtolovoi roshche: rasskaz sudebnogo sledovatelia* (*Murder in Mukhtolovaia Grove: The Tale of a Judicial Investigator*), we encounter a rare example of the investigator breaking away from the narration of his case to comment explicitly on his own authority. Midway through this story of how the peasant, Kuzma, is murdered with a pitchfork by his granddaughter's lover because he will not allow them to be together, the narrator notes:

> Закон вооружил следователей могучей властью: нет запоров, которые бы не открыли свои объятия при его первом появлении; нет власти, которая бы смела стать поперек пути его, если только требования его законны; нет экспертов, которые, ревнуя своим знанием, смели бы отказать ему в содействии.[20]

> [The law has armed investigators with mighty power: there are no locks that would not open their embrace at his first appearance; there is no power that would dare to stand across his path, so long as his demands are lawful; there are no experts who, envying his knowledge, would dare to refuse to cooperate with him.]

Such overt, and arrogant-sounding, commentary on the investigator's standing is a relative rarity in Russian crime fiction of the late Imperial period. In the case of Panov's investigator, it is also rather compromised by his less-than-professional conduct towards Kuzma's granddaughter, Tatiana, whom he cannot resist kissing on one occasion. However, what the lack of other similar examples demonstrates is that, more often than not, rather than simply declaiming it, investigators in the genre have to *earn* their authority by means of their attributes or conduct.

A significant factor in the detectives' performance of authority in crime fiction is their status as educated and erudite individuals, who can harness their various fields of knowledge to uncover the truth and re-establish order. So, for instance, in Poe's 'The Murders in the Rue Morgue', Auguste Dupin demonstrates a knowledge of subjects as varied as Greek philosophy and the work of Epicurus, the construction of a particular type of wooden shutter found on the victims' building, and the presence of syllabification as a marker of human language. Perhaps unsurprisingly, Russian crime fiction does not feature a criminal investigator with as eclectic a range of knowledge as Dupin; however, the genre is nevertheless keen to stress its protagonists as men in possession of both education and erudition. The desire to emphasize the investigators' education stems as much from the impulse towards verisimilitude as it does from the wish to bestow narrative authority. The legal reform of 8 June 1860 that instituted the position of judicial investigator in Russia required that they be men who had received higher education in the law, a situation quite different from the qualifications needed to be a policeman. The educated status of these new investigators was praised in contemporary *publitsistika* articles and is frequently highlighted in works of Russian crime fiction.[21] In Panov's 1872 novella *Pomoch': ocherk iz sel'skoi zhizni* (*The Harvest Gathering: A Sketch from Rural Life*), where the case involves the death of a peasant Sinitsyn during the stupendously drunken harvest gathering of the title, the reader's first impression of the investigator, Ivan Gerasimovich, comes from the description that his friend gives of his lodgings during an unannounced visit. The narrator knows that he must be in the right place because every available surface is strewn with legal books as well as various other papers, stamps and labels that are the tools of the investigator's trade.[22] Moreover, when Ivan Gerasimovich and his friend then travel together to the village where Sinitysn has died, the detective's first move is clearly symbolic: he asks for a large table and proceeds very deliberately to lay out on it his papers, extracts from the legal code, inks and quills.[23] Such a display of his education and, specifically, his literacy is obviously intended to establish his authority; and the table that is his workstation is presented in a fashion similar to that used by the doctor later to conduct an autopsy on the victim, clearly suggesting a parallel between their professional occupations.

In the same author's *Ubiistvo v derevne Medveditse: iuridicheskaia povest'* (*Murder in Medveditsa Village: A Juridical Story*), also published in 1872, the detective, Andrei Petrovich, is similarly depicted at the centre of an intricate web of written documents, all of which he masters, as part of his investigation into the murder of the peasant woman, Grosheva. As I have argued elsewhere, Andrei Petrovich almost obsessively advocates for the power of the written word and is repeatedly at pains to convert oral testimony into official documents with a minimum of delay.[24] One of the novella's more unusual features is its inclusion of numerous footnotes, almost all of which underscore the investigator's legal education and the foundation of his actions in legal statute. The main body of the narrative includes reference to an article of law that pertains in a given circumstance, and the footnote provides either an explanation or the full text of the given excerpt. So, for instance, we are told that Andrei Petrovich's criticism of the inordinate amount of time that his predecessor and a colleague have spent squabbling over the jurisdiction of a case is based on article 138 and the footnote explains that it states: 'следствия по уголовным преступлением должны быть производимы со всевозможною скоростью и оканчиваемы в месячный срок не изъемля дней воскресных и праздничных' ('criminal investigations must be conducted with all possible haste and completed within a month, including Sundays and holidays').[25] Not only do such references help to construct an image of the judicial investigator as an informed practitioner and honest agent of the law, but, in a move that recalls the instructive character of the works discussed in the previous chapter, they speak to a desire to educate the reader in post-reform legality.[26] *Murder in Medveditsa Village* makes the link between the investigator's legal education and his diegetic authority most explicit when Andrei Petrovich acts to correct the main suspect in the murder, the former army officer and now blacksmith, Avdei Ampleev Grishanin, who claims to have a similar knowledge of the law. When the detective questions Grishanin about the murder for the first time and pre-emptively warns him that he will subsequently have to corroborate his testimony under oath, Grishanin retorts that 'присягать ни в каком случае не будет, потому что «он-де и без того присяжный по службе»; а что без присяги он тоже не может отвечать без депутата' ('he will not swear an oath under any circumstances because "he is, if you like, under oath anyway because of his military service"; but that without swearing an oath he cannot respond to questions if there is no deputy present').[27] The investigator immediately rebuffs Grishanin's challenge by correcting him and stating that a deputy is not necessary because he is now a retired officer acting as a witness and not a serving soldier accused of a crime. The face-off here about relative legal knowledge functions as an early figuration of the subsequent battles for supremacy, including Grishanin's attempt to attack Andrei Petrovich with a hammer, that the novella portrays between detective and murderer.

In terms that more closely echo the practice in nineteenth-century English, French or American detective fiction, Russian investigators are also characterized as men in possession of a level of general erudition that benefits their criminal work. One manifestation of this erudition, and of the authority that flows from it, is the relatively frequent recourse that Russian fictional investigators make in their speech or narration to foreign words or phrases. So, for example, in Panov's *The Harvest Gathering*, at an early stage of his investigation into the murder of Sinitsyn, Ivan Gerasimovich speaks in German to invite his friend, the narrator, as well as the doctor to eavesdrop discreetly on the questioning that he is about to conduct with the local village elder.[28] The key here is that these three men's shared knowledge of German distinguishes them from the elder, as well as from all of the other inhabitants of the village, who are not able to understand them. Similarly, in Stepanov's story 'The Horse-Rustler's Bridle', the investigator and his boss, the governor, converse in French about the fact that they do not believe that Pakhom is guilty of the murder of his cousin for which he has been imprisoned.[29] The knowledge of a language other than Russian permits these men to instigate a reinvestigation of the case without bringing that fact to the attention of the other, less-educated characters around them in the prison. However, by far the most common way in which Russian fictional investigators claim apparent erudition is through their deliberate and repeated use of Latin. The use of Latin is arguably more marked in these Russian works than in those of Poe or Arthur Conan Doyle because it is the only text in the stories not to appear in Cyrillic script.[30] So, for instance, in Sokolovskii's *Prison and Life*, the narrator frequently uses Latin, including in the opening chapter, when he embellishes his discussion of how difficult he finds it to utter the words to deprive a suspect of their freedom, and to enact higher principles such as 'fiat justitia, pereat mundus' ('let there be justice, though the world fail').[31] Expressions in Latin are also regularly encountered in works by Stepanov, Timofeev, Panov and Shkliarevskii. However, although I have provided a translation into English above, none of these instances of Latin is ever accompanied by a rendering into Russian, and whilst some are easily understandable, others present more of a challenge to readers who lack a classical education.[32] The inclusion of these foreign languages is particularly effective in a genre that, especially in its earliest years of development, narrated stories of life in the lower social echelons, and it functions as a counterpart to the use of vernacular language that has been discussed in the previous chapter. Indeed, it is interesting to note that the few footnotes in Panov's *Murder in Medveditsa Village* that do not relate to legal statute are used to explain instances of the local dialect to the reader. However, whilst the reader is not expected to comprehend regional or rural variations in the Russian language, s/he is assumed to be able to cope with instances of Latin, French or German. So, not only does the use of these foreign languages characterize the investigator as sufficiently educated to employ them, it also serves to sketch the outlines of the implied reader as someone able to understand them without translation. As such, a degree of equivalence and empathy is established between the investigator and reader that encourages the latter to ascribe trust and authority to the former.

Unlike Dupin and Holmes, who both exemplify original approaches to the resolution of their criminal mysteries, many of the detectives in early Russian crime fiction are relatively conventional figures. The extrafictional reality, as outlined in Chapter 1, of judicial investigators having been introduced in Russia in an effort to improve the quality of criminal inquiries helps to explain the emphasis that many of these works place on their heroes' professionalism and incorruptibility. These are men who not only know the minute details of the relevant legal statutes, but who are keen to implement the law as judiciously as possible. Part of the performance of authority that derives from this preoccupation with professionalism is certainly related to the instructional element of the genre noted in the previous chapter. Russian crime fiction frequently encourages trust in its detective heroes by portraying them as delineating and then adhering to investigative protocol. For instance, in the first story in Popov's *The Guilty and the Innocent*, 'Konchina greshnitsy' ('A Sinner's End'), that revolves around the various crimes and eventual suicide in custody of a young woman, Irina, the narrator-investigator is seen to take especial care when organizing the questioning of both suspects and witnesses. He checks that the *sotskii* (a low-ranking rural police officer) knows the rules concerning the list of witnesses allowed to be present at interrogations: no relatives of the suspects; no minors; no people previously subject to fines; equal numbers of men and women.[33] However, perhaps the more telling index of these investigators' professionalism at this stage of the genre's development is their integrity. This 'independence' was an element of the new real-world judicial investigator's profile that was particularly lauded by contemporary commentators. The author of the 'Nashi domashnie dela' ('Our Domestic Affairs') section of *Vremia* for October 1862, for example, claimed that the foremost expectation of the forthcoming legal reforms was that 'власть судебная *отделяется* от исполнительной, административной и законодательной' ('judicial power will be *separated* from the executive, administrative and legislative powers').[34] The implications of this new legal statute are made clear in a speech apparently delivered by a Moscow procurator to a group of newly appointed investigators, which was cited in the 'Vnutrennie novosti' ('Internal News') section of the March 1861 volume of the same journal. Amongst the various exhortations that he makes to this crop of new recruits is that they should be able to claim, 'что вы служили делу, а не лицам' ('that you have served the case and not influential individuals').[35] Russian crime fiction responds to such discussion by furnishing a whole host of examples of investigators, whether in the post-1860 context or not, embodying this desire for unimpeachability.

To a certain extent, the detectives' ability to act independently in early examples of the genre is facilitated by the fact that they are often depicted as outsiders, usually as men dispatched to rural communities or the provinces from the city where they have been educated. As mentioned above, this is the situation of the narrator-investigator in Timofeev's *Notes of an Investigator* collection who has been nominated to serve in the extreme western regions of Russia in the immediate aftermath of the failed Polish insurrection of 1863–64. In the collection's third story, 'Podzhigateli' ('The Arsonists'), he is tasked with looking into an accusation that one of the most prominent Polish landowners in his district has been harbouring suspected arsonists on his estate. In the very earliest stages of his work, the detective receives a letter from the local governor ordering him to report on his progress every three days and warning him that, because of the political sensitivity of the case:

> всякий же неуспех в столь важном деле будет отнесен не только к нерачительности вашей в деле службы, но и к небрежности и невниманию к возлагаемым на вас поручениям.[36]

> [any failure in such an important case will be attributed not only to your carelessness in the matter of your service, but also to your negligence and inattention to the assignments entrusted to you.]

The investigator is annoyed by such an overt effort to interfere in his work and he resolutely refuses to bow to the pressure. The remainder of the story paints a picture of an investigator who patiently and impartially pursues the landowner's servant who has maliciously concocted the story of the arsonists having been sheltered. He is not afraid to disappoint his political masters by relying on the evidence of witness testimony rather than being swayed by the anti-Polish prejudice that was rife in the area at the time. In Stepanov's story 'They Wanted to Betray the Court and God's Will', set as it is in pre-Emancipation Russia, it is from the local landowner, Gulianov, that the investigator needs to distance himself. Even before he is convinced that Gulianov is somehow involved in sheltering the suspects in the murder of Zadornyi, the detective's instinct is to be wary of this character, and, in spite of the fact that he risks offending Gulianov by doing so, he firmly resists his offers of accommodation and food. This independence stands in stark contrast to the behaviour of the local police and judge who, we learn subsequently, were all enjoying a banquet at Gulianov's home on the night that Zadornyi was killed. The suggestion is clearly that the failure of the first investigation to solve the crime has much to do with these supposed agents of the law being in the pocket of the local landowner who does not want to lose the labour of the suspects from his estate. To avoid any such compromise to his work, the governor's secretary chooses to employ a clerk from a different district and relies on his own Kazak helpers rather than local people whom he imagines are also in thrall to Gulianov.

Knowledge of legal statute, education and incorruptibility are all important factors that contribute to the image of the investigator as the most authoritative character in the fictional text. However, it is their skill and ingenuity precisely as a detective capable of solving crimes that conventionally exert the greatest influence on the reader's assessment of their performance. As I have noted in the Introduction, the very earliest examples of Russian crime fiction choose not to construct complex criminal mysteries and frequently present the likely culprit for the crime without much delay. Such texts, where the tension in the narrative revolves around the question of 'whydunit' rather than 'whodunit', do not allow their protagonists a great deal of scope to prove themselves to be deductive geniuses in the mould of Poe's Dupin. The most significant factor in the authority of investigators in this context is emotional intelligence and psychological insight. These are attributes famously displayed by Dostoevskii's investigator, Porfirii Petrovich, in *Crime and Punishment* during his conversations with Raskolnikov. As will be discussed in more detail later in this chapter, Porfirii interacts with the murderer in a highly effective, albeit rather unconventional, fashion. He recognizes Raskolnikov's psychological and moral fragility, and refuses to provide him with the security that an immediate accusation and arrest might offer; as Raskolnikov himself acknowledges, the detective's ploy of being vague about what he does or does not know regarding the double murder and its perpetrator leaves the student unsure of who has the upper hand. As many scholars have noted, there is more than a hint of the psychologist to Porfirii's treatment of the murderer here. Although Dostoevskii's investigator might be the most famous example of this phenomenon in Russian crime fiction, he is neither the only one nor the first. In Sokolovskii's *Prison and Life*, the judicial investigator habitually displays his emotional intelligence, particularly as he allows his close observation of the affective reactions of the suspects in his cases to inform his thoughts on possible suspects and their guilt. In the story 'The Long-Suffering', the first half of the narrative recounts the investigation into the attempted murder of a young woman, Daria Iakovleva. She has had her throat cut and is lucky to survive, and she immediately points an accusatory finger at her lover, Stepan Prokofiev, whom she claims attacked her when she refused to give him money to buy alcohol. There is never any real doubt about the veracity of Daria's version of events, but Stepan proves to be reluctant to confess and so the investigator has to be both patient and persistent. During one of several interrogations of Stepan, the narrator carefully records the suspect's reaction as he tries to extract a confession by directly accusing him of having stabbed Daria:

> Видно было, что в Прокофье происходила страшная борьба, сознаться или нет в своем поступке: на подвижном лице Прокофьева можно было читать все симптомы этой борьбы. Наконец страх наказания превозмог.[37]

> [It was evident that a terrible battle was raging inside Prokofiev about whether or not to confess to his act: in the mobile features of Prokofiev's face one could read all of the symptoms of this battle. Eventually, fear of punishment won out.]

The investigator's ability to 'read' the external manifestations of the criminal's interior struggle is shown here to be as important as his power to read and apply legal statute when necessary. It is a skill that Sokolovskii's investigator and his counterparts showcase again and again.

As the genre in Russia develops, and the 'whydunit' gives way to more frequent appearances of the 'whodunit', the detectives' ability to earn authority through investigative ingenuity also comes more to the fore, and it obviously takes a variety of forms. In his numerous detective stories written in the early twentieth century, R. L. Antropov features a fictionalized version of the head of Russia's first detective bureau, Ivan Dmitrievich Putilin, who is portrayed as highly resourceful and fearless. In 'Potselui bronzovoi devy' ('Kiss of the Bronze Virgin') from 1908, for example, the fictional Putilin investigates the case of the Polish Count Boleslav Rzhevuskii, who has been abducted by Catholic priests intending to murder him because of his wish to marry a Russian woman and convert to Orthodoxy.[38] Having persuaded the victim's father to invite the head priest, Father Benedikt, to his house one evening, in a move not immediately revealed to the reader, Putilin takes the place of the priest, then somehow accesses the underground chamber where the execution is due to take place, frees the Count and hides himself behind a screen before confronting the other priests with a pair of revolvers. When the suspects try to deny their murderous intentions, Putilin challenges them to embrace the bronze statue of the title as they had planned for Rzhevuskii to do; however, he knows they will refuse because he has somehow discovered that it is equipped with a mechanism that ejects numerous daggers from various parts of its body when touched. In Putilin's almost super-heroic approach to crime-fighting, the influence of another popular genre, the adventure novel, can clearly be discerned. Antropov's Putilin is intelligent, inventive, athletic and courageous, attributes that leave the reader in no doubt that he will emerge victorious in his various investigations.

In a similar vein, many of A. E. Zarin's stories and novels, which were published in the same period as those of Antropov, feature the same private detective, Ivan Patmosov, whose skills and approach appear far more conventional to a contemporary reader of Western crime fiction. The opening to the story 'Propavshii artel'shchik' ('The Missing Worker') sees Patmosov perform the sort of feat of deduction so beloved of Dupin, when he predicts that someone is about to deliver him a telegram. In the same work, which recounts his efforts to find a railway employee who has gone missing with a large amount of money, the impressive Patmosov not only displays physical prowess as he climbs over a partition to inspect the safe in a locked room but also makes use of a range of tools (pincers, a screwdriver and a specially-fashioned metal probe) to ascertain that the worker's body has been buried in the cellar's dirt floor. In the story 'Chetvertyi: istoriia odnogo syska' ('The Fourth Man: The Story of an Investigation') from 1902, where Patmosov's case is the murder of the moneylender Dergachev in broad daylight, Zarin shows his detective to be a master not just of scientific methods (he uses a pedometer to measure the steps between the victim's house and the park where he was killed) but also of deduction and disguise. Unlike his colleagues, Patmosov works out that Dergachev's pocket has been ripped during the murder not because of the theft of money or a watch, but because it contained letters revealing the affair between the artist Sanin and the married Vera Andreevna that Dergachev is using to blackmail Sanin. At the conclusion of the story, Patmosov hides his real identity, which is already known to Sanin from a previous encounter, in order to pass himself off as a client simply wanting his portrait painted when he visits the artist at home. Once there, the investigator proceeds to present Sanin with a description of the murder of Dergachev as if it were the subject of a painting, leaving the culprit with no alternative but to admit his guilt.[39]

Most of the aspects of social identity discussed up until this point have been the type of intellectual or professional qualities that a reader might conventionally expect to find embodied in a criminal investigator. However, in the context of Russian crime fiction in the late Imperial period, it is a rather more 'soft' aspect of the detectives' performance that plays the most crucial role in earning them authority. Patmosov's reaction to Sanin's confession of having murdered Dergachev is absolutely typical of the genre in this regard. Whilst acting in accordance with the law, he is extremely sympathetic to Sanin's plight: he helps to keep Sanin's relationship with Vera, and the existence of their illegitimate son, a secret by replacing the stolen letters at the heart of the case with fakes when he has to produce them as evidence. Moreover, he opts not to arrest Sanin at that point but to permit him to confess of his own accord, a move that reduces his sentence. This humane approach, displaying considerable sympathy and compassion for the plight not just of victims but also of criminals whose actions can be explained by extenuating circumstances, is a distinguishing

feature of the genre in Russia in this period. Such behaviour earns authority for
the investigator by proving him to be not a mere functionary of the law, but an
empathetic character who is motivated by the human interests of both victims and
suspects. The roots of such an emphasis on compassion can perhaps be traced back
to Vissarion Belinskii's 1842 article on Eugène Sue's *Les Mystères de Paris* (a work
often cited as a precursor to crime fiction in Europe) in which he claims that the
work is redeemed from meretriciousness by Sue's 'humanitarian' and 'philanthropic'
pathos.[40] According to Joseph Frank, the first sign of the influence of Belinskii's
remarks is to be found in Dostoevskii's novella *Bednye liudi (Poor Folk)* which 'for the
first time in Russian literature, amidst an unsparing depiction of urban seediness
and lower-class misery, portrayed those who lived immersed in such conditions as
sensitive and suffering souls'.[41] The empathy displayed by investigators in Russian
crime fiction is undoubtedly one branch of the Natural School's call for critical
realism which was initiated in the 1840s. However, it is important to note in the
context of this genre that it is not simply that the victims or even perpetrators of
crime are shown to be 'sensitive and suffering souls', but that the law, embodied
in the figure of the investigator, is capable of giving expression to the necessary
sympathy and compassion.

What is more, the almost ubiquitous presence in examples of early Russian
crime fiction of such compassionate and humane investigators strongly suggests
that the figure is being held up as an archetype of desired behaviour. Indeed,
extrafictional evidence of the influence of compassion is to be found in the high
acquittal rates of suspects at Russian jury trials in the same period that are described
by McReynolds.[42] Evidence of such model behaviour can be found in almost
every crime story of the late nineteenth century, but we will highlight just a few
examples. In Sokolovskii's 'Posledniaia stranitsa' ('The Final Page'), a story that
picks up the narrative of the stabbing of Daria Iakovleva by her lover that was begun
in 'The Long-Suffering', the narrator-investigator's sympathy is not just restricted
to the victim who eventually succumbs to her wounds, but also extends to the
prostitute, Nadezhda Chobotova, who serves as the main witness in the case. In a
passage that recalls the narrator's earlier description of the thief, Dragunov's, squalid
living conditions in 'Unpleasant Moments', he here paints a picture of the abject
poverty in which Nadezhda lives and concludes:

> Я много видел страшных, поражающих картин бедности, одинокого,
> глухого страдания; видел как умирали арестанты в острогах, солдаты
> в госпиталях, но все это не оставляло по себе такого подавляющего
> впечатления, какое вынес я из жилища Чоботовой.[43]

> [I have seen many terrible, arresting scenes of poverty and of solitary, mute
> suffering. I have seen prisoners die in jail, soldiers die in hospital, but none of
> this left as overwhelming an impression as did that of Chobotova's hut.]

When the young Nadezhda dies as a direct result of her appalling living conditions,
the narrator expresses both compassion for her plight and frustration that such a
death should have passed almost unnoticed by the people living around her. In
Dostoevskii's *Crime and Punishment*, the emotional intelligence of Porfirii Petrovich

highlighted above can be seen to shade into compassion for Raskolnikov's plight, particularly in the decision to allow him to confess of his own accord. In Timofeev's story, 'The Prostitute', mentioned in Chapter 1 because of its use of lyricism, the narrator-investigator is given the case of a young prostitute, Tereza Pavlovna, whose dismembered body is found in the frozen river that runs through the town of Priazhsk. His investigation leads him to learn various details of Tereza's life, including: the way both she and her mother are violently mistreated by her father when she is a child; her forcible separation from her first love and the death of her son; her fall into prostitution in the town that eventually leads to her murder when she refuses to give up the gold cross that was gifted by her mother and that two potential clients attempt to steal. He reflects on her becoming a prostitute thus:

> Некоторые быть может осуждать несчастную за то, что она слишком легко решилась на такой резкий шаг. Но что, спрашивается, оставалось ей делать? [...] Чтобы осудить ее, нужно, мне кажется, самому побывать в той шкуре, в которой находилась она в то время.[44]

> [Some people might judge this unfortunate woman for having decided to take this drastic step too readily. But what else, one must ask, was there for her to do? [...] In order to be able to judge her, it seems to me, you would have to be in the same position she was at the time.]

Crucially, the detective not only empathizes with Tereza's fate, but also finds it hard to condemn the murderer, Stepan, because he too, in the narrator's eyes, is more of a victim of circumstance than an actively evil character. The judicial investigator in Shkliarevskii's 1872 story 'Kak liudi pogibaiut: rasskaz sledovatelia' ('How People Die: The Tale of an Investigator') is one of the few to voice explicitly an overt awareness of these compassionate tendencies and is bold enough to suggest that they might have constituted something of a weakness:

> мы были бы хорошие полицейские чиновники, если бы не мешала нам другая сторона: все мы [...] сознавали и по теории и по представлявшейся практике, необходимость смягчения наказаний, признания обстоятельств, уменьшающихся вину преступления; да, и молодые организмы наши были добродушны, а потому мы как-то спутывали действия судебных следователей с действием будущих мировых судей, и часто грешили против, данного нам «Наказ»...[45]

> [we would have made better police officials, if another aspect had not impeded us: all of us [...] acknowledged, both in theory and in practice, the necessity of alleviating punishment and the recognition of circumstances which reduced the guilt of the crime. Yes, our young souls were gentle-hearted and, as a result, we somehow confused our job as judicial investigators with that of the future justices of the peace and often sinned against our 'decree'...]

In spite of this reservation, the near *de facto* illustration of humanity and compassion in the Russian genre constructs an almost unambiguously positive image of the judicial investigator. In combination with his more professional and intellectual qualities, such empathy creates a picture of the criminal investigator as a rounded, experienced character who is, as the Moscow procurator in the March 1861 article in *Vremia* desired, a 'human being' first and not merely a 'functionary'.[46]

The professional dedication of investigators is established as such a given in Russian crime fiction of this period that when, on the odd occasion, one is depicted as less than skilful or impartial, it comes as quite a shock. Two such examples form the centrepiece of the discussion of parody in Russian crime fiction to come in Chapter 6, but they are worth mentioning briefly here. In Panov's 1876 story, *From the Life of a Provincial Town*, the protagonist, Vadim Vadimovich Polumordin, is portrayed as a dishonest and conniving character who is quite happy to pursue a spurious case of child abandonment against an obviously innocent woman in order to exact revenge on one of his enemies.[47] Polumordin is initially utterly disinterested in the circumstances surrounding the abandoned child's death and is only prompted to look into them when he is goaded into it by the local police inspector who agrees to wager a case of champagne on the outcome. In Chekhov's 'The Swedish Match', the detective duo of Chubikov and Diukovskii not only fail to check the veracity of the information about Mark Ivanych Kliauzov's murder, but also demonstrate a notable lack of empathy towards their various suspects. Finally, in a work only elliptically related to the genre of crime fiction, Dostoevskii's *The Brothers Karamazov* from 1880, the author departs from the more positive model for the characterization of judicial investigators in the portrait he draws of Nikolai Parfenovich Neliudov. Neliudov is described as being a 'шалун' ('a naughty man') who pursues a life of pleasure in the company of women and whose fingers are adorned with numerous sparkling rings.[48] He is undermined further on two counts: the first is that both he and the town's public prosecutor pursue and bring to trial the wrong man, entirely ignoring the actual culprit, Smerdiakov; the second is that Neliudov is often presented from the negatively disposed point of view of Dmitrii Karamazov as being a 'boy' not up to the task of recognizing the truth. Polumordin, Neliudov and Chekhov's protagonists are, however, rare exceptions amongst Russia's cast of gentleman detectives.

### Relative Authority: The Detective's Counterparts

The preceding part of this chapter has concentrated exclusively on the detective's individual possession of personal and professional qualities that earn him authority. However, none of these figures exists in isolation in the fictional world, so an almost equal measure of his power derives from the contrast drawn between his attributes and behaviour and those of other characters around him. This relative approach to social identity is not one considered by narratologists such as Lanser but, particularly in the context of crime fiction where the reader is asked to adjudicate between competing versions of the truth, it is one that assumes particular significance. A more nuanced understanding of the investigator's authority can be achieved by considering how he benefits from comparisons to characters who enjoy less power and to those who enjoy a similar social standing. This second section of the chapter will therefore look at how Russian crime fiction compares the detective to other representatives of the law, including the local police, doctors and priests.

As the *Russkoe slovo* article by Lokhvitskii referred to in the opening section of this chapter makes clear, the introduction of judicial investigators into the

Russian legal landscape in 1860 made members of the police force subservient
to this position in criminal investigations. This demotion of the police had two
motivating factors: the belief amongst reformers that their manpower would
be needed to deal with the social unrest that would probably result from the
Emancipation of the Serfs in 1861; and a general and long-standing dissatisfaction
with their professional abilities.[49] Stepanov's stories in *The Innocent and the Guilty*,
focused as they are on a series of rectifications of miscarriages of justice, function
as a damning indictment of the type of limited and lackadaisical investigations
conducted previously by the police. In 'The Horse-Rustler's Bridle', for example,
the account of the first investigation into the death of the horse-rustler Filka,
which has led to the wrongful imprisonment of Pakhom Karpov, is unremitting in
its criticism of various people, but particularly the *stanovoi* (district superintendent
of police). When he first arrives in the village of Nechaevo where the crime has
been committed, rather than immediately beginning the search for the culprit,
the superintendent is far more interested in organizing refreshments for himself
and his team. More suspiciously, having inspected the victim's body and the crime
scene, he orders that no mention of the all-important bridle should be made in the
official report and that the account should only refer to death as resulting from an
axe-blow. Throughout his various interrogations of witnesses and suspects, he is
depicted as drinking copious amounts of vodka. In contrast to the compassion that
is a byword for the investigators in the genre, this policeman repeatedly shouts at
the locals and threatens them in an attempt to get them to answer his questions. He
also treats Pakhom disrespectfully, pulling his beard when he speaks to him and,
in spite of the peasant's protestations of innocence, demanding to know how he
killed Filka. Because of the vodka, the police superintendent then proceeds to sleep
through the second half of the investigation and has himself replaced by his clerk.
When the clerk allows circumstantial evidence to convince him of Pakhom's guilt,
the policeman declares himself pleased that the investigation has been concluded
so satisfactorily because this allows him to go drinking again with his friend who
is celebrating his name day.[50] In such circumstances, the governor's secretary who
conducts the reinvestigation into Filka's murder needs to do little more than remain
sober and act with respect to earn authority for himself in the fictional world.

Works set in the post-1860 period see the depiction of members of the local police
force become no more positive, a fact that allows the judicial investigator to establish
his superior authority.[51] Sokolovskii's *Prison and Life* contains numerous examples
where the detective-protagonist deals with cases that have been compromised in
one way or another by the ineptitude of the police. In the story 'Chapurin', he
spends time interviewing the eponymous prisoner, who is already serving time
for numerous crimes, but who confesses to involvement in even more, including
the murder of the peasant Esai. The local police investigation into Esai's death is
so seriously flawed that the actual facts are never properly established. His carriage
and clothing are found next to a track he is supposed to have travelled along, and
a body is discovered not far away; however, a link between the body and Esai's
carriage take a long time to be established. Questions about why Esai's body is

found on one side of the track and his clothing on the other, about the location of his horse and how it managed to detach itself from the carriage, are neither posed by the police nor answered by their very limited interrogations.[52] They appear to be utterly disinterested in pursuing Esai's death as a crime, and the judicial investigator's criticism of the police report as 'laconic' is an obvious understatement. The shortcomings in the local police's handling of the case are precisely what allow Chapurin subsequently to retract his confession for Esai's murder and to remain unpunished for this particular crime.

In Timofeev's 'Ubiistvo i samoubiistvo' ('Murder and Suicide'), the humanity of the judicial investigator is established in large part by means of a comparison with his other, less empathetic colleagues. This excellent story, which will be referred to repeatedly in this study, revolves around the investigation into the attempted suicide of Marianna Bodresova that uncovers an appalling story of the years of violent abuse that she has suffered at the hands of her father and stepbrother, and that results in her premeditated murder of the latter. Marianna is arrested after her suicide attempt by the *pristav* (bailiff) and the narrator-detective describes his reaction to his colleague's approach thus: 'Бесцеремонность обращения представителя местной полицейской власти с несчастною Бодресовой, меня просто возмутила' ('The unceremonious attitude of this representative of the local police towards the unfortunate Bodresova made me simply indignant').[53] The adjective 'unfortunate' in this sentence is indicative of the narrator's compassionate conduct throughout. Whereas the bailiff thinks Bodresova should be treated entirely according to formal legal regulations, like Shkliarevskii's narrator cited above, Timofeev's investigator is willing to 'go against his decree' and bend the rule of law so as to offer her the reassurance she needs to agree to tell the story of her life. Compounding the negative portrayal of the local police, the *sotskii* then tries to impress the judicial investigator by insulting Bodresova and telling her that it is a shame that she was not successful in her suicide attempt because that would have saved the investigator work. When the narrator later decides to release Bodresova from arrest and return her to her children, the *sotskii* is dumbfounded and repeatedly reminds the narrator of the illegality of his actions. The terms of the narrator's reaction here are simultaneously damning and comprehending: 'простодушие его не дозволяло мне на него сердиться' ('his simple-mindedness did not allow me to be angry with him').[54] No comparison exists here between either the humanity or the professionalism displayed by the judicial investigator and that of the *pristav* and the *sotskii*. The moral authority of the former is further extended when he admits that the prospect of Bodresova being sentenced to hard labour for her crime seems unjust to him; and when she does succeed in killing herself before her court appearance, he calls it the end of the 'печальной истории несчастной Марианны' ('sad story of unfortunate Marianna').[55]

It should be noted that, in slightly later Russian crime stories, the judicial investigator can find himself surpassed in authority by another figure, the *syshchik* (detective). Although *syshchiki* had existed as far back as 1745, the first official department of detectives in Russia was founded in St Petersburg in 1868 under the directorship of Ivan Dmitrievich Putilin.[56] So, for example, in Zarin's 'The Fourth Man', the main protagonist, Ivan Patmosov, is a detective and his skills and motivations are compared favourably to the more plodding and self-interested approach of the judicial investigator, Viktor Ivanovich Iastrebov. Iastrebov is depicted as a largely passive character, almost an automaton, who, during his own investigation into Dergachev's murder, rarely leaves his office, poses the same questions mechanically to each of the witnesses and is really only interested in solving the crime as a means of gaining promotion. He is obsessed with issuing orders to his subordinates, is careless in his observations (he prematurely concludes that theft is not a motive before a *pristav* points out the ripped pocket on the victim's jacket), and is not capable of looking past the most obvious suspects in order to arrive at the truth of the matter. By contrast, Patmosov is characterized by his energetic activity and personal initiative: he has already visited the crime scene before calling on Iastrebov for the first time; he spends considerable time 'out in the field' gathering evidence in the form of cigarette butts in the park where Dergachev met his killer; he realizes the significance of the three love letters found amongst the victim's affairs that Iastrebov has dismissed as irrelevant; and the title of the story derives from the fact that it is Patmosov who correctly concludes that a fourth man, and none of Iastrebov's three suspects, is guilty of the murder. Whilst the depiction of Patmosov's skills and abilities in isolation might be enough to persuade the reader to confer considerable authority upon him, the positive comparison with Iastrebov is an effective means of putting the detective's position atop the hierarchy of authority beyond any doubt.[57]

Investigators in Russian crime fiction from this period earn authority not just by differentiating themselves from less reliable or adept figures but also by means of an association or comparison with characters who enhance their standing. In line with a convention that pertains throughout the history of the genre and irrespective of national provenance, the most common collaborator of the investigator in works of Russian crime fiction is the doctor. In the context of nineteenth-century society, the association between investigators and doctors was probably motivated, at least in part, by the popular view that crime was a 'disease or a degenerative aberration of nature's mechanism of evolution' that could be explained by medical biology.[58] It can also be traced to 'the fascination of the general public of the period with "objective science"'.[59] As Aaron Parrett explains:

> The rationalism of scientific investigation as it emerged in the nineteenth century offered a compelling model for medically-minded criminologists and detectives, with its emphasis on data and forensics, its meticulous obsession with details of evidence and accumulation of facts leading toward the solution of a crime. In this way, the *form* of the medical examination became the model for the form of the detective investigation.[60]

Arthur Conan Doyle responded to this environment by casting John Watson, a former army medic, in the role of sidekick to Sherlock Holmes. In the Russian context, this narrative set-up is borrowed by Antropov in his various stories featuring a fictional Putilin as the detective and which are narrated by one doctor Z. In the mid-twentieth century, many of the crime novels authored by Georges Simenon featured positive depictions of medical professionals who aided in the course of investigations. Later in the twentieth century, doctors or medically trained professionals increasingly came to take on the role of investigator themselves, as evidenced by Patricia Cornwell's medical-examiner heroine, Kay Scarpetta, and the popular *CSI* television series, where the main investigator is a forensic entomologist. In examples of late Imperial-period Russian crime fiction, the relationship between investigators and doctors is far from being standardized, but most frequently the latter help the former because their scientific knowledge and approach lend authority to the relatively new task of criminal detection.

The works of Semyon Panov in the 1870s are particularly notable for their nuanced portrayal of the relationship between detectives and doctors. The novella *The Harvest Gathering*, about the death of the peasant Sinitsyn, offers up an extended example of the cooperation that can exist between the two figures. Upon being informed of Sinitsyn's death, the judicial investigator's very first act is to send a request to the district doctor for him to conduct an autopsy on the body the following morning. The fact that the inebriation of all the villagers following the harvest gathering renders interrogation on that day impossible means that the five-hour autopsy on Sinitsyn's body represents the first significant stage of the investigation. The popular fascination with medical science is illustrated by the account of how, contrary to the investigator's orders, all of the villagers in Malyi-Neriushev crowd into the hut to witness the autopsy, which comes to seem like a piece of quasi-theatre. The procedure is described in considerable and realistic detail and the doctor's methodical and skilful approach is repeatedly stressed. Crucially, the narrator, who is the investigator's friend, notes that neither he nor the detective's limited training in judicial medicine is sufficient to allow them to assess the significance of what they observe on the body or to draw the correct conclusions: only the doctor is qualified to do this.[61] Once the autopsy is complete, the doctor does not rush to judgement: when the narrator asks him to state Sinitsyn's cause of death, he does not immediately reply, ensconced as he is in his own thoughts. The doctor's voice does open the following chapter, however, as he declares his readiness to give the investigator his considered opinion: although the amount of vodka Sinitsyn imbibed would have probably caused an apoplexy at about 10 pm, he actually died from suffocation some eight hours earlier. At this point, the doctor makes a declaration that lauds the power of science but doubts the potential of a criminal investigation in these circumstances:

> Ничего вам следствие не скажет [...] Наука непогрешима, когда она идет об руку с практикою. А ваши ухищрения останутся ничтожными перед показаниями пьяных и стакнувшихся мужиков.[62]

> [Your investigation will tell you nothing [...] Science is infallible when it is practised by an experienced hand. But your tricks will amount to nothing in the face of the testimony of drunken peasants who conspire against you.]

Over the remainder of the story, medicine and justice are shown to enjoy a playfully antagonistic relationship as the doctor and the judicial investigator each insists on the greater reliability of his own method. Ultimately, however, they remain united in their common cause of unmasking Sinitsyn's killers, and criminal detection and medical examination are shown to complement each other in the pursuit of justice. Crucially, in the eyes of both the local peasants and the judge who pronounces a guilty verdict on Sinitsyn and his accomplices, the judicial investigator's revelation of the true story of the crime depends for much of its authority upon the medical conclusions of the doctor.[63]

Russian crime fiction also features a number of instances when the judicial investigator is depicted as being more knowledgeable and skilful than his medical counterpart. Such illustrations suggest that criminal investigations have moved beyond, or improved upon, the rational deductive methods offered by medicine and that the detective has become the pre-eminent 'scientific' authority. The seeds of this development are sown as early as the opening chapter of Sokolovskii's *Prison and Life* where his analogy between the investigator and the anatomist underscores the far greater exposure to suffering, and thus somehow the moral supremacy, of the former. In a similar vein, Panov's novella *Tri suda, ili ubiistvo vo vremia bala: rasskaz sudebnogo sledovatelia v dvukh chastiakh* (*Three Courts, or Murder during the Ball: The Tale of a Judicial Investigator in Two Parts*) sees the narrator explicitly discuss the relative challenges of medical diagnosis and criminal investigation with a doctor. In this intriguing 'whodunit' from 1876, the narrator-detective investigates the murder of Elena Vladimirovna Ruslanova, who has had her throat slit and her diamond tiara stolen during a ball to mark her engagement. The investigator's challenge is that, even though the crime was committed during a party with scores of people present, none of the potential witnesses claims to have seen anything or to have any suspicions about a likely culprit. Three months after the murder, when there has still been almost no progress in the case, the investigator is visited by the doctor, Tarkhov, who has conducted the autopsy on the victim's body. As the two men examine a model of the tiara that has been stolen, Tarkhov compares their respective lines of work by remarking that, in medicine as in detective work, it is possible to observe and recognize symptoms but still not be able to arrive at a diagnosis of the illness. The investigator disagrees, however, and claims:

> Но в медицине вы по наружным признакам из ста случаев можете отгадать, по крайней мере, пять или десять раз, с какою болезнью вы имеете дело. А тут что ни дело, то новая наука.[64]

> [But at least in medicine, by observing the external symptoms, out of 100 cases, you can guess the illness you're dealing with at least five or ten times. But this is not the case here, this is a new science.]

The doctor does not contradict the detective and, although he makes a valuable observation about hairs he has observed on the razor used as the murder weapon, he plays no ongoing part in the investigator's attempts to solve the crime.

A more overtly negative portrayal of a doctor is to be found in Panov's story *From the Life of a Provincial Town*. As will be discussed in greater detail in Chapter 6, amongst the host of unreliable and unpleasant characters portrayed in this work, the doctor, Nikolai Nikolaevich Antonov, stands out for his incompetence and vindictiveness. In the spurious case of child abandonment that is concocted against a local woman identified only as Ampleeva, even when the reader and almost all of the characters in the diegesis have been persuaded that it is entirely fabricated, Antonov persists in his belief that she is guilty. He is shown to utterly betray his medical training by claiming, in the face of overwhelming evidence to the contrary, that a physical examination of Ampleeva has proved that she has recently given birth and so could be the mother of the dead abandoned child. Antonov thus functions as a complete inversion of the values conventionally associated with medical science in detective fiction: it is here not a tool for discovering the truth, but a method that can be corrupted by human malice. Although *From the Life of a Provincial Town* is unusual amongst Panov's stories for its depiction of an unreliable doctor, it chimes with the work of Shkliarevskii, which provides the clearest demonstration of the impulse to promote the authority of the judicial investigator at the expense of that granted to doctors. Shkliarevskii's 1878 story 'Neraskrytoe prestuplenie: rasskaz sudebnogo sledovatelia' ('An Undiscovered Crime: Tale of a Judicial Investigator') is arguably the most extreme iteration of this tendency with its portrayal of a doctor who, long after the fact, comes to be suspected of being a triple murderer. The suspect in question, Albert Vikentevich Vansovich, is the family doctor of a couple who are unhappily married, Vosnesenskii and his much younger wife, Klementina, who is possibly having an affair with a barrister. Even before suspicions are raised in the narrative about Vansovich, he is characterized in negative, almost clichéd, terms: his arrival into a room makes Klementina shudder; he is said to have a wholly unpleasant appearance, just like that of a Jesuit priest, with sly, sunken eyes, red hair that he combs over his bald spot in long strands, a constantly smiling face, and long bony hands with sharp nails. Rather than using his medical knowledge to promote the cause of justice, Vansovich initially supplies Klementina with undetectable poison in spite of knowing that it might be destined for use against her husband. In fact, he has appeared almost to suggest such a murderous intervention when he says: 'моя медицинская помощь только длит мучения... А для иных смерть — сущее благодеяние... Она избавляет несчастных от страданий... Особенно, если смерть мгновенна...' ('my medical assistance only prolongs suffering... But for some people, death is a real gift... It releases these unfortunate people from their sufferings... Especially when death is instantaneous...').[65] Klementina does not use the poison, and suspicion begins to fall on Vansovich because, after the old Vosnesenskii does suddenly die, the doctor threatens to tell the police that she is the culprit if she does not agree to marry him. Not content with the marriage that results from this blackmail, the doctor is then implicated in the poisoning first of his new wife's young son, Serezha, and then of Klementina herself a little while later. Significantly, the doctor's skill in selecting a means of murder that is virtually impossible to detect means that his crimes go undiscovered until the narrator-investigator comes into possession of Klementina's letters several years later, by which time any judicial retribution is impossible because the doctor himself has died.

To close this section on relative authority, it is important to draw attention to the relationship that is frequently constructed in early Russian crime fiction between investigators and members of the clergy. As with the other comparisons discussed here, the inclination to associate the investigator and the priest is, at least in part, historically determined. Throughout the late Imperial period, public confession, just like that required by Orthodox theology, remained a key part of the Russian judicial process. The 1857 legal code specified that a person could only be convicted of a crime if there was 'совершенные доказательства' ('complete proof'), which took the form of a judicial confession by the defendant — what was referred to as 'the best evidence in the world'. Indeed, it is the pre-eminent importance attached to this act of judicial confession that lends much of early Russian crime fiction its distinctive flavour. In works where the identity of the culprit is revealed at an early stage, the suspense typical of the genre frequently derives from the investigator's efforts to secure this much-needed confession. Based on the material provided by Russian crime stories of the time, there is scope for a much wider-ranging discussion of the role of religion in the genre than we have the space for here. It is perhaps sufficient to note in this regard that the title of Stepanov's story 'They Wanted to Betray the Court and God's Will' is typical of the construction of many, particularly early, Russian crime stories in which dual systems of justice — the secular and the religious — operate in tandem.[66] For the purposes of the present discussion, however, remarks will be limited to the depiction of the investigator figure as a quasi- or substitute religious figure or as someone who works in concert with priests.

Probably the best-known example of a judicial investigator casting himself in the role of a religious confessor is to be found in Dostoevskii's *Crime and Punishment*. From the outset, there is no doubt that Raskolnikov is guilty of the murder of the pawnbroker Aliona Ivanovna and her sister, Lizaveta. However, the novel still succeeds in generating a considerable degree of suspense thanks to the game of cat and mouse that ensues between Raskolnikov and the investigator, Porfirii Petrovich. Critics have long since noted the symbolic significance of the investigator's name and the fact that his attitude towards, and interactions with, Raskolnikov see him cast just as much as an agent of religious law as of secular law.[67] He very rarely treats Raskolnikov as a criminal who needs to be caught and far more often like a human being in need of salvation. He shies away from arresting Raskolnikov, even after he is convinced of his guilt, preferring to allow him the time and space to decide that he should voluntarily give himself up. And he keeps his word by not telling the prosecutor that he has identified the culprit before Raskolnikov confesses. In so doing, Porfirii ensures that Raskolnikov will receive a more lenient sentence as well as encouraging him, along with Sonia, to rejoin the human family through a process of spiritual redemption. Amy Ronner is right to point out that Raskolnikov never does confess to the detective, and that Sonia and Svidrigailov play equally important parts; however, Porfirii's role as something more than a statute-observing criminal investigator cannot be denied.[68] Although undoubtedly the most sophisticated depiction of the judicial investigator as quasi-priest, *Crime and Punishment* is not the first work to have featured such a characterization. In Sokolovskii's 'The Long-Suffering', for example, Daria Iakovleva promises the narrator-investigator that she will not lie about the details that led to her being stabbed because: 'что мне, батюшка, перед тобой таиться, может и жить-то мне час какой остался, у Бога не скроешься' ('why would I hide anything from you, sir, when I might only have an hour or so to live; I will not hide myself from God').[69] Furthermore, she informs the investigator that the story she is telling him is exactly the same as the one that she has just recounted to the priest, a remark that subtly draws an equivalence between these two roles. In Timofeev's story 'A Crime of Superstition', the man responsible for the disinterment of six corpses agrees to tell the narrator-detective the full story of the circumstances of his act 'как перед Богом' ('as if to God') and unambiguously considers his testimony to be an act of religious confession.[70]

In various other stories, including Panov's *Murder in Medveditsa Village*, the investigator actually joins forces with the local priest in order to advance his work. In this story, although suspicion for the murder of the peasant woman, Grosheva, falls relatively quickly on the retired army officer, Grishanin, the evidence is largely circumstantial and the suspect is extremely reluctant to confess. So the detective decides to enlist the help of the local priest and this latter becomes a part of the investigative team. The priest quickly shares the investigator's conviction regarding Grishanin's guilt and it is he who says: 'так вот и видно, что сознание у него на языке; но выговорить боится. Он, верно, страшится наказание' ('it is quite evident that a confession is on the tip of his tongue, but he is afraid to say it out loud. Most likely, he is fearful of the punishment').[71] In the final, public confrontation scene, when the investigator is still unable to coax a confession from Grishanin, it is the priest who steps in and takes the lead. The narrator describes how:

> Он объяснил ему всю важность совершенного преступления; ужасную ответственность, которую принял на себя виновный; мучения совести, которые неотступно будут преследовать его. При этом он объяснил и то, что виновник заслужил наказание, которое должен перенести, и перенести без отчаяния, с кротостью и смирением. Он доказывал ему, что только тогда, когда преступник сознается — он может почувствовать облегчение перед своей совестью [...].[72]

> [He explained to him the seriousness of the crime he had committed, the awful burden of responsibility that the guilty man had taken upon himself, and the torments of conscience that would forever trouble him. Then he also explained that the guilty man deserved his punishment, and that he should accept it without despair, with meekness and humility. He argued that only when the criminal confessed would he feel some relief from his conscience [...].]

And this does the trick: Grishanin requests to be allowed to go home and wash before returning and giving a full confession to the murder. The narrator is explicit at the close of the novella: Grishanin's confession would not have been secured without the help of the priest, and the collaboration between the two is instrumental in bringing the case to a successful conclusion.

As with the relationship between investigators and doctors, there are also instances where the detective's authority is promoted because he is shown to have greater professional or moral qualities than members of the clergy. Although relatively rare, such examples create the sense that over time rational, quasi-scientific criminal investigations gain the reputation of being more reliable and influential than religious systems of justice.[73] Panov's *The Harvest Gathering* paints a picture of the local religious figures in particularly unflattering colours. The local priest is characterized as a somewhat mercenary figure even before he directly appears in the story: the narrator is aghast at the investigator having to pay him 10 roubles a month for the cramped, low-ceilinged lodgings he inhabits in the village. The portrayal becomes more direct midway through the story, when the narrator leaves the village where Sinitsyn has died because of a lack of progress in the case, but when his carriage breaks down, he is forced to spend the night in another village and lodges with the priest and his family. Whilst in that village, the narrator overhears a conversation between two women, one of whom is betrothed to a man from Sinitsyn's village, that incriminates her fiancé as the likely culprit in the peasant's death. The narrator's immediate reaction is to ask the priest about which local girls are getting married and to whom. Although the priest does reveal that there are six impending marriages with local girls, when the narrator asks for their names, he declares that he has had enough and obliges the narrator to go off with him to inspect beehives. The narrator is particularly annoyed with himself because, as he says, he has forgotten that:

> сельский священник, живший лет тридцать с крестьянами, перенимает их обычай не доверять людям, предлагающим вопросы; подобно тому, как в городах не верят людям, просящим денег взаймы. Священник был задним умом крепок.[74]

> [the village priest, having lived amongst peasants for thirty years, adopts their habit of not trusting people who ask questions, just like townspeople do not trust people who ask for money. The priest has 20–20 hindsight.]

In spite of this initial misstep, the narrator manages to make some progress when he offers the priest some of his rum, and his interlocutor becomes more talkative. Although this conversation offers nothing of note with regard to the Sinitsyn case, it does serve to debase further the standing of the priest. He complains about the arguments he has with various deacons in his parish, laments his peasant parishioners' inability to understand his sermons and forces the narrator to listen as he reads aloud two sermons that he has had published in a church chronicle. The arrival of the local deacon at this point in the story only serves to reinforce the negative portrayal of representatives of the church. The narrator proceeds more carefully with him than with the priest and, as a result, manages to elicit the name and identity of the girl he has heard talking about her fiancé, even though the deacon cannot remember the name of her intended because 'водка память ошибла' ('his memory has been impaired by vodka').[75] In fact, whereas the priest's principal weakness appears to be for money, Panov's deacon has a real taste for alcohol. When the priest learns that the deacon has provided the narrator with the name of the betrothed girl, he gets angry and admonishes his colleague because 'кто его знает, что он такой? [...] Зачем ему знать? Кто его знает, что у него на уме' ('who knows who he is? [...] Why does he want to know? Who knows what he's planning').[76] Although neither the priest nor the deacon actively obstructs the narrator's quest to gather information relevant to the investigation, it is clear that they would rather not be involved. Indeed, when the two men are subsequently summoned for questioning by the investigator, the priest fails to turn up because he has not yet returned from the bazaar, and the deacon replies to a request to confirm that his parishioner and the suspect are betrothed with the single word directed at the narrator: 'измена!' ('betrayal!'). And, when he adds that, if there were a next time, he would choose not to provide any information, the narrator contents himself by remarking to the reader that the deacon is 'падок на ром' ('a sucker for rum').[77] In such circumstances, it is easy for the narrator of *The Harvest Gathering*, in his role as adjunct-detective, as well as the actual judicial investigator, to enjoy a position of elevated authority in the fictional world.

## Narrative Voice and Conventions of Authority

What the opening two sections of this chapter have demonstrated is that various aspects of social identity help to establish the authority of the detective in Russian crime fiction. Yet it is important not to lose sight of how such issues of characterization intersect with the question of narrative voice in the genre. In its discussion of the hybrid generic status of early works of Russian crime fiction, Chapter 1 has engaged with one aspect of what Lanser designates the 'authorisation' of the narrative voice: namely whether a text presents itself as a factual report or a fictional invention. However, the final section of the present chapter discusses authority in the light of two other aspects: 'representation' (whether a narrative voice is heterodiegetic, homodiegetic or autodiegetic) and 'privilege' (whether a narrative voice possesses omniscience or only a restricted level of access to knowledge). Put simply, we consider here how the issue of whether the detective in a particular work is also the main narrator or not affects his authority. Russian crime fiction of this period provides instances of each of the three basic models of narrative 'representation'. That is, there are examples of works in which the narrator is the detective (autodiegetic: e.g. the works of Sokolovskii, Stepanov and Timofeev discussed above and in Chapter 1); where the narrator is a figure in the story world but not the detective (homodiegetic: Panov's *The Harvest Gathering* and the various stories by Antropov); and where the narrator is not a character in the diegesis at all (heterodiegetic: e.g. Dostoevskii's *Crime and Punishment*, Chekhov's 'The Swedish Match' and all of Zarin's detective stories). The motivations behind the choice of one or other of these modes are probably manifold — historical, generic, stylistic. However, it is their consequences upon the mediation of authority that lies at the heart of the discussion here. The discussion below begins by considering how existing theory has envisaged the links between crime fiction, narrative mode and authority, before moving on to look at a number of examples of this relationship in practice. The chapter closes with an examination of how narrator privilege, in particular, can be effectively manipulated to affect authority.

Although the various sets of rules drawn up for detective fiction in the early part of the twentieth century, such as those by S. S. van Dine, unsurprisingly did not yet address the issue of narrative voice, subsequent scholarship has sketched out the genre's preferences in this regard. Most critics engage with questions related to representation and privilege in crime fiction from the point of view of the curiosity and suspense that are hallmarks of the genre, and the majority conclude that these ends are best served by using a narrator who is *not* the detective. The most valuable work undertaken to date in this regard is Donna Bennett's 1979 article, 'The Detective Story: Towards a Definition of Genre', and in particular the section on 'confidence' and 'confidentiality'. Building on remarks made by Dorothy Sayers regarding the various viewpoints (what Genette would call 'focalization') encountered in crime fiction, Bennett outlines her view of the genre's preferences:

> The greatest level of confidentiality between reader and detective exists at what Sayers calls 'Viewpoint No.4', in which the reader is allowed 'complete mental identification with the detective'. When confidentiality exists to this degree, then the reader does indeed see *through* the detective's eyes and become party to his internal judgements. Since the existence of this level of confidentiality involves surrender of many of the author's devices for masking information from the reader, this fourth degree of confidentiality is not often utilised.[78]

Although Sayers's and Bennett's terms both differ from those that we have adopted from Lanser, there is considerable overlap. The characteristics of Sayers's 'Viewpoint No. 4' are the same as those that (post-)structuralist theory attributes to autodiegetic representation, in which the narrator is the detective and the reader is privy to his/her thoughts. Bennett's belief that the degree of confidentiality between narrator and reader implied by autodiegesis problematizes the generation of suspense is one shared by other commentators. For example, in discussing Agatha Christie's controversial story, *The Murder of Roger Ackroyd*, Carl Lovitt makes clear his belief that autodiegetic narrators are, if not incompatible, then certainly undesirable in the genre:

> In compelling Sheppard to adopt Hastings' voice, the novel emphatically demonstrated the constraints imposed by formal detective fiction on the narrator. [...] the detective novel fundamentally restricted the narrator's access to privileged information. To sustain the mystery, the story had to be presented by someone who, like the reader, noted facts without initially grasping their significance.[79]

Beyond the specific issues of curiosity and suspense, explicit commentary on the mode of narrative representation has been even more scant and often has to be inferred from other statements. So, for example, from Kayman's discussion of how detective fiction insists that it is dealing in facts in part by employing an 'objective' narrator, we might imagine that he has in mind a heterodiegetic voice, but this is not stated explicitly.[80] Interestingly, even Bennett is sometimes rather oblique, such as in her discussion of the importance of 'confidence' to detective fiction where she says:

> The reader expects the author not to make misleading statements in his own voice and not to employ verbal ambiguity or trickery. The information he provides is taken as reliable, not to be doubted.[81]

This statement does no more than suggest that she believes that the detective story tends towards the use of a non-autodiegetic narrator, but it is not categorical.

More generally, critical theory has not definitively established a clear and indisputable correlation between the mode of narrative representation and the possession of narrative authority. On the one hand, certain critics consider the heterodiegetic narrative voice to generate the greatest degree of trust from the reader. As David Herman states, for instance:

> Generally speaking, fictional facts reported by third-person narrators have an authority, or mark a degree of certainty, lacking in first-person reports given by characters or character-narrators occupying specific positions in a storyworld.[82]

However, each of Genette's three categories (autodiegetic, homodiegetic, heterodiegetic) possesses features that generate an impression of authority. Chapter 1 has demonstrated, for example, how the autodiegetic narrators employed in the generically hybrid works of Sokolovskii, Stepanov and Timofeev are capable of earning considerable authority for themselves in a variety of ways. One of the most effective is the claim they make for their status as eyewitnesses to the characters, plots and worlds that they describe. This is what might be referred to as the 'I was there' authority of eyewitnesses that is, in fact, of such crucial importance to the judicial system. Such narrators give the reader the impression of experiencing not just the diegetic world, but also the criminal investigation, alongside the detective and almost at first hand. Both the emotional and educative effects of such proximity are precisely what is sought by the narrator in Sokolovskii's *Prison and Life* as he exposes the reader to the various victims and perpetrators of crime with whom he has to deal. There is a sense of immediacy in the presentation of such autodiegetic accounts that encourage the reader to bestow authority upon the narrator-detective. The use of this mode also permits the reader to be privy to the investigator's thought processes during an investigation and to hear the justification for certain decisions. So, for instance, in Timofeev's story 'Muzhniaia zhena: bytovoi ocherk' ('The Married Woman: A Sketch from Everyday Life'), taken from his 1878 collection *Iz vospominanii sudebnogo sledovatelia* (*From the Reminiscences of a Judicial Investigator*), the narrator reveals his investigative methodology as he tries to uncover the circumstances that have led an apparently happily married woman to poison her husband. In a manner that would seem contrived in an alternative narrative mode, the detective ponders how he tries to consider all of the possible ways in which the attempted murder of a husband by his wife might be interpreted, to take into account the importance of various circumstances, and to factor in the characters of the accused. When this does not work, he thinks about how he might attempt to find a basis or motivation for the crime and capture the thought that will allow his investigation to proceed in the correct direction. Such internal reflection on method, which is only possible in the autodiegetic mode, unmistakeably encourages the reader to put faith in the investigator. And Timofeev's detective's considered and rational approach does indeed pay dividends as he discovers that the wife's poison was not intended for her husband, but for her father-in-law who has been repeatedly raping her.[83]

Yet, the degree of authority accorded to such narrators, critical theory would argue, can equally be undermined by the very fact that their presence and participation in the story world renders them potentially subjective and unreliable. The reader is justified in asking whether the autodiegetic narrator's account is not influenced by his own involvement and the desire to depict his role as positively as possible. Indeed, it is precisely the lack of involvement in the story world that accounts for the authoritative standing conventionally accorded to heterodiegetic narrators. As the comments of Kayman and Bennett cited above suggest, the reader expects this type of narrative voice to provide a more objective, less personally motivated account of the criminal investigation, and one that is consequently deemed to be more reliable. This narrator's lack of involvement in the story world theoretically permits him to give a fuller, more representative picture not just of the detective's actions but of all the characters in the diegesis. In a sense, then, perhaps it is the homodiegetic narrator who commands the least authority: although a figure in the story world, he is not the detective and thus not as close to the action of the investigation; equally, as an embodied figure in the diegesis, he cannot enjoy the same objectivity and impartiality as a heterodiegetic voice. It would be interesting to consider whether, in fact, this mid-position of authority of the homodiegetic narrator, and not simply his position relative to epistemic knowledge, makes him such a favoured choice in much classic detective fiction.

The mention of epistemic knowledge brings us on to the question of narrative privilege. Although it is difficult to draw definitive conclusions about the authority granted to different types of narrator simply on the grounds of representation, the picture becomes clearer when the related issue of privilege is factored in. Whilst representation deals with the narrator's position in the diegesis, privilege reflects his relationship to knowledge, information and vision, factors that are self-evidently pertinent to the construction of authority. Lanser defines privilege as running between poles of omniscience and limitation. At one end are narrators who have complete access to knowledge and to the consciousness of other characters; and this unfettered knowledge is usually accompanied by the capacity for omnipresence. At the opposite end we find narrators whose privilege is limited to that possessed by ordinary human beings, incapable of seeing into the minds of others or of being simultaneously present in more than one space or time. The widely accepted convention states that omniscient privilege is associated with heterodiegetic narration, whilst auto- and homodiegetic narrators must, as embodied actors in the story world, enjoy only limited vision and access to knowledge. Consequently, a heterodiegetic narrator with omniscient privilege and the potential for omnipresence enjoys a greater degree of authority than do autodiegetic or homodiegetic narrators who are not endowed with these abilities.

The results of this intersection between narrative representation, privilege and authority can be better understood by means of a discussion of some actual examples. Early Russian crime fiction features relatively few works in the mode popularized by both Poe and Conan Doyle, where the homodiegetic narrator is a friend or colleague of the investigator. The homodiegetic, rather than autodiegetic, status of the narrator in Panov's *The Harvest Gathering* is open to question given the extent to which this character functions as an investigator, even though this is not his official role. However, Antropov's Putilin stories, narrated by doctor Z., are a more conventional instance of this narrative mode. In these works, it is abundantly clear that the voice of the narrator enjoys far less authority than do the detectives and/or narrators in either the autodiegetic or the heterodiegetic pattern. If we look again at Antropov's 'Kiss of the Bronze Virgin' that was discussed above, whilst ostensibly present during, and a participant in, the investigation, doctor Z. is portrayed as a far more marginalized and much less authoritative figure than Putilin. He is invited to accompany Putilin to Warsaw to investigate the disappearance of Count Rzhevuskii, but on the first night after their arrival he is abandoned by the detective who does not return until six o'clock the following morning. When he does return, the account he provides to the doctor of what he has discovered is incomplete: Putilin claims to know who is responsible for the abduction but does not say who, and he reveals very little about his plan for how the investigation should proceed. It is also the homodiegetic mode, and the consequent lack of either omniscience or omnipresence, that ensures that Putilin's assumption of the disguise of Father Benedikt referred to earlier is not revealed until after the fact. Such diegetic presentation certainly ensures that the reader experiences a heightened sense of curiosity and suspense, but it depicts the narrator's authority as very much subordinate to that of the detective. The position of doctor Z. in this story is similar to that of Dupin's friend in Poe's stories and of doctor Watson in the Sherlock Holmes mysteries: he is there occasionally to lend a hand during the investigation but primarily to bear witness to the far greater ability and authority of the detective.

Conversely, Zarin's story, 'The Fourth Man', provides an interesting illustration of the authority that can be constructed by a heterodiegetic narrator who possesses omnipresence and omniscience without destroying a sense of mystery. The narrator's omnipresence is signalled by the fact that the story's first three chapters focus in turn on a different character in a different location around St Petersburg as they learn of the murder of the moneylender Dergachev. In turn, the reader is introduced to Count Chekannyi and his young wife, Vera Andreevna (who is revealed subsequently to be Sanin's lover), at their luxurious dacha in Peterhof; someone called Katia and an unnamed woman she works for in a different apartment at a similar time of day as they both read of Dergachev's demise in the *Petersburg Gazette*; and then to a room in which Nikolai Nikolaevich Savelev is described waking up with a hangover. Only a narrator with omnipresent privilege would be able to describe these simultaneous but geographically distinct scenes. Meanwhile, the decision to withhold information about the relationship either between these characters or to the murder victim firmly establishes the reader as the narrator's inferior, as well as provoking his/her curiosity. The narrator reinforces his authority by demonstrating knowledge not only of Savelev's back story, but also that of his father: the son has been expelled from every educational establishment he has attended, including private gymnasia, but his father has now set him up as the director of a bank; meanwhile, Savelev Sr., although from humble origins, is said to now be the richest man in St Petersburg and famous in its business circles. At this point, the narrative voice proves its omniscience when, having described how Savelev Jr. reads of Dergachev's death in the newspaper, it reveals his inner reaction to be: 'Вот когда пропал, так пропал!' ('When you're gone, you're gone').[84] Similarly, when, in the fourth chapter, the narrative goes back in time to describe the judicial investigator, Iastrebov's, examination of Dergachev's body at the crime scene, the use of free indirect discourse gives access to his thoughts: 'вот сколько-нибудь интересное дело и, может быть, случай выдвинуться' ('here's an interesting case and, perhaps, the opportunity to move upwards').[85] However, the story's success in generating a significant degree of curiosity and suspense can be traced to the narrator's practice of frequently choosing not to employ this omniscience. Over much of its length, Zarin's story relies on an observation of characters from an external perspective, where access to their inner thoughts and emotions is not granted. So, for example, in the opening chapter, when a parcel is delivered that prompts Vera Andreevna to sigh with relief, the reader is not informed of the reasons for her reaction. Most importantly, the narrative voice does not keep the reader immediately abreast of Patmosov's thoughts and theories about the case in the way that an autodiegetic narrator might. Therefore, although it might not always be predictable or reliable, the performance of the narrator does create an image of that voice as knowledgeable and authoritative.

The most compelling evidence of the authority attributed to heterodiegetic representation and omniscient and omnipresent privilege, however, is the frequency with which works of Russian crime fiction narrated by autodiegetic voices attempt to claim it. That is, there are a striking number of works in the Russian genre that initially give the impression of being narrated by a heterodiegetic voice, only to reveal subsequently that they are, in fact, told by the embodied voice of the narrator-investigator. This deliberate confusion between two ostensibly distinct narrative positions proves to be very revealing about the level of authority that such autodiegetic narrator-detectives would like to claim for themselves. Take, for example, Stepanov's story 'The Horse-Rustler's Bridle'. As the discussion in Chapter 1 has shown, the story is part of a volume narrated by an autodiegetic narrator, the governor's secretary, who is given responsibility for investigating and rectifying a number of miscarriages of justice. However, this narrative set-up has not yet been revealed in the opening half of 'The Horse-Rustler's Bridle' and it reads very much as if it is told by a heterodiegetic, omniscient voice. Although the reader learns in the third chapter that the narrator is not assigned to the case until six months after Pakhom Karpov has been imprisoned, the story opens at a point in time before Filka has been murdered, with an idyllic scene of Pakhom peaceably mowing in a meadow before chasing Filka off after his attempt at theft. The story's second chapter is also focused on a period of time before the narrator becomes involved, describing as it does the incompetent local police investigation into Filka's death. In both of these chapters, the descriptions include a level of detail and carry a confidence of tone that suggest that the narrator has full knowledge of what happened and witnessed these various scenes directly at the time. Moreover, in the description of the governor's visit to the prison in the third chapter, the narrator demonstrates an ability to read Pakhom's thoughts and feelings:

> Измаялся, исхудал бедный Пахом, а душой словно окреп. Спокоен стал? Нет. Такой покой — обманчивая кора, как лед на бурном озере. И как спокойну быть, когда впереди такая погибель позорная! Какой покой, когда на душе истома, а на сердце страх.[86]

> [Poor Pakhom was exhausted and had lost weight, but his soul had hardened. Had he become calm? No. Such calm is a deceptive surface like ice on a stormy ocean. And how could he be calm when confronted by such a shameful end! What calm could there be when there was such languor in his soul and such fear in his heart?]

However, it is almost immediately after this description that the narrator first uses the pronoun 'я' ('I') and reveals that he is, in fact, a character in the diegetic world and the man who will lead the reinvestigation into Pakhom's case. Given that this voice has now been revealed to be autodiegetic, and conventionally in possession of only limited privilege, the reader is justified in asking how it is he could so confidently know the details of the night of Filka's murder, including the actions and speech of the villagers, and how he could report on the first investigation, to which he was not directly privy, with such certitude. In fact, even the revelation of his autodiegetic status does not prevent the narrator subsequently from including observations informed by omniscient privilege and from performing much like a heterodiegetic voice. The closing passage of the story, describing Pakhom's return to the village following his acquittal, is a case in point: this is a scene at which the narrator was not himself present, and we are given no details about how he learns about it, but this does not stop the narrator from giving full information in an utterly self-confident tone.[87]

   Such over-reaching of autodiegetic representation and limited privilege is also a technique encountered on more than one occasion in the work of Shkliarevskii. His 1872 story, 'Rasskaz sudebnogo sledovatelia' ('The Tale of a Judicial Investigator'), opens with descriptions that are typical of those provided by an omniscient heterodiegetic narrator. The first chapter informs the reader about the gossip in a provincial town surrounding the breakdown of the Pyl'nevs' marriage and Nastasia Pyl'neva's departure to St Petersburg, whilst the second shifts its focus to the capital. The description of the city scene appears to be informed by a birds'-eye visual perspective typical of heterodiegetic narration as actions occurring in different quarters of the city are observed apparently simultaneously: the yard-keeper at 36 Valdaiskaia Street is shown shouting for a policeman just as this latter is depicted in a wine merchant's some way off. However, at the close of this second chapter, the true autodiegetic status of this narrator is revealed as he states in relation to the discovery of Nastasia Pyl'neva's murdered body: 'описанное происшествие случилось в Петербурге, двадцатого ноября, в конце шестидесятых годов, и исследование его было поручено мне' ('the event described occurred in St Petersburg, on 20 November, in the late 1860s, and the investigation was assigned to me').[88] Whilst the inclusion of a relatively specific date and the matter-of-fact tone of the announcement are intended to encourage the reader to place trust in the voice of the narrator, it remains the case that reconciling the two contradictory narrative stances is problematic. If the narrator is actually the detective in charge of the case, how can he report on earlier events out in the provinces and describe two events some distance apart in St Petersburg simultaneously? Shkliarevskii's practice in another story, 'Sekretnoe sledstvie' ('The Secret Investigation'), follows exactly the same pattern with an apparently heterodiegetic voice subsequently revealed to be the autodiegetic narrator-investigator.[89]

It is possible to imagine cases where a narrator's decision either not to reveal unambiguously their diegetic status at an early stage or, perhaps more crucially, to abide by the level of privilege conventionally ascribed to their voice might entail a threat to the 'decorum' of the given text.[90] However, none of these examples taken from early Russian crime fiction actually does so. In fact, they bear out Lanser's claim that 'the conventions regarding the relationship between a narrator's privilege and the mode of representation are violated more frequently than one might expect'.[91] And Lanser specifically identifies auto-/homodiegetic narrators adopting the omniscient privilege of the heterodiegetic voice as one of the most frequently encountered violations. The frequency of such deviations in Russian crime fiction stands as a testament to the undoubted significance of the issue of authority in the genre. As Chapter 1 has shown, the stylization as memoirs of many of the earliest works of crime fiction in Russia established the autodiegetic narrator-investigator as the default voice in the genre; and this remained the convention throughout much of the 1870s and into the 1880s. Many aspects of the performance of these narrators, as have been outlined in the first two chapters here, are also designed to earn authority for their voices. However, the relatively frequent tendency for such autodiegetic voices initially to pass themselves off as heterodiegetic voices stands as an implicit acknowledgement that the latter are generally accorded greater diegetic authority. Even though the narrators in Stepanov's and Shkliarevskii's stories eventually reveal themselves to be characters in the fictional world endowed with no greater omniscience than the reader, the initial impression of God-like power created by their heterodiegetic performance leaves an indelible mark. The authority granted to these narrator-detectives is not simply the product of aspects of their social identity: their education, skill and humanity. The early adoption of a position of heterodiegetic representation and omniscient privilege gives these narrator-detectives the aura of an all-seeing, all-knowing 'I'; and the impression of their epistemic authority endures long after the revelation of their actual status as mere mortals.

## Conclusion

Crime fiction relies for much of its effect upon the generation of uncertainty in the mind of the reader, experienced as a sense of curiosity or suspense about various aspects of the crime and the subsequent investigation. However, what this chapter has clearly demonstrated is that the ways in which the reader is navigated through this uncertainty are significantly affected by the various matrices of authority that exist around the figure of the detective. By means of its primarily narratological approach, the discussion here has highlighted how this authority is the consequence of different, but intersecting, elements: social, relative and more purely diegetic. It is also vitally important, however, to acknowledge the considerable ideological significance that is implied by the creation of such authoritative figures in the context of post-1860s reform Russia. It is probably the case that the attributes of authority given to investigators in works of this era were intended, to some extent, to construct an ideal of the Russian citizen. In the radically altered social landscape of post-Emancipation Russia, such men acquired particular significance as guarantors of legal and moral justice, not only within the confines of literary fiction, but also in the world beyond. In this fashion, fictional investigators in the Russian context function in much the same way as Emma Bielecki sees both Sherlock Holmes and Maurice Leblanc's Arsène Lupin acting in their respective national and literary histories.[92] These figures become repositories for the types of abilities and attributes deemed desirable in their particular socio-historical context. It is highly likely that the presentation of such intelligent, professional and humane seekers of epistemic knowledge and 'truth' were intended by most examples of this conventionally conservative genre to function as the ideal archetype of the Russian man in the late Imperial period. Nevertheless, as the following two chapters of this monograph will demonstrate in greater detail, in more purely generic terms, the level of authority enjoyed by the voices at the forefront of much Russian crime fiction means that these works need to find ingenious ways to maintain curiosity and suspense.

## Notes to Chapter 2

1. William O. Aydelotte, 'The Detective Story as a Historical Source', in *The Mystery Writer's Art*, ed. by Francis M. Nevins (Bowling Green, OH: Bowling Green University Popular Press, 1971), pp. 306–25 (p. 311).
2. Martin A. Kayman, 'The Short Story from Poe to Chesterton', in *The Cambridge Companion to Crime Fiction*, ed. by Martin Priestman (Cambridge: Cambridge University Press, 2003), pp. 41–58 (p. 44).
3. Ronald R. Thomas, 'The Fingerprint of the Foreigner: Colonizing the Criminal Body in 1890s Detective Fiction and Criminal Anthropology', *English Literary History*, 61.3 (1994), 655–83 (p. 656).
4. Herzog, 'Crime Stories', p. 37.
5. Although the detective is most frequently viewed as the embodiment of authority in the text, it is also possible to see the criminal as enacting his own form of authority, via his crime, over other members of society. Peter Hühn views the criminal's act in terms of freedom when he notes, 'The criminal attempts to realize himself and to gratify his desires by freeing himself from the restraints of society and its defining norms' in 'The Detective as Reader: Narrativity and Reading Concepts in Detective Fiction', *Modern Fiction Studies*, 33.3 (1987), 451–66 (p. 460).
6. Peter Thoms, *Detection and its Designs: Narrative and Power in Nineteenth-Century Detective Fiction* (Athens, OH: Ohio University Press, 1998), p. 9.
7. Hühn, 'The Detective as Reader', p. 460; Kayman, 'The Short Story', p. 46; Thomas, 'The Fingerprint of the Foreigner', p. 656.

8. A. Lokhvitskii, 'Sudebnye sledovateli', *Russkoe slovo*, 9 (1860), p. 6.

9. Ibid., p. 14.

10. In this respect it is also possible to ascribe psychological significance to this figure in his position as 'ideal imago'. See Timothy R. Prchal, 'An Ideal Helpmate: The Detective Character as (Fictional) Object and Ideal Imago', in *Theory and Practice of Classic Detective Fiction*, ed. by Jerome Delamater and Ruth Prigozy (Westport, CT: Greenwood, 1997), pp. 29–37 (p. 30).

11. In 'The Detective as Reader', Hühn explains: 'In a manner of speaking the criminal *writes* the secret story of his crime into everyday "reality" in such a form that its text is partly hidden, partly distorted and misleading' (p. 455). Laura Marcus labels the detective a 'surrogate reader' in 'Detection and Literary Fiction', in *The Cambridge Companion to Crime Fiction*, ed. by Martin Priestman, pp. 245–67 (p. 254). In 'Detectives and Criminals as Players in "Le Théâtre du crime": A Reading of Émile Gaboriau's *Le Crime d'Orcival*', Gale MacLachlan argues: 'If the detective can be interpreted as the image of the (resistant) reader who produces an interpretation of the crime by reading against the grain of appearances, the criminal must necessarily double as his Other, the elusive and unidentified author of a sometimes duplicitous and always fragmentary "text"' (p. 48).

12. Thoms, *Detection and its Designs*, p. 2.

13. Eyal Segal, 'Closure in Detective Fiction', *Poetics Today*, 31.2 (2010), 153–215 (p. 164).

14. Lanser, *The Narrative Act*, pp. 150–69.

15. Susan Lanser, *Fictions of Authority: Women Writers and Narrative Voice* (Ithaca, NY: Cornell University Press, 1992), p. 6.

16. Lanser, *The Narrative Act*, p. 165. She adds later, on p. 168, that 'gender and other categories of social identity may affect presumptions of narrative authority and reliability'.

17. Ibid., p. 166.

18. Popov, *Vinovatye i pravye*, p. 10.

19. Stepanov, *Pravye i vinovatye*, p. 150.

20. S. A. Panov, *Ubiistvo v Mukhtolovoi roshche: rasskaz sudebnogo sledovatelia* (St Petersburg: Sokolov, 1876), pp. 18–19.

21. An article in the March 1861 volume of the journal *Vremia* underlined the belief in the value of the reform's requirement that judicial investigators be thus educated, stating:

> Это придает должности значительную почетность и уже возбудило общее сочувствие, как доказывают появившиеся из разных мест протесты и объяснения о назначении лиц, такого образования не получивших.

> It gives the post considerable respectability and has already aroused general sympathy, as is evidenced by the protests and explanations that have appeared in several quarters about the nomination of people who have not received this level of education.

See *Vremia*, 3 (1861), p. 9.

22. S. A. Panov, *Pomoch': ocherk iz sel'skoi zhizni* (St Petersburg: Bazunov, 1872), p. 270.

23. Ibid., p. 275.

24. See my article 'The Letter of the Law: Literacy and Orality in S. A. Panov's *Murder in Medveditsa Village*', *Slavonic and East European Review*, 89.1 (2011), 1–28. This practice will be discussed in more detail in Chapter 5 below.

25. S. A. Panov, *Ubiistvo v derevne Medveditse: iuridicheskaia povest'* (St Petersburg: Bazunov, 1872), p. 177.

26. As Shari Benstock explains in 'At the Margin of the Discourse: Footnotes in the Fictional Text', *PMLA*, 98.2 (1983), 204–25: 'Whatever specific services footnotes may render, they constantly remind us of the authority on which the text rests' (p. 206).

27. Panov, *Ubiistvo v derevne Medveditse*, p. 128.

28. Panov, *Pomoch'*, p. 281.

29. Stepanov, *Pravye i vinovatye*, p. 21.

30. The epigraph to Poe's 'The Purloined Letter' is taken from Seneca and reads 'nil sapientiae odiosius acumine nimio' (*Selected Tales*, p. 249) and in Doyle's *A Study in Scarlet*, the closing lines of the work belong to Watson who quotes Horace: 'Populus me sibilat, at mihi plaudo | Ipse

domi simul ac nummos contemplor in arca' (p. 96).

31. Sokolovskii, *Ostrog i zhizn'*, p. 15.

32. So, for instance, Stepanov's use of 'repetitia est mater studiorum' in 'They Wanted to Betray the Court and God's Will' (p. 134) is straightforward, whilst Panov's citation of 'Dolus praesumitur, donec probetur contrarium' in *Murder in Medveditsa Village* (p. 73) is rather more difficult.

33. Popov, *Vinovatye i pravye*, p. 12.

34. *Vremia*, 10 (1862), p. 34.

35. *Vremia*, 3 (1861), p. 11.

36. Timofeev, *Zapiski sledovatelia*, pp. 122–23.

37. Sokolovskii, *Ostrog i zhizn'*, p. 71.

38. Antropov's story appears in the collection *Taina Sukharevoi bashni: detektivnye rasskazy* (*The Secret of Sukharev Tower: Detective Stories*) (Tashkent: Adolat, 1992).

39. A. E. Zarin, 'Chetvertyi', in *V poiskakh ubiitsy*, pp. 384–88. Patmosov also uses disguise in the story 'Loss of Honour' from 1909.

40. Vissarion G. Belinskii, *Selected Philosophical Works* (Moscow: Foreign Languages Publishing House, 1948), pp. 323–24.

41. Joseph Frank, *Dostoevsky: The Stir of Liberation, 1860–1865* (Princeton, NJ: Princeton University Press, 1986), p. 67.

42. See McReynolds, *Murder Most Russian*, pp. 92–99.

43. Sokolovskii, *Ostrog i zhizn'*, p. 85.

44. Timofeev, *Zapiski sledovatelia*, p. 337.

45. A. A. Shkliarevskii, *Sochineniia A. Shkliarevskogo: rasskazy sledovatelia* (*The Works of A. Shkliarevskii: Tales of an Investigator*) (St Petersburg: Trub, 1872), p. 112.

46. *Vremia*, 3 (1861), p. 11.

47. Panov, *Iz zhizni uezdnogo gorodka: iz zapisok sudebnogo sledovatelia* (St Petersburg: Skariatin, 1876).

48. F. M. Dostoevskii, *Brat'ia Karamazovy*, in *Sobranie sochinenii v desiati tomakh*, IX (Moscow: Khudozhestvennaia literatura, 1958), p. 562. The translation is taken from *The Brothers Karamazov*, trans. by David Magarshack (London: Penguin, 1982), p. 532.

49. William Burnham, in 'The Legal Context and Contributions of Dostoevsky's *Crime and Punishment*', states that one of the aims behind the legal reform was to ensure 'greater professionalism, legality and objectivity in the investigatory stages of the case' (p. 1240).

50. Stepanov, *Pravye i vinovatye*, pp. 11–19.

51. As Donna Bennett points out, detectives are 'traditionally in benevolent rivalry' with the police. See 'The Detective Story: Towards a Definition of Genre', *PTL: A Journal for Descriptive Poetics and the Theory of Literature*, 4 (1979), 233–66 (p. 255). The judicial reform of 1860 in Russia motivates a rivalry between judicial investigators and the police that is particularly acute and not always entirely benevolent.

52. Sokolovskii, *Ostrog i zhizn'*, p. 166.

53. Timofeev, *Zapiski sledovatelia*, pp. 40–41.

54. Ibid., p. 56.

55. Ibid., p. 93.

56. For more information, see McReynolds, *Murder Most Russian*, pp. 26–29.

57. Establishing the authority of his recurring detective hero, Patmosov, by comparative means is a technique repeatedly favoured by Zarin. In the novel *V poiskakh ubiitsy* (*In Search of a Murderer*) from 1915, for example, the criminal investigation is initially handled by members of the 'сыскная полиция' (detective police) who make almost no progress before the case is transferred to Patmosov, who successfully solves it. In the story 'Loss of Honour', Patmosov acts as a mentor to his younger colleague, Pafnutev. He consistently displays superior knowledge, acting much like a teacher handing on his expertise, and the younger man follows him around diligently.

58. Aaron Parrett, 'The Medical Detective and the Victorian Fear of Degeneration', in *Formal Investigations: Aesthetic Style in Late-Victorian and Edwardian Detective Fiction*, ed. by Paul Fox and Koray Melikoğlu (Stuttgart: ibidem, 2007), pp. 97–114 (p. 99).

59. Régis Messac, *Le Detective-novel et l'influence de la pensée scientifique* (Paris: Slatkine Reprints, 1975), p. 185.
60. Parrett, 'The Medical Detective', p. 99.
61. Panov, *Pomoch'*, p. 289.
62. Ibid., p. 293.
63. Other examples of doctors and judicial investigators productively cooperating during an investigation can be found in Panov's *Murder in Medveditsa Village* as well as Timofeev's 'Tri zhizni' ('Three Lives') from 1878 and Zarin's *In Search of a Murderer*.
64. Panov's *Tri suda, ili ubiistvo vo vremia bala: rasskaz sudebnogo sledovatelia v dvukh chastiakh* (St Petersburg: Skariatin, 1876), p. 45.
65. Shkliarevskii, 'Neraskrytoe prestuplenie', in *Utro posle bala & Neraskrytoe prestuplenie: rasskazy iz ugolovnoi khroniki* (Moscow: Kudriavtsevaia, 1878), p. 149.
66. Panov's *Three Courts* provides a further illustration of the belief in a dual justice system: the work's first part is entitled 'Sud chelovecheskii' ('The Human Court') and the second is 'Sud bozhii' ('God's Court').
67. See, for example, Richard Weisberg, *The Failure of the Word: The Protagonist as Lawyer in Modern Fiction* (New Haven, CT: Yale University Press, 1984); Antony Johae, 'Towards an Iconography of "Crime and Punishment"', in *Fyodor Dostoevsky's Crime and Punishment*, ed. by Harold Bloom (Philadelphia, PA: Chelsea House, 2003), pp. 243–56 (pp. 247–48). 'Porfirii' equates to 'porphyry' which denotes purple in ancient Greece and therefore recalls the vestments of that colour worn by members of the clergy in the period before Easter. Moreover, Raskolnikov's friend, Razumikhin, reveals that Porfirii Petrovich has previously fooled him into thinking he was intending to become a monk (Part III, Chapter 5).
68. Amy Ronner, *Dostoevsky and the Law* (Durham, NC: Carolina Academic Press, 2015), p. 153.
69. Sokolovskii, *Ostrog i zhizn'*, p. 68.
70. Timofeev, *Zapiski sledovatelia*, p. 306.
71. Panov, *Ubiistvo v derevne Medveditse*, p. 234.
72. Ibid., pp. 239–40.
73. The numerous stories by Shkliarevskii and those by Zarin, for example, include no priests or other religious figures. The fact that the action in these stories is located primarily in urban, rather than rural, settings perhaps goes some way towards explaining their absence. However, the decision by these authors not to include religious figures speaks to a general move away from the more traditional belief systems operating in 1860s and 1870s rural Russia.
74. Panov, *Pomoch'*, p. 320.
75. Ibid., p. 322.
76. Ibid., p. 324.
77. Ibid., p. 348.
78. Bennett, 'The Detective Story', pp. 255–56.
79. Carl R. Lovitt, 'Controlling Discourse in Detective Fiction, or Caring Very Much Who Killed Roger Ackroyd', in *The Cunning Craft*, ed. by Walker and Frazer, p. 77.
80. Kayman, 'The Short Story from Poe to Chesterton', p. 42.
81. Bennett, 'The Detective Story', p. 238.
82. David Herman, 'Dialogue in a Discourse Context: Scenes of Talk in Fictional Narrative', *Narrative Inquiry*, 16.1 (2006), 75–84 (p. 76). Robert Scholes and Robert Kellogg express a similar idea in *The Nature of Narrative* (New York, NY: Oxford University Press, 1966) when they argue: 'The reason for this employment of third-person narrative in historical works may be that the reliability of the history seemed to the ancients clearly greater than that of the eyewitness. A document aspiring to achieve truth of fact had a better chance of being appreciated as factual if it did not seem too personal.' (p. 243)
83. Timofeev, 'Muzhniaia zhena', in *Iz vospominanii sudebnogo sledovatelia* (Moscow: Ioganson, 1878), p. 78.
84. Zarin, *V poiskakh ubiitsy*, p. 359.
85. Ibid.
86. Stepanov, *Pravye i vinovatye*, p. 19.

87. These remarks about the confusion of heterodiegetic/autodiegetic authorization apply equally to Stepanov's story 'They Wanted to Betray the Court and God's Will'.
88. Shkliarevskii, 'Rasskaz sudebnogo sledovatelia', in *Chto pobudilo k ubiistvu? Rasskazy sledovatelia (What Prompted the Murder? Tales of an Investigator)*, ed. by A. I. Reitblat (Moscow: Khudozhestvennaia literatura, 1993), p. 81.
89. The works of Antropov referenced earlier in this chapter offer a slight variation on this model. Although, as we have seen, there are times when the homodiegetic narrator, doctor Z., is left in the dark about Putilin's actions and motivations, at others he is able to record the inner thoughts of various characters and reports on scenes at which he was not physically present.
90. The term 'decorum of the text' is taken from David Hayman and Eric Rabkin's work *Form in Fiction: An Introduction to the Analysis of Narrative Prose* (New York, NY: St. Martin's Press, 1974). Decorum can be considered to exist in a text if the narrative voice observes, more or less, the rules of status which it has created for itself.
91. Lanser, *The Narrative Act*, p. 162.
92. Emma Bielecki, 'Arsene Lupin: Rewriting History', in *Rewriting Wrongs: French Crime Fiction and the Palimpsest*, ed. by Angela Kimyongür and Amy Wigelsworth (Newcastle: Cambridge Scholars Publishing, 2014), 47–61 (p. 54).

PART II

# Curiosity and Suspense

# CHAPTER 3

# Sifting for Clues amongst a Multiplicity of Voice

Part I has shown that authority is a key currency in crime fiction: Chapter 1 has highlighted how a text's presentation of itself as a quasi-factual account of authentic experience generates an aura of authority, whilst Chapter 2 has looked at the various ways in which the investigator is established as an authoritative and qualified pursuer of the truth. Authority remains a focus in this third chapter, but it is considered alongside another defining characteristic of the genre: mystery. Regardless of whether a work is a 'whodunit' or a 'whydunit', it still deals in some degree of mystery that manifests itself in the reader's experience of suspense and curiosity. The two chapters that form this book's second part focus on two particular methods of provoking a sense of curiosity and/or suspense in the mind of the reader: multiple voice and temporal construction. In 'The Typology of Detective Fiction', Tzvetan Todorov argues that two different 'forms of interest' are encouraged in the genre and he explains:

> The first can be called *curiosity*; it proceeds from effect to cause: starting from a certain effect (a corpse and certain clues) we must find its cause (the culprit and his motive). The second form is *suspense*, and here the move is from cause to effect: we are first shown the cause, the *données* (gangsters preparing a heist), and our interest is sustained by the expectation of what will happen, that is, certain effects (corpses, crimes, fights).[1]

Eyal Segal picks up this idea and, by combining it with work undertaken by Meir Sternberg on temporality and information gaps in narrative, provides the following helpful refinement: 'An awareness of not knowing would create an expectation for receiving the missing information. This would result either in suspense, if the expectation relates to the narrative future, or in curiosity, if it bears on the narrative past.'[2] The intimate relationship between suspense and the manipulation of temporality (and especially chronological order), which will be the focus of Chapter 4, is made clear by Susan Sweeney's remarks when she discusses the formal elements of detective fiction:

> Because detective fiction emphasizes a chronological, linear, sequential plot, it also emphasizes narrative suspense. [...] The suspense derives from this alternation between progression towards the ending and peripeteias such

as structural obstacles (parallel investigations and false solutions), characters (unsuccessful detectives, criminals, and false suspects), episodes (false clues), and the deceptive language of individual sentences.[3]

This third chapter approaches a discussion of how both this 'progression towards the ending' and the controlled revelation of information that might resolve the reader's sense of suspense and curiosity are affected by the use of multiple voice (and dialogue) in the narrative.

Why multiple voice? There has long been a recognition that works of crime and detective fiction feature a double story structure and that many of the genre's effects stem from the manipulation of the relationship between these two stories. Todorov argues:

> At the base of the whodunit we find a duality [...]. This novel contains not one but two stories: the story of the crime and the story of the investigation. In their purest form, these two stories have no point in common. [...] The first story, that of the crime, ends before the second begins. But what happens in the second? Not much. The characters of this second story, the story of the investigation, do not act, they learn. [...] The hundred and fifty pages which separate the discovery of the crime from the revelation of the killer are devoted to a slow apprenticeship: we examine clue after clue, lead after lead.[4]

Todorov acknowledges that there is nothing new in his insistence on the presence of two stories in a literary narrative: it was the Russian Formalists who first identified the existence of both a *fabula* (*histoire*) and a *siuzhet* (*discours*) in such texts. However, his notable contribution is to argue for their importance precisely to the genre of detective fiction. Building on the work of Todorov a decade or so later, Dennis Porter reiterates the presence of the double story but also emphasizes, primarily in temporal terms, how the relationship between the two is developed in such texts:

> In the process of telling one tale a classic detective story uncovers another. It purports to narrate the course of an investigation but the 'open' story of the investigation gradually unravels the 'hidden' story of the crime. In other words, the initial crime on which the tale of detection is predicated is an end as well as a beginning. It concludes the 'hidden' story of the events leading up to itself at the same time that it initiates the story of the process of detection. [...] This means that detective fiction is preoccupied with the closing of the logico-temporal gap that separates the present of the discovery of the crime from the past that prepared it.[5]

The present chapter contends that multiple voice — the inclusion of a variety of voices in a narrative — is a key strategy used in crime fiction to close this 'logico-temporal gap'. Picking up the terms employed by Todorov, not only does the 'second' story of the investigation examine 'clue after clue, lead after lead', but it does so by listening to the information provided by 'voice after voice'. Although the emphasis in this chapter is on the effects of multiple voice, the discussion also recognizes the relationship that exists between a variety of voices and points of view. As the references in Chapter 2 to Bennett's work on narrative authorization have shown, the use of different focalizing perspectives is crucial to the reader's experience of crime fiction. The decision to focus here primarily on multiple voice,

rather than point of view, is made in light of the significance that the genre ascribes
to various sorts of speech acts.

Although it is theoretically possible for all the details in the story of the
investigation to be narrated by a single voice, it is both more realistic and more
entertaining for this to be done by a variety of different voices, each of which
has a different part of the story to tell, sometimes complementary, sometimes
contradictory. Wilkie Collins recognizes the suitability of multiple voice to crime
fiction on the first page of *The Woman in White* (1859) when he writes:

> The story here presented will be told by more than one pen, as the story of an
> offence against the laws is told in Court by more than one witness — with the
> same object, in both cases, to present the truth always in its most direct and
> most intelligible aspect [...].[6]

Not only does multiple voice reflect the scenario of multiple witnesses in court,
it is a device that functions as a subtle but effective analogy of the various clues
which the detective (and the reader) needs to put together in order to construct
a single coherent narrative — the story of the crime. Just as the detective might
visit a series of different locations and collect various pieces of material evidence,
so he must also listen to a number of different voices that each has its own story to
recount. Moreover, the inclusion of a variety of different voices is a key device in
the generation of curiosity and, especially, suspense. Although, as Porter indicates,
detective fiction is concerned with the closing of the gap that separates the crime
from the end of the investigation, a considerable degree of the reader's enjoyment
is derived precisely from the postponement of such a resolution, from Sweeney's
'peripeteias'. One such 'structural obstacle' is the inclusion of a series of different
voices that supply piecemeal information about a crime; the presence of these
different voices is inherently a technique both of retardation and, to borrow a term
from Bennett, of 'fragmentation'.[7]

As a preface to her discussion of fragmentation, Bennett suggests that, in crime
fiction, although the *histoire* 'contains first the events of the criminal's narrative [...]
followed by the events of the detective's narrative', the *discours* 'contains only or
principally the second of these narratives'. What this means is that the narrative of
the crime therefore has 'a kind of shadowy existence; alluded to or evoked by the
text, it is never fully present there'. Bennett uses the term 'scionarrative' to refer to
this shadowy narrative, 'one which while not strictly within the text nevertheless
has a fully discernible existence'.[8] Moving on to the specific issue of fragmentation,
Bennett argues:

> The primary technique that allows presentation of the scionarrative within
> the *discours* while simultaneously limiting the reader's ability to perceive it as a
> coherent whole is the use of *fragmentation*. Fragmentation is the method whereby
> the whole of the scionarrative is broken into parts which may, at the author's
> discretion, be dispersed throughout the *discours* in various ways. The technique
> of fragmentation is the essential device of all mysteries, since it both permits a
> progressive discovery of the scionarrative and retards comprehension of it.[9]

Although Bennett does not mention multiple voice explicitly in this discussion, it is implied in her recognition that 'perspective is the most important means that the mystery author has at his disposal to modulate the extent of the reader's perceptions of scionarrative fragments when they appear in the text'.[10] Multiple voice is one element of perspective, providing as it does the opportunity for points of view other than those of the narrator to be provided through the voices of different characters in the fictional world. The object of the present chapter, therefore, is to examine the contribution that the exploitation of multiple voice makes both to the construction and to the unravelling of the mysteries presented in works of crime fiction. By taking into account the power relationships that pertain between the various speaking voices and the confidence that can consequently be placed in one or other account, this discussion continues to engage with the question of authority in crime fiction.

The chapter opens with a discussion of the status and significance of direct speech and dialogue in Russian crime fiction. Chapter 1 has briefly examined dialogue's contribution — via the inclusion of local dialect and instances of script-like presentation — to a sense of verisimilitude and immediacy. The discussion here begins by showing how the importance of direct speech and dialogue to crime fiction is implied by its prominent position in a significant number of works. It then discusses the dramatic impact of the depiction of 'ochnye stavki' (face-to-face confrontations) in dialogue before moving on to consider the power dynamics at play in scenes of direct speech in the genre. The third section of the chapter looks at some conventional examples of where multiple voice is used to fragment the story of the crime and the investigation in order to generate suspense and encourage the participation of an active reader. It considers, in particular, the relationship between the voice of the primary narrator and those of embedded narrators and the impact that this has upon the relative reliability ascribed to their accounts. Such examples are deemed conventional because their resolution affirms the position of the narrator (often the same voice as the investigator) atop this hierarchy of authority from where his voice and his version of the story of the crime can dominate. The chapter concludes with a section devoted to rather more unconventional instances of multiple voice. It looks at texts in which the authority of the narrator is challenged by voices that refuse to remain subservient to it, and it considers the risks run by, and the excitement generated in, such works.

## Direct Speech and Dialogue in Crime Fiction

In the introduction to a 2015 article in *The Guardian* newspaper on the top ten passages of dialogue in crime fiction, the author and critic Andrew Martin claims that 'some of the most brilliant speech in novels can be found in this genre. [...] Many of the best dialogue writers have been crime writers. Dialogue lends an immediacy that suits the genre.'[11] Although this chapter is not concerned with the *quality* of dialogue in crime fiction, Martin's statement nevertheless speaks to its significance in the genre. Bennett's identification of what she calls the 'interview tableau' as a key method of fragmentation in crime fiction makes equally clear the central role that is lent to direct speech in the genre.[12] Its role in the Russian context is no different:

during the late Imperial period, works feature substantial amounts of direct speech and dialogue and such passages often account for the moments of greatest tension and excitement in the text. Although a systematic study of the frequency with which direct speech occurs in its corpus of texts as compared to works in other genres is beyond the scope of this book, the contention here is that it is utilized more frequently, and in more prominent positions than in other genres such as the realist novel or the fantastic short story. The prominence of direct speech in crime fiction at this time is at least partially explained by the historical specificities of the era. As Stephen Lovell argues: 'This period [the 1860s–1880s] saw the creation of new institutions — municipal dumas, zemstvos, law courts — where the spoken word could be used to unprecedented effect by a wide range of participants'.[13] Anna Schur develops this claim further when she argues for the importance of the comcomitant act of listening in the post-1860 legal reform period:

> Replacing the written, inquisitorial procedure of the pre-reform era with the oral adversarial process, the reform made listening central to the process of legal judgment. It also spotlighted the individual person on trial. Like Athenian courts, Russian post-reform courts were also attentive to this person's particular life circumstances and sought understanding of his moral character.[14]

Although Schur has in mind here acts of speech that take place in the courtroom, I would argue that her remarks are equally applicable to the pre-trial stages of the investigation. Whilst criminal investigations had relied on oral testimony far more than courtrooms even before 1860, the emphasis placed by the reform upon the need for direct and open processes of justice finds expression in the extent to which dialogue is foregrounded in works of crime fiction during this period.

One key indicator of dialogue's importance to the genre is the frequency with which acts of direct speech or dialogue either open works or appear in their earliest stages. So, for example, Popov's story 'A Sinner's End' begins *in medias res*, plunging the reader immediately into a one-and-a-half-page passage of direct dialogue between, firstly, the narrator-investigator and the coachman who is driving him to the village of Nizov'e to investigate a case of theft and then with the stationmaster, Gradov, with whom he is already acquainted. The style of this opening section serves to characterize the narrator as a man of action who appears well acquainted with inhabitants in his area of jurisdiction more effectively than could a passage of description. Dialogue is also used to open Antropov's story 'Kiss of the Bronze Virgin' where it indicates implicitly the significance of the conversation that takes place in the confession box between Rzhevuskii, the future victim, and his Catholic priest, who is plotting to kidnap and murder him. There are also very many examples of stories that introduce direct dialogue after the most peremptory passage of orienting narration. This is the case in all of the other stories in Popov's collection, *The Guilty and the Innocent*, in several of Sokolovskii's stories, including 'Soap Bubbles' and 'Diadia Foma' ('Old Man Foma'), in Panov's *Three Courts*, in Shkliarevskii's stories 'The Tale of a Judicial Investigator', 'An Undiscovered Crime' and 'Sekretnoe sledstvie' ('A Secret Investigation'), as well as in Zarin's 'The Fourth Man' and 'The Missing Worker'. In these works, following a very brief description of the location and time of the action, sometimes lasting only two or three lines, the narrative switches to an extended section of dialogue between characters largely unknown to the reader. Such passages of non-contextualized dialogue are, of course, a highly effective means of arousing the reader's curiosity.

Not only does direct speech or dialogue appear early on in many works of crime fiction, it also occupies a dominant position over the course of the narratives as a whole. Very many of these works feature at least as much direct dialogue as they do descriptive narration or indirectly reported speech. Furthermore, in what are often relatively short, novella-length works, crime fiction presents a high number of different voices within these passages of direct speech. Popov's 'A Sinner's End' provides an interesting, if extreme, example of crime fiction's desire to foreground direct speech. At least 90 per cent of the story is reported in direct speech, interspersed with short passages of orienting description in which the narrator-investigator provides details of a couple of characters' physical appearances, his own actions as well as several brief summaries of reported speech. Over the course of a story that lasts only thirty-seven pages, the reader gets to hear directly the voices of no fewer than eighteen different characters as they engage in dialogue either with the narrator or with another character in his presence. These include: the stationmaster's wife and young daughter; the victim of the theft, Matvei Negodiaev; the three suspects in the case, including the main protagonists, Irina Negodiaeva and Liutikov the carpenter; the local treasurer, Viktor Ivanovich, who serves as the investigator's assistant; various witnesses from both Nizov'e and neighbouring villages; the *sotskii*; and the local priest. The most significant amongst these voices make multiple direct appearances in the text and that of Irina Negodiaeva, in particular, is permitted to give accounts of her life and actions that remain uninterrupted by any other voice for relatively long passages. The inclusion of such a chorus of different voices directly in the text, rather than in indirect summary form, unquestionably provides the reader with a sense of the fictional world as one populated by living characters. As Bronwen Thomas claims, 'dialogue plays a crucial role in helping to create and populate credible fictional worlds'.[15] Not only is the inclusion of direct speech linked to credibility, as Thomas argues elsewhere, it is also linked to the question of authority:

> as well as adding variety to a narrative, representing the speech of those who take part in a narrated event, or who are somehow qualified to comment on what takes place, may also contribute importantly to the authenticity and authority of the story, as we appear to be told what happened 'from the horse's mouth'.[16]

As mentioned in Chapter 1, the fact that the speech of many of these characters, particularly in the earlier, rurally-set works, carries markers of style, pronunciation or dialect/idiom related to geographical region or social class encourages the reader to consider them to be realistic representations of authentic characters.[17]

Examples from our corpus of texts also provide excellent illustration of the widespread and longstanding belief held in literary studies that '[dialogue] contribut[es] drama and vitality to the actions and situations located within those worlds'.[18] Many works of Russian crime fiction underscore the drama inherent in direct speech by employing it to communicate the essential discovery, revelation or progress in an investigation. So, for example, in Sokolovskii's 'The Long-Suffering', Daria Iakovleva's accusation of her lover Stepan as the man who has attempted to murder her is not paraphrased but comes in a passage of direct dialogue when the narrator-investigator first goes to question her. The exchanges between Raskolnikov and Porfirii Petrovich in *Crime and Punishment* will be discussed later in this chapter, but it is worth noting that the hero's confession (of sorts) to Lizaveta in Part IV of the novel is made during a charged conversation between the two that is presented in direct speech. Meanwhile, in Panov's *Murder in Medveditsa Village*, the investigator's eventual victory in his long struggle to get the suspect, Grishanin, to confess to the murder of his neighbour, Grosheva, comes when the blacksmith utters the word, reported directly, 'виноват' ('guilty').[19] As if to accentuate the dramatic import of providing a confession in direct speech, the narrative then quickly switches to an indirect report from the narrative voice of the further details that Grishanin provides about the circumstances of his crime. Whilst informative, this account possesses nowhere near the same affective impact as does the direct confession.

To conclude this opening section on the status of dialogue in Russian crime fiction, it is pertinent to discuss briefly the role of the historically and culturally specific concept of the 'ochnaia stavka' (face-to-face confrontation) in the Russian judicial landscape. The *Brockhaus-Efron Encyclopaedic Dictionary* defines these face-to-face confrontations thus:

> Одновременный допрос двух лиц по одним и тем же вопросам. На предварительном следствии очные ставки даются свидетелям в тех случаях, когда от разъяснения противоречий в их показаниях зависит дальнейшее направление следствия.

> [The simultaneous interrogation of two people on the same questions. In a preliminary investigation, face-to-face confrontations are staged between witnesses when the subsequent development of the investigation depends upon the clarification of contradictions in their respective testimonies.]

Timofeev's story 'The Arsonists' in *Notes of an Investigator*, about the narrator's investigation into what turns out to be a false accusation that the prominent Polish landowner is harbouring the titular criminals on his estate, contains an embedded explanation of the role of these confrontations and of what the investigator hopes to gain from them. The narrator-investigator explains that, as far as he is concerned, their value is to be found in psychological more than formal or procedural terms:

> Обыкновенно, одна сторона говорит свое, другая свое, и следователь, извлекая из взаимных возражений то, что нужно к делу, переносит это на бумагу. Гораздо более значения имеет очная ставка как нравственное доказательство правдивости одной и лживости другой стороны.[20]

> [Usually, one side gives his version and the other side gives his, and the investigator, extracting what is necessary for the case from each side's answers, transfers it onto paper. But the face-to-face confrontation is far more significant

in terms of offering moral proof of the honesty of one side and the mendacity of the other.]

Although reports of such face-to-face confrontations in Russian crime fiction do not necessarily have to appear in direct dialogue, their very nature means that this is usually the case. And such direct confrontations between witnesses in the presence of the investigator provide the narrative with moments of considerable drama and tension. Illustrative examples of the potential to create effect by means of dialogue in these face-to-face confrontations are to be found in the work of Sokolovskii, Timofeev and Panov, amongst others. We will restrict ourselves here to discussing the scene of 'ochnaia stavka' that is staged between Daria Iakovleva and Stepan Prokofiev in Sokolovskii's 'The Long-Suffering'. The investigator explains that Prokofiev's allegation that Daria has accidentally stabbed herself during one of their many arguments (that contradicts her accusation of him) means that he is obliged to stage a confrontation between the two. He describes how, when the two come face to face, it seems to him that Daria is pleased to see her lover, whilst Prokofiev appears affected as he frowns and sucks in his lips. The narrative then switches into a passage of direct dialogue between the two in which the drama of the confrontation is communicated by means of a rapid to-and-fro of untagged speech acts that are staccato in nature. They accuse each other of having gone mad, before Daria asks Prokofiev what she has done to deserve such brutal treatment at his hands and tells him that his denial constitutes a great sin. When he repeats his accusation, she asks where his conscience is before he accuses her of being a prostitute. Although she openly acknowledges this fact, she protests: 'Почто же ты тиранствовал надо мной, коли денег тебе не давала? Почто-ж ты кровь мою день деньской пил?' ('Why on earth did you terrorize me when I wouldn't give you the money? Why did you drink my blood from morning until night?').[21] Whilst her words appear to have some effect on Prokofiev, he sticks to his story. The combative nature of the relationship and the sheer strength of the emotion captured in this passage of dialogue functions as a quasi-restaging in front of the narrator and reader of the original crime. Although no physical blows are exchanged, the vehemence of the direct verbal exchange succeeds in effectively representing the violence of their previous confrontation. Indeed, the fact that, in spite of the narrator-investigator's best intentions and the reassurances of the medics, Daria dies very soon afterwards reinforces the impression that it functions as a re-enactment of the crime. There is no doubt that the impact of this scene is enhanced by its presentation in direct dialogue; the unmediated speech of the two characters brings the reader into much more immediate contact with the fractured relationship between Daria and Prokofiev and ensures that the announcement of her death when it comes creates a considerable shock.

## Dialogue and Power Relations

As Wilkie Collins's justification for the inclusion of multiple voice in *The Woman in White* cited above makes clear, it is commonly assumed that acts of direct speech give characters the opportunity to speak for themselves and to have their voice and their version of events heard. Such a positive interpretation of the value of direct speech chimes with opinions expressed in much scholarship on the theory of listening (in which dialogue is clearly implicated) that has developed since the 1990s. As Schur points out, much work in this area:

> presents listening as the quintessential ethical stance: as a stance that is uniquely responsive to the claims of the Other, accepting of difference, promoting sensitivity, inclusiveness, care, and other progressive values. Listening [...] is often credited with socially and politically transformative powers and is contrasted to desires for power, dominance and superiority [...]. Qualified with such descriptors as 'real,' 'active,' 'genuine,' 'deep,' and 'receptive,' listening figures not just as an activity of another's communication but as a commitment to responsiveness, acceptance, empathy, obedience and self-transcendence.[22]

She goes on to point out quite correctly, however, the weaknesses in and exceptions to this positive and idealizing view of listening, focusing in particular on Dostoevskii's *Notes from the House of the Dead*. In fact, as the examples of 'face-to-face confrontations' suggest, crime fiction provides numerous examples of how the ethical dimension of listening can become complicated. Although direct speech may well bestow a more visible status upon a fictional character than if their speech act is ventriloquized by the narrator, the particular context of many of the direct speech acts in crime fiction must also be acknowledged. Although the epistemic challenge proffered by crime fiction means that the reader's attention is likely to be focused on the *content* of a particular speech act, and of what it might reveal about the circumstances of the crime, it is essential to keep context in mind. Specifically, the dynamics of power and authority that pertain in the verbal exchanges between characters in the fictional world (particularly between the detective and others) need to remain in focus. The labels for three of the four of Bennett's subcategories of the 'interview tableau' make these dynamics clear: all apart from 'encounter' suggest that coercion is key to their existence and functioning.

Critical work to date has not stated sufficiently starkly that many acts of speech (both direct and indirect) in crime fiction arise in situations in which one participant (the witness or suspect) is forced to speak by the investigator. Crucially, the investigator is, in many instances, not a neutral listener, but one whose professional role not only compels others to speak, but forces him into the position of being an active and judgemental listener. While the context of the criminal investigation might be seen to place the act of dialogue under particular pressure, it arguably speaks to a more widespread critical suspicion of dialogue's status that finds its echo in Schur's article. According to Bronwen Thomas, critics such as Lennard J. Davis and Aaron Fogel 'offer a critique of theories of dialogue that associate it only with the "fun" and the "free", arguing that they neglect the extent to which conversation can be coercive and authoritarian'.[23] For Fogel, 'dialogues display a kind of miniaturised, static social constitution' that is 'used and imposed' on those who do not have power by those who do.[24] As Thomas herself argues, crime fiction provides extreme examples of a fact that applies to all acts of speech because: 'conversation is about the exercise of power, and because linguistic exchanges do not take place in a vacuum but are shaped and constrained by the "larger, governing shapes" of any given society'.[25] Ronald Thomas correctly identifies the investigator as the embodiment of that power and authority in the context of crime fiction when he argues that:

> the literary detective gains the power to discover 'the truth' by acquiring the right to tell someone else's story against his or her will. [...] The work the literary detective performs is an act of narrative usurpation in which he converts stories told by subjects about themselves into alibis proffered by suspects.[26]

Popov's 'A Sinner's End' and Panov's *The Harvest Gathering* are just two of the texts that effectively illustrate the power dynamics that relate to the use of dialogue in Russian crime fiction. As mentioned above, Popov's story opens with direct dialogue between the narrator-investigator and the coachman who refers to him immediately and repeatedly as 'your Excellency'. Although this coachman plays no direct role in the criminal investigation, the fact of his being in the service of the narrator-investigator as well as his use of the respectful epithet denote their exchange as being between unequal participants. Indeed, whether or not the narrator-investigator's acts of dialogue are with suspects/witnesses in the case, or just with incidental characters, this power dynamic, in which the investigator enjoys a higher social and professional standing and is therefore the ultimate authority, remains unchanged. Many of the direct verbal exchanges in the story involve the narrator-investigator issuing orders to his subordinates and checking that they understand both what is required of them and the relevant legal protocols. So, for instance, the dialogue between the narrator and the middle-aged woman who serves as the *desiatskii* (peasant police helper) involves him instructing her to find him the *sotskii* immediately and not to gossip and dawdle along the way, whilst her speech is restricted to promising to try to fulfil his orders. Even as regards Viktor Ivanovich, who acts as unofficial assistant to, and comes closest to standing on an equal footing with, the investigator, his passages of dialogue do little more than carry out the orders of the narrator. For example, his early speech about the three suspects in the theft is entirely coloured by the fact that the narrator has asked him to provide details of the backgrounds of those who are under suspicion. This is no spontaneous act of verbal description but a framing account that has the potential to influence much of the subsequent investigation. Similarly, the central parts of the story are structured around the acts of speech of the victim of the theft and, most especially, these three suspects. Each of the suspects speaks only because they have been compelled to do so by the narrator-investigator: they are rounded up by the *sotskii*, brought to the interrogation room and then placed face to face with the investigator. The detective's opening lines to the carpenter, Liutikov, are indicative of the combative tone throughout: 'тебе обвиняют в краже у Матвея Негодяева [...] не хочешь ли чего еще сказать к своему оправданию?' ('you are accused of stealing from Matvei Negodiaev [...] don't you want to say something else in your defence?').[27] During many of the dialogues in Popov's story, particularly these first interrogations, the sense of compulsion and, consequently, of tension, is achieved by means of the staccato exchanges in which the narrator-investigator poses direct, often accusatory, questions and the suspect attempts to avoid self-incrimination by giving as brief a response as possible. The most significant exceptions to this pattern, as mentioned above, come in relation to the voice of Irina, who, on two occasions, is permitted to give a longer account of her circumstances and life in response to the narrator's prompts. Nevertheless, these passages of direct speech still need to be viewed in the context of a suspect giving testimony to a judicial investigator who, in spite of sympathy for her plight, ultimately ends up writing reports on her actions that lead to her being tried and sentenced to hard labour.

Panov's *The Harvest Gathering* offers up somewhat different examples of the power relationships that exist between the various voices in the diegesis, most likely because it is narrated not by the judicial investigator, but by his friend who accompanies him during the case. In contrast to Popov's story, the reader does encounter voices here that enjoy at least as much authority as that of the investigator. His friend, the narrator, assumes the guise of an adjunct investigator when he stumbles upon crucial evidence in the case of Sinitsyn's murder that leads him to challenge the interpretation of the detective and to propose an alternative approach to solving the case. As mentioned in Chapter 2, the investigator is also aided in the case by the doctor whose autopsy establishes the cause and time of death; throughout the story, their two voices spar about the relative value of medicine and justice in a manner that bestows a very similar degree of authority upon each. Nevertheless, the overwhelming majority of speech acts depicted in the story involve situations in which one voice (usually that of either the narrator or the detective) compels another to speak as part of the investigation. The reluctance of the villagers to be subjected to an investigation into the death of Sinitsyn is made clear by the village elder's attempt to persuade the detective that the victim has died simply from drinking impure vodka and that no crime has been committed. Over the course of the investigation, some fifteen or so characters are compelled to appear before the detective and recount what they know about the events of the night that Sinitsyn died. All of these characters, with the exception of the members of Sinitsyn's own family, perform this action reluctantly. These include the local priest, who refuses to answer the narrator's questions about which couples are due to get married, as well as the main suspect in the case, Gvozdev, who repeatedly attempts not to answer questions in a full manner, particularly about his injured thumb. However, the most striking example of coerced speech comes in the story's closing pages where the narrator's rather outlandish idea of staging a 'coup d'état' is enacted so as to force Gvozdev into providing a confession. The plan consists in detaining Gvozdev overnight in a barn in order to keep him unaware of progress made in the case before bringing him out into a scene staged to make it look as if his accomplices have already confessed to their part in the murder in front of a priest and the necessary witnesses. The success of the 'coup d'état' is demonstrated when Gvozdev almost immediately utters the word 'виноват' ('guilty') in direct speech before the assembled company, a word that he has been determined not to say before this point. It is this act of direct speech, again swiftly followed by a switch into indirect report, which indicates the effective resolution of the case and the victory of the investigators.[28] However, it is clear that Gvozdev would never have admitted his guilt if he had not been forced into doing so by the investigators' act of duplicity and the pressure applied by the public scene.

Although the scenario of coerced speech applies in very many situations depicted in crime fiction, it should not be confused with a depiction of criminal investigators as unsympathetic. Chapter 2 has shown how, in the Russian context, the humanity and compassion of the detectives is a significant characteristic contributing to their authority. What one can say, however, is that this sense of humanity and empathy is more effectively created precisely when the sense of coerced speech is minimized. So, for example, Russian crime fiction of this period does offer examples of works in which voices belonging to characters other than the judicial investigator, particularly to victims or suspects, can dominate for relatively long passages of the text, and these passages are of interest not merely in terms of the empathy that they generate. Anticipating a preoccupation of the later sections of the present chapter, it is worth noting that such passages of extended direct speech occur in works that tend to create less suspense with regard to the criminal case. Such a situation is a logical consequence of the fact that the dominance of a single character's voice implies both a lesser role for the criminal investigator and fewer possibilities to introduce a network of competing and contradictory voices. This is not to say that such characters' acts of speech cannot themselves contain other voices; it is simply that when they do, these other voices tend to coincide to construct a unified story of confession.

Striking examples of less coercive, and hence more sympathetic, speech situations can be found in Timofeev's 'Murder and Suicide' and in Shkliarevskii's 'Otchego on ubil ikh? Rasskaz sledovatelia' ('Why Did He Kill Them? The Tale of an Investigator') both from 1872. In Timofeev's story, which is fifty-eight pages long, the voice of the criminal/victim, Marianna Bodresova, dominates in direct speech for seven pages towards the close of the narrative. Whereas the first part of her life story has been reported by the narrator in indirect speech earlier in the narrative, at this later point, she provides details of her abusive relationship with, and eventual murder of, her half-brother directly. Her account of how she is raped by her half-brother, bears him three children, is made to promise not to reveal that he is their father, is cruelly mistreated and then abandoned by him before she decides to murder him creates a powerful impression on both the judicial investigator and the reader. Here, to borrow Schur's terms, it is possible to view the narrator's decision to step back and to allow Bodresova to speak for herself as one that promotes a sense of 'commitment to responsiveness, acceptance, empathy'.[29] It also serves to individualize Marianna to some extent, depicting her as the victim not so much of the institution of serfdom but of the exceptional cruelty and violence of her half-brother. This sense of a less coerced act of speech combined with an ethical act of listening is created even more powerfully in Shkliarevskii's story. 'Why Did He Kill Them?' recounts events surrounding the double murder of his wife and his lover, as well as his own attempted suicide, committed by the narrator's friend, the local teacher, Sergei Antonovich Narostov.[30] The friendship between the narrator-investigator and Narostov goes a long way to explaining the rather different power dynamics revealed to be at work, and that find expression in the configuration of speech acts contained in the story. Of its ten chapters, seven and a half are dominated by the voice of Narostov telling his own life story in direct speech. Indeed, from midway through the third chapter until the conclusion of Chapter 9, the voice of the narrator intervenes on only three, very brief occasions before his voice returns to the fore in the final chapter. Although Narostov's act of extended speech is unambiguously part of the narrator's investigation, its duration and its dominance without interruption ensure that it suggests to the reader a status as more voluntary speech. The decision to allow Narostov's direct discourse to stand at the fore of the narrative with almost no interruption can be interpreted as promoting a sense of the teacher as a victim of both circumstance and education, and thus not entirely to blame for his crimes. The narrator here conducts only the most limited active investigation before the facts of the case are laid out before him with the minimum of fuss and suspense in Narostov's act of direct speech.

## Multiple Voice and Levels of Authority: Shkliarevskii's 'A Secret Investigation'

Moving on from a discussion of the impact of dialogue in crime fiction, the third section of this chapter examines the organization of multiple voices from a narratological perspective in order to consider the interrelated notions of authority and suspense. As mentioned above, the particular relevance of multiple voice to crime fiction lies in the contribution it makes to the fragmentation of the *discours* that is key to the provocation of suspense. Although it is possible to find examples of single voices that dominate for long stretches in Russian crime fiction, such texts neither provoke much suspense nor encourage the participation of an active reader. It is more conventionally the case that the story of the investigation features a chorus of different voices by means of which the story of the crime is broken up into smaller sections that then need to be reassembled into a coherent whole by the investigator (and the reader). In his discussion of Edgar Allan Poe, Martin Priestman invokes the related concepts of metaphor and metonymy and argues that it is the latter that plays a significant role in much detective fiction:

> In metonymy [...] one thing stands next to another in a temporal sequence, and this in turn involves a use of synecdoche whereby an aspect or fragment of a whole 'stands in' for it as an exemplary instance: realistic narratives expect us to relate these fragmentary instances back to the known wholes from which they come. This can be seen as one of the key procedures of the detective story, where our ability to deduce the whole ape or sailor from a scrap of fur or greasy ribbon is constantly put to the test.[31]

The argument put forward in the remainder of this chapter is that the genre's exploitation of multiple voice operates in a similar fashion. Each voice has a fragment of the whole story to recount and gives the investigator and the reader an opportunity to perceive the whole behind the fragment; but it is conventionally the case that a multiplicity of voice is required to reconstruct the entirety of the story of the crime.

One crucial facet of the reconstruction of the 'whole' story is that the various voices that participate in this process do not necessarily enjoy equal degrees of authority and reliability. Narratologists conventionally map the different voices in a text onto a framework of narrative levels. Genette offers the following definition of the distinction between the various narrative levels operating within a text: 'tout événement raconté par un récit est à un niveau diégétique immédiatement supérieur à celui où se situe l'acte narratif producteur de ce récit' ('each event narrated by an account is at a diegetic level immediately superior to that in which the narrative act producing this account is situated').[32] He identifies three such levels and labels them 'extradiegetic', 'diegetic/intradiegetic' and 'metadiegetic' (or what Mieke Bal calls, perhaps more helpfully, 'hypodiegetic').[33] An extradiegetic narrative act is one that exists externally to the diegesis and where the voice does not figure as a character in the story world; an intradiegetic narrator is one who narrates events in the primary narrative; the hypodiegetic level is made up of narrative acts that are embedded within the intradiegetic level. Lanser acknowledges the importance of this idea of levels to the reader's interpretation of the text: '[it] is structurally significant because it signals differences among narrative voices that must be clarified if we are to recognize the relations of subordination and authority generated by a given text'.[34] So, for example, a hypodiegetic narrative voice is likely to be considered subordinate to that of an intradiegetic voice unless there are good reasons for it to be granted greater authority. The reader's assessment of the authority and reliability of any given voice in the diegesis is informed not just by level, therefore, but also by the evaluative information provided about it, either implicitly or explicitly. In order to consider how the fragmentation necessary to curiosity and suspense can be generated by multiple voice in Russian crime fiction, this section of the chapter will examine one text as a detailed case study: Shkliarevskii's 'A Secret Investigation'.

Aleksandr Alekseevich Shkliarevskii deserves recognition as one of the most productive writers of early Russian crime fiction. Between 1870 and 1883, Shkliarevskii wrote some two dozen works, many of which are high-quality examples of the genre. He had a biographical link to crime which might reasonably be seen to have influenced his literary creation: although he did not work as an investigator like Sokolovskii, Stepanov and Timofeev, Shkliarevskii was employed as a clerk, first for the police and later in the local court. Reitblat, Shkliarevskii's champion in contemporary Russia, claims that this period of employment provided him with an especially rich stock of impressions on which he frequently drew in his subsequent literary career.[35] In about 1862, he started to send correspondence to local journals, and this eventually led to his first literary publications: observational sketches of life in Voronezh, firmly rooted in everyday realism.[36] Influenced by his reading of the journals, *Sovremennik* and *Russkoe slovo*, especially the work of Dobroliubov, Shkliarevskii dreamt of escaping the provinces so as to be able to make a meaningful contribution to the enlightenment of society. Thus, in 1869 he moved to St Petersburg to try to become a professional writer where Anatolii Fedorovich Koni, the celebrated prosecutor, who was acquainted with his early work, took him under his wing. Koni found him work as a court clerk and then as a legal attaché in various provinces; however, this employment was short-lived as illness forced Shkliarevskii to return to the capital. There he resumed his writing and published stories such as 'Neproshloe' ('Unpast') (1867) and 'Shevel'nulos' teploe chuvstvo' ('There Stirred a Warm Feeling') (1870) in Petersburg journals. Over time, Shkliarevskii turned increasingly towards detective fiction and, whilst influenced by the earlier documentary tradition established by Sokolovskii, his detectives were the heroes crucially of 'rasskazy' ('tales') and not 'zapiski' ('notes'). Although Shkliarevskii was frequently published in popular newspapers and illustrated journals in the 1870s (including *Novoe vremia* (*New Time*), and *Pchela* (*The Bee*)), the reluctance of the 'thick journals' to publish crime fiction meant that his financial position was always precarious. He quickly became one of countless minor writers of the period whose recognition of their own unfashionability in both literary and 'society' terms was accompanied by a descent into alcoholism. In spite of numerous efforts to help him break the vicious circle he found himself in, Shkliarevskii's life continued upon its downward spiral until his death in 1883. By his own admission, Shkliarevskii's principal role model in his artistic endeavours was Dostoevskii. In a letter addressed to the author in the early 1870s, he confessed:

> Я принадлежу к числу самых жарких поклонников ваших сочинений за их глубокий психологический анализ, какого ни у кого нет из наших современных писателей [...] Если я кому и подражаю из писателей, то Вам...[37]

> [I number amongst the most ardent disciples of your works for their deep psychological analysis, which is shared by none of our other contemporary writers [...] If I imitate any writer, then it is You...]

This was no empty expression of admiration: as I have explored elsewhere, the influence of Dostoevskii can be discerned in a number of different aspects of Shkliarevskii's writing.[38] Here, however, attention will remain more tightly focused upon the internal functioning of one of Shkliarevskii's works in terms of its exploitation of multiple voice.

Shkliarevskii's story 'A Secret Investigation' was first published in 1876 and recounts the narrator-detective's investigation into the death of Zinaida Aleksandrovna Mozharovskaia. She is brought back to her temporary residence in St Petersburg in a carriage following a night out with a female friend, Avdotia Nikanorovna Kriukovskaia; but when a servant opens the door, she is found slumped on the floor and very recently deceased. As mentioned briefly in Chapter 2, the initial descriptions of the discovery of Mozharovskaia's death and the reactions to it are narrated from the perspective of what appears to be an uninvolved heterodiegetic narrator. However, towards the end of the second page the narrator notes how a crowd gathers around the house and that eventually senior police officers and the local judicial investigator arrive — and that he is that judicial investigator. He then commences his investigation by reading the medical report into Mozharovskaia's death and accompanying the doctor and the victim's body to the hospital. The story's title is explained by the fact that Mozharovskaia's death is initially ruled to be due to natural causes: although she is said to have previously been in relatively good health, neither the first doctor nor subsequent medical experts can find any evidence of foul play and this decision leaves the narrator with no investigation to conduct. It is only six months later that the narrator receives further information that convinces him that Mozharovskaia was in fact poisoned and he then begins an unofficial, 'secret' investigation in order to find the culprit(s). The centrality of multiple voice to this story is demonstrated by the fact that almost the entirety of the autodiegetic narrator's investigation consists in soliciting and listening to the testimony of a cast of different characters who are somehow linked to the case: as McReynolds notes, the work is 'structured [...] as a series of imbricated personal stories'.[39] In line with remarks made in Chapter 2, it would be hard to argue that Shkliarevskii's detective acts here as a brilliant analyst in the mould of Poe's Dupin. He is more of a facilitator, a linking character who gathers testimony from the right witnesses and then pieces the bits together. Aside from the descriptions of the narrator's brief examination of Mozharovskaia's body, a visit to the Mariinskii Theatre where Kriukovskaia is a season ticket holder and a search of another character's apartment, the narrative is exclusively made up of the various different acts of speech that eventually combine to tell the story of the crime. In order to understand how curiosity and suspense are generated and how knowledge is acquired in a piecemeal fashion in this story, it is necessary to consider in some detail how this constellation of different voices is arranged and exploited.

Over the course of 'A Secret Investigation', which is eighty pages long, the reader hears at least thirteen different voices in the narrative, including Mozharovskaia's maid, her husband, and various other witnesses and suspects, including her best friend, the main suspect, Avdotia Kriukovskaia. What makes multiple voice such a striking feature of this work, however, is the fact that five of these voices are given the opportunity to narrate embedded accounts of a significant duration. Whilst the first chapter incorporates a number of different voices in both direct and indirect speech, it is the voice of the autodiegetic narrator that dominates as he describes the initial investigation that was conducted immediately after Mozharovskaia's death. However, beginning in Chapter 2, this narrator repeatedly gives the floor to other characters who recount what they know of the victim and the main suspect, and of the network of characters that surround them. All these five voices (as well as the others) are examples of hypodiegetic narrators: their narrative acts are embedded within that of the investigator who is responsible for the intradiegetic level. However, the fact that their speech acts are permitted to dominate for an extended period lends them a notable degree of authority. So, for instance, in Chapter 2 the narrator describes how, during a visit to his father sometime after Mozharovskaia's death, he spends a good deal of time with the local army doctor, Mitrofanii Stratonovich Mikhailovskii. One day after lunch, Mikhailovskii asks to look through the narrator's album and quickly cries out in surprise when he comes across the picture of Mozharovskaia that the narrator has been given by her husband following her death. In the subsequent passage of direct dialogue between the two,

Mikhailovskii categorically rejects the idea that she has died of natural causes and claims not only that she has been poisoned with curare but that he has unwittingly been an accessory to her murder. Following this relatively short exchange in dialogue, Mikhailovskii begins his embedded narrative act and his 'I' effectively replaces that of the narrator for fourteen pages. During this time, there are no interruptions from the narrator as his voice falls entirely silent. Mikhailovskii's story reaches back to a time when he was at the military academy and recounts how a fellow student, Ivan Il'ich Belotserkovskii, experiments on himself with curare, appearing to come extremely close to death before being revived by fellow students, including Mikhailovskii. Closer to the present moment of the crime, Mikhailovskii recounts how one night he is compelled by some strange feeling to walk to Mozharovskaia's house and, once there, he witnesses the alarm being raised on the occasion when she has apparently previously been poisoned. Mikhailovskii's story about Belotserkovskii, and specifically the similarities between his symptoms and those of Mozharovskaia, suggests that there is a strong basis to his claim that she has been poisoned with curare. His story about the earlier attempt to poison Mozharovskaia is implicitly ratified as reliable because it repeats many of the details previously given to the narrator-investigator by her maid. Moreover, the fact that Mikhailovskii's voice here functions as a double of that of the narrator, because he voices the same suspicions about the crime but can likewise provide no proof, earns it authority. The narrator explicitly attaches some reliability to Mikhailovskii's account when he says, 'я не сомневался ни в честности, ни в благородстве его и верил, что он говорил с полным убеждением в подлинности отравления' ('I doubted neither his honesty nor his honour and I believed that he spoke with full conviction about the truth of the poisoning').[40] Nevertheless, the investigator also expounds upon the reasons for Mikhailovskii's potential unreliability: most notably the fact that the doctor is clearly in love with Mozharovskaia and that this might cloud his judgement but also that the detective considers Mikhailovskii's medical investigations to be 'сомнительны' ('doubtful'). So, at the close of Mikhailovskii's fragment of the story, the investigator and the reader have learned about the likely manner of death and heard suspicions voiced against Kriukovskaia, but they are still not in possession of either proof or a motive. The suggestion from Mikhailovskii that Mozharovskaia's death is not natural but a murder, combined with the doubts voiced by the narrator-investigator about the reliability of his version of events, effectively generates a good dose of both curiosity about past events and suspense about their future resolution.

The second embedded voice we encounter belongs to the narrator's second cousin, Bystrov, who quite fortuitously happens to be at the Mariinskii Theatre with Kriukovskaia and her mother when the investigator visits to try to learn more about this main suspect. The narrator and his cousin go off to a restaurant together where, in the relative privacy of a separate room, Bystrov tells the narrator what he knows of Kriukovskaia and her mother. His narration reaches back into a more distant past than that of Mikhailovskii in order to give details of how Kriukovskaia's mother's marriage was driven by her desire for wealth rather than love and of the negative effect of this arrangement on her daughter during childhood; it also describes the circumstances of Kriukovskaia's first marriage. Just as Mikhailovskii's narrative has introduced the previously unknown figure of Belotserkovskii, so Bystrov's account introduces the previously unheard-of, and shadowy, figure of Kebmezakh, a sixty-year-old retired state councillor, who is responsible for the scandalous reputation that Kriukovskaia enjoys after the breakdown of her first marriage and before she later becomes engaged to Mozharovskaia's widow. In a sense, although Bystrov's narrative allows the investigator and the reader to piece together certain fragments of Kriukovskaia's past, and possibly provides a motive for the murder given her eventual romance with the victim's husband, it also deepens the mystery and generates further suspense by introducing the fragment related to Kebmezakh. The reader certainly has the sense here of confronting the sort of 'structural obstacles' that Sweeney identifies as being among the formal characteristics of detective fiction. Progress along the path towards a resolution for this criminal mystery seems to be a case of one step forward and two steps back. Moreover, whilst Bystrov's voice technically exists at the same embedded (hypodiegetic) level as that of Mikhailovskii, his authority and reliability are inferior to it. This subordinate position can be accounted for by three reasons: most simply, Bystrov's voice does not dominate the narrative for as long as does Mikhailovskii's; it is also interrupted on several occasions by questions from the intradiegetic narrator; and the information that Bystrov provides about Kriukovskaia's mother is not directly sourced but reported on the basis of what he has learned from another, unnamed character. Nevertheless, the fact that, again, the narrator-investigator and the reader are able to map certain of his story's details back onto the account provided previously by Mikhailovskii means that Bystrov's voice cannot be dismissed as wholly unreliable. What should be clear, however, is that the reader is confronted here by a process of quite deliberate fragmentation designed to increase the suspense experienced with regard to the ultimate resolution of the investigation.

Even greater suspense is generated in the run-up to the introduction of the third embedded voice that belongs to a retired soldier, Sergei Panteleimonovich Atomanichenkov. If, as the reader of this summarized account of Shkliarevskii's story, you are feeling somewhat confused about the characters, their interrelationships and relevance to the plot, then you are approaching the experience of the actual reader of 'A Secret Investigation'! Initially, the introduction of Atomanichenkov appears to take the story off at another slight tangent, similar to those featuring Belotserkovskii and Kebmezakh. Having become interested in Kebmezakh because of Bystrov's story, the narrator-investigator learns, in another fortuitous coincidence, that he lives in an apartment opposite his own. The investigator therefore starts to observe the comings and goings at his apartment and notices that one daily visitor is never allowed in. He then stages an apparently accidental meeting with this man, Atomanichenkov, who reveals that he wishes to see Kebmezakh to claim money that is owed to him since the death of his sister. The narrator quickly vouches for the reliability of Atomanichenkov by saying that he believes his story, not least because he can back up his claims with written documents. Unlike the other four embedded voices in 'A Secret Investigation', however, that of Atomanichenkov does not speak directly but has his story paraphrased by the intradiegetic narrator because it 'отличался такими длиннотами и хвастливостями, вовсе неинтересными вставками о собственных любовных похождениях' ('was distinguished by its verbosities and boastfulness as well as its completely uninteresting digressions about his romantic adventures').[41] Although Atomanichenkov's voice enjoys a status inferior to the other embedded voices in the story, in part because of the indirect presentation of his voice but also because he is linked to Kebmezakh rather than to either the victim or the suspect, his account nevertheless provides more useful clues to the murder. Again, it reaches back in time to reveal that he and Kebmezakh were friends at school, and later visited Berlin together, before Kebmezakh travelled from England to America and Guyana — a possible source of the curare. It further reveals Kebmezakh to be a powerful personality, drawn to the darker side of life and capable of exerting considerable influence upon those around him (as has been suggested by Bystrov in his description of the relationship between Kebmezakh and Kriukovskaia). Most significantly for the reader's sense of suspense about the future progress of the investigation, whilst the narrator-detective explicitly advises Atomanichenkov on how best to deal with Kebmezakh in terms of retrieving his stolen money, he does not reveal the manner in which he will be of most use to the resolution of the murder case.

By the time that the fourth embedded voice appears in the story, the narrator-investigator has revealed his conviction that Mozharovskaia has been poisoned by her so-called friend, Kriukovskaia. However, uncertainty and suspense continue to reign not only because he still has little more than circumstantial evidence for this accusation but also because, as he admits, he is not sure whether Kriukovskaia might have been abetted by Mozharovskii or Kebmezakh. Such doubt means that the stakes are high when the fourth hypodiegetic voice, that of Mozharovskii, the victim's husband and now fiancé of the main suspect, is introduced in Chapter 6. The status of the narrator's investigation as 'secret' and therefore unofficial means that each voice tells their story under circumstances that might be perceived as somewhat less coercive than would be the case if they were being formally questioned. That said, the narrator is adept at applying pressure when he needs to: in order to lure Mozharovskii into coming to see him he visits his house when he knows he is absent and leaves his calling card. When Mozharovskii then visits him the following day, the narrator begins by revealing his belief that Kriukovskaia was involved in the death not only of her first husband, but also of a business acquaintance of his, both of whom have been poisoned. At the end of this brief passage of dialogue, the narrator-investigator invites Mozharovskii to tell his own story so that 'он может объяснить мне некоторые места в этой загадочной истории, над которыми я тщетно ломаю себе голову' ('he might clarify for me a couple of points in this mysterious story about which I am banging my head against a brick wall').[42] Mozharovskii agrees and begins to tell the story of his relationships with his deceased wife and with Kriukovskaia and his voice dominates the narrative, without interruption, for eight pages. Following the rather more subordinate narrative acts of Bystrov and Atomanichenkov, the voice of Mozharovskii enjoys a similar degree of authority and reliability as did that of Mikhailovskii previously. In spite of the narrator's earlier suspicions about his potential involvement, Mozharovskii appears to give a full and frank account of his relationships and, in particular, of his blindness to what was happening to his wife because of having fallen under the influence of Kriukovskaia. Again, the fact that elements of Mozharovskii's story tally with the account of events given by Mikhailovskii as well as with the narrator's own suspicions encourages the reader to place considerable faith in it. Moreover, Mozharovskii's reference to his account as an 'исповедь' ('confession') further promotes the sense of him holding nothing back and telling the complete truth, as if to a priest. Nevertheless, although his account provides more clarity about some of the fragments of the story, it is still not a full version and does not provide incontrovertible evidence of Kriukovskaia's guilt. Most crucially, as we have known from the outset, Mozharovskii was not in St Petersburg on the night of his wife's death and so is unable to provide definitive information about Kriukovskaia's involvement. Therefore, his account can be seen to resolve a good deal of the reader's curiosity, but the sense of suspense about how Kriukovskaia might actually be brought to justice persists.

At a slightly earlier point in the story, the narrator has explicitly acknowledged the work he has to do in uniting the fragments of the story of Mozharovskaia's murder when, after Atomanichenkov's account has been summarized, he describes how he forms an impression of Kebmezakh by 'сверяя рассказы Быстрова, Атоманиченкова и собранные мною лично сведения' ('tying together the stories of Bystrov and Atomanichenkov with other information I had collected myself').[43] In a more implicit, but arguably more effective, expression of his method, the narrator also describes how, upon visiting the Mariinskii Theatre for a second time, and seeing Kebmezakh approach Kriukovskaia in her box to give her what appears to be a letter, he invents an excuse to go to the box and gather up the ripped pieces of paper that are lying on the floor. Not only is this torn-up letter an important clue in itself, containing potentially incriminating information passed from Kebmezakh to Kriukovskaia, it functions as an iconic equivalent to the narrator's job throughout his investigation. Just as he tries to place the pieces of the letter back together and decipher the smudged writing they reveal, so he must link together the various bits of information that are provided in the different embedded voices to make a whole story. However, just as he is unable to reconstruct anything more than portions of words and disjointed phrases in Kebmezakh's letter, so the accounts of the first four embedded voices in the narrative provide only an incomplete account of Kriukovskaia's crime in which much remains indecipherable. The fragments of the first four voices are only successfully pieced back together when the voice of Kriukovskaia herself comes to the fore to give her version of events.

Kriukovskaia is compelled to speak after the narrator visits her, on the pretext of coming on behalf of Mozharovskii, only to announce promptly that he is actually there on behalf of the procurator of the local court. In a passage of dialogue, the narrator-investigator reveals that, during a search of Kebmezakh's apartment, he has found not only fifteen letters from her but also a vial of poison hidden in the compartment of a suitcase. After Kriukovskaia seeks to implore the narrator and his police colleagues to hide her crime and to save her, the narrator reports how he tells her that he knows she has poisoned her first husband, his business associate, as well as Mozharovskaia. In direct speech again, she protests her quasi-innocence in the murder of the business associate given that she did not know what she was doing, but then claims that she can say no more at the present time. In a departure from the style in which the first four embedded voices have been presented, she says that she will go away and compose a full written account of the crime for the investigator. The following day, as is recounted at the beginning of Chapter 9, the narrator does indeed receive Kriukovskaia's testimony, which he describes as 'изложено в форме полуписьма, полурассказа' ('laid out in the form of a half-letter, half-story').[44] The narrator then gives way again, this time to Kriukovskaia, whose voice comes to the fore and dominates, uninterruptedly, for ten pages. The narrator's characterization of the form of Kriukovskaia's written testimony is accurate: during the account she provides summarized descriptions of her early life and her relationship with Kebmezakh, but also more vivid and detailed accounts of particular events that themselves include passages of direct dialogue at key moments. In its storytelling competence, the voice of Kriukovskaia undoubtedly rivals that of the intradiegetic narrator which it replaces for an extended period. Her account has the effect of more coherently uniting many of the fragments of the case that the narrator-investigator has begun to piece together: she reveals how she and her mother were robbed by Kebmezakh and became entirely dependent upon him; she provides a full account of the murder of her first husband's business associate, confessing that he ate a poisoned sweet that she gave him but which was originally provided by Kebmezakh who has denied that it is dangerous; and she describes her love for Mozharovskii and her relationship with and eventual murder of his wife, her rival. Throughout Kriukovskaia's version of events, the reader is again invited to superimpose the details that she provides onto the information that has already been gleaned both from the other embedded narratives and from the intradiegetic narrator's own interpretation. So, for instance, her description of how she poisons her husband's business associate tallies with the conjectures made by the narrator-investigator on the basis of accounts he has heard elsewhere; her confession to the murder of Mozharovskaia using a poisoned pin confirms the suggestion of method made by Mikhailovskii in his account; and her reproduction of the full text of the letter from Kebmezakh that the narrator has found ripped up reveals its actual contents and those places where the investigator has mistakenly interpreted it.[45] The inclusion of the full text of this letter functions as a powerful, though covert, indication that Kriukovskaia's narrative establishes the most complete 'truth' of the murder and unites all of the various fragments gathered by the investigation. This status is further confirmed by the fact that the final chapter of the story consists in a relatively brief summary of the aftermath of this confession, given in the voice of the narrator. He reveals how he gives Mozharovskii the letter to read, establishes Kriukovskaia's mother's innocence, and hears Kebmezakh's confession that he has used the curare to murder seven people in addition to the three killed by Kriukovskaia. The narrator's closing sentence reveals how, given the length of time his investigation has taken, he feels a great weight lifted from his shoulders when he passes it to the local court for prosecution.

It might be tempting to take the fact that the fullest version of the story of the crime is provided by a hypodiegetic narrator, Kriukovskaia, as an indication that the authority and position of the intradiegetic narrator-detective are undermined in Shkliarevskii's story. A similar interpretation might be encouraged by the fact that, because of the presence of multiple embedded narrative voices, that of the intradiegetic narrator is effectively absent for almost half of the story's eighty pages. However, whilst 'A Secret Investigation' might figure as a rather extreme example of the possibilities extended by the exploitation of multiple voice in crime fiction, it remains representative of the conventional organization of this heteroglossia. Although the different voices are permitted to dominate the narrative for a period, and each provides proof of its reliability and honesty to a degree, they all ultimately remain subordinate to the authority of the voice of the narrator-detective. His intradiegetic voice always functions as both facilitator (the others only speak because he asks them to) and regulator (he provides an introduction, occasional interruptions, and an evaluative conclusion to their accounts). Both the story of the crime and the story of the investigation are fragmented to great effect by means of this network of different voices; curiosity and suspense are generated and modulated as the various characters take their turn to speak and reveal the information in their possession. Yet, even though it is Kriukovskaia who provides the fullest account of the story of the crime, the story of the successful investigation remains resolutely in the grasp of the narrator-investigator. His decision to give the floor to various witnesses and suspects proves to be justified. However, he supplements this role as receptive listener with that of a more active seeker, reading newspaper reports, staging apparently fortuitous meetings and undertaking official searches. Each of the various embedded voices has only part of the story to tell and, equally importantly, each one hears only their own fragment, or, in the case of Mozharovskii, one other. It is the narrator-investigator who occupies the most privileged position, and it is one of his own making. Only he has the opportunity and ability to piece all of the various fragments together in order to produce a story of the crime that is full enough to present to the local court for prosecution. And it is worth remembering that the ultimate revelation of Kriukovskaia's guilt affirms his earliest suspicions that Mozharovskaia's death is not natural and that her friend's conduct is dubious. Ultimately, therefore, the various embedded voices in the text are marshalled by the narrator-investigator to establish what Mikhail Bakhtin has called 'cognitive monologism', in which one version of the truth is constructed and possessed by the most authoritative voice. Indeed, this is the overarching convention for works of crime fiction: the fragmentation that guarantees retardation of the solution and the provocation of suspense ultimately gets resolved into such a uni-voiced version of the truth of the crime.

### Unconventional Multiple Voice: Dostoevskii's *Crime and Punishment*

Russian crime fiction also features notable instances, however, where its multiplicity of voice is not marshalled into such monologism and where the authority of the narrator or the investigator is not ultimately and definitively affirmed. The final sections of this chapter discuss two works that depart from generic convention and offer up more original and inventive models of multiple voice. The mention of Bakhtin above leads neatly to the first example, that of Dostoevskii's *Crime and Punishment*. Dostoevskii's novel of 1866 is quite distinct, in terms of its ambition, scope and structure, from any of the other works of crime fiction discussed in this monograph. Indeed, unlike almost all of the others, the novel's genre can be, and frequently has been, categorized as something other than crime fiction: scholars view it variously as primarily rather more of an existential, psychological, philosophical or ideological novel, or as one with a strong sociological or religious component. Even within the genre of crime fiction, *Crime and Punishment* represents a case apart. Although it conforms in some respects to the 'whydunit' model favoured by other early Russian writers, the experience of accompanying the central protagonist, Raskolnikov, as he prepares and then commits the murders is unusual. As mentioned in Chapter 2, in spite of the fact that there is no doubt about his guilt, *Crime and Punishment* still succeeds in generating suspense about Raskolnikov's simultaneous evasion of justice and path towards spiritual redemption. The suspense and tension experienced by the reader are, in large part, a consequence of the novel's unusual approach to the organization and exploitation of narrative voice and perspective.

The narrative set-up in *Crime and Punishment* is different from that encountered in the other works of crime fiction discussed so far in this chapter. Not only is the judicial investigator, Porfirii Petrovich, not the main intradiegetic narrator in the text, he is not even the central protagonist through whom the action is focalized. Although the novel was originally planned as a first-person narrative in the voice of Raskolnikov (the consequences of which will be mentioned below), it actually features an omniscient heterodiegetic narrator who is not a part of the story world. The diegesis contains a large number of different speaking voices — commensurate with an ostensibly realist novel — and a variety of different styles of presentation of this speech. The reader encounters passages of direct dialogue between pairs or sets of characters; there is the use of both indirect and free indirect discourse; and, as with other works of Dostoevskii's, there is the striking use of the main protagonist's internal dialogue as Raskolnikov constantly debates with himself, imagines conversations with other characters, and anticipates the speech of others in a series of postulated or imagined interactions. The simple fact that the judicial investigator is just one of these many voices, and neither the main narrator nor focalizer, makes it less likely that his voice will be unequivocally established as the most authoritative in the text. However, the originality of Dostoevskii's approach is more marked, and more productively disruptive, even than that. It will suffice to examine the organization of voice in a couple of chapters from the novel to demonstrate the success of its unconventionality for the production of suspense and the complication of conventional authority patterns.

Part II, Chapter 4 of *Crime and Punishment* depicts a conversation between Raskolnikov's friend, Razumikhin, and Zosimov, a doctor, about developments in the investigation into the murder of Aliona and Lizaveta that takes place in Raskolnikov's room as he lies on the couch, still ill and drifting in and out of consciousness following his crime. The scene is interesting not just because it discusses the crime and various purported suspects, but because of the presentation of voice and the claims for authority and reliability that are made therein. The two men's discussion of the case begins when Razumikhin asks for Zosimov's help in saving the decorator, Mikolai, who has been taken in for questioning on suspicion of the murders. Although Razumikhin is sure that Mikolai is entirely innocent of any involvement in the crime, Zosimov is more sceptical. Crucially, Razumikhin's unhappiness with Mikolai's detention leads him to voice his disappointment with the investigator: 'Я Порфирия уважаю, но... Ведь что их, например, перво-наперво с толку сбило?' ('Porfirii's a man I respect, but... Just think: what was it that threw them off from the very start?').[46] Razumikhin and Zosimov's discussion is presented in direct dialogue, with very few speech tags from the heterodiegetic narrator to provide commentary on their remarks. Following a passage of fairly rapid to-and-fro between the two men, with a very occasional interjection from Raskolnikov or the maid, Nastasia, who is also present, Razumikhin launches into a longer act of speech. He intends his narrative to demonstrate the mistakes made by the investigation in seemingly heeding the accusations made against Mikolai by the peasant Dushkin. However, the reader is justified in finding passages of Razumikhin's speech confusing because of the way in which they give voice to the words of various other characters. In effect, Razumikhin's embedded act of hypodiegetic narration has another, more subordinate, hypodiegetic voice contained within it (that of Dushkin), and then Dushkin's embedded voice itself presents the speech of Mikolai, at an even more subordinate level. Therefore, although the boundaries between the different voices are ostensibly indicated through the use of speech marks, particularly towards the end of Razumikhin's account it becomes difficult for the reader to disentangle the voices of Razumikhin, Dushkin and Mikolai. The problem of assigning authority is explicitly raised by Razumikhin when he attempts to use this network of different voices to claim reliability for his contention of Mikolai's innocence. Razumikhin provides a report of the exchanges between Mikolai and police officers after his detention in a highly staccato, back-and-forth manner, with the inclusion of no speech tags to identify the speakers. When he reports that they have asked Mikolai why he should fear 'getting done' by the police when he has done nothing wrong, Razumikhin states, 'Ну веришь или не веришь, Зосимов, этот вопрос был предложен, и буквально в таких выражениях, я положительно знаю, мне верно передали' ('Believe it or not, Zosimov, that was the question they put to him, in those same words. I know this for a fact, from a good source').[47] A couple of pages later, as he recounts how Mikolai and his colleague Mitrei are found fighting 'like little boys' in the victims' building, Razumikhin claims that these were 'буквальное выражение свидетелей' ('the witnesses' precise words').[48] However, the problem here is that the voices that

Razumikhin is reporting are both embedded at such a subordinate level within his own voice and stem from such unidentified sources that they cannot be deemed reliable by the reader (or, if he is honest, by Razumikhin). There is a profound irony here that, in attempting to establish the reliability of his sources so as to make his defence of Mikolai more persuasive, Razumikhin is actually pointing up the lack of confidence that can be placed in these embedded and unidentified statements. His failure is effectively demonstrated when Zosimov objects to Razumikhin's explanation, saying: 'слишком уж все удачно сошлось... и сплелось... точно так на театре' ('It's far too tidy the way it comes together... and falls into place... like in the theatre').[49] For the reader, this exchange creates tension and a measure of suspense because, even though s/he knows that Raskolnikov is the murderer, the complicated organization of the voices and the embedded accounts creates confusion about why Mikolai should be suspected and has apparently offered some sort of confession to the crime. Crucially also, given the dominance here of acts of direct dialogue, the voice of the heterodiegetic narrator, which ought ostensibly to be serving as an aid to comprehension, is effectively absent.

The second passage selected to demonstrate the impact of the unconventional organization of voices in *Crime and Punishment* spans the fourth and fifth chapters of Part III and describes the first face-to-face meeting between Raskolnikov and Porfirii Petrovich. In Chapter 4, Raskolnikov tells Razumikhin that he has pawned items with Aliona Ivanovna and suggests that, because the police are interviewing all such people, he should go and see Porfirii Petrovich. In light of the discussion of dialogue in crime fiction presented in the second section of this chapter, it is important to note that, given that Raskolnikov himself suggests going to see Porfirii, the dialogue that ensues between the two men should not be considered to represent an act of coerced speech, as is commonly encountered in the genre.[50] However, it is precisely the voluntary nature of the murderer's visit to the judicial investigator that injects such intrigue and suspense into the description of their encounter. The performance of the heterodiegetic narrator is crucial here. Towards the end of Chapter 4, the narrator provides omniscient access to the thoughts of Raskolnikov as he debates with himself the wisdom of having suggested that he meet Porfirii. The internal dialogue that he conducts with himself is typical of much of the mental and emotional wrangling in which Raskolnikov engages throughout the length of the novel and contributes to the sense of a cacophony of voices being at play:

> «Этому тоже надо Лазаря петь, — думал он, бледнея и с постукивающим сердцем, — и натуральнее петь. Натуральнее всего ничего бы не петь. Усиленно ничего не петь! Нет, *усиленно* было бы опять не натурально... Ну, да там как обернется... посмотрим... сейчас... хорошо иль не хорошо, что я иду? Бабочка сама на свечку летит. Сердце стучит, вот что нехорошо! . .»[51]

> ['I'll have to play Lazarus for him as well,' he thought with a hammering heart, 'and make it look natural. It would be more natural not to pretend anything. Go out of my way not to pretend! No, *going out of my way* wouldn't be natural either... Well, let's see how it goes... Let's see... Right now... Am I sure this is

such a good idea? A moth making straight for the flame. My heart's thumping — that's bad...']

As many critics have noted, however, omniscience of the type displayed here is enacted unevenly and unpredictably by the heterodiegetic narrator in *Crime and Punishment*. As Sarah Young points out, the novel retains traces of its originally-planned first-person narrative form in its 'insistent focalisation on Raskolnikov' and it is a focalization that means that access to other characters' inner thoughts is frequently missing.[52] In the exchanges between Raskolnikov and Porfirii depicted in Chapter 5, a heightened sense of suspense is created by the fact that, in spite of being technically capable of doing so, the narrator provides no insight into the motivations, inner thoughts and, especially, suspicions of the latter. The description of the encounter is firmly focalized from the perspective of Raskolnikov, a decision that ensures that considerable attention is paid to the way in which Porfirii speaks and reacts to him, but that sees the narrator refuse to supplement this limited perspective in any helpful manner. So, for example, when Porfirii responds to Razumikhin's description of how Raskolnikov disappeared off somewhere the previous night by repeating some of Razumikhin's own words ('И неужели в *совершеннейшем бреду*? Скажите пожалуйста!' ('*Completely and utterly delirious!* Really? Well I never!')),[53] the narrator does nothing to clarify the reasons for Porfirii's exclamatory interest. Similarly, when Porfirii says to Raskolnikov in direct speech, 'Если бы вы знали, как вы меня интересуете! Любопытно и смотреть и слушать...' ('If only you knew how much you intrigue me! How interesting it is to observe and listen to you...'),[54] the narrator provides no speech tag whatsoever to explain the reasons for Porfirii's apparent fascination. Such uneven omniscience has interesting consequences for an assessment of the relative authority of the voices of Raskolnikov and Porfirii, as criminal and investigator square up to one another. On the one hand, the access to Raskolnikov's inner thoughts gives the reader a sense of intimacy that might encourage the bestowal of a greater level of authority upon him. However, the lack of insight into Porfirii's thoughts means that the reader finds it practically impossible at this stage to assess whether the words and looks that he addresses to Raskolnikov indicate that he suspects his guilt in the murders or not. Similarly, just as Raskolnikov's troubled emotional state after the killings compromises the authority and reliability of his voice, so the pre-posed criticism of Porfirii by Razumikhin in his story of the detention of Mikolai places doubts in the reader's mind about his authority and professional competence. Crucially, therefore, in the cat-and-mouse game that is played out between Raskolnikov and Porfirii, their voices can be said to enjoy a similar degree of authority in the eyes of the reader.

However, it is not simply the absence or unhelpfulness of the heterodiegetic narrator's voice that poses interpretive problems for the reader. Not only is the narrative perspective intimately aligned with Raskolnikov both here and elsewhere, there is an almost constant slippage between, or merging of, his voice and that of the narrator. The description of how Porfirii Petrovich welcomes Raskolnikov and Razumikhin into his rooms provides an eloquent example of such confusion:

Порфирий Петрович, как только услышал, что гость имеет до него «дельце», тотчас же попросил его сесть на диван, сам уселся на другом конце и уставился в гостя, в немедленном ожидании изложения дела, с тем усиленным и уж слишком серьезным вниманием, которое даже тяготит и смущает с первого раза, особенно по незнакомству, и особенно если то, что вы излагаете, по собственному вашему мнению, далеко не в пропорции с таким необыкновенно важным, оказываемым вам вниманием. Но Раскольников в коротких и связных словах, ясно и точно изъяснил свое дело и собой остался доволен так, что даже успел довольно хорошо осмотреть Порфирия.[55]

[As soon as Porfirii Petrovich heard that his visitor had 'come on a bit of business', he immediately offered him a seat on the couch, sat himself down at the other end and stared at his guest, eagerly waiting for him to explain what this business was, with that emphatically and excessively serious attention which can be quite oppressive and disconcerting when first encountered, especially in a stranger and especially when what you are explaining is, in your own opinion, completely incommensurate with the unusual solicitude being shown to you. But Raskolnikov, in a few brief and coherent sentences, lucidly and precisely explained the matter and was so satisfied with his efforts that he even managed to take a good look at Porfirii.]

The opening half of the first sentence above appears to be given from both the perspective and the voice of the heterodiegetic narrator. However, as the sentence continues, the presence of subjectively inflected adverbs and adjectives ('emphatically', 'excessively', 'oppressive', 'disconcerting', etc.), and their somewhat superfluous accumulation, hints that the voice becomes influenced by the emotional perspective of Raskolnikov. Indeed, the inclusion of references to 'вы' ('you') in the latter half of the sentence suggests that the reader is now dealing not with the voice of the narrator but with that of Raskolnikov in free indirect discourse. The unequivocally positive characterization of Raskolnikov's brief speech in the closing sentence also seems to confirm this shift from the voice and perspective of the narrator to that of the protagonist. The slippage observed here is not confined to this encounter between Raskolnikov and Porfirii, but is a characteristic of the entirety of the novel. What it means is that the reader is frequently left unable to grant authority to statements apparently made in the voice of the heterodiegetic narrator. The descriptions of how Porfirii looks at Raskolnikov during this first encounter 'как-то явно насмешливо' ('with a sort of blatant mockery'),[56] for instance, cannot be taken as definitive proof of the investigator's suspicions because they are informed by the criminal's perspective. This confusion of voice and perspective therefore means that the reader is unable to construct with any certainty the conventional hierarchy of authority between the various voices that are presented within *Crime and Punishment*.

In place of the conventional model of different levels of voices, each granted a distinct (or at least identifiable) degree of authority, Dostoevskii's novel, particularly through the performance of the heterodiegetic narrator, collapses the hierarchy and flattens out many of the distinctions. Although it remains possible for the well-informed reader to identify characters whose speech is undermined through the exercise of parody, those belonging to many of the central protagonists (Raskolnikov, Razumikhin, Dunia, Sonia and Porfirii) exist on a very similar level of authority and, crucially, are not rendered subordinate to the voice of the heterodiegetic narrator. Bakhtin claims that the chief characteristic of Dostoevskii's novels is the presence of 'a plurality of independent and unmerged voices and consciousnesses, a genuine polyphony of fully valid voices'.[57] He makes explicit the absence, in a work such as *Crime and Punishment*, of a single, authoritative narrative voice when he argues that what unfolds in Dostoevskii is:

> not a multitude of characters and fates in a single objective world, illuminated by a single authorial consciousness; rather a plurality of consciousnesses, with equal rights and each with its own world, [which] combine but are not merged in the unity of the event.[58]

Returning to the issue of suspense that is so key to crime fiction, such polyphony makes a highly original contribution to the sustained tension experienced by the reader of the novel. The inability to attribute greater authority to the voice of either Raskolnikov or Porfirii during their various encounters means that the reader can never be sure which, if either, of the two is going to prevail in their battle. However, beyond the confrontation of these two voices, the novel's polyphony also ensures continuing suspense surrounding the reader's search for a motive for the crime. The reader hears Raskolnikov express an ever-shifting panoply of motives for his crime, including opportunity, poverty, natural justice, ideology and existential ambition, but no single one of these ever establishes itself as the 'truth'. Similarly, we are presented with the various theories of other characters such as Zosimov and Lebeziatnikov regarding the identity of the criminal and the reasons that might be used to explain the crime. Detective fiction boasts just such a multitude of possible interpretive avenues as its very lifeblood; in Dostoevskii, however, the various voices that express such possibilities are never reconciled in order to tell the sort of unified, monologic story that has been discussed in Shkliarevskii's 'A Secret Investigation'.[59]

## The Rebellious Voice: Shkliarevskii's 'The Tale of a Judicial Investigator'

The extent to which Dostoevskii adopts an original approach to the conventions of crime fiction is unrivalled throughout the history of the genre's development in Russia. However, he is not the only Russian author to offer up unconventional experiments with multiple voice during this period. This chapter concludes with a reading of the entertaining example provided by Shkliarevskii's 'The Tale of a Judicial Investigator' from 1872. For much of its length, it appears that the story will observe the type of orthodox organization of multiple voice encountered in 'A Secret Investigation'. As outlined in Chapter 2, the work is recounted by an autodiegetic narrator-investigator (who nevertheless initially demonstrates heterodiegetic privilege) assigned to the case of the violent strangling of Nastasia Pavlovna Pyl'neva. The 23-year-old victim is found lying on the bed in her rented lodgings and appears to have been asphyxiated with a belt while asleep. Just as in

'A Secret Investigation', following a detailed examination of the crime scene and attempts to identify the provenance of the murder weapon, the majority of the narrator's investigation comprises listening to witness testimony from a variety of different characters. Prior to gathering these statements, the narrator-investigator's strongest suspicions fall on the victim's estranged husband and, to a lesser extent, her former guardian as well as her current male companion. However, the story of the crime that is fragmented amongst these three different voices points to a different and unexpected culprit, and it is the performance of that fourth voice that makes the story so interesting. Specifically, in its exploitation of multiple voice, 'The Tale of a Judicial Investigator' proves to be an original exception to Segal's claim that 'the detective story is generally recognized to be a paradigm case of strong closure'.[60]

The first person to be interviewed by the narrator-investigator is Aleksandra Vasil'evna Lastova, the victim's half-sister, who turns up unexpectedly at his office. Following a brief conversation about the circumstances in which Pyl'neva's body has been found, the narrator invites Lastova to tell him the story of her sister's life, with which she is probably better acquainted than anyone else. Lastova agrees, attempting to earn pre-emptive authority for her voice by noting that, although there are family secrets, she will ensure her account is full and frank. Thus begins Lastova's act of embedded narration that, just as many of those in 'A Secret Investigation', lasts for a considerable amount of time (seventeen pages, spanning two chapters) and during which the voice of the intradiegetic narrator-investigator is almost entirely absent. The dominant theme in Lastova's account is the tension between the sisters' early aristocratic upbringing and their subsequent transformation into provincial, uneducated children after being abandoned by their father and taken in by their mother. It is the fear of the consequences of social difference that makes their neighbour and guardian in St Petersburg, Nikolai Ivanovich Zarubin, hesitant to introduce them to two of his former pupils, Lastov and Arkadii Ivanych Pyl'nev. Lastova recounts how her and her sister's marriages to these two men turn out quite differently, again for reasons of social distinction. Whereas Lastov treats his wife well, educating her slowly and not taking her out into society too quickly, Pyl'nev rushes his wife out into provincial society where she makes numerous gaffes to their mutual embarrassment. Lastova goes on to reveal how, after some four years of marriage, her sister meets the student Garnitskii and the pair fall in love. By the time of her death, Pyl'neva has moved back to St Petersburg with Garnitskii having been beaten unconscious by her husband who has learned of the relationship. Aside from the authority earned simply by dint of the length of her account, Lastova's voice makes other claims for its reliability: she refers to her story as the 'истинн[ая] правд[а]' ('honest truth');[61] she embeds the back story of Zarubin's life into her own, thereby demonstrating considerable knowledge; and she permits herself the same adoption of heterodiegetic privilege as the intradiegetic narrator has done at the start of the story, when she appears capable of reading the thoughts and emotions of her sister's husband. When his voice reappears, the intradiegetic narrator is not entirely explicit in his reaction to Lastova's testimony. He records his surprise at how she is shocked by the news that Pyl'nev visited his wife on the night of her death and he further notes that this reaction prompts him to wonder whether there is not some sort of relationship between Lastova and Pyl'nev. However, he gives voice to no overt suspicions against Lastova for involvement in the crime and the story moves on immediately at the beginning of Chapter 6 to the testimony of the neighbour, Zarubin, and then the student, Garnitskii. Lastova's narrative has satisfied a degree of the reader's curiosity about the circumstances of the victim's life before her murder, but only generates more suspense about who, from the cast of characters, the perpetrator might be.

Although the next two voices provide different perspectives on Pyl'neva's life and the crime, they do not actually serve to advance the investigation in any meaningful way. The direct dialogue between Zarubin and the narrator confirms many of the details of Pyl'neva's life that have already been provided by Lastova and establishes that he has a reliable alibi for the night of the murder. When the narrator asks Zarubin what he would make of the fact that Pyl'nev was seen with his wife on the night she was killed, Zarubin replies that he would suspect him of involvement given his 'вспыльчивый и бешеный характер' ('hot-tempered and violent personality').[62] This allegation only serves, however, to reinforce a suspicion already held by the narrator about Pyl'nev's possible guilt. Moving on to Garnitskii, the first part of the student's testimony is briefly summarized in indirect speech by the narrator because it is a 'repetition'[63] of the details given by both Lastova and Zarubin. However, when Pyl'neva's lover begins to talk about events on the day of the murder, his voice is presented in direct speech. Garnitskii speaks uninterruptedly for more than a page to recount how he spent much of the day with Zarubin before going to the theatre with Pyl'neva, walking her home and then leaving because she was so tired. The narrator appears sympathetic towards Garnitskii, recording how he begins to sob at the end of this first speech that he characterizes as a 'печальный рассказ' ('sad story').[64] However, his doubts about Garnitskii remain, particularly because, given that her body was found in bed, he is convinced that Pyl'neva has been murdered by a lover, and so he decides to arrest the student as a precaution, albeit apologizing for doing so. The next voice to provide evidence in the case of Pyl'neva is that of her estranged husband and, crucially, he speaks twice, on consecutive days, to quite different effect. On the first occasion, he is combative, demanding to know why he has been detained and brought in front of the investigator. During the ensuing coerced dialogue, Pyl'nev claims that he met his wife by chance in a restaurant on the night of her murder, following which he visited her at home where he found her asleep and left without waking her. During a brisk exchange with the narrator, Pyl'nev expresses shock at his wife's death, acknowledges that the murder weapon might be the belt he has lost, and asks for further questioning to be put off until the following day to allow him to gather his thoughts. Pyl'nev's second act of speech, by contrast, is an embedded narrative that lasts five pages with no interruption from the narrator, and that is preceded by his claim that he is 'невинен в убийстве жены' ('not guilty of murdering [his] wife').[65] The reader is encouraged to place some faith in the reliability of Pyl'nev's second account because the narrator notes that, in spite of certain evidence against him, he is reluctant to believe that he has actually killed his wife. Pyl'nev's version of events is most useful in revealing that, whilst he was at his wife's lodgings, another visitor arrived, rang on the door but then apparently left. Further suspense is generated when Pyl'nev recounts how, from the limited perspective of his position hidden down in the courtyard after he had left, he saw a female figure move past the window in Pyl'neva's room.

Although the investigator is able to plot certain of the details from these various accounts back on to the others, it is not the case that these different voices combine to tell a complete story of the crime. That said, it *is* the act of reading and thinking back over these acts of testimony that leads the narrator to make a chance remark that decisively changes the course of his investigation. Musing on the evidentiary importance of the signet ring that Pyl'nev claims to have lost in his wife's room, the investigator realizes that if robbery was not a motive in the crime then Pyl'neva's murder must have been perpetrated by someone for whom her life was a nuisance. The narrator then ensures that further suspense is introduced into the story when he shifts from his prior position of not being entirely explicit with the reader to actively withholding crucial information about who this new suspect might be. For a couple of pages as he prepares his approach to this person, including a visit to the local police chief, and the summoning of a priest and another witness in the case, the reader is kept in the dark about what precisely the narrator is planning and against whom. That is, until he includes the text of a letter he sends to Lastova informing her that he has solved the case, thanks largely to the details she has provided, and inviting her to visit him so that she might correct any mistakes he has made. Both the letter and the narrator's subsequent remarks about not wishing to arouse her suspicions make clear that Lastova is now the prime suspect in her sister's murder. It is from this point onwards that the execution of multiple voice in 'The Tale of a Judicial Investigator' becomes highly original and entertaining. Initially, the voice of the narrator is to the fore as he describes how he begins to read out his case report to Lastova. Maintaining his position of withholding information, when the narrator describes how he is called out of his office by a police officer who informs him that they have found 'it', the reader is not told what the object in question is. However, the announcement prompts the narrator to return to his room and inform Lastova in a brief act of direct speech that 'больше нечего читать [...] вы убили ее' ('there is no need to read any more [...] you killed her').[66] He then embarks on a concise and confident summary of the steps that have led him to this conclusion: his interrogation of her coachman who confirmed she visited her sister on the night of the murder and has voiced his own suspicions as to her guilt; Pyl'nev's story of a woman being present in the room; and the discovery of the signet ring during a search of Lastova's house which he now places in front of her. His speech has the desired effect because the detective records that, whether it is thanks to his sudden accusation or for some other reason, Lastova 'сделала полное признание' ('made a full confession').[67] This confession is soon followed by Lastova's second embedded act of narration (after the first in Chapters 4 and 5 of the story) in which she provides a full and convincing account of how she has killed her sister, motivated by the shame she believes is occasioned to her by Pyl'neva's fall from grace through her extra-marital relationship with Garnitskii. Her account appears to establish the voice of the investigator-narrator as the highest authority within the text: it knits together the fragments of the case provided in the testimony of the other voices that he has gathered and, most importantly, proves the veracity of the suppositions about both motive and culprit that he has previously made. At this point the narrator has succeeded in unifying the various partial accounts of the night of the murder into a single and compelling story of the crime.

However, the narrator-investigator does not get to retain this diegetic superiority in the same way as in 'A Secret Investigation' because when he offers to read her testimony back to her, Lastova's reply is 'Какое показание?' ('What testimony?').[68] In direct speech, Lastova completely wrong-foots the narrator by claiming not only to have had no involvement in the murder, but to having been tricked by the narrator into thinking that she was being summoned to help in the investigation rather than being accused of being guilty. She calmly informs him that his one piece of physical evidence (the signet ring) has disappeared and, when the narrator threatens to retrieve what she has swallowed, she tells him that he has gone mad and that she will scream if he touches her. She proves true to her word when, having been asked by the narrator to give back the key to the locked office where they now find themselves, she runs into the corner of the room, rips her own dress and cries out 'спасите, спасите меня' ('Save me, save me') to the voices she can hear on the other side.[69] The narrator realizes how Lastova has turned the tables on him and remarks 'Я посмотрел на нее просто с отчаянием [...] из следователя я обращался в просителя' ('I just looked at her in amazement [...] I had turned from an investigator into a supplicant').[70] Although the final words in the story belong to the intradiegetic narrator, he uses them to confirm the utter failure of his investigation: Lastova remains free and moves abroad; Garnitskii and Pyl'nev remain under suspicion; and he is removed from the case and suspected of concocting Lastova's confession as a means of forcing her into an illicit relationship with him. 'The Tale of a Judicial Investigator' thereby demonstrates how multiple voice can be manipulated not only *not* to close the gap between the story of the crime and the story of the investigation, but to ensure that two alternative versions of the story remain forever in existence and unresolved. By means of her unexpected move, Lastova's voice refuses subordination to the authority of the narrator-detective that is the conventional pattern in crime fiction and, in so doing, denies the story closure. By withdrawing her confession, an act that denies the veracity of her earlier speech act, and by providing an alternative (and, whilst unlikely, still persuasive) narrative, Lastova effectively constructs two distinct and irreconcilable readings. The narrator-detective is unable to impose his voice at the pinnacle of the hierarchy of authority and so Lastova's voice ultimately remains free and independent. Although it is not as novel an approach as Dostoevskii's device of polyphony, Shkliarevskii nevertheless provides readers with an instructive demonstration of the potential for open-endedness in an unconventional exploitation of multiple voice that makes for a wonderfully compelling story.[71]

## Conclusion

The discussion of dialogue and multiple voice offered in this chapter has shown how devices ostensibly related to the creation of a verisimilar fictional world are harnessed to great effect in crime fiction for the provocation of curiosity, but most particularly, suspense. Although it might appear at first sight that the genre allows myriad characters involved in the stories of a crime and an investigation to speak 'for themselves', it is crucial to acknowledge the coerced speech situation that pertains in many of these exchanges. The analysis of Shkliarevskii's 'A Secret Investigation' has served as a paradigm for the conventional functioning of multiple voice in a work of crime fiction. The course of the investigation, and its inclusion of various obstacles and moments of retardation, is structured around the introduction of numerous different voices, whose accounts of the crime ultimately remain subordinate to the voice of the investigator. The various acts of embedded narration that frequently bestow temporary superiority on the different witnesses and suspects function as an iconic representation of the different clues that the detective has to piece together. Much of the detective's authority derives from his marshalling of these various voices into a single, coherent and truthful version of the story of the crime. Nevertheless, there exist other works that defy the genre's apparent desire for closure by refusing to abide by the conventions of hierarchy that usually pertain to a multiplicity of voice. Such works demonstrate both the promise and the threat extended to both fictional and extrafictional worlds by a voice that refuses to be ventriloquized and rendered subordinate to another. This type of freedom of voice ensures that suspense is maintained for as long as possible in the story of the investigation, sometimes even beyond the close of the narrative.

## Notes to Chapter 3

1. Tzvetan Todorov, 'The Typology of Detective Fiction', in *The Poetics of Prose*, trans. by Richard Howard (Ithaca, NY: Cornell University Press, 1977), pp. 42–52 (p. 47). Originally published as *Poétique de la prose* (Paris: Seuil, 1971).
2. Segal, 'Closure in Detective Fiction', p. 159.
3. S. E. Sweeney, 'Locked Rooms: Detective Fiction, Narrative Theory, and Self-Reflexivity', in *The Cunning Craft*, ed. by Walker and Frazer, pp. 1–14 (p. 5).
4. Todorov, 'The Typology of Detective Fiction', pp. 44–45.
5. Dennis Porter, *The Pursuit of Crime: Art and Ideology in Detective Fiction* (New Haven, CT: Yale University Press, 1981), p. 29.
6. Wilkie Collins, *The Woman in White*, ed. by Matthew Sweet (London: Penguin, 2003), p. 9.
7. The function of 'retardatory structures' is discussed at some length by Viktor Shklovskii in *Theory of Prose*, trans. by Benjamin Sher (Normal, IL: Dalkey Archive Press, 1991), pp. 22–46.
8. Bennett, 'The Detective Story', p. 241.
9. Ibid., p. 244.
10. Ibid., p. 250.
11. Andrew Martin, 'Top 10: The Best Dialogue in Crime Fiction', <http://www.theguardian.com/books/2015/nov/25/top-10-crime-fiction-dialogue-agatha-christie-chandler-amis> [accessed 15 December 2016].
12. Bennett, 'The Detective Story', pp. 247–48. She divides the 'interview tableau' into the four categories of interview, encounter, confrontation and confession.
13. Stephen Lovell, 'Looking at Listening in Late Imperial Russia', *The Russian Review*, 72.4 (2013), 551–55 (p. 552).

14. Anna Schur, 'The Limits of Listening: Particularity, Compassion and Dostoevsky's "Bookish Humaneness"', *The Russian Review*, 72.4 (2013), 573–89 (pp. 576–77).

15. Bronwen Thomas, *Fictional Dialogue: Speech and Conversation in the Modern and Postmodern Novel* (Lincoln, NE: University of Nebraska Press, 2012), p. 15.

16. Bronwen Thomas, 'Dialogue', in *The Cambridge Companion to Narrative*, ed. by David Herman (Cambridge: Cambridge University Press, 2007), pp. 80–93 (p. 80).

17. Popov's 'A Sinner's End' represents an excellent example of the 'demotic' nature of much crime fiction featuring, as it does, the verbal idiosyncrasies of many of the inhabitants of the fictional world. The speech of the stationmaster's young daughter, for instance, reveals clear 'eye dialect' markers to indicate her immature speech: she tells the narrator-investigator 'юбью' (for 'люблю'; 'I love you') and reassures him that he is not like a wood goblin because 'ти биеньку денезку дав' (an approximation of 'ты денег дав' ('you've given us money')) (p. 11). The voice of the main suspect in the theft, Irina, also carries markers appropriate to her social class and rural upbringing: frequent uses of the '-то' suffix, archaic phrases (экий (this), почто (why)), obscure vocabulary that has to be explained in footnotes (e.g. бутора (a snowstorm)), as well as frequent ellipsis and unnecessary repetition.

18. Thomas, *Fictional Dialogue*, p. 15.

19. Panov, *Ubiistvo v derevne Medveditse*, p. 244.

20. Timofeev, *Zapiski sledovatelia*, p. 134.

21. See Sokolovskii, *Ostrog i zhizn'*, pp. 74–75.

22. Schur, 'The Limits of Listening', p. 575.

23. Thomas, *Fictional Dialogue*, p. 39.

24. Aaron Fogel, *Coercion to Speak: Conrad's Poetics of Dialogue* (Cambridge, MA: Harvard University Press, 1985), pp. 13 and 233–34.

25. Thomas, *Fictional Dialogue*, p. 118.

26. Ronald Thomas, 'The Fingerprint of the Foreigner', p. 656.

27. Popov, *Vinovatye i pravye*, p. 17.

28. Panov, *Pomoch'*, pp. 350–52. A similar act of forced confession is to be found in Panov's *Murder in Medveditsa Village* where the culprit, Grishanin, is emotionally tortured into a confession by means of repeated confrontations with the young daughter of his victim who reacts with terror at the sight of him.

29. Schur, 'The Limits of Listening', p. 575.

30. Shkliarevskii, *Povesti i rasskazy (Tales and Stories)* (Moscow: Bakhmetev, 1872).

31. Martin Priestman, *Detective Fiction and Literature: The Figure in the Carpet* (Basingstoke: Macmillan, 1990), p. 48.

32. Genette, *Figures III*, p. 238.

33. Mieke Bal, *Narratologie: Les instances du récit* (Paris: Klincksieck, 1977), p. 35. Bal also helpfully suggests that we should think of these various levels not as being 'superior' to one another, as in Genette's formulation, but as being dependent upon one another.

34. Lanser, *The Narrative Act*, p. 136.

35. See Reitblat's preface, '«Russkii Gaboriau» ili uchenik Dostoevskogo?', to the *Chto pobudilo k ubiistvu?* collection (Moscow: Khudozhestvennaia literatura, 1993), pp. 5–13 (p. 6). Reitblat is Shkliarevskii's principal promoter in Russia and considers that this 'father of Russian detective fiction' deserves to have his modest reputation restored.

36. From 1864 onwards, Shkliarevskii contributed a chronicle of local theatrical life in Voronezh, entitled 'Russkaia stsena' ('Russian Stage'); in 1867, he published the short story 'Otpetyi' ('The Inveterate') in the St Petersburg journal *Delo*, which won him some popularity with readers.

37. *Literaturnoe nasledstvo*, 86 (1973), p. 429.

38. For a discussion of the points of comparison between the work of Dostoevskii and Shkliarevskii, see my chapter 'Shkliarevskii and Russian Detective Fiction: The Influence of Dostoevskii', in *Dostoevskii: Influence, Comparison and Transposition*, ed. by Joe Andrew and Robert Reid (Amsterdam: Rodopi, 2013), pp. 101–21.

39. McReynolds, *Murder Most Russian*, p. 123.

40. Shkliarevskii, 'Sekretnoe sledstvie', in *Chto pobudilo k ubiistvu?*, p. 160.

41. Ibid., p. 174.

42. Ibid., p. 188.
43. Ibid., p. 179.
44. Ibid., p. 203.
45. For instance, the narrator-investigator has been convinced that one fragmented and smudged part of the letter must read 'жду ее' ('I am waiting for her') when it actually says 'жду сегодня' ('I am waiting today') (p. 213).
46. F. M. Dostoevskii, *Prestuplenie i nakazanie*, p. 142/p. 163. Quotations are taken from *Sobranie sochinenii v desiati tomakh*, v (Moscow: Khudozhestvennaia literatura, 1957). English quotations are taken from Oliver Ready's 2014 translation, published by Penguin, unless otherwise stated. In subsequent footnotes, page references refer first to the Russian original and then to the English translation.
47. Ibid., p. 145/p. 167.
48. Ibid., p. 147/p. 169.
49. Ibid., p. 149/p. 172.
50. That said, the fact that Porfirii mentions Raskolnikov's article from the *Periodicheskaia rech'* (*Periodical Review*) during their conversation effectively forces the protagonist into an explanation and defence of his ideas that he was not planning to give.
51. *Prestuplenie i nakazanie*, p. 256/p. 295.
52. Sarah J. Young, 'Fyodor Dostoevsky (1821–1881): "Fantastic Realism"', in *The Cambridge Companion to European Novelists*, ed. by Michael Bell (Cambridge: Cambridge University Press, 2012), pp. 259–76 (p. 266).
53. *Prestuplenie i nakazanie*, p. 262/p. 302.
54. Ibid., p. 263/pp. 303–04.
55. Ibid., p. 259/p. 299.
56. Ibid., p. 260/p. 300.
57. Mikhail Bakhtin, *Problems of Dostoevsky's Poetics*, trans. by Caryl Emerson (Minneapolis, MN: University of Minnesota Press, 1984), p. 6. I take Bakhtin's use of 'consciousness' to be an equivalent to 'voice'.
58. Ibid.
59. Similar comments regarding the combination of polyphony, indistinct levels of authority and suspense could be made with regard to Dostoevskii's *The Brothers Karamazov*.
60. Segal, 'Closure in Detective Fiction', p. 154.
61. Shkliarevskii, 'Rasskaz sudebnogo sledovatelia', in *Chto pobudilo k ubiistvu?*, p. 87.
62. Ibid., p. 107.
63. Ibid., p. 108.
64. Ibid., p. 110.
65. Ibid., p. 115.
66. Ibid., p. 125.
67. Ibid., p. 126.
68. Ibid., p. 131.
69. Ibid., p. 133.
70. Ibid.
71. It is worth noting here that the fact that the voice of the narrator-investigator is defeated by a woman is not insignificant. Although an extended discussion of gender is outside the scope of this monograph, it is likely that Shkliarevskii's story implicitly suggests that the power to maintain mystery and freedom belongs primarily to the female sex. There is the implication here that, although the role of the detective is to render everything 'explicit and accountable' (in the same way that Catherine Belsey argues happens in the Sherlock Holmes stories), there are areas of human experience that remain in darkness for the male detective, and these often relate to female activity and motive. See Catherine Belsey, *Critical Practice* (London: Methuen, 1980), p. 111.

# CHAPTER 4

# Doing Time: Temporal Organization in Russian Crime Fiction

This chapter illustrates how, in a manner similar to multiple voice that has been the subject of the previous chapter, structures of time constitute an effective means of provoking curiosity and suspense by producing 'fragmentation'. In his discussion of the double story structure that characterizes detective fiction, Todorov's first reference to the role of temporality is only oblique: he says, 'the first story, that of the crime, ends before the second begins'.[1] A little later in the same article, Todorov uses lines from Michel Butor's *Emploi du temps* to reinforce his claim as to the presence of two stories in the genre and this excerpt makes the temporal aspect of that dualistic structure unmistakeable: Butor's quote reads 'the narrative [...] superimposes two temporal series: the days of the investigation which begin with the crime, and the days of the drama which lead up to it'.[2] A consideration of the ways in which this superimposition actually functions permits Todorov to declare that 'temporal inversions' are one of the two 'literary devices' that characterize the story of the crime which is initially missing from the text (the other is 'point of view').[3] Echoing Todorov, Bennett argues that 'temporal deformation is the principal (though not the only) agency through which [...] *histoire* is transformed into *discours*' in detective fiction.[4] Porter brings the part that time plays in the genre into even sharper focus when he describes the job of the literary detective in the following terms: '[he] encounters effects without apparent causes, events in a jumbled chronological order, significant clues hidden among the insignificant. And his role is to re-establish sequence and causality'.[5] This view of the centrality of (chronological) order to crime fiction, and of the job of the detective as entailing some degree of temporal reorganization, is one that enjoys considerable currency amongst critics. Sweeney, for instance, argues:

> Detective fiction is unusually preoccupied with establishing linear sequences, perhaps because the crime has already happened [...] before the story begins. If a plot is a series of related incidents culminating in a climax, then the stages in the detective's investigation — the discovery and analysis of each successive clue, which ultimately leads to the solution of the crime — provide the plot of a detective story. If the investigation makes the detective story a coherent narrative, then that investigation, in turn, establishes a coherent narrative to explain the crime. The detective accomplishes this by deconstructing the

mystery — that is, by revealing it to be a logical, chronologically ordered sequence of causes and effects.[6]

The present chapter seeks to give a more detailed picture, especially with regard to Russian crime fiction, of how temporal devices play a role in both the construction of a mystery and the detective's efforts to re-establish order.

Beyond identifying the drive exhibited by detective fiction towards establishing chronological order, understood as one facet of epistemic knowledge, the role of time in the genre has been predominantly discussed in relation to two particular issues. These are, firstly, the notion of retardation and, secondly, that of information gaps (both of which pertain to questions of curiosity and suspense). It should be noted, however, that such discussions tend to refer to time in a predominantly broad and conceptual fashion, rather than focusing on specific temporal devices. For example, in his comprehensive consideration of time in fiction, Meir Sternberg contends that:

> One of the prime means of creating, intensifying, or prolonging suspense consists in the author temporarily impeding ('suspending') the natural progression of the action, especially its onward rush toward some expected climax, by the interposition of more or less extraneous matter.[7]

He labels this extraneous matter 'retardatory material'. Of course, as Sternberg makes clear, retardation produced by the inclusion of non-necessary information is a feature of almost all literary genres. The uniqueness of detective fiction is to be found in the scale of retardation it deploys: it accounts for not just a part or parts, but for the whole. For Sternberg, the detective story is 'a retardatory structure'[8] in its entirety. Porter, in contextualizing his own claims about retardation, appears to agree with Sternberg's notion of scale when he argues that the detective novel, more obviously than other genres, is composed of two contradictory impulses. He explains:

> On the one hand, it is made up of verbal units that combine to close the logico-temporal gap between a crime and its solution. On the other hand, it also contains at least an equal number of units that impede progress toward a solution.[9]

Of course, as both Sternberg and Porter understand, in the literary text, the very act of making the desired progress towards a solution necessarily delays the point in time at which this destination is reached. Porter explains: 'every action sequence that occurs in a detective novel between a crime and its solution delays for a time that solution even when it appears logically required by it'.[10] There exist, however, more intentional and specific ways of delaying progress that authors can exploit in order to introduce 'that minimum of impediments required for the production of the thrills of suspense'.[11] Whilst Sternberg acknowledges that such delaying tactics might take manifold forms, he contends that amongst the most important are 'temporal shifts (whether in the form of doubling back into the past or plunging into the future)'.[12] Similarly, in her discussion of fragmentation (a device that, according to Porter, is associated to retardation), Bennett identifies achrony as a significant element in that process. It seems reasonable, therefore, to claim, in an expansion of the Todorov/Sternberg view, that temporal devices constitute one of the primary means of deliberately impeding progress towards knowledge. Rather than proceeding in an entirely linear and chronological fashion, the journey towards a solution in detective fiction frequently encounters retardatory obstacles; and these obstacles include instances of temporal deformation, particularly but not only in the form of what Genette calls 'anachronies', that is disruptions between the order of events as presented in the *fabula* and the order in which they occur in the *siuzhet*. An examination of various examples of anachrony and their impact is undertaken in the third section of this chapter.

The process of impeding the investigator's and reader's progress towards a solution for the criminal mystery creates suspense. The creation of information gaps — the other type of temporal device to be discussed here — generates both suspense and curiosity, depending on how they are used. Unlike the larger-scale 'logico-temporal gap' envisaged by Porter that exists at the macro-level of crime fiction, these information gaps can be rather more limited in scope. Many such gaps in knowledge might appear over the course of a narrative, varying in significance, and their individual resolution need not necessarily equate to the solution of the overarching mystery. Indeed, although this chapter concerns itself with gaps that are primarily temporal in nature, not all gaps necessarily relate to time; the reader might also confront missing information regarding the cause of death or the murder weapon that are more purely epistemic. In work undertaken on the contribution that temporal gaps make to narrativity in literature in general, Sternberg is again a key figure; but his work has been more recently complemented, specifically in regard to detective fiction, by that of Segal. The relationship between gaps and temporality is made clear when Sternberg claims:

> There is no shock of discovery without a *hidden* gap in plot continuity for the reader to discover behind time, no reversal of narrative expectation without a more or less imperceptible reversal of chronology in the narrative: late before early, effect before cause, deed before doer's (real) motive [...].[13]

Referring back to the *fabula/siuzhet* binary identified by the Russian Formalists, Segal argues that such gaps 'result from the interplay between two temporalities: that of the lifelike sequence of represented events [*fabula*] and that of its artful disclosure along the telling/reading sequence [*siuzhet*]'.[14] Specifically, they arise when information is withheld from the reader: as Sternberg explains, if the gap relates to the narrative past it provokes curiosity; if it pertains to the narrative future, the result is suspense.[15] Mapping Sternberg's system of gaps onto detective fiction specifically, Segal explains:

> The narrative [...] present of the detective story moves, as a rule, along the axis of the story of the investigation, which aims at solving the crime mystery; and because the goal of the investigation is, naturally, to fill in gaps related to *past* events, the dominant kind of interest generated by the detective plot is curiosity. However, there is also a fundamental element of suspense built into this type of plot related to the reader's expectations concerning the progress of the investigation toward a solution — that is, regarding the narrative *future*.[16]

Whilst the expectation amongst most readers that the mystery of the crime will ultimately be resolved might seem to reduce the scope for suspense, information gaps related to the narrative future are in fact commonly encountered. As Segal makes clear, this series of gaps 'revolves around the character of the detective and his actions, many of which remain puzzling, thus creating a mystery that is sometimes as powerful and intriguing as that of the crime itself'.[17] Segal here claims that suspense gaps surrounding the thoughts and actions of the detective are primarily generated by the manipulation of point of view. However, as with curiosity gaps, it is possible to see that temporal deformation, and temporal devices more broadly, make a key contribution to the generation of both types of blanks.

This chapter gives consideration to the impact of both retardation and information gaps in crime fiction; its ultimate aim, however, is to achieve a comprehensive analysis of the impact of a broader variety of temporal devices in crime fiction. In order to do so, it offers a narratological examination of these devices, informed primarily by the work of Genette. Genette proposes a tripartite model for the consideration of time in narrative, organized around the categories of order, frequency and duration. The present chapter takes these three categories in turn and considers how temporal devices related to each contribute to the epistemic games played in the genre and, consequently, to the reader's experience of curiosity and suspense. The third part of the chapter looks at various examples of how Russian crime fiction employs disruptions to the chronological order of the narratives (anachronies), specifically the use of analepsis and prolepsis, to great effect. The fourth section turns its attention to the question of frequency, most notably the effects created by the instances of repeated temporality that have been mentioned implicitly in the discussion of multiple voice in Chapter 3. The final part of the chapter moves on to examine the impact of devices related to duration. It discusses issues of pace in crime fiction, and most especially the role of ellipsis and its relationship to information gaps. The chapter also aims to reach beyond questions of narratology and epistemology, however, in order to consider how elements of temporal arrangement engage with the thematic or ideological concerns not solely of crime fiction but of late Imperial Russian literature more generally. In so doing, this analysis of temporal devices in crime fiction highlights the structural and thematic wealth of the genre in Russia during this period.

## Preliminary Remarks on Temporal Stance

By way of preparation for the discussion of the exploitation of chronological order in Russian crime fiction to follow, it is worth considering two preliminary temporal factors that affect the reader's experience of the text. The first is the temporal stance of the narrator vis-à-vis the action described; i.e. what is the position of the narrating instance in the *siuzhet* relative to the action of the story in the *fabula*? The second, which is much more specific to crime fiction than the first, is the relationship between the opening of the literary narrative and the temporal location of the crime. With regard to the position of the narrator, Genette identifies four basic temporal stances (subsequent, prior, simultaneous and interpolated to the time of the *fabula*) and without exception works of Russian crime fiction in the late Imperial period all fall into the first of these.[18] That is, by the time that the act of narration that constitutes the *siuzhet* begins, all of the action in the *fabula* has been completed. A subsequent temporal stance has long been the default setting in literature of all kinds; however, it is one that engenders particular interpretive expectations in crime fiction. Crucially, the fact that all of the action of the *fabula* has elapsed before narration begins encourages the reader to expect that, at least in a temporal sense, the narrator is in full possession of the facts relevant to the story before he begins to recount it. In a genre as end-oriented as crime fiction, this temporal stance therefore implicitly suggests that the *siuzhet* will reach a satisfactory conclusion, most conventionally by means of the detective solving the case. Otherwise, the reader might legitimately inquire, if such an end point has not been reached, what is the point in the narrator telling the tale? Indeed, even in the rare examples in this Russian corpus where detectives fail, such as Shkliarevskii's 'The Tale of a Judicial Investigator', the fact remains that the moment of this defeat has passed before the point in time at which the narration begins. Crucially, subsequent temporal orientation encourages the reader to expect that a full exposition of all facts relevant to the case ought, in principle, to be possible. Therefore, moments at which full information is not imparted to the reader are generally taken to be the consequence of deliberate acts of obfuscation on the part of the narrator in order to pique curiosity or suspense.

In contrast to the uniformity across the genre of this basic temporal stance, there exists much greater variety when it comes to the relationship between the beginning of action in the *siuzhet* and the temporal location of the crime. Simply put, it is not the case that all works of early Russian crime fiction open at a point in time when the crime has already been committed; in some, the crime has yet to happen. Moreover, even if the timing of the crime does precede the moment at which the *siuzhet* opens (or is almost simultaneous with it), a narrator may choose not to reveal this fact immediately. The best-known example of a work in which the narrative begins at a point in time prior to the crime is *Crime and Punishment*, where, as mentioned previously, the reader meets Raskolnikov as he is preparing the murder of Aliona Ivanovna. However, Dostoevskii's novel is not unique in this regard. In Panov's *Murder in Mukhtolovaia Grove* from 1876, the first two chapters describe the narrator-investigator's meeting with the peasant, Kuzma, during a hunt and some unexplained knocking at the door of his hut in the dead of night. A year later, the narrator sets out again to hunt: it is only at this point that he and his companion discover the body of Kuzma lying partially hidden in the forest and an investigation ensues. An intriguingly unconventional example is to be found in N. D. Akhsharumov's novel of 1872, *Kontsy v vodu* (*And None Will Be the Wiser*), where the title's hint at a lack of resolution presages the delayed revelation of a crime.[19] The novel, which features an amateur detective figure, does not announce the crime at its centre, the death of the narrator's cousin, Olga, until Chapter 7, by which time the reader has already witnessed her meeting with the narrator and heard her complaining of an unhappy marriage. As in Shkliarevskii's 'A Secret Investigation', the use of undetectable poison as the weapon means that the judicial investigation conducted immediately after her death fails to conclude definitively that a crime has even been committed.[20] Meanwhile, in A. I. Sokolova's 1892 novella, *Spetaia pesnia: iz zapisok starogo sledovatelia* (*The Song Has Been Sung: From the Notes of an Old Investigator*), the narrator-detective spends almost a quarter of the text describing his acquaintance with the Osinskii family, and relations between its various members, before revealing how the family tutor, Bazhlanov, is found murdered outside his lodgings on the estate.

The delayed revelation of a crime in works such as these ensures that they succeed in generating a considerable degree of suspense in the mind of the reader. In the case of Sokolova's novel, *The Song Has Been Sung*, in particular, although the fact of a crime is obviously hinted at in the subtitle, neither the nature nor the eventual victim of that crime is initially known, ensuring that the suspicious reader considers each character introduced as potentially either victim or perpetrator. Moreover, the postposed revelation of the crime ensures that a considerable degree of sympathy is encouraged for the participants in the drama because the reader witnesses them as living and breathing characters before the crime occurs. As such, the reader's reaction to the crime and its aftermath is invariably altered. In *Crime and Punishment*, the reader's likely desire that Raskolnikov get away with his crime stems precisely from his/her acquaintance with the protagonist and his circumstances prior to the commission of his crime. In Akhsharumov's *And None Will Be the Wiser*, the considerable empathy with, and sympathy for, Olga that is encouraged in the reader only heightens the sense of shock that s/he then experiences when her murder is revealed. In *The Song Has Been Sung*, the narrator hears Bazhlanov express the fear that he is doomed to die on the Osinskii estate, but the tutor fails to offer any justification for this conviction. Indeed, Bazhlanov's enigmatic claim foreshadows the conclusion of the story in which Osinskii's daughter, Bella, who has been shown to be capricious and vindictive, confesses to the murder and subsequently kills herself, but fails to offer any explanation of motive.

The majority of works in the Russian corpus, however, opt for a temporal structure in which the moment of the crime occurs either prior to, or almost simultaneously with, the time identified as the opening of the narration. So, for example, Popov's story, 'A Sinner's End', opens with a description of the narrator-investigator travelling to the village of Nizov'e, having already received the order to investigate the case of theft that has occurred there. Similarly, in Panov's *The Harvest Gathering*, the communication about the death of Sinitsyn is received very shortly after the narrator has arrived at the investigator's house. The opening paragraph of Chekhov's 'The Swedish Match' describes how a young man appears in the local police office to announce that his landowner has been killed. Antropov's story 'Belye golubi i sizye gorlitsy' ('White and Turtle Doves') from 1908 features an opening dialogue between the detective, Putilin, and the narrator that is interrupted by the visit of the millionaire Vakhrushinskii who alleges that his son has been abducted.[21] And in Zarin's 'The Missing Worker', the detective, Patmosov's, first words are spoken to announce that he is being brought a telegram, which turns out to summon him to the town of Nezhin on a case.[22] Such works create a quite different initial effect upon the reader than those in which the revelation of the crime is delayed. The former type immediately places the figure of the investigator and, most especially, his responsibility for attempting to solve the crime, centre stage. Although this model of temporal construction is to be found in both 'whydunit' and 'whodunit' narratives, the manner in which it encourages the reader to focus on the investigator rather than the victim or perpetrator makes it more appropriate to the 'whodunit'. In emphasizing the interpretive challenge that this early revelation of the commission of a crime represents to the investigator, such stories place a premium on curiosity as the reader is encouraged to participate in the resolution of the presented mystery. It is significant that no stories conforming to this temporal model remain without a resolution at the close or see the investigator defeated. Such a lack of a satisfactory resolution is, however, a feature of works in which the occurrence of the crime is delayed, particularly *And None Will Be the Wiser* and *The Song Has Been Sung*. It also occurs in certain works belonging to a different, third category in which, although the crime precedes the time of the opening of the narrative, it is not immediately revealed. Two notable works in this group are Shkliarevskii's 'The Tale of a Judicial Investigator' and Panov's *From the Life of a Provincial Town*.

## Analepsis, Prolepsis and their Various Effects

Turning more closely now to the first aspect of Genette's model, 'order', this section of the chapter examines issues related to what he defines as the relationship between 'the order in which events or temporal sections are arranged in the narrative discourse (*discours*) [and] the order of succession these same events or temporal segments have in the story (*histoire*)'.[23] Genette explains that, whilst the timeline of the *histoire/fabula* has to be chronological, that of the *discours/siuzhet* does not. In fact, it is far more common practice for a narrator to create discordances between the two. These anachronies, as he calls them, are of two main types: analepsis, which is constituted by 'any evocation after the fact of an event that took place earlier than the point in the story where we are at any given moment'; and prolepsis, which is 'any narrative manoeuvre that consists of narrating or evoking in advance an event that will take place later'.[24] Further to this basic division, Genette proposes that both analepsis and prolepsis can be classified in two additional ways: in terms of their point of reference and of their temporal reach. The first of these subcategories, concerning whether or not the anachrony refers to the same character, event or storyline as the one that is the subject of the narrative when the anachrony occurs, is not one that will be addressed here. The second, however, which addresses the question of whether the anachrony refers to a point of time outside the start or end point of the *siuzhet*, is pertinent. To begin, then, this section will consider the exploitation of analepsis in Russian crime fiction, its role in the mediation of the reader's sense of curiosity as well as how it relates to certain of the genre's thematic concerns.

The significance of analepsis to detective fiction is revealed by Porter's instructive claim that 'it is a genre committed to an act of recovery, moving forward in order to move back'.[25] Albert D. Hutter's description of the detective stories written by Poe and Conan Doyle is one that is equally pertinent to the genre more broadly: '[they] begin with the recent impact of a crime and work backwards to restructure the incomplete fragments of present knowledge into a more intelligible whole and consequently to explain the past'.[26] As readers tacitly understand, in order to be able to solve a crime, an investigation must look back to the time that preceded its commission for possible causes, motives and explanations. Given that many texts open at the moment when the crime has (just) been committed and when the investigation is starting, such an examination necessitates disruptions in the temporal order of the *siuzhet* in the form of analepsis. So, for example, if we refer again to Shkliarevskii's 'A Secret Investigation', which has been examined in some detail in Chapter 3, it is obvious that the 'present' time of the story of the investigation is repeatedly enriched by references to a whole range of moments in the past, before the crime has been committed. Closest in time to the start of the investigation are the details given by the maid about Mozharovskaia's recent activities in St Petersburg and her friendship with Kriukovskaia. As the investigation continues, the narrator hears details from the doctor, Mikhailovskii, about experiments with poison that date back to his time at the military academy, from Bystrov about Kriukovskaia's mother's marriage at a more distant moment in the past, from Atomanichenkov about his acquaintance with Kebmezakh when at school, as well as from Mozharovskii about the history of his relationship with his wife. It is information contained within these references to various times prior to Mozharovskaia's death that permits the investigator to build a case against Kriukovskaia, by understanding both her possible motives and her ability to have committed the crime.

The exploitation and effect of such analepsis in crime fiction can be approached from any number of angles, but the present discussion will concentrate on two of the most pertinent in the Russian context. These are, firstly, the temporal reach of the instances of analepsis encountered; and, secondly, the relationship between analepsis and the reader's experience of curiosity, and particularly how temporal retrospection relates to the categories of the 'whydunit' and the 'whodunit'. As Shkliarevskii's story demonstrates, the criminal investigation frequently consists of listening to stories that refer to times stretching back to relatively distant points in the past. Although difficult to establish definitively, the analepsis with the greatest reach in 'A Secret Investigation' is most likely the report that the sixty-year-old Atomanichenkov gives of his friendship with Kebmezakh at school, presumably some fifty years before the time of the 'present' investigation.[27] The use of 'external' analepsis with a considerable temporal reach is a feature shared by many works of Russian crime fiction. So, for example, in Timofeev's story 'A Gang of Thieves', from the *Notes of an Investigator* collection, the narrator-detective investigates not only the recent past that has led to the theft of 4,000 roubles, but also what might be called the narrative's 'pluperfect', that is, the circumstances that led the thieves to become members of this gang in the first place. These sections of the narrative take the reader back to a time some twenty years before the investigation to provide descriptions of the unhappy and deprived childhoods that left these men with little choice but to fall into a life of crime.[28] Similarly, the story 'Murder and Suicide' in the same collection moves from the investigation into Marianna Bodresova's attempt on her own life, initially back through the details of her life in the village of Gostitsa where she currently lives, before hearing details of her earliest childhood and the suffering meted out to her at the hands of her parents. However, the narrative makes use of an analepsis with even greater reach when the investigator is informed that Marianna's father also had a son, her half-brother, born five years before her, who was sent away when his stepmother, Marianna's mother, did not want to look after him. Given that we are told that Marianna is about twenty-seven years old, it is then possible to state that the analeptic reach of the narrative is roughly thirty-two years.

One explanation for the impulse behind the use of passages of analepsis with such temporal reach is offered by the work of Sokolovskii. In his story 'The Long-Suffering', the narrator-investigator explains that, in order to understand crimes such as Stepan Prokofiev's stabbing of Daria Iakovleva, it is necessary to take a longer-perspective chronological look at the circumstances of the lives that have led up to them:

> На такие преступления нельзя смотреть как на нечто зародившееся и развившееся мгновенно; напротив того путь их развития чрезвычайно медленный, последняя, видимая причина есть только прикосновение к свежей ране, вырвавшее у больного мучительный крик боли; это песчинка заставившая весы потерять равновесие; вся суть не в ней; само по себе прикосновение могло быть ничтожном, при других условиях прошло бы незаметном, но дело в том, что до этого времени организм то настолько наболел, что и ничтожное прикосновение для него было равносильно прикосновению раскаленным железом.[29]

> [One should not look upon such crimes as events that have appeared in an instant. On the contrary, the path of their development is strikingly slow and the final, visible reason is just like when you touch a recent wound and it prompts a cry of pain from the victim. It is the grain of sand that makes the scales tip out of balance, but the whole story is not contained in it. In itself, that touch might be negligible; in different circumstances it would go unnoticed. But the fact is that, up until that moment, the organism has been suffering to such a degree that, for it, even the faintest touch is equivalent to that of a hot poker.]

By way of further illustration, Sokolovskii explains that the blow that the barge hauler, Kariag, strikes to the head of the publican who has seized him by the neck when he refuses to pay for some vodka contains 'все пережитое бурлаком прошлое, все ожидаемое им будущее' ('everything the barge hauler had experienced in the past and everything he expected in the future'), and this is why its violence is such that it proves fatal.[30] Sokolovskii's narrator gives voice here to an opinion seemingly shared by many writers of Russian crime fiction. In *Crime and Punishment*, Dostoevskii depicts Raskolnikov's crime not as the product of a single moment, but as an act that has been prepared over a much longer period with references to his own past in St Petersburg, the experiences of Dunia and his mother back in the provinces, as well as the history of characters such as Marmeladov that reach further back in time. Similarly, Sokolova's *The Song Has Been Sung* sees the narrator-investigator gather information that relates to a time at least seven years prior to the murder of Bazhlanov when this tutor's employer, Osinskii, entered into a second marriage with a woman who was only two years older than his daughter. The strained relationship that exists between the second wife, the daughter and her new half-brother, Bazhlanov's pupil, not only provides the backdrop to the murder but greatly complicates the search for the culprit.

However, it is not the case that all works of Russian crime fiction in the late Imperial period feature the use of this type of analepsis. Counter-examples would include Chekhov's 'The Swedish Match', stories by Zarin, including 'The Missing Worker' and 'The Fourth Man', and many of the works written by Antropov. The fact that these counter-examples all date from rather later in the genre's development in Russia and can be categorized as 'whodunits' allows a broad conclusion to be drawn regarding the use of analepsis in this particular national context. Although 'whodunits' might employ analepsis of either restricted or extended reach, works belonging to the category of the 'whydunit', or which mix the two categories, invariably employ analepsis with an extensive temporal reach. So, for instance, in Chekhov's 'The Swedish Match', a 'whodunit', analeptic references during the investigation, with only one or two exceptions, stretch no further back in time than the 'murder' a week previously, with the investigators focusing on the immediate circumstances surrounding Mark Ivanych Kliauzov's disappearance and betraying no interest whatsoever in the longer-term question of motive.[31] Similarly, in Antropov's 'Kiss of the Bronze Virgin', the search for the culprit in the disappearance of Count Boleslav Rzhevuskii remains firmly focused on the present time, with one of the few instances of analepsis reaching back only a matter of months into the past to record a disagreement between the victim's father and his fiancée's father. Zarin's 'The Fourth Man' represents an interesting example of a mid-point along the 'whydunit'/'whodunit' spectrum. For much of the story, the narrative keeps the temporal focus on the present of Patmosov's investigation, delving backwards to only relatively close moments in the past. However, once the artist Sanin has been unmasked as the culprit in Dergachev's murder, his explanation includes an analepsis that takes the reader considerably further back. He describes how Vera, who is the author of the love letters stolen by Sanin's servant and bought by Dergachev, married Count Chekannyi upon the death of her parents at some unspecified point in the past. Then, four years prior to the murder, Sanin met Vera for the first time and immediately fell in love with her when Chekannyi asked him to paint her portrait. They began an affair, Vera fell pregnant and gave birth to a son, who was raised in secret, while she and Sanin conducted a correspondence that gave rise to the incriminating letters with which Dergachev attempts to blackmail Vera. Here, then, although the analepsis stretches further back in time than in the Chekhov and Antropov stories mentioned, it is still more restricted than the examples from either Sokolovskii or Timofeev. Not only that, but such extensive analeptic reference is not a recurrent feature of the story; it is presented only at the point at which Patmosov has successfully identified the 'who', and at which this culprit is then permitted to provide a justification for his actions by explaining the 'why'.

In works that are more straightforwardly classified as 'whydunits', the analeptic reach is not only greater but the instances of such analepsis tend to be repeated. So, for example, in Timofeev's 'Murder and Suicide', the details of Marianna Bodresova's appalling life of abuse are provided initially in the testimony that she has given during her first interrogation, then again in evidence that the detective hears from witnesses during his investigation in her former village of Dereshi, and once again in the account that is provided in her own voice during the third interrogation. In a similar vein, as has been mentioned above, Sokolovskii's story 'Chapurin' sees the narrator-investigator interview the eponymous protagonist in the prison where he has been incarcerated for four years for a series of murders. There is no doubt that Chapurin is guilty of these crimes and probably more, but the investigator attempts to gain a greater understanding of his path into crime and his experience of committing the acts. The narrative alternates between the 'present' moment of the investigator's conversation with Chapurin and repeated analeptic forays into the past, including not only the times at which he committed his various crimes, but also the more distant point of his early family circumstances.[32]

In the context of nineteenth-century Russian crime writing, the popularity of the device of repeated extensive analepsis is significant. In terms of the manner in which it insistently directs the reader's curiosity to the historical reasons for crime, analepsis of extended reach emphasizes the role of upbringing and environment in particular as explanatory factors. Bodresova's murder of her half-brother and attempt on her own life come to seem entirely justified when the reader has been referred repeatedly back to the horrific suffering that she has experienced over such a long period. The men described as members of 'A Gang of Thieves' in Timofeev's story, the narrator notes, could easily have turned out differently had they been exposed to a more benevolent influence during their childhoods. And in Shkliarevskii's story 'Why Did He Kill Them?', although the narrator voices some scepticism, the protagonist Narostov explicitly attributes his crime and 'нравственн[ое] падени[е]' ('moral downfall') to his 'воспитание' ('upbringing').[33] At the same time as acknowledging that other people who received the same upbringing and education did not turn out to be double murderers, Narostov uses the story of his life in analepsis as a means of convincing himself that his own dénouement was inevitable.

As such, the use of extended-reach analepsis in Russian crime fiction of the period enters into dialogue with contemporary debates surrounding determinism. Related to the belief in scientific materialism, as espoused by the narrator in Sokolovskii's *Prison and Life*, notions of determinism with regard to crime were relatively frequently invoked and debated in the second half of the nineteenth century in Russia. Although it predated him, it was Nikolai Chernyshevskii who gave some of the most forceful expression to the belief that people are the product of their physiological composition and environment, that their actions can be described as reactions to various stimuli, that they have no independent will, and that they are not, therefore, morally responsible for their actions. From this determinism flows the view of crime as a consequence of material hardship, social inequality or institutional failings and, as such, individual responsibility for 'bad actions' (as Chernyshevskii labelled crime) is diminished. None of the authors of crime fiction discussed here express such strident views as Chernyshevskii about the moral absolution from crime offered by determinism. However, it is equally the case that few of the early authors display such a commitment to the belief in the existence of individual free will as does Dostoevskii in *Crime and Punishment*. Precisely by having the narrative offer up a variety of equally inconclusive possible motives for Raskolnikov's murders, Dostoevskii argues that his crime cannot be explained or excused by any single material, or other, factor. Dostoevskii argues even more forcefully against the deterministic view of crime in his article 'Среда' ('Environment') that appeared in *A Writer's Diary* in 1873. There, he writes:

> мало-помалу придем к заключению, что и вовсе нет преступлений, а во всем среда виновата [...] Ведь вот что говорит учение о среде в противоположность христианству, которое, вполне признавая давление среды и провозгласивши милосердие к согрешившему, ставит, однако же, нравственным долгом человеку борьбу со средой, ставит предел тому, где среда кончается, а долг начинается.[34]

> [we slowly and surely come to the conclusion that there are no crimes at all and, 'the environment is to blame' for everything [...] So runs the doctrine of the environment, as opposed to Christianity which, fully recognizing the pressure of the environment and having proclaimed mercy for the sinner, still places a moral duty on the individual to struggle with the environment and marks the line where the environment ends and duty begins.]

In the works by Sokolovskii, Timofeev, Shkliarevskii and others mentioned here, the illustration of the role of environment and determinism is rather more ambiguous. What the use of analepsis implies is that the crime that gives rise to the 'present' story of the investigation is not a freely or randomly occurring event, but one that is inescapably linked to the (long-term) past that has prepared it. As such, a number of the empathetic, humane investigators encountered in works of the 'whydunit' variety seem to lean towards the belief that criminals should not invariably be held morally accountable for their actions. For Sokolovskii's narrator, Chapurin's lack of remorse undermines his implicit claim that his upbringing has determined his path into crime, whilst Kariag's life of suffering partially exonerates him; for Shkliarevskii's narrator-investigator, it is Narostov's self-conscious invocation of his upbringing as an excuse that undermines his attempt at moral self-absolution; while in Timofeev's 'Murder and Suicide', the narrator expressly desires the acquittal of Bodresova and bitterly regrets her eventually successful suicide.

If analepsis is primarily a means of prompting the reader's curiosity about factors in the past that might have motivated a crime, prolepsis, or the flashforward, is most frequently used to build up a sense of suspense about the future course of the investigation. Just as with analepsis, the use of prolepsis is, of course, not a feature unique to crime fiction. However, in a genre that places such emphasis on the eventual success of the investigation, its role assumes a particular significance. From the opening of every work of crime fiction, the reader is primed to expect that the temporal end-point of the narrative will be the resolution of the mystery of the crime and the triumph of the investigator.[35] It thus becomes interesting to consider the role of determinism not just as it relates to the past that has prepared the crime but also to the future progress of the investigation. Such future-oriented determinism affects the experience of the reader at least in the sense that, in spite of the illusion of being invited to act as a quasi-investigator with an equal chance of solving the mystery, the authority of the detective, but most especially that of the narrator, remains absolutely paramount in almost all cases. It is informative, therefore, to look at how prolepsis is exploited in crime fiction not only from the point of view of suspense, but also in terms of the authority and control that is demonstrated by the narrator and experienced by the reader.

Because all the works of crime fiction from the late Imperial period in Russia discussed here employ a subsequent temporal stance, when the narrator begins his story of the investigation, he already possesses information about its outcome. It is precisely this temporal position that allows the narrator to employ prolepsis to heighten the reader's sense of anticipation. For example, as mentioned in Chapter 2 above, Panov's 1876 novella, *Three Courts, or Murder During the Ball*, recounts the narrator's investigation into the murder of Elena Vladimirovna Ruslanova during a ball to celebrate her engagement, and the simultaneous theft of her tiara. In spite of the fact that the killing takes place during a party attended by scores of guests, there are no witnesses to either crime and no immediate suggestion as to the identity of the culprit. As if responding to a sense that the reader might find this initial lack of information frustrating, the narrator-investigator repeatedly employs prolepsis to extend the promise of future revelations. So, the novella's second chapter opens with his announcement that, although this point in time has not yet been reached in the *siuzhet*, 'следующий день принес с собой открытие новых обстоятельств, которые на балу не были обнаружены' ('the following day brought with it the discovery of new circumstances which had not been detected at the ball').[36] Such proleptic announcements that relevant information will soon be revealed are a recurrent feature not just of this work, but of many others. For instance, in Timofeev's story 'The Married Woman', from 1878, the narrator informs the reader on the second day of the case that the following morning will bring the most interesting period of the investigation because it is then that he will interview the alleged poisoner, the victim's wife, Irina.[37] Equally, at the close of the sixth chapter in Stepanov's 'They Wanted to Betray the Court and God's Will', the narrator-investigator heightens suspense by informing the reader that the case into the murder of Zadornyi is about to take an unexpected turn (and what is revealed is that the narrator's detective sidekick has found an army deserter hiding in a hut in the forest who has crucial information about why the landowner, Gulianov, has not wanted the perpetrators of the crime to be found).[38] The use of this type of prolepsis is clearly part of a strategy, not confined to crime fiction, to encourage the reader to continue reading by promising that the narrative contains interesting revelations in the pages to come.

Although prolepsis in such instances necessarily depends upon the narrator's possession of knowledge about the course that future events will take, there are also occasions where the device is used to create a stronger sense of the authority of this voice. It is in these contexts where its appearance can mediate the relationship between the narrator and reader in interesting ways. From the very earliest days of critical commentary on crime fiction, the belief has existed that one reason for the genre's popularity is that readers derive pleasure from participating in its epistemic games. Moreover, the oft-cited notion of 'fair play' in the genre implies that there exists, or should exist, some sort of level playing field between the narrator (or implied author) and the reader that means that each one is equally capable of solving the crime. Fortunately, since the period in the early twentieth century when there was a vogue for 'rules' of the genre, this idea has been frequently, and correctly, debunked.[39] The use of prolepsis ought to be seen to function precisely as an implicit, but persuasive, indication of the lack of equality between narrator/investigator and reader and the fallacy that such a level playing field ever exists. So, for example, in Timofeev's story, 'Tri zhizni' ('Three Lives'), that appears in the same 1878 collection as 'The Married Woman', the narrator-investigator is tasked with examining the case of an apparently happily married woman who has committed suicide by drowning herself in a lake. At the close of the fourth chapter, the narrator makes a proleptic comment about the secret that has disrupted the couple's conjugal harmony, which the victim has carried with her to the grave and about which her husband has sworn to say nothing:

> Не менее того эта тайна не осталась тайной. Тут же у гроба покойницы, в тот же самый вечер, когда я собирался уезжать из дома Погожевых, она была выдана мне... третьим лицом.[40]

> [Nevertheless, this secret did not remain a secret. Right next to the coffin of the deceased, on the very evening I was intending to leave the Pogozhevs' house, it was passed to me... by a third party.]

The narrator thus clearly demonstrates that he already possesses the knowledge which the reader also desires; and whilst suggesting that he will soon reveal more details, he refuses immediately to do so, hence the use of elliptical points. In a similar fashion, in Sokolovskii's 'The Long-Suffering', the narrator-detective's announcement that Daria Iakovleva's wish (expressed as 'God forgive you, Stepan'), during her face-to-face confrontation with her lover, were to be her final words because she dies soon afterwards profoundly shocks the reader who anticipates a more positive outcome.[41] This proleptic reference comes as a surprise not simply because of the information that it contains, but because such leaps into a future time have not been a feature of the narrative up until this point. In Panov's *The Harvest Gathering* meanwhile, the narrator exploits prolepsis to demonstrate his superiority not only over the reader but also over his friend who is the official investigator. Having outlined his idea for staging a 'coup d'état' to force a confession from the murderer, the narrator describes how the investigator, Ivan Gerasimovich, dismisses it as a waste of time, and chooses instead to summon more witnesses. The narrator's comment at this point is: 'к несчастью, несмотря на все мои доводы, он немного торопился' ('unfortunately, in spite all of my arguments, he rushed rather').[42] The presence of 'unfortunately' here functions as an implicit proleptic indication that Ivan Gerasimovich's choice of action will not pay dividends and that the narrator's 'coup d'état' will eventually secure the necessary confession. As Teresa Bridgeman argues, 'explicit flashforward can establish a narrator's mastery of his or her tale or can generate suspense'.[43] Such deviations from the chronological order of the *fabula* are designed, on the one hand, to instil confidence by demonstrating that the narrator has full control over his material. However, they are also a means of establishing the narrator's superiority over the reader: the narrator possesses information about the future development of the story that the reader cannot have. As such, prolepsis lays bare the fundamental inequality of the positions occupied by narrator and reader as they approach the mystery presented in crime fiction. Indeed, the narrator in Timofeev's 'The Married Woman' recognizes the potentially negative impact of prolepsis when he remarks: 'впрочем, зачем говорить выводами; пусть дело скажется само собою, фактами' ('in any case, why am I speaking of conclusions; let the case tell itself, by means of facts').[44]

Given the manner in which such proleptic references suggest that the future trajectory of the story is already mapped out in advance, it becomes instructive to consider how this temporal device feeds into debates on determinism, and ideas of fate more generally. Albeit in a somewhat different tone than that associated with the use of analepsis, prolepsis makes clear that the course of the future (certainly of the narrative, but perhaps also of the extratextual world) is already decided and cannot be changed. Occasionally the two devices can be combined to convey a sense of predestination. So, for example, in Shkliarevskii's 'The Tale of a Judicial Investigator', during a passage of analeptic recollection, Zarubin expresses his fear about what might come of the relationship between his two young neighbours and their suitors in the future.[45] Although at the time that he experiences this fear Zarubin cannot know that the outcome will be the murder of Pyl'neva, his remarks are shown to function as an accurate anticipation of future misfortune. In Zarin's 'Poteria chesti: tragicheskaia istoriia' ('Loss of Honour: A Tragic Story'), the detective, Patmosov, reveals his premonition that the case of the card sharp, Kolychev, whose father has asked the investigator to find out how and why his son is losing so much money, will not end well and that he should have refused to take it on: 'Отчего томит меня злое предчувствие [...] чувствую, чувствую, что бесполезен' ('Why am I afflicted with this evil presentiment [...] I feel, I feel that it's useless').[46] His prediction, as hinted by the story's subtitle, proves to be correct when Kolychev, who has double-crossed the group of card sharps that recruited him, commits suicide having been publicly shamed by these other gamblers. Crucially, however, Patmosov's words represent a case of anticipation or foreshadowing rather than prolepsis: his ominous presentiment does not function as a chronological disruption in the *siuzhet* of the order of events from the *fabula*.

Nevertheless, the inclusion of anticipation into the temporal patchwork of crime fiction significantly affects the reader's experience of the genre. In his discussion of foreshadowing in literature, Gary Saul Morson explains the relationship between knowledge and the sense of a predetermined future in the following terms:

> Readers are aware that authors can know things about their characters that characters cannot know about themselves or each other. Most obviously, the author can know what will happen to a character. In life, we do not have that information about others any more than we have it about ourselves. [...] But in literature the author does have godlike power; the future is part of his image of a character. The author normally knows a character's destiny for certain and beyond the possibility of revision by the character. For the author, the character's life is in effect already over before it has begun.[47]

In our corpus of Russian crime fiction, this foreshadowing finds its fullest expression in the work of Dostoevskii. In fact, a far denser use of the device is one of the aspects that marks Dostoevskii's writing out from other authors in the genre. Not only that, but the orientation of the foreshadowing his works include is frequently dualistic — it relates to two different categories of future. The first is the more typical one of a future time, from a past moment of speaking, which is still located at a point prior to the crime (as illustrated in the Zarubin example from Shkliarevskii); the other, more significantly, relates to a time that is post-crime, and sometimes even post-resolution of the criminal mystery. It can be argued, therefore, that by such a use of foreshadowing, Dostoevskii's work not only moves in two directions (à la Porter) but attempts to *control* time in two directions: backwards by reconstructing the past, but also forwards by predicting the future. The importance of anticipation in *Crime and Punishment* is clearly established early on when Part One of the novel is peppered with veiled allusions from Raskolnikov about what he is planning to do: 'Ну зачем я теперь иду? Разве я способен на *это*? Разве *это* серьезно? Совсем не серьезно' ('So why am I going now? Am I really capable of *that*? Can *that* be serious? It's not serious at all').[48] At a later stage, Raskolnikov's article on crime in *Periodicheskaia rech'* possesses an interesting dual temporal status. When it is paraphrased by the protagonist in Part III, Chapter 5 in response to provocation by Porfirii Petrovich, it should be seen to constitute an act of retrospective reading of the murder. The murder is at this point an event in the past and Raskolnikov's article effectively reaches into a pre-crime past in order to unveil a potential motive or motives: a utilitarian view of the division of society. Yet, if we position ourselves temporally at the time of the writing of the article, some six months prior to the murders, it functions as a predictive account of the crime. Indeed, this anticipatory status is obliquely suggested by Raskolnikov's eavesdropping on the conversation between the student and the officer in Part I, Chapter 6 which echoes so many of his own ideas: it takes place after he has written the article but before he becomes the author of the crime.

The second category of anticipation is most apparent during Raskolnikov's conversations with Porfirii Petrovich. One of the judicial investigator's favoured strategies with the protagonist is to outline his own counter-theory regarding what a criminal *will* do in a particular set of circumstances. For instance, in Part

IV, Chapter 5 of the novel, Porfirii suggests, during a much longer sketch of his method: 'Да пусть, пусть его погуляет пока, пусть; я ведь и без того знаю, что он моя жертвочка и никуда не убежит от меня! Да и куда ему убежать?' ('Let him wander as much as he likes, for now; after all, I already know I've got my catch and he won't run away! I mean, where would he run to?').[49] The use of three verbs in the future perfective aspect in the original Russian is more marked than in the translation. Porfirii's strategy of anticipation and the interest he shows in the future that still awaits Raskolnikov is key to his symbolic role in the novel and is what distinguishes him from more conventional detective figures. Having eventually revealed in Part VI, Chapter 2 that he believes Raskolnikov to be the murderer, Porfirii's speech is heavily inflected with references not just to a hypothetical future, but to a definite future that God intends for him. By looking towards a post-confession future, and by functioning as a secular priest, Porfirii contributes to the religious-philosophical content of the novel that is obviously concerned with very much more than the simple reconstruction of the circumstances of a past event.

Diane Oenning Thompson believes that Dostoevskii's striving to divine the future 'finds its fullest, most voiced and urgent expression in his last novel', *The Brothers Karamazov*.[50] The crime at the centre of this famous work is the murder of Fedor Karamazov, apparently by his son Dmitrii, who is charged, goes on trial and is convicted, even though it is revealed that the actual culprit is his half-brother, Smerdiakov. The novel's dual chronology is crucial to its impulses towards divination because the 'present' of most of the novel's action (located some thirteen years before the 'present' of the narrative voice) includes so many hints, clues and discussions about the future. On the one hand, as Maria Kanevskaia suggests, such clues can really only be activated upon a second reading, once the resolution of the *fabula* has been reached.[51] On the other, even on a first encounter with the text, the reader is assailed by the frequency with which the speech of both the narrator and the characters is coloured by references towards, or predictions of, a future time or future events. For example, all of Alesha's actions in the first half of the novel are carried out under the pressure of the predicted imminent death of Father Zosima. Most significant, however, is the temporal orientation of Smerdiakov's dialogue with his half-brother Ivan in the chapter 'Пока еще очень неясная' ('So Far Still A Very Obscure One') in Book Five, where he predicts that Dmitrii might come to the house to steal his father's money and possibly kill him whilst he, Smerdiakov, might have an epileptic fit that will incapacitate him for several days. Tellingly, this suggestion prompts Ivan to ask: 'да ты сам уж не хочешь ли так подвести, чтобы сошлось' ('You're not by any chance planning it all to happen like that?'),[52] a question that, with hindsight, clearly indicates the real culprit — Smerdiakov himself. And, as Kanevskaia claims:

> Предзнаменования делают будущее не только неизбежным, но и активно учавствующим в настоящем. В структуре повествования настоящее и будущее меняются ролями, между ними нарушаются причинно-следственные связи, и будущее начинает определять предшествующие ему события.[53]

[Omens make the future not only inevitable, but also actively a part of the present. In the structure of the narrative the present and the future switch roles, cause–effect links between them break down and the future begins to determine events that precede it.]

Such an apparent desire to suggest that the future is controlled might appear to stand at odds with Dostoevskii's anti-determinist relationship to 'open' time but, as Morson has shown, authors such as Dostoevskii can create a persuasive vision of the future 'as many different things'.[54]

Albeit with a less religious and eschatological focus than Dostoevskii, many of Shkliarevskii's works also include an examination of the past that is predicated on a sharply enunciated presence of the future. That is, many of the embedded narratives encountered in his stories not only look backwards through analepsis but also attempt to manipulate the future by claiming to anticipate the crime and its immediate aftermath. To take just one example, in 'A Secret Investigation', the ostensibly retrospective story told in the first embedded narrative by the doctor, Mikhailovskii, is heavily imbued with anticipation of the circumstances of the future demise of Mozharovskaia, even though he knows very few of the actual details. Immediately upon hearing of her death, he claims that Mozharovskaia must have been poisoned with curare by her friend Kriukovskaia. As justification for this allegation, he recounts the story of Belotserskii, who experimented with the same poison as a student. The evidence provided by a story from some thirty years previously does indeed foreshadow the eventual circumstances of Mozharovskaia's death. This future-oriented temporality also helps to explain the recurrence throughout the narrative of vocabulary marked with the prefix 'пред' ('pre' or 'fore'). For instance, Mikhailovskii attributes his visit to the Mozharovskii household on the night that the victim is first, non-fatally poisoned to a 'предчувстви[е]' ('premonition') that something untoward was happening. He reveals that he feared at the time that this first incident would be repeated in the future and that, these fears having been borne out, he is justified in claiming: 'я предупредил бы теперешнее преступление' ('I could have predicted the present crime').[55] The detective himself admits that Mikhailovskii's story chimes with his own 'инстинктивное предубеждение' ('instinctive prejudice') towards Kriukovskaia.[56] With the death having initially been ruled unsuspicious and the poisoner still at large, the story is lent a far greater urgency because it is not simply a question of reconstructing the past but of preventing a potentially murderous future. So, in both Dostoevskii and Shkliarevskii, the temporal planes of present and past that are most naturally associated with crime fiction are productively and intriguingly supplemented with a potent sense of the future. In one sense, such heterochrony (or multi-temporality) might be considered to be nothing more than the natural accompaniment to the heteroglossia discussed in Chapter 3. After all, the interrelationship of multiple voices, as Stacy Burton has claimed, can be understood in significant ways as a dialogue of chronotopes.[57] That said, the often-complicated tapestry of temporal reference encountered in crime fiction can offer a significant challenge to the investigator (and reader) interested in uniting the various fragments.

Indeed, it is informative to consider how devices of temporal order can be exploited precisely to disorient the reader and reinforce the sense of his/her inferiority vis-à-vis the narrator or investigator. The corpus of early Russian crime fiction features works that fragment temporal presentation in a manner that not only imitates the profusion of clues confronted by the investigator, but also ensures that the search for the truth is significantly problematized. Sokolovskii's story 'Chapurin' clearly illustrates how switches between various temporal locations by means of anachronies can disorient and confuse the reader. The story does not involve a standard criminal investigation, given that the eponymous hero is already sitting in prison convicted of a number of murders. Nevertheless, the narrator-investigator's interviews with him do pose an interpretive and epistemic problem because of the multiple confessions and then retractions that the convict makes to additional crimes. Chapurin is deeply unreliable, and neither narrator nor reader are able to establish with any certainty when he is telling the truth and when he is just inventing a story so as to delay further the execution of justice against him. The instability of truth in the narrative is mirrored and reinforced by the temporal disorientation that results from the constant toing and froing between the various episodes of his life that he recounts. The anachronies in the story include, as noted above, references back to Chapurin's earliest childhood, other instances of analepsis back to the various criminal incidents in which he alleges he has been involved, closer analepses to his time in prison since his incarceration, as well as examples of prolepsis about his future fate in prison. It is not the case that the reader's confusion arises out of a lack of clear temporal markers during these various passages; rather, it is simply the proliferation of instances of departure from the chronological order of the *fabula* in the *siuzhet* that creates this disorientation. Ultimately, the reader finds it difficult to reorder the chronological jumble of events presented by Chapurin and, therefore, to ascertain the truth value of his claims.

Stepanov's story 'Forced Marriage' in the *Innocent and the Guilty* volume offers a similarly persuasive example of the complication that can arise out of the use of multiple anachronies. Its opening wrongfoots the reader in its description of Pakhom Ermolaich out ploughing in the fields the evening before the murder of his cousin, Andrei. Given that the previous story in the collection, 'The Horse-Rustler's Bridle', has revealed that Pakhom is in prison having been arrested for Andrei's killing, this scene must qualify as an immediate example of analepsis, albeit from a present moment that has not yet been detailed in this specific narrative. Such a temporal set-up ensures that, as the narrative in 'Forced Marriage' moves on to describe events that evening, there is a strong sense of determinism, or even fatalism, because the reader already knows that Andrei will not return from his ride alive. The false sense of contemporaneity constructed here between the moments of action and narration is reinforced by the fact that the description of this opening pastoral scene repeatedly employs the historic present tense. Moreover, as the story goes on to narrate the course of the first criminal investigation, the reader experiences a keener sense of frustration with its flaws than might otherwise have been the case, given that s/he already knows that it has resulted in Pakhom's false arrest and conviction. The account of this first investigation, itself an analepsis, is punctuated by numerous instances of additional embedded analepsis, as Pakhom and other characters are asked to account for their actions on the night of the murder. The story moves closer to its real 'present' at the close of the second chapter when the narrator reveals that he has been charged by the governor with going to the village and establishing the correct back story to this particular drama.

The narrator in 'Forced Marriage' makes clear the importance of analepsis to his undertaking when he explains that murder should be considered to be a 'dénouement' and that 'чтобы развить [развязку], нужен был пролог' ('in order to unravel this dénouement, there must have been a prologue').[58] One of the first parts of this 'prologue' is provided by an analeptic passage with greater reach than previously offered in the story, as the investigator listens to the coachman's story about Andrei's daughter-in-law, Akulina's, background and the details of the circumstances surrounding her marriage to his son, Vasilii. From here onwards, the narrative is constructed around numerous instances of analepsis that relate to an almost endless variety of past times, the order and significance of which the reader has to try to establish and which the narrator does not explain. Akulina — whom the coachman has indicated is a likely suspect in the murder — is asked to account, not necessarily in this order, for: the details of her prior relationship with a different man, Sergei; the reason she subsequently agreed to marry Andrei's son; the family set-up in her new family after the marriage; her relations with her mother; the numerous times when she has absconded from her father-in-law's home; her actions on the night of the murder and the time immediately preceding that; as well as her movements thereafter. However, analepsis, as well as prolepsis presented within analepsis, is also provided by a host of other voices, including Akulina's mother and, crucially, her niece (who provides evidence of Akulina's theft from Andrei), various of the villagers, members of Andrei's family, the innkeeper and, finally, the shepherd whose testimony is crucial in substantiating the accusations against her.

Stepanov's narrator-investigator is also adept at employing prolepsis and anticipation to achieve his aims during the case. In particular, his efforts to persuade Pakhom to implicate Akulina in the murder rely upon his assurances that his deceased cousin will forgive him for doing so; he also constructs a vision of the future that is designed to instil considerable fear in Akulina herself. Part of his strategy in the later stages of the story, after Akulina has been detained on suspicion of the murder, is to ask the prison guards outside her cell to recount various stories of victims returning to haunt their murderers and exacting vengeance upon them. These stories, which are intended to force a confession from Akulina, contain implicit predictions about her future damnation in the eyes of God for her crime. Although there is little doubt in 'Forced Marriage' that Akulina is indeed the culprit, the proliferation of various temporal anachronies ensures not only that the narrator succeeds in painting an accurate picture of the complexities surrounding the crime and the investigation, but also that the path towards her eventual confession is anything but straightforward and assured. By means of the complicated web of temporal discordances presented in the narrative, the reader is given an acute sense of the various threads of a story that need to be united in order to ensure a satisfactory conclusion to a criminal investigation. The reader's disorientation mirrors closely the narrator-investigator's sense of frustration and impotence in the face of a lack of physical evidence and the determination of a reticent suspect.

## Frequency: The Role of Repeated Temporality

Given the recognition by scholars that crime fiction narratives are conventionally constructed around temporal movements both forwards and backwards, it is no surprise that an analysis of analepsis and prolepsis should prove so fruitful. However, what a more extensive discussion of time in crime fiction can reveal is the as-yet unremarked importance of frequency, and specifically repeated temporality, to the genre. Genette defines frequency as 'a system of relationships between [the] capacities for "repetition" on the part of both the narrated events (the story) and the narrative statements (of the text)'.[59] He identifies four possible categories of frequency: two types of 'singulative', where each time an event occurs in the story, it is narrated in the discourse (whether that be one event or many); 'iterative', where an event occurs more than once in the story, but the discourse narrates it only once; and 'repetitive', where an event occurs only once in the story, but is narrated more than once in the discourse. What a reading of Russian crime fiction demonstrates is that, amongst these three categories, it is repetitive frequency that is the most influential device of temporal organization. Indeed, the claim that the use of repeated temporality is a definitive feature of the genre is one that can be applied to crime fiction from all national traditions. Repetition is generically characteristic because the central aim of these works is to gain an understanding of one particularly significant moment in time (the crime); and one obvious means of doing so is to revisit it on multiple occasions. A striking example of the inclusion of such repetition in crime fiction is to be found in the accounts of trial scenes, such as that in Book Twelve of *The Brothers Karamazov*, where the time of the murder is rehearsed over and over in the various acts of witness testimony. As Genette points out in *Narrative Discourse*, repetitive frequency is often combined with the exploitation of various points of view so as to give slightly altered versions in the *siuzhet* of one and the same event. In fact, it is almost impossible to disentangle the issue of repeated temporality from a discussion of point of view in crime fiction, whose role has been briefly acknowledged in Chapter 3. What this section of the present chapter offers, therefore, is an examination of the various ways in which repetitive frequency can be employed in crime fiction. It will focus upon three works in particular that showcase especially effective uses of repetition, but that are nevertheless representative of the device's impact in the genre more broadly.

Timofeev's 'Murder and Suicide' is a story that has been discussed previously in this book, but it is one that provides an excellent example of how repetitive frequency can be used both to underscore the significance of certain events and to emphasize the professional competence of the detective. As noted earlier, the story records the narrator-investigator's efforts to understand the circumstances surrounding Marianna Bodresova's unsuccessful attempt to commit suicide. During the course of his investigation, not only does the detective uncover the story of a life blighted by innumerable acts of violence meted out to Marianna by members of her own family, but also that she has murdered her half-brother who is the father of her three children. Although this previously undiscovered murder comes to form the centre-piece of the narrator's investigation, it is not the only event in the *fabula* that is described on multiple occasions in the *siuzhet*. During the narrator's first conversation with Marianna, she reveals in direct speech that, in addition to her three illegitimate children, she also had another son who died when he was eight months old having caught a cold whilst he lay on the ground next to her as she washed clothes in a pond. A few pages later, in a longer and more detailed account of Marianna's life that is given in the voice of the narrator but informed by her perspective, the death of this infant son is reported again. On this occasion, the reader is told that the boy has been sired by Marianna's own father and that he dies after lying on damp linen as his mother, who has been banished to the back yard by her father, Grondzevskii, is doing the family washing during inclement weather. The fact of the boy's death is then narrated for a third time in a report of testimony that the investigator has gathered from witnesses in the village of Dereshi where Grondzevskii's estate is located. This time, the account is much more peremptory, because it is informed by the perspective of people who were not themselves participants in the drama. Nevertheless, the fact that this death is described on at least three occasions during the story, informed by a variety of voices and perspectives, means not only that it is established as a fact, but that the reader is left in no doubt as to the indelible trace that it imprints upon Marianna's life and her future recourse to violence.

As 'Murder and Suicide' develops, the judicial investigator is confronted by several unfurling and interlocking mysteries that need to be resolved. At the outset is the question of why Marianna has attempted to kill herself. Thereafter, and at a relatively early stage of this investigation, the detective becomes intrigued about why she refuses to reveal the identity of her children's father, either to them or to him. This question then becomes inextricably linked to the mystery surrounding the disappearance of Marianna's half-brother, Grondzevskii Jr, during the Polish insurrection in 1863. It is this disappearance, which the investigator discovers to be due to his murder at Marianna's hands, that constitutes the most significant event to be repeatedly narrated during the story. The first mention of it comes in the narrator's report of the witness testimony that he has gathered from villagers in Dereshi. They do not ascribe any particular importance to the disappearance, and there is no suggestion from the villagers that Grondzevskii Jr has fallen victim to a crime; they think it more likely he has just left the area following the insurrection. However, the narrator-investigator is already convinced that the disappearance is significant and so, during his next interrogation of Marianna, he provokes her by stating baldly that he believes her half-brother to be the father of her children. When she denies that this is the case, the investigator feigns belief in her words so as to tempt her into revealing more details. His approach pays dividends because, in direct speech, although Marianna claims not to know where Grondzevskii Jr is, she uses a particularly telling phrase to describe his disappearance and becomes the first to suggest that he might be dead. She says: 'пошел в мятеж, да с той поры — как в воду канул, видно где-нибудь убили его, а может куда и ушел' ('he went off to the rebellion and since then, it's as if he has sunk into water; he's evidently been killed somewhere, or perhaps has just gone off somewhere').[60] These words convince the investigator that Marianna harbours a considerable sense of guilt related to her half-brother, and that this sentiment is focused precisely on the fact of his disappearance. The third account of Grondzevskii Jr's disappearance comes when the narrator reports on his consultation of the official notes compiled during the military investigation that had previously been conducted into it. This written record provides an external and contemporary perspective on the case, informed by multiple witness accounts. The reports state that Grondzevskii made no secret of his intention to join up with a gang in the forest but that, when its members were arrested the following day, he was not with them and they claimed never to have seen him. The fourth account of this same event comes during the narrator's third interrogation of Marianna in response to his direct accusation that she has killed her half-brother on the night he leaves to join the rebellion. At this point, the passage of repeated temporality expands on the simple fact of the disappearance to describe first how Marianna plans her revenge on her half-brother for another particularly violent attack he has launched upon her and then enacts this plan by murdering him. Within her description, there are also other instances of repetitive frequency as the reader hears her confirm and elaborate upon details that have been previously narrated of how she is perturbed by her eldest son's questions about his father and about how she was often used as a bet in Grondzevskii Jr's card games, meaning that she was passed around various of his friends and acquaintances for their sexual gratification.

The repeated descriptions of Grondzevskii's disappearance, which eventually develop into an account of his murder by Marianna, serve a number of functions within 'Murder and Suicide'. Given that they emanate from a number of different sources (local witnesses, Marianna herself, military case notes, etc.), a strong sense of reliability emerges from the points of convergence between these various accounts. However, most significantly, the device serves to characterize the narrator's investigation as one that proceeds methodically and intelligently from one account to another of the same, centrally important event. His ability to 'read' Marianna and her reactions combines with a logical return to the question of Grondzevskii Jr's disappearance to solve a mystery that evaded the military commission and is initially still hidden at the moment of Marianna's suicide attempt. Repeated temporality plays a central role in satisfying the reader's curiosity about various of the story's mysteries by means of its piecemeal revelation of relevant information. Equally, though, it generates a certain degree of suspense by implying that the fact of the initially obscure disappearance of Grondzevskii Jr is a central element of Marianna's story and her crime.

Such repetition of one and the same event is employed to markedly different effect in Panov's *Three Courts* from 1876. The novella features a bipartite structure (it is divided into two parts entitled respectively 'The Human Court' and 'God's Court') and it is this construction that is a primary enabling factor in the exploitation of repetition. In a reflection of this overarching structure, this is a work in which duality, given various expressions, is the dominant motif. The murder of Elena Ruslanova subsequently reveals another, simultaneously committed crime: the theft of her tiara. The job of investigating these crimes is divided between the judicial investigator, who serves as the narrator, and his sidekick, the *syshchik* (detective), Kokorin. In spite of their concerted efforts, these detectives make a fundamental mistake in their investigation when they attribute both crimes to a single perpetrator when there are in fact two. Having identified Nikandr Petrovich Ichalov as the likely thief of the diamond tiara, and despite physical evidence speaking against him as the murderer, he is charged with both crimes. During the description of his trial at the end of the novella's first part, and just at the point at which he has been pronounced guilty of both crimes, the victim's friend, Anna Bobrova, appears in an agitated state and announces, in an act of brilliant drama, that she, in fact, is the murderer. So, the first part ends with the announcement of a new beginning: that of a re-investigation into the crime intended to corroborate Bobrova's confession. In something of a metatextual twist, both the narrator-investigator and the reader are thereby invited to perform an act of re-reading (and perhaps rewriting in the case of the former) of the first investigation into the crimes; and it is a re-reading that, whilst confirming the validity of one part of the case (the guilt of Ichalov in the theft of the tiara), indicates the mistakes and misreadings that have meant that Bobrova was not initially identified as the killer.

In the early part of the investigation, the moment of Elena's murder, preceded by an audible scream from her, is described from a number of different perspectives. The first report is provided by Kokorin, who visits the narrator late at night to announce the crime and to request that he come and investigate. Kokorin informs the investigator of what he knows of the case: in the midst of the dancing, Elena felt unwell and went to her room to freshen up; fewer than five minutes later a scream was heard and when people, including her fiancé, Petrovskii, went running to the noise, they found her dying on her couch with her throat slit. These same events, of Elena withdrawing and then a scream being heard, are then reported on two further occasions in the form of testimony from unidentified witnesses, conveyed by the narrator. They are subsequently narrated again in the reported speech of the soldier, Norbakh, who was dancing with Elena at the moment that she left the room. Finally, when the narrator comes to question Anna Bobrova, she declares in her direct speech that she remembers hearing Elena cry out but maintains that she has no memory of anything else. In spite of the fact that the event is narrated on multiple occasions from a variety of perspectives, all of these accounts remain only partial as no one claims to have more directly witnessed either the scream or the murder. As the narrator reports a little later: 'никто ничего не знал, и никого заподозрить свидетели не могли' ('nobody knew anything and the witnesses could not indicate any suspects').[61] However, the narrator-detective's own shortcomings in these early stages of the first investigation are implicitly indicated by an act of quasi-repeated temporality that he stages but does not follow through effectively. On this first night of the investigation, he asks the guests at the party, who have been ordered not to leave the house, to reassume their positions and activities as they were at the moment that the scream was heard. What this reconstruction demonstrates is that the person in closest proximity to Elena at the moment of her death was her friend, Anna Bobrova. Whilst not precisely an example of repetitive narration, this restaging nevertheless functions as a form of replication of events, and the narrator-investigator's fundamental mistake is not to follow sufficiently carefully the lead it gives him with regard to a suspect. Were he to have paid more attention to Anna Bobrova at this stage, he might have avoided the spectacle of his first investigation being entirely undone by her confession at Ichalov's trial.

The most original and influential use of repetitive frequency comes, however, in the second part of Panov's novella. As the narrator remarks, the second investigation into the murder of Elena Ruslanova involves an inversion of normal procedure: suspects are usually asked to prove their innocence, but in this instance, Anna Bobrova is asked to substantiate her claim to be guilty. The novella's second part is largely comprised of two acts of testimony, given in direct speech for the most part: the first from Anna Bobrova herself; and the second by Ichalov. Initially, Bobrova gives very few details of the murder, concentrating instead on the aftermath of the crime and how she hides in the neighbouring room and then faints at the sight of the victim. The narrator-investigator has to coax her into describing more fully the act of murder, but when she does so, her account contains not just important new information but also numerous instances of repetition of details that the reader has heard at least once previously. So, for example, we hear her describe how Elena entered her room having left the dancing, how she, Anna, reaches from behind to stab her repeatedly in the neck with a razor blade, and how Elena screams before dying. She describes how she throws both the blade and the tiara out of the window for Ichalov to pick up and dispose of. Crucially, the reader's impression here of the investigator is influenced by Anna's repeated criticism of him as a sub-par interpreter of the crime even during her re-telling of it. When he asks her, for instance, why she needed Ichalov to be present, she replies 'неужели вы так недогадливы, что вам все надо объяснять?' ('are you really so incapable of guessing that you need to have everything explained to you?').[62]

However, the narrator does, in the closing stages of the novella, demonstrate that he understands the value of repeated temporality. Following the close of Anna's testimony, he announces that her guilt will be proven beyond doubt if, the following day, Ichalov tells the same story of the night of the murder without having heard her version of events. And this is indeed what happens. While also giving further details related specifically to his courtship with Anna and of their movements on the day leading up to the fateful ball, his testimony focuses on and repeats many of the same details that she has previously provided and that have also been learned in the first part of the story. In spite of the limited perspective that his position on a ladder outside the window gives on the crime, he reports in considerable detail how he saw Anna move from a position behind Elena to slit her throat, how the victim then screams out, how she throws the razor and the tiara out of the window, how people come running towards the room before he manages to slide down the ladder out of sight. What the use of repeated temporality in this second part of the novella achieves, therefore, is the construction of a full and reliable story of the crime, in which all clues and evidence are accounted for and all motives are explained. In so doing, it offers up an exemplary reading of the crime in which the narrator-investigator plays an entirely passive role: he is, at this stage, merely a listener who does nothing more than prompt the retelling and record its details. Furthermore, the repetition in this second part makes clear the relative incompetence of the narrator during the first investigation, when he not only allowed evidence pointing to Ichalov's innocence of the murder to stand untested, but also paid no attention to the person indicated as a prime suspect by the reconstruction of the crime scene. It is crucial in this regard that, in contrast to Timofeev's story, none of the repetitions of the most significant events are given in the narrator's voice; the fact that they come in the voice of other intradiegetic characters implicitly indicates both his impotence and his incompetence.

The final example of the impact of repetitive frequency to be discussed here is provided by Akhsharumov's *And None Will Be the Wiser*. This novel is a relatively unconventional work, not least because it does not feature a professional detective figure. Rather, the circumstances surrounding the death of Olga Bodiagina are investigated informally by her cousin, the narrator, Cherezov. Much of the originality of *And None Will Be the Wiser*, as well as its effective use of repeated temporality, stems from the fact that Cherezov is only one of the work's two narrators, the other being the main suspect, Iuliia Shtevicha. The novel's structure is designed to extract maximum effect from these twin narrative voices: it is divided into three parts, with the first narrated only by Cherezov; the second described solely in the voice of Iuliia; and the third featuring sixteen chapters in which these two voices take turns to narrate. Although there is some repeated narration of events during the first part (such as of the visit by a mysterious Madame Vogel to Olga to counsel her on her marriage, as well as descriptions of the night of Olga's death), it is really in Parts Two and Three of the novel that the device makes its most striking impression. At the opening of Part Two, the identity of the new female narrative voice is not immediately revealed and so the temporal relationship (like all other relationships) between this part and Part One is not initially clear to the reader. Cast in the role of surrogate detective, it is up to the reader to piece together the (admittedly not terribly difficult) clues because there is no uninvolved narrative voice to do so. The first such clue comes at the close of the first chapter when this second narrator's marriage to Ksaverii Osipovich Shtevich is announced, a fact that gives her the same initials (Iu.Sh.) as the enigmatic stranger that Cherezov has met on the train to Moscow and to whom he is so attracted. More explicit is the revelation in the fourth chapter that, in spite of her marriage, she meets a man with whom she believes she is destined to have a romantic relationship. When he is revealed to be Pavel Ivanovich Bodiagin, Olga's husband, the reader is further encouraged to believe that this narrator is the woman that Cherezov has met on the train and whom he suspects of having visited his cousin and of having killed her. The timelines of the two parts of the novel first directly intersect in Part Two, Chapter 9 when this female narrator relates how she meets a man on a train as she is travelling home from seeing Olga. This description is an unmistakeable example of repeated temporality as it reproduces Cherezov's earlier account of the same encounter. Thereafter, in the following chapter, the second narrator, Iuliia, recounts in some detail the meetings that she has with Olga during her first visit when she presents herself falsely as a distant relative of Pavel Bodiagin, Madame Vogel; and the reader again recognizes these as a repetition of the description previously given by Cherezov. In the twelfth chapter, Iuliia relates the aftermath of the crime and her fears that she is going to be caught at any moment. It is here that the primary effect of the repeated temporality in Akhsharumov's novel begins to make itself felt: combined with the alternation of narrative perspective between Cherezov and Iuliia, this repetitive frequency places the reader in a position of superior knowledge relative to the fictional characters. Thanks to Cherezov's account in the first part, the reader can be entirely confident that Iuliia will escape the crime scene successfully because s/he knows that no suspect has ever been apprehended for Olga's murder. The reader's confidence when reading about the escape after the fact stands in stark contrast to the almost crippling fear experienced by Iuliia at the time of the action.

This sense of superiority on the part of the reader, deriving precisely from the exploitation of repeated narration, endures through much of the third part of the novella as well. Each chapter in turn features significant passages of repetition of events that have previously been related by the narrative voice in the preceding chapter. So, for example, the opening chapter of Part Three, voiced by Cherezov, gives details of the marriage between Iuliia and Olga's widower, Bodiagin, as well as the birth of their daughter, that she herself has recounted in the closing chapter of Part Two. In Part Three, Chapter 2, Iuliia not only describes her past encounter with Cherezov on the train once more, but also gives an account of how they met again at a party, an encounter of which the reader is already aware thanks to Cherezov's account in the first chapter. Each subsequent chapter, at least in part, provides a depiction of a period of time, and of its constituent events, that has already been accounted for from the other narrator's perspective in the preceding chapter. The significance of the reader's superior knowledge during this third part of the novel is related, on the one hand, to the fact that, whilst Cherezov now begins to doubt Iuliia's involvement in Olga's death, the reader knows it to be the truth thanks to her narration in Part Two; and, on the other hand, to the fact that Iuliia is not sure either whether Cherezov recognizes her from their first meeting (as the reader knows he does) or about the nature of his intentions towards her (about which the reader is far less certain). As a consequence, the reader is implicitly invited to criticize Cherezov's credulity and emotional weakness as he allows himself to be seduced by Iuliia as part of her plan to avoid being accused by him of the murder. Simultaneously, the reader's repeated exposure to different accounts of the same events forces him/her to experience both sympathy and antipathy towards

Iuliia as her actions are shown to be sometimes calculated and sometimes more spontaneous.

What makes Akhsharumov's novel particularly fascinating is the fact that the sense of superiority it encourages in the reader by means of its use of repetitive frequency and switches in point of view ultimately proves to be entirely illusory. Depending upon which voice is to the fore, the reader is persuaded by the presence of repetition to expect either that Cherezov is going to secure a confession from Iuliia and 'solve' the crime, or that Iuliia will succeed in persuading an enamoured Cherezov to absolve her of her guilt and allow her to remain free. In fact, neither of these two scenarios comes to pass as the malevolent figure of Olga's widow, Bodiagin, emerges from the shadows, first to have Iuliia declared insane and confined to her room and then to murder Cherezov by stabbing him repeatedly. Therefore, although Iuliia technically remains unpunished for the murder, her account of how her daughter slowly wastes away and dies soon after Cherezov, and of how, at the moment of the girl's death, she imagines seeing Olga taking her daughter away from her clearly demonstrates how she continues to be profoundly affected by her guilt. Crucially, although the sustained use of repeated temporality in the novel's third part has enabled the reader to have advance knowledge of many of the events described in one or other account, the withdrawal of Cherezov's voice at the close of Chapter 15 leaves the reader entirely incapable of predicting his murder. Moreover, the fact that the narrative depends on two points of view, both of which are external to the consciousness of Bodiagin, ensures that these two characters and the reader are in a position of significant inferiority when it comes to understanding and foreseeing his behaviour and actions. The sense of predictability of action promoted by the sustained use of repetitive frequency in the novel is thus shown to have functioned as an extremely effective red herring. The reader's shock at the dénouement is exacerbated by the fact that the temporal device has, until very close to the end of the narrative, encouraged a belief in his/her superiority vis-à-vis the intradiegetic characters.

## Duration: Crime Fiction's Use of 'Summary' and 'Scene'

Genette argues that the difficulties posed by written literature to the notion of the 'time of the narrative'[63] make themselves most keenly felt in relation to the category of duration. Even though he recognizes that it is an abstraction to talk about the duration of a literary narrative *per se*, Genette argues that it is nevertheless possible to posit that a temporal relationship exists between *fabula* duration and *siuzhet* duration. He proposes that the question of duration can be most easily considered in terms of 'speed', by which term is intended:

> the relationship between a temporal dimension and a spatial dimension [...] the speed of a narrative will be defined by the relationship between a duration (that of the story, measured in seconds, minutes, hours, days, months and years) and a length (that of the text, measured in lines and in pages).[64]

In considering the aspect of duration in a text, he claims, the reader will have in mind a hypothetic degree-zero text (that cannot exist in actuality) in which the relationship between the duration of the *fabula* and the length of the *siuzhet* would be constantly steady. Genette proposes four categories of what he calls 'narrative movement' or duration: (i) pause, where there is a passage (often of description) in the *siuzhet* that does not actually refer to an element of the *fabula*; (ii) scene, where the duration of the *siuzhet* is the 'same' as the duration of the *fabula*; (iii) summary, where the duration of the *siuzhet* is less than the duration of the *fabula*; and (iv) ellipsis, where there is an event of some duration in the *fabula* but which is passed over completely in the *siuzhet*. Although it is possible to argue that each of these 'movements' makes a notable contribution to the effect of crime fiction, discussion here will be largely restricted to the categories of 'scene' and 'ellipsis' as producing the greatest impact.

There is a significant sense in which, just as in other literary genres, the exploitation of 'scene' and 'summary' in Russian crime fiction is implicitly linked to the importance that the narrative wishes to ascribe to particular events. Predictably, those events that are deemed to be relatively less important tend to get summarized whilst those that carry greater significance are given more time and space by means of a scene-type treatment. Looking back to the discussion of analepsis earlier in this chapter, it is obvious that the long temporal reach that features in many Russian crime narratives carries with it the necessity to employ a good deal of summary. So, for example, in Sokolova's *The Song Has Been Sung*, although it occupies a not insignificant portion of the text, the narrator's account of Osinskii's relationship with his second wife, Rozaliia, and the reaction to it of his daughter, Bella, is still given in summary form. Far less space in the text is devoted to the years covered by this part of the *fabula* than to the months over which the narrator's direct acquaintance with the family occurs and the story of Bazhlanov's murder unfolds. Similarly, in Zarin's 'The Fourth Man', Sanin's account of Vera's marriage and his subsequent love affair with her is condensed into just two of the story's thirty-seven pages, whilst the investigation of the murder which takes no more than a couple of weeks occupies the remainder. The use of summary is not restricted to analeptic accounts of the past, however. It is also quite possible for elements of the 'present' time of the investigation to be treated in a similar fashion. This is the case, for example, in Panov's *Three Courts*, when the narrator-investigator informs the reader at the end of the second chapter that he has interviewed seventy-two witnesses over the course of one day and that their testimony has revealed absolutely nothing.[65] Indeed, the use of summary is a necessary element of almost all crime fiction narratives, where there is usually not the space to record each and every action with the same equivalence between story time and narrative time. Nevertheless, it remains instructive to consider which events or episodes are treated in summary and which are lent greater temporal equivalence (and arguably, significance) through the use of scene.

The use of scene duration in crime fiction is particularly worthy of note because of the influence it exerts over the suspense experienced by the reader. As Genette remarks in *Narrative Discourse*, 'the contrast between detailed scene and summary

almost always reflect[s] a contrast of content between dramatic and nondramatic'.[66]
The previous chapter has discussed the pre-eminent position granted in Russian
crime fiction to direct speech and dialogue, narrative forms that are obviously
closely aligned with scenic duration. As we have noted in that discussion, it is
frequently the case that such exchanges boast the essential discovery or revelation
in the criminal investigation, including the all-important direct confession of
guilt. The 'real-time' recording of the to-and-fro between the participants in such
passages of dialogue (or in the face-to-face confrontations also discussed) emphasizes
the game of cat and mouse between investigator and suspect and, consequently,
increases the reader's sense of suspense about the possible outcome. However, as
the following examples will demonstrate, the use of scene in literary narrative is
by no means restricted to the presentation of dialogue. Part One of Dostoevskii's
*Crime and Punishment*, for instance, provides a number of illustrations of the effects
to which a quasi-equivalence between story time and narrative time can be put.
This device is to the fore, for instance, in the opening chapter of the novel during
the description of how Raskolnikov carries out a dress-rehearsal visit to his victim,
the pawnbroker Aliona Ivanovna. The account of Raskolnikov leaving his lodgings
and heading towards the K___ bridge features moments of scene, such as in the
access to the protagonist's thoughts as he mulls over his actions, but also passages
of summary as he covers the 700 or so steps between his and Aliona's apartment.
However, once he arrives at the building itself, the pace of the narrative decelerates
and becomes more sustainedly scene-like as Raskolnikov is described climbing
the stairs to the fourth floor and ringing at her door. The visual perspective is
aligned closely with the protagonist here, and the fact that his progress through
the building is marked by an acute degree of observation ensures that the reader
has the impression of narrative time equating with story time. The description of
the appearance of the back stairs, the porters carrying furniture out of the other
fourth-floor apartment and Raskolnikov ringing the bell are imbued with a level
of detail that corresponds to the time that the protagonist would have taken to
observe them. Moreover, the provision of access to Raskolnikov's inner thoughts
as he considers how scared he might be if he ever decided actually to commit 'the
thing', as well as of the implications of the German civil servant moving out of the
neighbouring apartment, reinforces the sense of the appropriate amount of time
elapsing in the *siuzhet* to correspond to the actions in the *fabula*. This scene-type
pacing continues throughout the description of Raskolnikov's time in Aliona's
apartment, aided by the inclusion of the direct dialogue between them as he pawns
his father's watch. The use of this type of narrative 'movement' at this stage of the
novel makes a crucial contribution to the reader's sense of anticipation and suspense
as s/he considers what it is that Raskolnikov intends to do and whether he will
go through with it. It implicitly underscores the sense of Raskolnikov as a careful
planner, but also as a man filled with fear at his potential act and utterly preoccupied
by the present moment as it unfolds.

A further example of scene pacing comes in the final chapter of the novel's first
part in the description of how Raskolnikov executes his double murder. The visual

and emotional perspective during this scene is located very close to that of the main protagonist, but the use of scene presentation makes a similarly significant contribution to the reader's impressions during these passages. Raskolnikov's act of striking Aliona Ivanovna twice with the butt of the axe on the crown of her head is described in considerable detail, for instance. The reader is told that the first blow is dealt 'почти без усилия, почти машинально' ('almost effortlessly, almost mechanically') and the temporal gap between this first attack and the second strike is filled with details of the appearance of her hair: 'по обыкновению жирно смазанные маслом, были заплетены в крысиную косичку и подобраны под осколок роговой гребенки, торчавшей на ее затылке' ('thickly greased as usual, [it] was plaited in a pigtail and tucked up with a fragment of a tortoiseshell comb, which stuck out from the back of her head').[67] The second blow is followed by a description of how 'кровь хлынула, как из опрокинутого стакана и тело повалилось навзничь' ('blood poured out, as from a toppled glass, and the body fell back'). The inclusion of such detailed descriptions, as if in extremely close-up focus, and the time it takes the reader to read them ensures considerable equivalence between narrative and story time. The more obvious shift to focalization internal to Raskolnikov (and the inclusion of some free indirect speech) in the account of how he then goes off into the bedroom to try to unlock drawers containing other pawned items further underscores the use of scene here. The reader is told how Raskolnikov struggles to cut through the string with which a purse is tied around Aliona's neck, how he opens a box with a red morocco leather lid and stuffs its varied contents into his pockets, and the anxiety that permeates these descriptions is a consequence of equivalent or scene pacing. The device has arguably its greatest impact in the account of how Raskolnikov hears a voice from the other room, runs in to find Lizaveta standing over the body of her murdered sister and then rushes at her, striking her in the forehead with the axe. The inclusion here of details of how she quivers, half-raises a hand, fails to scream, backs into a corner, of how her lips twist and how she 'только чуть-чуть приподняла свою свободную левую руку, далеко не до лица, и медленно протянула ее к нему вперед, как бы отстраняя его' ('just lifted her free left arm an inch or two, nowhere near her face, and slowly held it out towards him, as if pushing him away')[68] ensure that the reader has the sense of experiencing the horrific scene at the same pace as both perpetrator and victim. This use of scene, coupled with the point of view so closely associated with that of Raskolnikov, ensures that the reader reacts with a significant sense of horror to the specific way in which the murders are committed. Moreover, as this pacing is maintained through the description of Raskolnikov's tortuous efforts to leave the apartment building without being apprehended, the reader also feels a strong sense of suspense and fear.

Antropov's 1908 story 'White and Turtle Doves', which has been briefly mentioned above, provides a quite different, but equally effective example of the impact of scene pacing. The story forms something of a pair with another of his stories, 'Kiss of the Bronze Virgin', because both feature an investigation by the detective, Putilin, into the disappearance of a man at the hands of the church. In

'White and Turtle Doves', the case begins when Putilin is visited by the millionaire Vakhrushinskii Sr who presents a letter from his son in which Vakhrushinskii Jr claims to have joined the church and to have taken 80,000 roubles with him for the service of God. The father is deeply suspicious of the truth of the letter's contents and pleads with Putilin to look into the disappearance. Like many of Antropov's Putilin stories, this one is narrated by Putilin's friend, doctor Z, who often accompanies him on his cases to lend a hand. However, just as the description of the climactic scenes in 'White and Turtle Doves' is about to begin, this narrator informs the reader that he will continue his account temporarily in the words and voice of Putilin, who has informed him of the events to which he was not himself directly privy. This shift in both voice and point of view is accompanied by a crucial switch to scene-type presentation during the account of how Putilin disguises himself and then enters a large house in Moscow using a memorized password, before descending into a subterranean room that he believes is key to the case. As Putilin describes in detail how he negotiates the labyrinthine path into this room and how he then, from his position hidden under a table, sees numerous members of a religious sect dressed in long white robes become increasingly deranged until the scene descends into an orgy, a far greater equivalence of pace between story time and narrative time is introduced than has been the case up until this point. Putilin describes:

> Страшная комната задрожала. Отрывочные слова песни, ужасная топотня голых ног о пол, шелестение в воздухе подолов рубах, свист мелькавших в воздухе платков и полотенец — все это образовало один нестройный, страшный, адский концерт. Казалось, в одном из кругов ада дьяволы и дьяволицы справляют свой бесовский праздник.
> — Ах, Дух! ай Дух! царь Дух! Бог дух! — гремели одни.
> — О, Ега! О, Ега! Гоп-та! — исступленно кричали другие.[69]

> [The terrifying room began to shake. Disjointed words from a song; the awful tread of bare feet against the floor; the rustling of sleeve hems in the air; the whistle of capes and towels that flitted in the air — all of this formed a single discordant, fearful, diabolical concert. It seemed as though, in one of the circles of Hell, the he- and she-devils were celebrating their demonic holiday.
> 'Ah, Spirit! Oh, Spirit! Lord Spirit! God Spirit!', railed some.
> 'Oh, Ega! Oh, Ega! Gop-ta!', raved others.]

The equivalence between story time and narrative time is achieved here not simply by the inclusion of acts of direct speech, but also by the use of relatively succinct clauses, strong punctuation and the insertion of multiple adjectives and adverbs to describe single objects or actions.

In the next, and final, chapter of the story, this scene speed is again to the fore as the narrative voice and perspective switches back to doctor Z in the description of how, the next day, he and Putilin enter a bathhouse in the garden of a nearby property and conceal themselves under one of the shelves so as not to be seen. The combination here of a restricted visual point of view and the scene pace ensures that the reader experiences a strong sense of anticipation and fear as the events that unfold are recounted. The narrator and Putilin observe how the door opens to the sound of an old voice singing about killing, hell and cutting and they then see how Vakhrushinskii's old servant, Prokl Onufrievich, who has previously been identified as a member of the Skoptsy sect, leads the abducted man into the bathhouse and prepares to castrate him with a heated knife. The direct inclusion in the text of the four-line song, as well as the acts of speech of both Onufrievich and Vakhrushinskii, in addition to the detailed description of the layout of the room and of how the servant slowly approaches his victim, all serve to decelerate the pace of the narrative, whilst simultaneously injecting considerable drama. As the young Vakhrushinskii repeatedly cries out for salvation, and the old servant tells him that no one other than Christ can save him, Putilin suddenly jumps out from his hiding place 'быстрее молнии' ('quicker than lightning') and announces, 'я спасу!' ('I'll save you!').[70] Scenes such as these contrast markedly with the various summaries that the narrator provides of Putilin's actions, particularly at moments when the detective has just returned from periods of absence from the doctor as he investigates the case. Whilst such summaries give the reader a sense of being somewhat distanced from elements of Putilin's detective work, the repeated use of scene pacing at moments of dramatic climax ensure that s/he feels much more directly involved when matters are at their most thrilling. The use of dialogue and the detailed enumeration of actions in such passages are an effective means of introducing suspense by drawing out the descriptions in the narrative to an equivalence of story time. Combined with the shift to a restricted point of view, the use of scene during these passages gives the reader the sense of experiencing the drama not only from the same point of view, but also at the same tempo, as the characters in the text.

## Filling in the Blanks: Ellipsis

In spite of the validity of Porter's claim, cited in both Chapter 3 and at the head of this chapter, that crime fiction is a genre committed to closing the 'logico-temporal gap' that lies at its heart, the reader encounters plenty of occasions in such texts where smaller gaps in the timeline of the narrative are either introduced or allowed to persist. That is, as per Genette's definition of ellipsis, there are events in the *fabula* that take up a certain amount of time to which no time at all is dedicated in the *siuzhet*. In crime fiction, these ellipses may relate to the 'past' story of the crime or to the 'present' story of the investigation and can, therefore, borrowing Sternberg and Segal's terminology, be referred to as either 'curiosity gaps' or 'suspense gaps'. It is important to make clear, however, that, whilst Sternberg and Segal's gaps can be generated in a number of different ways, following Genette, the term 'ellipsis' is employed here to refer only to gaps in time. Such temporal ellipsis needs to be distinguished from what Genette refers to as 'paralipsis', in which the moment in time is not skipped over, but sidestepped somehow.[71] Such 'paralipsis', particularly achieved through the manipulation of point of view, is what critics such as Sternberg and Segal primarily have in mind when they talk about the generation of gaps in crime fiction. And this device unquestionably has an important role to play in the modulation of the reader's curiosity and suspense. So, for example, in Zarin's story 'The Missing Worker', where a railway worker responsible for delivering the money used to pay the company's employees suddenly disappears, the heterodiegetic narrator frequently describes the detective, Patmosov, carrying out certain actions but fails to provide the reader with full information either about why he does so or what conclusions he draws from them. Although theoretically this narrator does have access to Patmosov's inner thoughts, he chooses not to exercise this privilege on repeated occasions. In Chapter 4 of the short story, for instance, Patmosov is said to inspect a trunk carefully and then squat down beside it before letting out a whistle; however, the narrator opts not to reveal either what he sees or what he thinks, leaving the reader at a loss to know what of interest the detective has observed and why it prompts this reaction. Similarly, when Patmosov later asks for a metal probe to be made for him and disappears into the cellar with it for half an hour, the reader is not told what he does with the tool because the narrative point of view does not accompany him during this time. The lack of full disclosure about the detective's actions and motivations here creates an epistemic gap that generates suspense for the reader. However, in instances such as these, the gaps do not arise because of lacunae in the timeline of the narrative but due to the effective manipulation of point of view. They are not, therefore, examples of temporal ellipsis.

One significant, and nationally specific, use to which actual temporal ellipsis is put in Russian crime fiction is the provision of codas or postscripts at the end of works. These postscripts are most often included either to provide details about the outcome of the criminal trial that results from the detective's investigation, or to describe the post-crime or post-conviction life of criminals and/or victims when the investigator returns to the location of the action after a period of time. Timofeev is a particular fan of such codas, for instance. In 'Murder and Suicide', the penultimate paragraph of the story begins 'прошел год' ('a year passed') and proceeds to describe how Marianna's former boyfriend, Stepan, is now living in a new house close to where she is buried, and is caring for her three children. Meanwhile, in his story 'Three Lives', where Lidiia Pogozheva has apparently inexplicably drowned herself in a lake, the narrator returns by chance to the family estate some six years after the case. He learns that Masha, the servant who was seduced by Lidiia's husband and who provided the clue that unlocked the mystery of the suicide, has 'buried herself alive' in a monastery.[72] He also discovers that Lidiia's widower, the third figure implied by the title, is now held in a mental asylum in which he is likely to spend the remainder of his life, enjoying only infrequent moments of clarity in his thoughts. So, although the coda provides the reader with information about these characters' fates, not all of the intervening period between the suicide and this visit is provided in the *siuzhet*. In his story 'The Married Woman', which appears in the same collection and deals with a woman's inadvertent poisoning of her husband, following a line break in the text, the penultimate section of the story begins 'месяца четыре спустя' ('about four months later') and provides details of the trial of Irina and her abusive father-in-law Pankratov, for whom the poison was intended. There is then another temporal ellipsis before the final section opens 'спустя около года' ('about a year later') to describe how much happier a now pregnant Irina and her husband are when the judicial investigator meets them again.[73] The lack of details regarding the intervening periods implies that, even after considerable suffering, life goes on and that, thanks to the efforts of the investigator and the jury during the trial, justice in this case has been done. Similarly, in Zarin's 'The Fourth Man', the final paragraph of the story is typographically separated off from the remainder of the narrative and relates how 'two years later' Vera Andreevna's husband dies and she and her son travel to Siberia to join Sanin in his exile. In none of these cases is any information given about the events that have occurred in the missing periods of time. The year or two (or whatever period has elapsed), is given no textual representation and they simply stand as an ellipsis in the narrative. Although the presentation of such gaps is not related to the mystery of the crime or to the conduct of the criminal investigation, their effect should not be underestimated. Their inclusion as part of the provision of information from the subsequent timeline of the story serves to underscore the humanity and sense of responsibility that is demonstrated by the judicial investigators and that has been commented upon in Chapter 2. For these men, the story of the victims and perpetrators frequently does not end with the securing of a confession or the uncovering of a culprit. There are lives still to be lived, and the investigators demonstrate, by means of this use of ellipsis, a continued interest in the fates of those with whom they have been involved.

The inclusion of such instances of temporal ellipsis in the form of postscripts responds to the reader's perceived curiosity about the continuation of the story after the resolution of the central mystery. However, in terms of an effect upon the reader, it is rather examples of ellipsis encountered prior to this peak moment of resolution that are most powerful. Panov's novella *The Harvest Gathering* provides an excellent demonstration of how temporal ellipsis can be employed to increase the reader's sense of suspense regarding the future course of the investigation. The work depicts how something of a power struggle develops between the narrator and the judicial investigator, with the former convinced, particularly in the second part of the work, that his friend is adopting the wrong approach to trying to unmask the culprits in the death of Sinitsyn. His own idea, which is initially dismissed as being akin to 'something out of a novel', is to stage what he refers to as a 'coup d'état'. At the close of the seventh chapter, the judicial investigator eventually asks the narrator to outline what he has in mind, and the following chapter opens with the statement 'я ему рассказал' ('I told him').[74] However, instead of this declaration then being followed by an account of the details that the narrator gives of his plan, the very next line simply states: 'Иван Герасимович улыбнулся' ('Ivan Gerasimovich smiled'). It is clear therefore that, the space between these two lines, which provides no explicit acknowledgement of a time lapse, is precisely the period during which the narrator's explanation took place. Here, then, is a clear example of a significant passage of time in the *fabula* receiving no representation or space in the *siuzhet*. Supplementing, therefore, the central mystery of the identity of the culprit(s) in the murder of Sinitsyn, comes the question of what it is that the narrator and detective have devised to try to extract a confession and of how it is going to play out. The use of temporal ellipsis here not only means that the reader is kept in the dark, and denied information possessed by the narrator and the detective, but that s/he is placed in a position comparable to that of the suspects in the case. Although s/he is party to the description of the preparations for the 'coup d'état' in a way denied to these characters, it is nevertheless the case that the eventual revelation of the scene of confrontation produces a much stronger effect because of the previous use of ellipsis and the consequently missing information.

In Zarin's *V poiskakh ubiitsy* (*In Search of a Murderer*), a novel published in 1915, temporal ellipsis is used repeatedly to prevent the reader from gaining a full picture of the actions of the protagonist, Grigorii Vladimirovich Chemizov, and, therefore, from deciding whether or not he should be considered to be a criminal. The novel opens with the grotesque image of a dog unearthing part of a dismembered body from a rubbish dump and taking it home to gnaw under a kitchen table. What Patmosov's investigation discovers is that the body belongs to Berta Eduardovna Shvartzmann who has been murdered by her love rival Stefaniia Kazimorovna Plintusa. However, this plotline is intersected and complicated by another, simultaneously less abject but somehow more intriguing, that involves the seemingly nefarious control that Chemizov exerts over two women. In Chapter 11, the narrative point of view is aligned with the female protagonist, Elena Semenovna Diakova, as she receives a visit from Chemizov. Although there are repeated hints in the text that Chemizov might have hypnotized Diakova, these are never definitively confirmed by the narrator as fact. In the account of this particular visit, the narrator describes how: 'Дьякова упала в кресло. Голова ее кружилась, губы улыбались; ей казалось, что в вихре страсти она теряет сознание' ('Diakova fell into an armchair. Her head was spinning and her lips were smiling. It seemed to her, that in the swirl of passion she was losing consciousness').[75] It is at this point that a period of temporal ellipsis is introduced into the narrative as the time between this bout of faintness and Chemizov's departure from her apartment goes entirely undescribed. Although the subsequent illustration of how Chemizov takes bank notes out of his pocket suggests that he might have just stolen from Diakova, this suspicion cannot be confirmed because of the missing period of time. Moreover, although subsequent information in the work does prove that Chemizov has been exerting a criminal influence over Diakova, this temporal gap is never filled and so the particular suspicion of theft is never clarified. This information blank is the consequence of an effective combination of point of view and temporal ellipsis that magnifies the reader's sense of being unable to judge the character and conduct of Chemizov reliably.

The work of Antropov shares a number of similarities with that of Zarin, and the withholding of information in order to generate suspense about the detective's actions and knowledge is a particularly notable one. In Antropov's story 'Kiss of the Bronze Virgin', for example, as has been discussed in Chapter 2, the narrator inserts a temporal ellipsis that covers the period of his and Putilin's first night in Warsaw. The reader is informed that the detective returns to the room he shares with the narrator at six o'clock in the morning, but no description of what happens during the hours of the preceding night is provided. The reader's sense of suspense derives from the fact that, having returned, Putilin states that he now knows where the victim, Rzhevuskii, is being held and that he needs to be rescued at once, but refuses to elaborate on this claim or how he came by the information. Again, then, the effectiveness of a combination of point of view and temporal ellipsis is apparent. As a character within the diegesis, the narrator-doctor does not have access to Putilin's inner thoughts and so is not in a position to reveal to the reader what it is that the detective has discovered. Putilin's own reticence, taken together with the narrator's inability to provide an account of the hours that have elapsed, leaves the reader without the answers to address the epistemic gap. The use of such temporal ellipsis serves, as in the example from Panov's *The Harvest Gathering*, to place the fictional detective in a position of considerable authority over the reader. There is no level interpretive playing field here; the reader not only has to 'read' the facts of the crime but is also left to try to guess what it is that the detective has been up to and what he has discovered. Temporal ellipsis used in this way becomes, therefore, like prolepsis, an effective means of encouraging the reader to continue reading in the hope that the text will ultimately reveal the answers to his/her questions.

By way of contrast, Sokolova's *The Song Has Been Sung* provides a striking example of how temporal ellipsis can be employed to provoke not suspense, but curiosity in the mind of the reader with regard to a past event. It is, of course, frequently the case in works of crime fiction that the period of time in the *fabula* during which the crime is committed is not immediately described in the *siuzhet*. The mystery that lies at the heart of the genre often arises precisely out of the fact that, whilst the circumstances leading up to the crime are described (often in analepsis) and its discovery and aftermath are accounted for, the actual moment of the crime is left, initially, as a blank. Sometimes, it is not simply a question of the events not being directly witnessed by anyone other than the (deceased) victim and the (unknown) perpetrator, but of the period of time during which the crime takes place being temporarily absent from the narrative. However, as stated in the first part of this chapter, the role of the fictional detective is not just to reorder chronologically jumbled events, but also to uncover and account for the missing period of time of the crime. Sokolova's novel is different, however. In it, the period of time covering the murder of Bazhlanov is presented as an ellipsis, but that ellipsis is never filled. It will be recalled that *The Song Has Been Sung* is an example of a text in which the murder has not yet been committed by the point in time at which the narrative opens. Rather, the narrator not only relates details of his acquaintance and conversations with the tutor Bazhlanov but also describes how, having been awoken one night by a banging window as he sleeps in the tutor's cottage, he hears whispers in the bushes below. The narrator then reports the emotionally charged conversation he overhears between a voice he recognizes as Bazhlanov's and another, which frequently sobs, but which he is unable to identify. From his restricted visual perspective, the narrator describes how the voices then fall silent and he returns to bed, before leaving for home at first light the following morning. However, as the narrator-investigator discovers a couple of days later when he is summoned to Osinskii's estate in great haste, Bazhlanov is found dead by gardeners on the very morning of this departure. The narrator then sets about questioning the various inhabitants and employees of the estate and collecting and comparing their testimony about events on the night of the murder. However, what a careful reading of the novel reveals is that none of these accounts actually cover the precise passage of time during which the murder has taken place. Just as the narrator lets the period between his return to bed in the cottage on the night in question and his departure the following morning pass entirely uncommented, so all the other inhabitants of the estate describe the period before and after, but never during, the crime. In fact, the reader's strong sense of curiosity provoked by this entirely absent time period mutates into frustration when, even though Osinskii's daughter, Bella, confesses to Bazhlanov's murder, she provides no account of the missing time period either. Thus, the temporal ellipsis that often initially exists in works of crime fiction but that is subsequently filled remains a permanent blank in Sokolova's novel. The investigator and the reader hear Bella confess to the murder, but she provides no details of the actual killing or of her motive for the crime. It is as if the crucial period of time has simply evaporated, never to be accounted for, leaving the investigator at a loss to explain what actually occurred during it, and the reader with a profound sense of exasperation. In this case, the temporal ellipsis is inextricably linked with Bella's refusal to account for her crime and satisfy the detective and the reader's curiosity. The ellipsis represents the missing piece of the puzzle that is the secret of the murder that Bella takes with her to her grave.

## Conclusion

In his article on 'Sherlock Holmes and the Mystery Story', Viktor Shklovskii claims that:

> A story may [...] be told in such a way that what is happening is incomprehensible to the reader. The 'mysteries' taking place in the story are only later resolved. [...] Characteristic of this second type of narration is temporal transposition. As a matter of fact, a single temporal transposition such as the omission of a particular incident and its appearance after the consequences of this incident have already been revealed is often quite sufficient to create such a mystery.[76]

What this fourth chapter has demonstrated, however, is that this claim, just like those regarding the way in which crime narratives move forwards and backwards in time, tells only a very partial story of the role played by temporal structures in the genre. The discussion here of the impact of a raft of different elements related to narrative temporal construction in crime fiction is more comprehensive than any attempted previously, certainly with regard to the Russian context. It has revealed the variety of different, sometimes seemingly contradictory, effects that they can create within the narrative text. Amongst the most significant discoveries offered by this chapter are the understanding achieved of the part played by passages of analepsis with considerable temporal reach in the construction of a sense of realism as well as in the expression of social criticism. Such analepsis not only points an accusatory finger at the various social pressures that have apparently made the crime in question inevitable, but also enters into dialogue with ideas about determinism that were popularly debated in the late Imperial era. The distinction between the relative reach of analepsis in the 'whydunit' and 'whodunit' models of Russian detective fiction is also meaningful for the poetics of the genre more broadly. The use of prolepsis, meanwhile, sees the more conventional past and present time lines of crime fiction supplemented by a sense of urgency about the future, not just of the investigation, but also of future crimes yet to be committed.

However, the mastery of various devices of temporal organization demonstrated here is perhaps most important for the reflections it provides about the textual, rather than extratextual, experience. Without exception, these various devices of time have impacted upon the sense of curiosity and suspense generated by the text with regard particularly to the search for epistemic knowledge. Analepsis fills in gaps in the back story, and prolepsis encourages anticipation about revelations to come from the future unravelling of the mystery. Moreover, the often complex relationship between various moments of the past, the present and the future serves to obfuscate the investigator's and the reader's access to the true and complete story of the crime. Similarly, repeated temporality can fragment and complicate the narrative of a crime, but it can also help to reconstruct a full and persuasive account of it, although, as in Panov's *Three Courts* not always in a manner that flatters the detective. Examples from writers as different as Dostoevskii and Antropov have demonstrated how effectively shifts in visual perspective can be combined with scene-type pace to achieve a sense of verisimilitude and heightened drama. However, what is most striking in this analysis is the influence that these temporal devices exert upon the reader's sense of superiority or inferiority vis-à-vis the intradiegetic characters. Repeated temporality can sometimes serve to encourage the reader to believe that he or she sits above fictional characters in the hierarchy of authority. However, as Akhsharumov's *And None Will Be the Wiser* has shown, the same technique can very quickly be exploited to deprive the reader of this sense. Ellipsis, by means of the gaps that it leaves in the narrative timeline, most frequently places the reader at a disadvantage in terms of the information that s/he possesses relative to intradiegetic characters or the narrator. Whatever the situation, however, these devices underscore the fundamental importance to the genre of the reader's sense of his/her access to knowledge, not just for its own sake but for the perception of authority it promotes relative to other figures in the diegesis.

## Notes to Chapter 4

1. Todorov, 'The Typology of Detective Fiction', p. 44.
2. Ibid., p. 44.
3. Ibid., p. 46.
4. Bennett, 'The Detective Story', p. 240.
5. Porter, *The Pursuit of Crime*, p. 29.
6. Sweeney, 'Locked Rooms', p. 4. Bennett makes a similar point in 'The Detective Story' when she states on pp. 244–45: 'Reconstruction of the missing narrative thus requires temporal

reordering and interpolation or extrapolation of missing narrative links. Many mysteries emphasise the detective's ability to perform exactly these acts of reconstruction in reaching his solution.'

7. Meir Sternberg, *Expositional Modes and Temporal Ordering in Fiction* (Baltimore, MD: The Johns Hopkins University Press, 1978), p. 159.

8. Ibid., p. 182.

9. Porter, *The Pursuit of Crime*, p. 31. Porter notes that similar notions have been suggested by Boris Tomashevskii ('bound and free motifs') as well as by Umberto Eco ('fundamental and incidental moves').

10. Ibid., p.41.

11. Ibid.

12. Sternberg, *Expositional Modes*, p. 161. Although Sternberg does not acknowledge it here, the relationship between these temporal shifts and Todorov's 'temporal inversions' is clear. Other retardatory means mentioned by Sternberg include the suspension of the expected ending, spatial shifts and authorial commentary.

13. Meir Sternberg, 'Telling in Time (II): Chronology, Teleology, Narrativity', *Poetics Today*, 13.3 (1992), 463–541 (p. 519).

14. Segal, 'Closure in Detective Fiction', p. 159.

15. Sternberg, 'Telling in Time (II)', pp. 524–26.

16. Segal, 'Closure in Detective Fiction', pp. 163–64.

17. Ibid., p. 176.

18. In fact, this temporal stance pertains in the vast majority of works of crime fiction, whatever their historical period or geographical provenance.

19. Akhsharumov's novel first appeared in serialized form in the journal *Otechestvennye zapiski* in three volumes, 10–12, in late 1872. The version I refer to for quotations is Moscow: Sovremennik, 1996.

20. Undetectable poison, in the form of curare, also features in Shkliarevskii's 'An Undiscovered Crime' from 1878. In contrast to that story, in Akhsharumov's *And None Will Be the Wiser*, Olga's death is considered to be a crime and there is an investigation; in contrast to 'A Secret Investigation', there is no satisfactory outcome.

21. Both this story and 'Ognennyi krest' ('The Burning Cross') are republished in the collection, R. L. Antropov, *Shef sysknoi politsii Sankt-Peterburga Ivan Dmitrievich Putilin (Sochineniia v dvukh tomakh)* (*The Head of the St Petersburg Detective Division, Ivan Dmitrievich Putilin (Collected Works in Two Volumes)*) (Moscow: Olma, 2003).

22. In stories belonging to this type, the early receipt of a written summons is a recurrent trope. The first action narrated in Antropov's 'Ognennyi krest' is the receipt by Putilin of a letter from a priest alleging either criminal or otherworldly activity in his monastery. Shkliarevskii's 'Samoubiitsa li ona?' ('Is She a Suicide?') opens with the delivery of a 'пакет' ('official document') that reports the crime, whilst in Timofeev's 'Murder and Suicide', the document announcing the crime of attempted suicide is accompanied by the arrival in the investigator's lodgings of the alleged perpetrator/victim herself.

23. Gérard Genette, *Narrative Discourse: An Essay in Method*, trans. by Jane E. Lewin (Ithaca, NY: Cornell University Press, 1980), p. 35.

24. Ibid., p. 40. Genette explains that he prefers these more neutral terms to those with a greater psychological connotation, such as 'anticipation' and 'retrospection'. This chapter will, however, make use of both sets of terms.

25. Porter, *The Pursuit of Crime*, p. 29.

26. Albert D. Hutter, 'Dreams, Transformations, and Literature: The Implications of Detective Fiction', in *The Poetics of Murder: Detective Fiction and Literary Theory*, ed. by Glenn W. Most and William M. Stowe (New York, NY: Harcourt Brace Jovanovich, 1983), pp. 230–51 (pp. 231–32). Originally published in *Victorian Studies*, 19.2 (1975), 181–209.

27. Atomanichenkov's story of his acquaintance with Kebmezakh at school is a good example of what Genette would label 'external analepsis', in which the flashback refers to a time entirely prior to the point in time at which the *siuzhet* has opened. Genette has two further categories

of reach: 'internal', where the analepsis refers to a point in time prior to the 'present' moment in the narrative, but after the point in time at which the *siuzhet* has opened; and 'mixed', where the analepsis denotes a time that is initially prior to that at which the *siuzhet* has opened, but stretches to beyond that point. Explanations and examples of these categories can be found on pp. 48–61 of *Narrative Discourse*.

28. Timofeev, *Zapiski sledovatelia*, pp. 273–74.
29. Sokolovskii, *Ostrog i zhizn'*, pp. 76–77.
30. Ibid., p. 80.
31. In the course of the investigation, the detective, Chubikov, makes one very brief reference to a similar-seeming case he worked on in 1870, fifteen years before the 'present' time of the story, and reminds one of the suspects that he has twice been sentenced for theft, in 1879 and 1882. However, these are both fleeting references that are not expanded and that relate only tangentially to the present investigation.
32. Sokolovskii, *Ostrog i zhizn'*, p. 148. The narrator reports that Chapurin comes from a relatively prosperous peasant family, but one that is strictly ruled over by his eighty-year-old grandfather who has little interest in him.
33. Shkliarevskii, *Rasskazy i povesti*, p. 121.
34. Dostoevskii, 'Sreda', in *Dnevnik pisatelia* (St Petersburg: Lenizdat, 1999), p. 17. The English translation is taken from *A Writer's Diary, Volume 1 1873–1876*, trans. by Kenneth Lantz (Evanston, IL: Northwestern University Press, 1997), p. 136.
35. Occasionally, a coda might be provided in the form of information about the outcome of a trial or the subsequent fates of the characters.
36. Panov, *Tri suda*, p. 17.
37. Timofeev, *Iz vospominanii sudebnogo sledovatelia*, p. 111.
38. Stepanov, *Pravye i vinovatye*, p. 131.
39. In 'The Detective Story as a Historical Source', Aydelotte argues: 'the reader does not generally compete intellectually with the detective. A detective story is not an invitation to intellectual exercise or exertion, not a puzzle to which the reader must guess the answer. On the contrary, the claim of detective stories to be puzzle literature is in large part a fraud, and the reader, far from attempting to solve the mystery himself, depends on the detective to do it for him.' (p. 317)
40. Timofeev, *Iz vospominanii sudebnogo sledovatelia*, p. 42.
41. Sokolovskii, *Ostrog i zhizn'*, pp. 75–76.
42. Panov, *Pomoch'*, p. 335.
43. Teresa Bridgeman, 'Time and Space', in *The Cambridge Companion to Narrative*, ed. by David Herman (Cambridge: Cambridge University Press), pp. 52–65 (p. 57).
44. *Iz vospominanii sudebnogo sledovatelia*, p. 95.
45. Shkliarevskii, 'Rasskaz sudebnogo sledovatelia', in *Chto pobudilo k ubiistvu?*, p. 91.
46. Zarin, *V poiskakh ubiitsy*, pp. 397 and 398.
47. Gary Saul Morson, *Narrative and Freedom: The Shadows of Time* (New Haven, CT: Yale University Press, 1994), p. 44.
48. Dostoevskii, *Prestuplenie i nakazanie*, p. 6/p. 6.
49. Ibid., p. 353/p. 407. The use of the future tense is more explicit in the original Russian quotation. Porfirii makes clear his concern for a time yet to come when he introduces his examples to Raskolnikov by saying: 'Ну, так вот вам, так сказать, и примерчик на будущее' ('Well, here's a little example, as it were, for the future [...])' (p. 352/p. 405).
50. Dianne Oenning Thompson, *The Brothers Karamazov and the Poetics of Memory* (Cambridge: Cambridge University Press, 1991), p. 212.
51. Maria Kanevskaia, 'Struktura detektivnogo siuzheta v "Brat'ia Karamazovykh"', *Russkaia literatura deviatnadtsatogo veka*, 1 (2002), 46–63 (p. 48).
52. Dostoevskii, *Brat'ia Karamazovy*, p. 342/p. 319.
53. Kanevskaia, 'Struktura', p. 52.
54. Morson, *Narrative and Freedom*, p. 45.
55. Shkliarevskii, 'Sekretnoe sledstvie', in *Chto pobudilo k ubiistvu?*, p. 160.

56. Ibid.
57. Stacy Burton, 'Bakhtin, Temporality and Modern Narrative: Writing "The Whole Triumphant Murderous Unstoppable Chute"', *Comparative Literature*, 48.1 (1996), 39–62.
58. Stepanov, *Pravye i vinovatye*, p. 70.
59. Genette, *Narrative Discourse*, p. 114.
60. Timofeev, *Zapiski sledovatelia*, p. 67. The fact that Grondzevskii's body is eventually found dumped at the bottom of a well retrospectively casts Marianna's description as a quasi-acknowledgement of the details of her crime.
61. Panov, *Tri suda*, p. 25.
62. Ibid., p. 142.
63. Genette, *Narrative Discourse*, p. 86.
64. Ibid., pp. 87–88.
65. Panov, *Tri suda*, p. 28.
66. Genette, *Narrative Discourse*, p. 109.
67. Dostoevskii, *Prestuplenie i nakazanie*, pp. 83/p. 94.
68. Ibid., p. 86/p. 98.
69. Antropov, *Shef sysknoi politsii Sankt-Peterburga Ivan Dmitrievich Putilin* II, pp. 63–64. The language used in places in the direct speech in the original resembles that of Old Church Slavonic liturgy.
70. Ibid., p. 69.
71. Genette, *Narrative Discourse*, p. 52.
72. Timofeev, *Iz vospominanii sudebnogo sledovatelia*, p. 65.
73. Ibid., p. 152.
74. Panov, *Pomoch'*, pp. 337–38.
75. Zarin, *V poiskakh ubiitsy*, p. 257.
76. Shklovskii, *Theory of Prose*, p. 101.

PART III

# Textual Games

# CHAPTER 5

# Textual Clues:
# Intertextuality and Metatextuality

The third and final part of this study turns its attention to what might broadly be labelled the more 'ludic' or playful aspects of late Imperial Russian crime fiction. The two chapters that comprise this section consider how works reflect upon themselves as literary texts, how they interact with a variety of other texts, and how they interrogate the conventions of the genre in search of originality and effect. As David Gascoigne notes, 'the act of reading can always, and quite usefully, be understood as play or interplay, delimited in time, between reader and text'.[1] This idea of play or gaming is particularly frequently linked with the genre of detective fiction. George N. Dove argues: 'Of the several analogies that have been used to account for the individuality of the detective story, the most common one is that of the tale of detection as play or game [...].'[2] The assumption of this association is revealed in certain of the titles selected for critical studies of the genre. For instance, the quotation used in Kathleen Belin Owen's chapter, '"The Game's Afoot": Predecessors and Pursuits of a Postmodern Detective Novel', picks up on a remark made by Sherlock Holmes to Dr Watson as they embark on an investigation in the 1904 story, *The Adventure of the Abbey Grange*. The very same phrase is used by Patricia Merivale and Susan Sweeney in the introductory chapter, 'The Game's Afoot: On the Trail of the Metaphysical Detective Story', to their 1999 edited collection, *Detecting Texts*.[3] However, as Marty Roth's 1995 monograph, *Foul and Fair Play: Reading Genre in Classic Detective Fiction*, makes clear, the positing of a relationship between detective fiction and game-playing is not restricted to postmodern iterations of the genre. Scholarly approaches that associate detective fiction and play most frequently refer to an analogy between the acts of reading and puzzle-solving. As R. Gordon Kelly notes in *Mystery Fiction and Modern Life*, 'such theories locate the appeal of the fiction in the battle of wits, conducted within the rules of fair play, between author and reader'.[4] And the various sets of rules for the genre elaborated in the early part of the twentieth century, by critics such as S. S. van Dine, are perhaps the most obvious expression of such a view. However, what this final part of the present monograph has in mind is a slightly different conception of the ludic where, as Gascoigne argues, it functions as 'one of the ways in which writing can be seen as reflecting on its own production'.[5]

Chapter 6 will examine the most acute expression of the tendency towards play by means of a reading of two parodies of detective fiction: Panov's *From the Life of a Provincial Town* and Chekhov's 'The Swedish Match'. Before that, however, this chapter discusses the various ways in which works of Russian crime fiction demonstrate an awareness of themselves as both linguistic constructs and literary artefacts, and the impact that these gestures have upon the reader's interpretation. Based on a reading of Poe's early detective stories, Sweeney is one of the critics to argue that detective fiction displays 'inherent self-reflexivity'.[6] With reference to the apartment depicted in 'The Murders in the Rue Morgue' where Madame L'Espanaye and her daughter are brutally killed, she contends:

> the locked room — with its imagery of enclosure and entrapment, and its reference only to elements within its own finite space — provides a perfect metaphor for the inherent self-reflexivity of the genre [...]. Detective fiction, with its streamlined structure, its emphasis on interpretation at all levels of plot and narration, and its peculiar focus on the relationship between writer and reader — represents narrativity in its purest form. [...] Indeed, in its formal elements, such as sequence, suspense, and closure, as well as in content, the detective story dramatizes the workings of narrative itself.[7]

Albeit with an eye more firmly fixed on detective fiction's relationship to realism, Peter Thoms echoes these remarks closely when he argues that: 'for the inventors and earliest practitioners of detective fiction, narrative is not what *is* — an unproblematic mirroring of events — but what *is made*, and that process of construction becomes the very subject of these works'.[8] What Sweeney's discussion of Poe and Thoms's examination of works including William Godwin's *Caleb Williams* (1794) and Charles Dickens' *Bleak House* (1853) demonstrate is that self-reflexivity has been inscribed into works of detective fiction since the very inception of the genre. This self-reflexivity can express itself in various ways. With regard to Poe, Sweeney identifies the interplay of different narrative levels as well as the presence of various embedded narratives as two possible manifestations. Other instances of the practice include the fact that, in 'The Murders in the Rue Morgue', Dupin and the narrator first meet in a library, that the detective is able to 'read' the narrator's mind as they walk through the streets together; that the story cites newspaper reports from the *Gazette des Tribunaux* about the double murder, and that, in all three of his detective stories, Poe repeatedly insists on the significance of language and human speech.[9] Similarly, Gaboriau's *Le Crime d'Orcival*, which was first serialized in 1866–67, contains numerous references to the theatre and role-playing, and includes at an early stage a long explanation from the detective, Monsieur Lecoq, about the similarities between the judicial process of an investigation and the writing and production of a play.[10] Moreover, the novel contains a substantial embedded narrative (occupying ten of the twenty-eight chapters) in the form of a manuscript co-authored by the victim and her first husband that provides the story of the origins of the crime in question. As a final example, Wilkie Collins's *The Moonstone* (1868) includes narratives from multiple different voices, including Betteredge, Bruff, Cuff and Blake, as well as extracts from Jennings's journal and the letter of Rosanna Spearman. Such heteroglossia prompts Thoms to claim that 'instead of attempting to obscure its own textuality, the novel self-consciously flaunts it, emphasizing how stories are carefully assembled for particular reasons'.[11]

In the Russian context, previous work has shown how self-reflexivity and play is a key facet of the writing of one of Russia's most popular contemporary crime fiction authors, Boris Akunin.[12] Although works from the late Imperial period do not demonstrate the same degree of metafictional irony that is deployed in Akunin's postmodern novels, they do nevertheless invite the reader into a network of intertextual references and metatextual reflections that enrich the reading experience. Chapter 1 of this monograph has established how the desire that early works of Russian crime fiction exhibit to straddle the boundary between fact and fiction implicitly speaks to a sense of themselves as textual constructs engaging with literary history. It has also argued that the presence of metatextual commentary, such as Sokolovskii's narrator's complaint about the inadequacy of language to render the experience of judicial investigators, contributes to an interpretation of the work as a literary-fictional text rather than a factual memoir. In the light of Sweeney's identification of narrative levels and embedded narratives as devices permitting self-reflexivity, it becomes possible to consider the exploitation of multiple voice and temporal organization that has been discussed in the previous two chapters as instances of the same practice. The approach in the present chapter, however, is to consider self-reflexivity in early Russian detective fiction in terms of three broad categories: narrative self-consciousness, intertextuality and, finally, metatextuality. The next section of the chapter discusses examples of narrator self-consciousness in terms of its role as a frequent precursor or adjunct to the practice of inter- and metatextuality. The following section turns its attention to examples of intertextuality in a variety of guises: reference to more canonical works of literature; nods to other works of detective fiction and their investigator figures; and the crucial intertext of newspapers. It considers the various ways in which such allusions encourage a reflection upon the status of the genre as well as on other facets of both literary production and judicial investigation. The chapter concludes with an analysis of the role of metatextuality, placing particular emphasis on the figural depiction of the investigator as both reader and writer, as well as on the performative power of language.

## Knowing Detectives: Self-consciousness in Russian Crime Fiction

Chapter 1 has illustrated how the figure of the narrator-investigator looms large in the earliest works of Russian crime fiction. Each of the narrators in the works by Sokolovskii, Stepanov and Timofeev demonstrates self-consciousness with regard to their role as a judicial investigator and provides passages of explicit reflection upon the nature of their professional duties. In fact, this readiness to discuss the functions and responsibilities of the judicial investigator is a feature shared by many examples of Russian crime fiction throughout this late Imperial period, including, amongst others, Shkliarevskii's 'How People Die', Panov's *Three Courts* and Sokolova's *The Song Has Been Sung*.[13] Where the earliest works are more unusual, however, is in their narrators' self-consciousness about their role specifically as storytellers. Such explicit discursive self-consciousness is a feature that does not endure beyond these first examples and so it is instructive to consider how it functions when it does appear, and to discuss why it does not establish itself as a more lasting trait.

Amongst the three earliest practitioners of Russian crime fiction discussed in Chapter 1, it is only the narrators in Sokolovskii and Timofeev who demonstrate self-consciousness as storytellers; Stepanov's narrator voices no such explicit self-awareness. In Timofeev's *Notes of an Investigator*, the investigator makes various metanarrational interventions in both the foreword and the main body of the text to reveal that he is cognizant of his role and responsibilities as a narrator. The voice in the foreword displays rather formulaic self-awareness as it offers an apologia for the account to come, arguing that it might be of use and interest to the field of Russian letters.[14] This overt reflection subsequently translates into a relatively elevated degree of explicit self-consciousness on the part of the narrator in the main body of the text. So, for example, in the opening chapter, 'First Impressions', as he travels to his first posting in the T*** district in western Russia, the narrator explains to the reader: 'описывать свои дорожные впечатления не буду: они слишком общим для того, чтобы быть интересными' ('I am not going to describe my impressions during the journey because they are too mundane to be of any interest').[15] A little later in the same chapter, following a proleptic digression to record the future retirement of the unfriendly German president of the local court, the narrator again nods to his role as a storyteller when he says: 'Возвращаюсь к своему прерванному рассказу' ('I'll get back to my interrupted story').[16] Ansgar Nünning identifies instances of analepsis and prolepsis, as seen here, as metanarrative utterances that not only lead to a higher degree of self-reflexivity but that also foreground the act of narrating.[17] Although such comments speak only obliquely to an awareness of the presence of a reader, Timofeev's collection also features numerous instances when this figure is more directly acknowledged or addressed. For example, in the story 'A Gang of Thieves', the narrator-investigator describes how, upon his arrival in a town, he moves immediately to question a recently-arrested man, Petr Podpletnevoi, who turns out to be the main suspect in the robbery of 4,000 roubles around which the narrative revolves. However, having announced this intention, the narrator then states: 'но прежде чем знакомить читателя с сущностью его показаний, я опишу его личность' ('but before informing the reader of the content of his testimony, I will first describe his appearance').[18] Later in the same story, the narrator indulges in another act of self-consciousness in order to point out to the reader the interpretive links that s/he should be making between elements of the plot. In describing the physical appearance of another character, Ivan, who is missing two teeth, the narrator justifies his suspicion about this man's acquaintance with the main suspect, and hence of his belonging to the gang of thieves, in the following terms: 'так как в записной книжке последнего были записаны, если припомнит читатель, чьи то приметы об отсутствии двух передних зубов' ('because in the notebook of [the main suspect] there was a note, if the reader remembers, about the absence of two front teeth as someone's distinguishing features').[19]

Although such moments of self-consciousness are relatively conventional here, in the efforts they make towards orienting the reader in the diegesis, they form something of a complement to the sense that these same early texts provide of their desire to familiarize the reader with the new, post-1860 judicial landscape. Whilst not as frequent, similar examples of narrator self-consciousness are to be found in Sokolovskii's *Prison and Life*. For example, towards the end of his first account of the story of the recidivist thief, Dragunov, in 'Unpleasant Moments', the narrator explicitly acknowledges a sense of his limitations as a storyteller, as well as a respect for his reader, when he says: 'Это история одного «преступника», вора. Сознаюсь, она неполна; я представил только голый остов ее, внешнюю сторону [...] Но недостающее предоставлю дополнить читателем' ('This is the story of one "criminal", a thief. I recognize that it is incomplete. I have presented only its naked form, its external appearance [...]. But I would suggest that the remainder can be filled in by the reader').[20] The self-consciousness here not only encourages the participation of an active reader but, like others of Sokolovskii's techniques, seeks to draw this figure more directly into the diegesis. It is crucial to underline the distinction that needs to be drawn here between self-consciousness/metanarration and metafictional practice. Although certain instances of metanarration might emphasize the fictionality of a situation or characters in the narrative, it is equally possible, Nünning argues, that, 'depending on the type and context, [it] can [...] support the illusion of authenticity created in a text and in the act of narration'.[21] This is certainly the case in Timofeev and Sokolovskii where the overt references made by the narrator either to his own role or to that of the reader do not point up fictionality but 'reinforce [the] claim to truth according to the convention of realism'.[22]

In spite of the model for overt self-consciousness established by Timofeev and Sokolovskii, Russian detective fiction proves to be reluctant to replicate it through its subsequent history. There are no examples of such explicit self-awareness of the storytelling role in the work of Stepanov, Popov, Dostoevskii, Panov, Sokolova or Zarin, for instance. It is also largely absent from the numerous detective stories written by Shkliarevskii, although there are a couple of exceptions, including 'Liudskoe uchastie: rasskaz sledovatelia' ('Human Involvement: An Investigator's Story') from 1872. The plot of this early work revolves around a case of double infanticide, where the perpetrator is the twins' mother, Liubov Nikolaevna Krasova, who is married to one man who does not love her but has conceived her children with another. The title of the story refers to the fact that Liubov's marriage to Vaskov, by whom she has previously been pregnant on two occasions, is forced upon both of them by the provincial 'high' society who think that they are doing a good deed but are actually just heaping more misery upon her. At the start of a brief six-line epilogue, the narrator makes the type of remark, which is both metanarrational and metafictional, that has been completely absent from the main body of the text. He states: 'Два слова к читателям. Все главные события этой истории не вымышлены авторы. Брак по приговору уголовной палаты был действительно совершен' ('A couple of words to my readers. None of the main events in this story have been dreamt up by the author. The marriage on the order of the local court did actually take place').[23] Fleeting metanarration also appears in the second part of Akhsharumov's *And None Will Be the Wiser*, when the female narrator, Iuliia, makes one very concise reference to her own narrative practice at the precise moment that she describes administering poison to her victim, Olga, saying 'все это длилось не дольше, чем я рассказываю' ('all of this took no longer than it takes me to narrate it').[24] Finally, although explicit self-consciousness is absent from the main body of Antropov's collection, *Genii russkogo syska I. D. Putilin: rasskazy o ego pokhozheniiakh* (*I. D. Putilin, a Genius of Russian Detection: Stories of his Adventures*), it does feature a highly conventional 'Predislovie avtora' ('Author's Foreword') that accounts for the stories' provenance. This narrative frame, which evokes memories of Romantic-era story cycles, features a collective narrative voice, 'мы', that describes a brief conversation between a group of friends and an unnamed 'старый престарый доктор' ('very elderly doctor'). This doctor explains that he had the honour of being a close friend and sometime associate of the now-deceased Ivan Dmitrievich Putilin.[25] In a remark that can be seen to link back to the claim made in Timofeev's much earlier foreword, the unnamed doctor justifies the value of his stories by saying:

> Мы, вот, русское общество, набрасываемся с какой-то лихорадочной страстностью на похождения всевозможных иноземных сыщиков, нередко существовавших лишь в фантазии господ романистов. А вот свое, родное, забываем, игнорируем. А между тем это родное будет куда позанимательнее иностранных чудес.[26]

> [We, that is Russian society, devour with passionate fervour the adventures of various foreign detectives, who are often merely the product of the writers' imaginations. Whilst at the same time, we forget and ignore our very own, native detectives. And yet these home-grown examples are probably far more entertaining than these foreign wonders.]

However, within the main body of the text, where the doctor acts as the narrator, there is no metanarrative commentary upon his role as storyteller or his responsibilities with regard to the reader.

Why should it be that metanarrative gestures are a feature in the early works of detective fiction by Timofeev and Sokolovskii but largely disappear in the subsequent development of the genre in Russia? The absence of such overt self-consciousness in many of the later works can be traced to what Monika Fludernik calls the conventional belief, espoused in much narrative theory, of the device as being 'especially intrusive and as puncturing the illusion of reality'.[27] Given that, during the period 1860–1900 especially, examples of detective fiction were appearing on a Russian literary scene dominated by works embodying a strong belief in various types of realism (critical, psychological, social, etc.), it is not surprising that they kept such potentially non-mimetic commentary to an absolute minimum. Nevertheless, as Fludernik states, building on work undertaken by Nünning, such self-consciousness need not disrupt the apparent realism of the fictional world; rather: 'the mediation level of narration even serves the purpose of creating a mimesis of the narrative process'. Fludernik elaborates:

> The level of mediation is in itself so realistic that the reader feels s/he is in direct communion with the narrator. This results in a build-up of trust between reader and narrator, a feeling of closeness and reliability, which — in contrast to the stereotypical view of an intrusive narrator — helps to put across a convincing picture of the fictional world. Metanarrative comments enhance the credibility of the narrator: her/his difficulties in teasing out the truth of what happened or the search for the right words to use are taken by the reader as proof of authenticity.[28]

The self-conscious interjections made by the narrators in the works cited here work in exactly this credibility-enhancing manner. Such enhancement achieved through self-consciousness functions in a very similar way to the broader issue of generic hybridity discussed in Chapter 1. Just as *Notes of an Investigator* and *Prison and Life* argue for their literary validity by straddling the boundary between fact and fiction, so such moments of metanarration are intended to reassure the reader that the narrative voice in the nascent genre of detective fiction is fully aware of his storytelling responsibilities. The narrator here is not just a judicial investigator drawing on authentic lived experience, but a storyteller aware of how to retain and reward the interest of the reader. As such, once the genre has established its credentials a little better by the middle of the 1870s, such explicit indications of literary and discursive aptitude become less necessary as a means of self-validation. Interestingly, however, whilst such explicit self-consciousness is a feature of Russian crime fiction that fades over time, the practice of including intertextual and/or metatextual reference is one that remains relatively constant over the genre's history in this period.

## Intertextuality and Detective Fiction

Julia Kristeva's discussion of intertextuality teaches us that the literary word exists as: 'an *intersection of textual surfaces* rather than a *point* (a fixed meaning), as a dialogue among several writings: that of the writer, the addressee (or the character), and the contemporary or earlier cultural context'.[29] In a review of the history of intertextuality theory, María Jesús Martínez Alfaro provides a useful elaboration upon how the practice should be viewed:

> There are always other words in a word, other texts in a text. The concept of intertextuality requires, therefore, that we understand texts not as self-contained systems but as differential and historical, as traces and tracings of otherness, since they are shaped by the repetition and transformation of other textual structures.[30]

To a greater degree, arguably, than other literary genres, detective fiction invites the reader to consider its texts as open systems, embellished with various intertextual references that lend them an almost 'palimpsestic quality'.[31] Hanna Charney has claimed that 'detective novels are often filled with allusions to books' and that 'the use of a book in some form — the whole work, or the title, or quotations from it, or the main themes — as a symbolic reference' is a hallmark of the genre.[32] Certainly, intertextual reference is a striking feature of early works of detective fiction outside the Russian context. In Poe's 'The Murders in the Rue Morgue', for example,

Dupin makes reference to the work of Epicurus on atoms and invites the narrator to read Georges Cuvier's 'minute anatomical and generally descriptive account'[33] of an orang-utan, which he claims is the animal guilty of the double murder, whilst the narrator himself quotes from Jean-Jacques Rousseau's *La Nouvelle Héloïse*. However, most notably, Dupin also demonstrates that he is aware of the memoirs written by his non-fictional predecessor, Vidocq, when he criticizes their author thus:

> Vidocq, for example, was a good guesser, and a persevering man. But, without educated thought, he erred continually by the very intensity of his investigations. He impaired his vision by holding the object too close. He might see, perhaps, one or two points with unusual clearness, but in doing so he, necessarily, lost sight of the matter as a whole.[34]

What Dupin does here, even without explicitly mentioning the title of Vidocq's memoirs, is to place not just his investigative methods but Poe's story as a whole into dialogue with the earlier French work and to open both texts up to mutual influence. In a less specific, yet still highly generative fashion, the narrator in Collins's *The Moonstone* argues: 'It's only in books that the officers of the detective force are superior to making a mistake.'[35] As these examples demonstrate, intertextuality can take a number of different forms: it can be explicit or implicit; serious or ludic; literary or non-literary (even textual or non-textual); macrotextual or microtextual (i.e. relating to the entirety of a text, or only sections of, or brief comments in a narrative). The aim of this section of the chapter, therefore, is to examine a number of different manifestations of intertextuality in early Russian detective fiction, and to consider their use and potential effect upon the reader's interpretation of the text.

The efforts that Russian detective fiction makes to be considered as a literary genre worthy of the readership's attention have been discussed at various points in this book up to now. These include the cultivation of generic hybridity in the works of Sokolovskii and Timofeev, as well as the exploitation of a range of techniques used to earn authority for the narrative voice. The first instances of intertextuality to be analysed here fulfil a similar function, as the texts provide evidence of their desire to earn authority or 'prestige' by 'quoting examples from the works of the greats'.[36] Numerous works of crime fiction from the late Imperial era feature obvious references to more 'canonical' texts and authors from the Russian and European literary pantheon. So, for example, in Sokolovskii's 'Samoubiitsa' ('The Suicide'), first published in 1863, the story of the long-suffering civil servant, Sinitsyn (not to be confused with the murder victim in Panov's novella *The Harvest Gathering*), is accompanied by numerous implicit intertextual references to Nikolai Gogol's 'Shinel'' ('The Overcoat') from 1842. The narrator constructs repeated echoes between the account of the life of the lowly scribe who has stabbed himself to death and that of Gogol's Akakii Akakievich, albeit without any of the irony of the original. Sinitsyn is described as working for many years in the same position with no promotion and only a single rise in his wages after twenty years of service; he is relentlessly ridiculed by his colleagues until, like Gogol's hero, he cries out in protest: 'Ведь я никого из вас, господа, не трогаю, что же вы-то ко мне с такими все пакостями лезете?' ('Seeing as I am not troubling any of you, gentlemen, why do you play such mean tricks on me?'). In Gogol's story, Akakii Akakievich repeatedly pleads with his co-workers: 'Оставьте меня, зачем вы меня обижаете?' ('Leave me alone. Why are you tormenting me?').[37] Although Sinitsyn's heavy drinking, religious mysticism and role as an exploitative moneylender distinguish him from Akakii Akakievich, his physical resemblance to his predecessor is unmistakeable to the informed reader:

> Во время совершившейся катастрофы Синицыну было уже лет около сорока, невысокого роста, рябоватый, с жидкими темно-русыми волосами, с крупными чертами, с обыкновенным, гемороидально-зеленым цветом лица, всегда нахмуренный, молчаливый, Синицын никак не мог остановить на себе внимания.[38]

> [At the time of the catastrophe that took place Sinitsyn was already about forty years old, not particularly tall, slightly pockmarked, with thin dark ginger hair, coarse features, and with the usual haemorrhoidal-green complexion. Perpetually frowning and taciturn, Sinitsyn was incapable of attracting anyone's attention.]

Although the degree of similarity constructed between Sinitsyn and Gogol's Akakii Akakievich might lead the reader to expect the later text to stand as a parody of its predecessor, this is not in fact the case. Rather, Sokolovskii's narrative of the unenviable life and horrific death of Sinitsyn offers an earnest restatement of the critical-realist reading of 'The Overcoat'.

In Shkliarevskii's story, 'Why Did He Kill Them?' from 1872, meanwhile, the intertextuality is far more explicit and the principal point of reference is Dostoevskii, and one highly relevant novella, in particular. In the very first lines of his account of events, Shkliarevskii's protagonist, Sergei Antonovich Narostov, who has strangled his wife and shot his mistress, refers to himself thus: 'Я теперь член не здешнего общества, но «Мертвого дома», в разряде убийц...' ('I am no longer a member of this world, but of the "House of the Dead", in the ranks of murderers...').[39] Narostov then elaborates on the appropriateness of his reference to Dostoevskii's 1860 depiction of a prison camp in *Notes from the House of the Dead* when he says:

> Достоевский нарисовал целый мир страдающих, искалеченных нравственно и физически людей, задумывался над этим вопросом, и не решил его... Вы не найдете у него ничего определенного, кроме намеков на злополучную судьбу, как бы наталкивающую на преступление...[40]

> [Dostoevskii sketched an entire world of suffering, morally and physically mutilated people and thought long and hard on this question [of why people commit crime] and did not come up with an answer... You will not find in his work anything definite, apart from hints at an accursed fate that might have had some influence on the crime...]

Given the prominent role that Narostov the schoolteacher ascribes to literature and culture in his all-important 'upbringing', it is hardly surprising that Dostoevskii is not the only point of intertextual reference. A little later, as he discusses how he makes efforts to improve his reading when still a child, Narostov describes how his father criticizes him for being primarily interested in the process of reading rather than the subject matter, 'как гоголевского Петрушку' ('like Gogol's Petrushka'), in reference to the servant character in *Dead Souls* (1842).[41] Such explicit reference to the work of writers belonging to the Russian canon sees Sokolovskii and Shkliarevskii 'inscribing themselves in *Tradition*'.[42] In so doing, they attempt to earn a more elevated reputation for their own writing by demonstrating their knowledge and appreciation of works and authors that enjoy an established position in the world of letters. Such a use of intertextual reference can also be seen to offer an implied characterization of the figure of the ideal reader envisaged by these works. That is, by including references to authors such as Gogol and Dostoevskii, the lesser-known writers are suggesting that their ideal reader is one who is able to recognize and understand the meaning and significance of such intertextual allusions.

The role that intertextual reference to the canon can play in the characterization of the implied reader and to the sense of literary play is even more notable when it functions as an implicit *mise en abyme* in the text. Zarin's 1915 novella, *In Search of a Murderer*, for instance, includes a description of how Chemizov, the shadowy central protagonist, and his intended victim, Elena Diakova, attend the theatre to watch an operatic production of Mikhail Lermontov's poem 'Demon'.[43] What the informed reader is invited to understand from the reference to 'Demon' is that, in its depiction of the powerful and tyrannical demon's possession of Tamara, the poem and the opera reflect the roles and story being constructed between Chemizov and Elena in Zarin's narrative. The similarity in the content of the two works is effectively illustrated when the lines between the two are blurred in a description of a dialogue between Chemizov and Elena as they watch the opera:

> — Я сразу почувствовал, что вы станете на моей дороге, едва увидел вас, — тихо продолжал Чемизов. — До этих пор я считал себя свободным, как сокол.
> — А теперь? — тихо спросила молодая вдовушка.
> — Теперь я связан...
> Эти слова, сказанные почти шепотом, были для Дьяковой слаще всей прослушанной музыки. Она взглянула на своего спутника и увидела строго сжатые губы, нахмуренный лоб и сосредоточенно смотрящие пред собою глаза. Что-то роковое показалось ей в его лице, и она почувствовала власть этого человека над собой. Спектакль окончился.[44]

> ['I immediately sensed, having only just seen you, that you would be mine', continued Chemizov quietly. 'Up until then, I had considered myself as free as a bird.'
> 'And now?' asked the young widow quietly.
> 'Now, I am bound...'
> These words, uttered almost in a whisper, were sweeter to Diakova than all the music she had heard. She looked at her companion and noticed his strictly pursed lips, his furrowed forehead and his eyes that were staring straight ahead. It seemed to her as if there was something fateful in his face and she sensed the power that he had over her. The performance ended.]

Knowledge of the plot of Lermontov's poem, in which the demon destroys Tamara because of his obsession with her, creates a horizon of expectations in the mind of the reader about how the relationship between Elena and Chemizov might play out and, specifically, a sense of fear for the former's life. As it turns out, in fact, these expectations are not met because, although Chemizov exerts a 'demonic' influence over Elena by means of hypnotism, his crimes are restricted to theft, and do not extend to murder. Nevertheless, Zarin adroitly employs *mise en abyme* to manipulate the informed reader's responses and to play with the fear that this literary knowledge instils in him/her.

A similar, if less extensive, use of *mise en abyme* is encountered in Akhsharumov's *And None Will Be the Wiser*, where Lermontov's poem is again used, as well as a reference to Pushkin's *Kamennyi gost'* (*The Stone Guest*, 1830). In Akhsharumov's novella, the female protagonist, Iuliia, admits to styling herself after Lermontov's heroine and casts her lover, Pavel Bodiagin, in the role of the demon. Ultimately, however, although Bodiagin murders the narrator, Cherezov, in an echo of the original poem, Iuliia herself survives, albeit to live out her days in a monastery. The references to Pushkin's drama appear on a couple of different levels in the work. First, at a paratextual level, the third part of Akhsharumov's novella is given the same subtitle as the title of Pushkin's tragedy. The reference receives no immediate or overt elaboration in the first chapter of that part and so the reader remains rather intrigued by it. A little later, however, in the third chapter of Part Three, Cherezov describes how he is profoundly affected by watching a performance of *Don Giovanni* (the Mozart opera on which the Pushkin drama is based), to which he has been taken by his rival, Bodiagin, and where he joins Iuliia and her adoptive mother in a box. Initially Cherezov is captivated by the music, but his mood changes as he watches the scene of Don Juan imagining Donna Anna. He notes: 'Моя поэма, впрочем, была в связи если не с подлинным содержанием драмы, происходившей на сцене, то, по крайней мере, с одним из лучших ее мотивов' ('My poem, however, had links if not to the actual content of the drama being acted out on the stage, then at least to one of its best motifs').[45] Although Cherezov explicitly acknowledges this coincidence between the opera and his own life, it is left to the reader to draw out the potential implications: the victim, Olga (and perhaps also Iuliia), can be seen to be represented in the character of Donna Anna, whilst Bodiagin resembles Don Giovanni; Cherezov himself is represented by facets of the Commendatore, Don Giovanni and Leporello, given the morally dubious position he occupies with regard to both Iuliia and Olga. Little wonder then, that Cherezov later tells Iuliia that the opera has made a considerable impression upon him, precisely because he felt so implicated in it.

In anticipation of the consideration to be given to parody in detective fiction in the next chapter, it is important to note here that not all instances of what might be called 'legitimizing' intertextual reference are employed so earnestly. Whilst the mention of works belonging to the canon of Russian literature, or the pantheon of European culture more broadly, is generally intended to characterize the voice responsible for them as well-educated and informed, certain instances reveal a more ludic incongruity between voice/context and reference that creates a humorous effect. In Panov's *Three Courts*, for example, the narrator-investigator compares the beauty of Anna Bobrova, when she explains her desire to murder Elena Vladimirovna out of jealousy, to that of Judith who beheaded Holofernes.[46] The informed reader might acknowledge some resemblance between the aggressive and sexualized image of Judith that became popular in European art and that of Bobrova, who is determined to get rid of her rival; however, the fact that such a classical reference is voiced by a narrator who is generally not portrayed positively in terms either of his education or his ability as a detective strikes the reader as misplaced. The dissonance between the register of the reference and the abilities of the narrator-investigator is therefore designed to criticize implicitly the latter's tendency to be too easily seduced by feminine beauty. In Chekhov's 'The Swedish Match' meanwhile, the equally ironic use of intertextual reference offers implicit clues to the fundamental misdirection that underpins the entire story. For example, in the early part of the story, the local policeman describes the apparent victim, Mark Ivanych Kliauzov, thus: 'дворянин, богатый человек... любимец богов, можно сказать, как выразился Пушкин' ('a landowner, a rich man... beloved by the Gods, one might say, as Pushkin expressed it').[47] Yet this suggestion of Kliauzov as a favoured soul is ironically out of place given that it would appear that the repeated warnings about the risks involved in his debauched behaviour have now materialized. Later in the story, as I have argued elsewhere, a quotation by one of the investigators, Diukovskii, citing the work of Dostoevskii, Leskov (and Pecherskii) as proof of the guilt of the victim's sister, Maria Ivanovna, functions as an implied criticism of his ability. Rather than using first-hand knowledge of the situation and actual proof to pursue the case, Diukovskii has his status ironically undermined by referring instead to literary stereotypes of Old Believers as popularized by these writers.[48] However, whether they are intended to be interpreted more seriously or more ludically or ironically, such references to works of canonical Russian literature serve a broadly legitimizing function. What the frequency of such allusions to the classics makes clear is that, in the earliest period of its existence, Russian detective fiction sought to establish its literary credentials by means of the demonstration of a knowledge and appreciation of the work of its most illustrious forebears.

Early Russian detective fiction does not, however, restrict its intertextual references to highly regarded works from the European canon. What its development demonstrates is the equal appropriateness in the Russian context of a contention that Gale MacLachlan makes about the French and British genres in the light of Gaboriau's use of the theatre as a setting in *Le Crime d'Orcival*. She argues: 'Once the *roman policier* is established as a genre, the reference point is not only the theatre, but also commonly the genre itself, textual performance being measured implicitly against the preestablished rules of the game.'[49] MacLachlan cites the example of Conan Doyle's *A Study in Scarlet*, from 1887, in which Sherlock Holmes responds to Watson's remark that he reminds him of Poe's detective by saying:

'No doubt you think you are complimenting me in comparing me to Dupin [...] Now, in my opinion, Dupin was a very inferior fellow. That trick of his of breaking in on his friends' thoughts with an apropos remark after a quarter of an hour's silence is really very showy and superficial. He had some analytical genius, no doubt; but he was by no means such a phenomenon as Poe appeared to imagine.'[50]

Holmes is even more critical of Gaboriau's Lecoq, whom he dismisses in the same conversation as 'a miserable bungler' whose only redeeming feature is his energy. In a similar fashion, Russian detective fiction in the late Imperial period makes frequent reference to other fictional detectives, usually also Lecoq and Holmes, as it endeavours to insert its protagonists into the literary family tree of their chosen profession.[51] And these nods can express a range of attitudes to their generic predecessors, not simply the arrogance voiced by Holmes here. So, for example, in Sokolova's *Without a Trace* from 1890, which recounts the investigation into the murder of a Frenchwoman, Laura Grey, and the conviction of the wrong suspect, the detective (*syshchik*), Argunin, who works alongside a judicial investigator, describes himself to the victim's sister thus:

> Вам лично, по всей вероятности, в первый еще раз в вашей жизни, приходится лицом к лицу сталкиваться с тем, что вы, с таким неподдельным ужасом назвали нелестным именем «сыщика», но я смело уверяю вас, что далеко не всегда слово это служит синонимом слову «бесчестный человек»... Вспомните хотя бы знаменитого предшественника моего Лекока, имя которого наверное известно вам, благодаря французским романистам, создавшим ему такую легендарную славу!...[52]

> [This is most likely the first time in your life that you have had to come face to face with the figure to whom you, with such unmistakeable horror, gave the unflattering label 'detective'. But I would make so bold as to say that it is far from always being the case that this term is a synonym for 'dishonourable man'... Recall, if you will, my famous predecessor, Lecoq, whose name is probably known to you thanks to the French novelist who established such a glorious reputation for him!...]

At an earlier stage in the genre's history, Cherezov, in Akhsharumov's *And None Will Be the Wiser*, who is an interested amateur rather than a professional investigator, acknowledges as he attempts nevertheless to identify his cousin's murderer that he is no 'Lecoq'.[53] Meanwhile, in Zarin's story 'Loss of Honour', the heterodiegetic narrator characterizes the investigator protagonist, Patmosov, as a man who has honed his skills through hundreds of cases before adding: 'рассказы о его делах не менее занимательны, чем рассказы о подвигах фантастического Шерлока Холмса' ('stories about his cases are no less entertaining than those about the feats of the fantastic Sherlock Holmes').[54]

Just as with the canonical references discussed above, the intertextual nods to other fictional detectives can be deployed playfully or ironically. In Panov's *The Harvest Gathering*, for instance, the judicial investigator initially dismisses the idea of a 'coup d'état' to trap the culprit by telling the narrator: 'Ну брат — это все хорошо в каком-нибудь романе Габорио' ('now, old man, that's all very well in one of Gaboriau's novels'), before eventually agreeing and seeing the idea prompt the necessary confession.[55] Ivan Gerasimovich's implied criticism here that fictionally inspired notions of how to solve a crime are inappropriate to a real-life context is thus shown to be misplaced. Moreover, the fact that this dismissal of an idea gleaned from literary fiction itself appears in a work of literary fiction suggests that an element of metatextual irony is also at play. Gaboriau and his novels are also the point of reference in an ironic characterization of Diukovskii in Chekhov's 'The Swedish Match'. In the context of Diukovskii's claim that he is beginning to believe in his own genius as a criminal investigator, his remark that he is a former student kicked out of seminary and who subsequently read lots and lots of the French detective author's novels can only be taken to underscore ironically his lack of appropriate professional training. Meanwhile, in the frame narrative of *The Shooting Party* from 1884–85, Chekhov's editor figure offers what might initially appear to be an earnest critique of previous detective stories; however, in the light of the criminal plotting constructed by Kamyshev in the main body of the narrative, it is one that comes to seem deeply ironic. The editor-narrator says:

> 'Дело в том, что наша бедная публика давно уже набила оскомину на Габорио и Шкляревском. Ей надоели все эти таинственные убийства, хитросплетения сыщиков и необыкновенная находчивость допрашивающих следователей.'[56]

> ['The point is, for far too long now our poor readers have had their teeth set on edge by Gaboriau and Shkliarevskii. They're sick and tired of all these mysterious murders, these detectives' artful ruses, the phenomenal quick-wittedness of investigating magistrates.']

Finally, the works of Zarin make frequent mention of Gaboriau and his detective protagonist, Lecoq. In 'The Missing Worker', one of the characters inappropriately compares the local judicial investigator to Lecoq, and mispronounces the Frenchman's name, when it is an epithet far more accurately applied to the main protagonist and principal detective, Patmosov. *In Search of a Murderer* sees members of the local police force refer to Lecoq as the 'ideal investigator'.[57] However, they subsequently claim that whereas Lecoq solved crimes using 'intuition' ('чутье')[58], they will employ only their rationality; ironically, of course, these police prove to be entirely incapable of doing so and have to rely on the expertise of Patmosov in order to make any progress in the case.

Zarin's various works also provide intriguing examples of how crime fiction can create a sense of play by means of reference not only to literary-fictional detectives, but also to historical figures such as Ivan Dmitrievich Putilin. Putilin (1830–93) was an actual historical figure who became the head of the first detective police force in St Petersburg in 1866 and worked for this service in various capacities well into the 1880s. The historical Putilin is a frequent point of reference in Zarin's works, but one who appears to take on a certain literary-fictional status in the process. Early on in *In Search of a Murderer*, for instance, the local police bemoan the lack of clues in the case of the dismembered body and declare that even Putilin would find it difficult to solve.[59] The narrative proceeds to provide a summary of Putilin's career with a footnote informing the reader that he was responsible for successfully solving hundreds of complicated cases. Later on, when one of the initial investigators, Prokhorov, sends a colleague out to fetch Patmosov, the colleague asks who this man is and receives the following reply:

> 'Он — знаменитейший сыщик. Сыщик по призванию. Покойный Путилин пред ним — мальчик, Лекок — ничтожество, а все эти Холмсы и Пинкертоны — выдуманные писателями фантастические сказки, тогда как мой Патмосов жив, и вы завтра увидите его.'[60]

> ['He is the most outstanding detective. He is a detective by calling. In comparison to him, the late Putilin is a boy, and Lecoq is nothing, just like all these Holmeses and Pinkertons thought up by the writers of fantastic tales, whereas my Patmosov is real, and tomorrow you will meet him.']

There is obvious irony here in having an intradiegetic character claim that another character who exists in a literary-fictional world, Patmosov, is so much more realistic than his fictional counterparts. However, it is also significant that the historical Putilin gets lumped together in this dismissive comparison with three entirely fictional figures. In Zarin's 'The Fourth Man', Patmosov is again associated closely with Putilin, who is said to have valued him for his exceptional ability.[61] Furthermore, the father of one of the possible suspects in the murder of the moneylender, Dergachev, notes that he has been advised specifically by Putilin to seek Patmosov out as the best investigator around. This blurring of the historical/fictional lines around Putilin can in part be explained by the fact that he inscribed himself into Russian literary history by penning a memoir of his own experience as an investigator, but also by his appearance as a fictionalized figure in other works dating from as early as 1898.

Putilin first appeared in that year in a collection of stories published by Mikhail Shevliakov who was personally acquainted with the investigator.[62] In 1904, I. A. Safonov published a collection claiming to be based on actual cases from Putilin's career, whilst 1908 saw the publication of a collection entitled *Putilin I. D. Znamenityi russkii syshchik* (*I. D. Putilin: A Famous Russian Detective*) by P. A. Fedorov.[63] Another key figure in the development of this hybrid status for Putilin is Antropov who, as we have seen, casts a fictionalized version of him as the hero of his numerous literary detective works published between 1907 and 1917.[64] Antropov's protagonist may share certain biographical details and professional attributes with the historical Putilin, but he is nothing other than a literary creation, just like Zarin's Patmosov. Like Patmosov, Antropov's Putilin is referred to as the 'Russian Lecoq', but in fact he has more in common with Conan Doyle's Sherlock Holmes. As mentioned previously, like Conan Doyle's works, Antropov's stories are narrated by a doctor friend of the detective. And as with Holmes's Watson, doctor Z functions not just as storyteller but also as a sidekick, whose lesser abilities serve to point up the ingenuity of Putilin. More broadly, Antropov's Putilin stories involve the detective in numerous adventures where he employs his skills of disguise as well as his ingenuity to solve cases that have something to say about modernity and a changing social landscape. However, in spite of the doctor's claim in the foreword that there is value in home-grown detective stories, as well as a degree of originality and considerable enjoyment in Antropov's work, there is no denying that there is something rather derivative about them. Whilst not exactly a pastiche of Conan Doyle's work, the stories do, at the very least, speak to a certain fascination with naturalizing, by means of the figure of Putilin, a more foreign model of detective fiction. Rather closer to the status of pastiche are the detective stories of Petr Orlovets that were also written in the first decade or so of the twentieth century. Orlovets employs Conan Doyle's hero in *Pokhozhdenie Sherloka Kholmsa v Rossii* (*The Adventure of Sherlock Holmes in Russia*) from 1908 and pitches the Englishman against an American counterpart in his *Prikliucheniia Sherloka Kholmsa protiv Nata Pinkertona v Rossii* (*The Adventures of Sherlock Holmes versus Nat Pinkerton in Russia*) of the following year. In Orlovets's stories, which have little to recommend them either in originality or in internal construction, Sherlock Holmes is characterized precisely by his English qualities and reveals many of the behavioural and procedurals ticks well known to readers of Doyle's stories, whilst Pinkerton represents clichéd American capitalism in his perpetual interest in money and financial gain. In 'Taina Fontanki' ('The Secret of the Fontanka'), for instance, which appears in the second of these volumes, Holmes and Pinkerton compete with each other to solve the mystery of the disappearance of a young Countess which appears to be connected to sightings of a strange underwater boat that surfaces in the Neva close to where she lives. Pinkerton, as the quintessential American, bets $500 that he will solve the crime before Holmes and reminds his team during the investigation that 'время — деньги' ('time is money').[65] Holmes, meanwhile, dons the disguise of a workman to find out more details of the Countess's house; deduces, thanks to his interest in science and new inventions, that the boat in the Neva must be a submarine; and then displays his adventurous credentials by diving down in scuba gear to get a closer look at the vessel. Orlovets's stories capitalize on the Russian public's love of Holmes and Pinkerton in the early twentieth century, relocating their escapades onto Russian soil, but adding little in the way of quality to the originals.

## Detective Fiction and Newspapers

Detective fiction's exploitation of intertextuality is not of course limited to allusions to literary texts. In fact, one striking feature of the genre is the manner in which it both references, and directly includes excerpts from, all manner of different texts, including: police reports, autopsy reports, witness statements, summonses, letters, telegrams, diaries and newspaper reports, amongst many others. The extent to which this overt textuality casts the detective as both a reader and a writer will be considered in the next part of the present chapter. However, the discussion here will focus upon the intertextual relationship between detective fiction and newspaper reports. As with intertextuality more generally, the link between newspapers and detective fiction was established at the earliest stages of the genre thanks to their prominent appearance in the work of Poe. As mentioned above, for instance, in 'The Murders in the Rue Morgue', Dupin reads about the murders of Madame L'Espanaye and her daughter in the *Gazette des Tribunaux* before beginning his own investigation. The story includes lengthy excerpts from the newspaper quoted directly in the text that, in their incorporation not only of reporting but also of cited witness statements, function as an embedded narrative. In 'The Mystery of Marie Rogêt' meanwhile, the reader is presented with a series of excerpts from contradictory newspaper reports that highlight the degree of confusion surrounding the case.[66]

Before moving on to consider the various ways in which newspaper reports are referenced in the Russian genre, it is worth noting that close biographical connections existed between journalism and many of the first detective fiction writers in Russia. For instance, Panov worked as the courtroom correspondent for the *Peterburgskii listok* during the 1870s and published his detective novellas in serialized form in the same newspaper.[67] Similarly, Shkliarevskii was first a provincial journalist before moving to St Petersburg where, alongside this work, he published his detective stories 'below the fold' in the urban press. In the early twentieth century, Orlovets, the author of the Sherlock Holmes series, was a journalist who reported on criminal investigations and trials for various newspapers. Both Poe and Gaboriau also had experience working as journalists; however, the difference in the Russian context is that Panov, Shkliarevskii and Orlovets all reported on crime specifically, rather than acting as literary critics. As with the investigators-turned-writers discussed in Chapter 1, this is not the place to examine whether the factual cases that these authors reported on found their way into their fictional writing.[68] It suffices to say that there is a strong likelihood that the concern with *fait divers* that formed the basis for their journalistic work exerted some influence on their literary exploits. In a broader sense than these specific biographical examples, it is important to acknowledge, as has been done in both the Introduction and Chapter 1 above, that newspapers played a significant role in the historical development of the genre of detective fiction in Russia, as they did in various other countries.

However, let us turn attention now to specific examples of how works of Russian detective fiction make intertextual reference to newspapers and their reporting of crime. One of the most striking is to be found in Zarin's story 'The Fourth Man', where the opening pages are structured around a description of how various characters learn of the murder of Dergachev by reading the newspaper. In the opening paragraph of the first chapter, count Chekannyi exclaims in front of his wife, Vera Andreevna, that Dergachev has been killed and is said to 'drop the newspaper' in his shock at the news. Vera, in turn, drops a spoon and turns very pale before attempting to compose herself and asking her husband for more details. Chekannyi is then described as he reads aloud from the newspaper: he initially paraphrases part of the report but then quotes directly from it at the point where it states that, given that one of the victim's pockets has been ripped, the motive for the murder is assumed to be theft. The newspaper account also includes the supposition that a large amount of money must have been stolen because the victim's other valuable belongings (his watch, signet ring and wallet) have not been taken. After her husband has left the veranda, Vera asks her maid to bring the newspaper to her in her own room where she is said to read it extremely attentively, and this description includes another directly quoted excerpt. It is by means of this extract that the reader receives the first more detailed account of the discovery of the body: its location, who found it, the fact that it is immediately obvious that a crime has been committed, as well as the fact that the police have arrived on the scene and that 'следствие ведется энергично...' ('the investigation is being pursued energetically...').[69]

The second chapter opens with a description of a character named Katia running into a room holding a copy of the *Peterburgskii listok* and announcing to her mistress that Dergachev has been murdered with an axe. She says that she was initially told about the murder in a shop and that she bought the newspaper expressly so as to find out more details. Katia's unnamed mistress is as shocked as Chekannyi and Vera by the news and is described unfolding the newspaper and reading the headline that announces in big letters, 'Убийство ростовщика' ('Murder of a Moneylender').[70] At Katia's request, she reads aloud, with the report here appearing to pick up exactly where the one cited in the previous chapter left off (with mention of an energetic investigation), although the reader is not told explicitly that they are the same newspaper. It then moves on to provide further information in another direct citation: a detective is on the scene and, although nothing is yet clear, the agent's skill will soon unmask the murderer.[71] Chapter 3 switches its focus to the character, Nikolai Nikolaevich Savelev, who is woken up at midday by a servant who brings him some coffee and the newspaper. He, like the characters before him, is shocked by the news, jumping up in bed having read of the murder. The illustration of three different characters in three consecutive chapters each learning about the crime by reading newspaper reports lends a striking symmetry to the opening of 'The Fourth Man'. In view of the fact that, ultimately, Patmosov's investigation discovers that Dergachev has been murdered in order to retrieve stolen love letters, this early focus on newspaper reports functions in part as an implicit indication of the importance of written documents to the plot (of both the *fabula* and the *siuzhet*). However, there are other possible interpretations for the manner in which newspaper reports are thrust to the forefront of Zarin's narrative. Firstly, the presentation and repetition of the fact of Dergachev's murder in these newspaper reports serves to depersonalize the victim in a manner that prejudices the reader against him. Whilst intrigued by the case, the reader is not encouraged to feel sympathy for Dergachev, a man who has suffered a violent death but who is referred to repeatedly by his profession as if this fact somehow rationalizes or justifies his murder. By means of these reports, Dergachev's body is shown to be public property where the interest lies not in his life but in the facts surrounding his death. Secondly, the repeated references to the reports in the first three chapters creates a community amongst the intradiegetic readers who all appear not only interested in, but also somehow affected by the murder. These are characters that never actually meet in person in the narrative, but who are shown to be associated by their common act of reading the newspaper and their shared concern at the fact of Dergachev's killing. At this early stage of the story, in fact, this shared activity is the only thing that links them because the reader is given no information regarding how else they might be related to one another. Finally, the repeated inclusion of these reports underscores the crucial role that journalism had come to play in the mediation of reality by the early twentieth century. None of these opening descriptions of the murder is provided in direct witness testimony, either by the criminal investigator or by another character, or indeed in the voice of the narrator, but rather in a form that suggests it has been passed through many pairs of eyes, lips and hands before it is read by the intradiegetic characters and the extradiegetic reader.

Certain of the intertextual references to newspaper reports in Russian detective fiction speak more to their role in stimulating a sense of public interest, or perhaps even sensation, in criminal investigations. As such, they suggest a tendency in journalism to present crime as a legitimate form of entertainment and a simultaneous blurring of the boundary between newspapers and literary fictions. So, for instance, in Shkliarevskii's 'The Tale of a Judicial Investigator', the narrator-detective informs the German shopkeeper he visits on the trail of the belt that has been used to strangle Nastasia Pyl'neva, that his interest in the items he has sold recently is part of a criminal investigation that, if so inclined, the shopkeeper will be able to read about in the following day's edition of *Politseiskie vedemosti* (*The Police Gazette*).[72] The investigator intentionally uses mention of newspaper reporting of the case as bait to encourage the shopkeeper to cooperate by suggesting that any help he gives might earn him a degree of fame. A similar situation pertains in Shkliarevskii's 1878 work 'Utro posle bala: rasskaz prisiazhnogo poverennogo' ('The Morning after the Ball: A Barrister's Tale'). The story tells of the case of Count Wilhelm von Grossberg who is accused and eventually found rightly guilty of the brutal murder and mutilation of his lover, Laura. Shkliarevskii's narrator-barrister announces that the work's main interest consists in a psychological study of the culprit, who has initially escaped capture under the pre-reform, closed system of justice, and whom he subsequently defends in court following his arrest. As part of preparations for the trial, the narrator informs von Grossberg that both the case and his court appearance will be described in detail in the press, and the accused seems to be pleased by, rather than apprehensive of, this information. Moreover, in spite of the gravity of the charges he faces, there is a clear sense that von Grossberg enjoys the public notoriety that his case earns him thanks to it being reported in the press. As if to reinforce the view that it is the press that generates public interest around criminal investigations more than any other factor, later in the work the narrator describes how it is almost impossible to get into the courtroom during the trial such is the level of attendance by members of both the press and the public.[73]

In certain examples of Russian detective fiction, reference is made to employing newspapers more directly as tools during the criminal investigation. In Panov's *Three Courts*, for instance, the diamond dealer, Khaim Faivelovich Aaron, who is suspected of having received Elena Ruslanova's stolen tiara, is effectively trapped by the investigator when he answers an advertisement that has been posted in a newspaper by the police offering to buy jewellery. Because of his response, the police are able to suggest that, as a reader of newspapers, he would have been aware both of the initial murder of Elena and the theft of her tiara, and of her father's offer of a reward for the return of the diamonds.[74] A little later, when the investigator visits Aaron's lodgings, the dealer is further incriminated by the presence of newspapers in which reports on the Ruslanova case have been marked up in red ink. Panov's investigator's method of using an advert in a newspaper to try to find the recipient of the stolen diamond tiara clearly echoes that of Dupin in 'The Murders in the Rue Morgue', where he lures the sailor owner of the orang-utan by means of an advert placed in *Le Monde*.[75] Rachman's contention that 'as a master-reader the detective can harness the power of the press to his own ends' is as applicable to Panov's story as it is to Poe's.[76] The caveat in this interpretation of the Russian investigator, however, is that references to newspaper reports in *Three Courts* do not cast him in an unequivocally positive light. As mentioned in the previous chapter, at the outset of his investigation into Elena's murder, the detective makes very little progress in spite of interviewing more than 200 witnesses. He then describes how, as a consequence, he comes in for considerable criticism both from the local population and in articles published in domestic and foreign newspapers that cite his lack of talent. Whilst there can be no doubt that this investigator is driven, from the outset, by a desire to identify the murderer, it also cannot be denied that a wish to prove that this press criticism is misplaced also acts as a motivating factor. In the context of Panov's story, then, the depiction of a public easily seduced by the newspaper reporting of crime is one that ironically extends to include the figure of the professional investigator himself.

Indeed, as with the literary intertextual references discussed in the previous section, allusions to newspaper reports in Russian crime fiction can also be deployed to ironic ends. Shkliarevskii's story 'Semeinoe neschastie' ('Family Misfortune'), published in 1878, provides the most effective illustration of this potential. The narrator-investigator in this work, whilst ostensibly reliable and respectful in his attitude towards the reader, also uses newspaper reports to play games with and manipulate his/her expectations and reactions. He opens the narrative with a description of how a recent edition of *Politseiskie vedemosti* has published details of an almost simultaneous double suicide: Aleksandra Ivanovna Lavrova has been found poisoned and Iegudiil Engel'gardt, a student lodger in Lavrova's apartment, has shot himself to death at the university. The narrator then comments that another, unnamed newspaper in Moscow has noted that there is much mystery surrounding this case. Given the structure of almost every other crime story in this corpus of early Russian detective fiction, it is entirely reasonable for the reader to expect that it will be the case of Lavrova and Engel'gardt that forms the basis of the narrative to follow. However, a few pages later, following a detailed description of the circumstances surrounding this apparent double suicide, the narrator announces that this is not in fact the case in which he is principally interested, but that his subject is a different, albeit similar, one from twenty-five years previously. The reader thus realizes that mention of the Lavrova/Engel'gardt case, and the associated newspaper reports, constitutes a substantial misdirection of his/her interest towards a case that ultimately receives no full explanation. Moreover, the irony directed at the reader is compounded by the fact that details from this first case exert a significant complicating or distracting influence upon how the reader is primed to interpret the second (though chronologically prior) case. Precisely because the narrator has explicitly stated that the first case, in which Engel'gardt shoots himself dead, is similar to the one he goes on to relate, the reader is primed to anticipate that the male protagonist in the second case, Liubarskii, has also died. In fact, this proves not to be true when the narrator reveals that a third case, chronologically positioned seventeen years after the first and eight years before that of Lavrova and Engel'gardt, and in a completely different geographical region, has led him to hear the confession of a vagrant who turns out to be Liubarskii. The narrator thus harnesses the power of newspaper reporting on crime to create a set of expectations in the informed reader's mind that he then thwarts in order to establish his diegetic superiority. This ironic misdirection can thus be read as an implied warning about the dangers inherent in considering newspaper accounts of crime to possess a privileged relationship to the truth. Indeed, this is the comment that the diamond dealer, Aaron, makes in Panov's *Three Courts* when he complains that newspapers should not be used to incriminate him because 'газеты часто передают известия о событиях вовсе не бывалых' ('newspapers often include information about events that never actually happened').[77] At least part of the intention in Shkliarevskii's work, therefore, is to demonstrate how any narrative, whether it be literary or journalistic, is a construction in which the truth of a criminal case can readily be manipulated so as to create an effect upon the reader.

## Metatextuality and Detective Fiction

The fact that Shkliarevskii's narrator's misdirection can be read as a reflection on the constructed nature of any narrative underlines the difficulty we confront in definitively categorizing such references as either intertextual or metatextual (does the mention of the newspaper article in 'Family Misfortune' primarily reflect on another text or on the literary text itself?). What is clear, though, is that, just as much as detective fiction features examples of texts that refer to other texts, it is also 'almost without exception, a story about a story'.[78] The sense of play that is present within the genre owes much to its tendency towards an elevated degree of self-reflection, whether that is overt or covert. It is to examples of such textual self-reflexivity that this final section of the fifth chapter dedicates itself. The metatextual tendency in detective fiction repeatedly prompts the reader to consider implications beyond those of the basic plot; as such, it is a key device in broadening out the impact of works to permit a consideration of more universal themes and issues. One aspect of the metatextual status of detective fiction has been noted briefly in Chapter 2 with mention of its exploitation of the etymological links between 'authority' and 'authoring'. This facet of the genre is discussed in more detail below, with a specific focus on the various examples of detectives (rather than criminals) that are depicted as writers. That discussion will also consider how detective fiction reflects upon the performative power of language, a phenomenon that, while of the utmost importance in the judicial system, is also one that is shown to be of relevance in the literary context. It is preceded by an analysis of the illustration of detectives as readers in works of Russian detective fiction, a role that has been referred to obliquely throughout this study, but most directly in the instance in Panov's *Three Courts* where the narrator-investigator is invited to re-read his first, flawed investigation. The discussion of metatextuality begins here, however, with an exploration of instances where works of Russian detective fiction reflect upon the influence of literature. As with the examples of intertextuality discussed above, such self-reflexivity often produces an ironic effect.

The discussion of detective fiction's exploitation of intertextuality above has stressed the legitimizing function fulfilled by such references. However, the genre also features many moments when the effect of literature is suggested as being far less laudable. The work of Shkliarevskii, in particular, provides various examples of protagonists whose criminal or inhumane behaviour is presented precisely as a consequence of their interest in literature. In 'Why Did He Kill Them?', for instance, the narrator-investigator's friend, Narostov, who is accused of killing both his wife and his lover, stands as an example of what Bakhtin calls the 'literary man', that is 'one who sees life through the eyes of literature and tries to live according to it'.[79] Providing a broader context to his self-identification as a member of 'the house of the dead' that has been mentioned above, Narostov explains to the narrator that his only pleasure during childhood was to be found in reading books.[80] He goes on to list the journals and books that he read as a young man and he states explicitly that 'такое чтение не могло не оказать вредного влияния на мою нравственность' ('this reading could not but exert a pernicious moral effect upon me').[81] Moreover, he acknowledges that he reads the theory of the utopian socialist Charles Fourier selectively and chooses only those bits that suit him.[82] A little later on, when he describes how his lover, Chastova, begins to lose interest in him soon after their affair has resumed, Narostov acknowledges that he is influenced in his jealousy and desire to exact revenge by his reading of 'старые романы' ('old novels').[83] Finally, Narostov is depicted presenting himself as a dramatic hero during his appearances in court, as a man who grows into his role whilst members of the public watch the spectacle of his trial through their 'лорнетки' ('opera glasses').[84] It is important to note the shift here between Narostov's evocation of various literary influences and the more dramatic analogy of himself as an actor on the stage. Whilst there is a distinction between these two frames of reference, the discussion here ranges across both and recognizes that a sense of the aesthetically artificial and performative unites the two. There is the unmistakeable sense in Shkliarevskii's story that Narostov is at least partly driven to commit the double murder because he allows his life to become confused with, or overly influenced by, the depiction of life to be found in literary works. He is shown to be unable to differentiate sufficiently clearly between the models of behaviour provided in literature and those that are appropriate for real life.

Shkliarevskii depicts one of the male characters in his story 'Human Involvement' in similarly unflattering terms. Literature is used as the tool to characterize negatively the officer, Valentin Svistul'skii, who is the father of the murdered newborn twins.

During his first inspection of the crime scene, the narrator-investigator spots a book of poetry and prose that Svistul'skii has written lying on the bed in the accused mother's room. When the narrator comes to look at it more closely later in his investigation, he describes how it contains poetry that features far too many empty phrases as well as 'вирши с непростительными грамматическими промахами, бессодержательны и ни в одном из них не проглядывала искра чувств' ('verses with unforgiveable grammatical mistakes, meaningless and lacking the least spark of feeling').[85] Somehow, the narrator notes, the prose is even worse: it expresses no intelligence, no observational skill nor any talent on the part of the author, and is full of empty romanticism. Again, whilst other factors such as upbringing and social interference are implicated, an accusatory finger is clearly pointed most directly at literature and its potential influence in the description of Svistul'skii's criminal behaviour. The very clear allegation behind these depictions is that Narostov and Svistul'skii are not simply the criminal protagonists in works of literary fiction, but that they are criminal protagonists in part produced by literature, whose fate might have been different if they had been less influenced by the art form.

As certain of the intertextual references to other fictional detectives have hinted, a more diffuse and less personally focused criticism of the role of literature is also a feature of works in the genre. So, for instance, in Panov's *Three Courts*, Anna Bobrova tries to deny her guilt in the murder of Elena Ruslanova by telling the narrator-investigator that he spends too much time reading novels.[86] In its early pages, Zarin's *In Search of a Murderer* features a conversation about the virtual impossibility of someone committing a crime and leaving no trace. Chemizov says that such untraceability might be possible if a crime was committed under hypnosis, but the procurator dismisses this idea by saying 'это уже из области романа' ('this is something from the realm of fiction').[87] However, Chemizov counters by saying, 'Роман — это жизнь, а жизнь часто дает темы, которые не решается обрабатывать романист; они кажутся слишком фантастичны' ('the novel is life, and life often provides plots that a novelist would choose not to develop because they seem too fantastic').[88] The irony of such metatextual commentary is obvious. In the case of Panov's story, Bobrova's criticism of the narrator-investigator functions as a bluff: although it might well seem that the suggestion of her involvement derives from the plot of a novel, it is in fact the truth presented in this literary fiction. Zarin's novella, meanwhile, is replete with metatextual elements, including the heading 'действующие лица' ('characters/cast') for the chapter in which the above-quoted conversation takes place. To a certain extent, Chemizov is correct: in the case of this criminal plot the hypnosis theory should not be discounted because it is too fantastical to be true. However, the fact that it exists as a reality in life depicted only in a literary fiction sees it take on the status of a metatextual loop, where the referent constantly slips out of the interpreter's grasp.

## Detectives as Readers

The examples from Shkliarevskii above provide evidence of how the genre frequently casts various characters, but most frequently either the detective or the criminal, in the role of reader or writer. These associations, whether implicit or explicit, lie at the heart of much of the genre's metatextual practice, and are far from unique to the Russian context. In much detective fiction, there is a figurative sense of the investigator as a reader who deciphers the clues to a crime in order to unmask the culprit. As Sweeney argues:

> the relationship between criminal and detective, mediated by the crime which one commits and the other resolves, suggests the relationship in any fiction between writer and reader, mediated by the text. At the metadiegetic level, in other words, the criminal is the author of a crime that the detective must interpret.[89]

As such, the investigator comes to function as a textual representative of the extradiegetic reader, often providing a model of ideal interpretation. Again, it is Poe who establishes the blueprint for such a characterization when the narrator in 'The Murders in the Rue Morgue' introduces Dupin as a man remarkable for 'the vast extent of his reading', whom he meets in a library where both were 'in search of the same very rare and very remarkable volume'.[90] Early Russian detective fiction picks up on this portrayal of Dupin as a reader and builds upon it in a number of different ways. For instance, in the opening chapter of Timofeev's *Notes of an Investigator*, the narrator records how his interest in investigative work comes about almost by accident: in the office where he works as a civil servant, he is asked to look for a document in an old case file and his curiosity is piqued by its contents. He is described very much as an amateur, who teaches himself the job of being an investigator specifically by reading about the practice of his predecessors as they are described in these cases. He explicitly states that it is the act of reading over these old cases that instils in him the desire to become an investigator even though he understands he might not be successful.[91] Sometime later in this same chapter, when the now-qualified narrator-investigator arrives on his first assignment, he is described as spending a day with the local court assessor reading through the current cases in his district. What is more, he is shown to have grown into a critical reader when he expresses his shock at the overly florid titles that have been given to the cases on which he now has to work.[92]

Although it is not presented as directly in the text, an act of reading is demonstrated to be of central significance to Porfirii Petrovich's pursuit of Raskolnikov in *Crime and Punishment*. In Part III, Chapter 5 of the novel, Raskolnikov and Razumikhin visit the judicial investigator in his lodgings. In the midst of a conversation that recalls a discussion the previous evening to which Raskolnikov has not been privy, about whether or not crime exists, Porfirii apparently casually says:

> 'мне вспомнилась теперь, — а впрочем, и всегда интересовала меня, — одна ваша статейка: «О преступлении»... или как там у вас, забыл название, не помню. Два месяца назад имел удовольствие в «Периодической речи» прочесть.'[93]

['I'm suddenly reminded — though, in fact, it has always intrigued me — of a little article of yours: "On Crime"... was that the title? I'm afraid it's slipped my mind. I had the pleasure of reading it two months ago in the *Periodical Review*.']

Porfirii then demonstrates his perspicacity as a reader when he informs Raskolnikov that he was most intrigued by 'некоторая мысль, пропущенная в конце статьи, но которую вы, к сожалению, проводите только намеком, неясно' ('a certain thought which you let slip at the end, but which, unfortunately, is only hinted at and remains rather obscure') about certain individuals who are fully entitled to commit crimes.[94] What follows thereafter is an analytical standoff between Porfirii, as reader, who presents intentionally and provocatively naïve interpretations of the article's contents in the form of questions, and Raskolnikov, as author, who seeks to explicate and defend what he has written. It is significant that the first serious, although unofficial, interrogation of Raskolnikov by the investigator is thus constructed around the roles of reader and writer, where what is superficially at stake is the correct comprehension of a written text. It is Porfirii's queries as a reader seeking to understand the article more fully that prompt Raskolnikov into acts of prolonged speech as he effectively re-authors his article and explains it to the gathered audience. In spite of Porfirii's claim towards the end of the exchange that he is only posing his questions 'для уразумения вашей статьи, в литературном только одном отношении-с...' ('to gain a better understanding of your article, in a purely literary respect'),[95] both Raskolnikov and the reader see this remark as disingenuous. The presentation of this first interrogation of Raskolnikov the criminal as an act of literary analysis clearly, though implicitly, illustrates a degree of metatextual preoccupation in Dostoevskii's novel. The figuration of Raskolnikov as an author who is interested in those who are able 'сказать [...] *новое слово*' ('to utter [...] *a new word*')[96] should be taken as a reflection upon the position of the extradiegetic writer, Dostoevskii, who is similarly interested in originality. By extension, therefore, the position and role of the extradiegetic reader should be seen to find a reflection of itself, however idiosyncratic, in the character of Porfirii.

The metatextual impulse in detective fiction is also clearly in evidence in those many works in which written documents play a central role in the deciphering of the crime. In Shkliarevskii's 'A Secret Investigation', as we have seen earlier, the narrator-investigator picks up the pieces of a torn-up note that has been left behind by the suspect, Avdotia Kriukovskaia, in a box at the Mariinskii Theatre. He is then described as spending some time attempting to work out what has been written in the note, a task complicated not just by the fragmented pieces but by the fact that some of the writing has been partially erased or is missing entirely. As has been argued in Chapter 3 above, the detective's reading of this letter stands as a metonymical representation of his broader investigative act: the ripped and partially erased writing stands for all of the various clues that he has to try to fit back together and read if he is to solve the crime. To flesh this example out with more detail: the detective describes in some detail at one point what he thinks he is able to read and the various interpretive questions he confronts: he can read 'жду ее'

('I await her') but is unsure whether this 'жду' is a separate word or part of another, such as 'между' ('between').[97] There is clear metatextual irony in the fact that the investigator only receives confirmation of what the note actually says when he reads the written confession provided by Kriukovskaia later in the narrative. In describing the card that Kebmezakh gave to her in the theatre box, and that she subsequently rips up, she cites the message in full. And whilst the narrator-detective does not comment explicitly upon how the contents map onto the pieces he has earlier tried to decipher, it becomes clear to the active reader that the presumed 'жду ее' was actually 'жду сегодня' ('I am waiting today'), where the first letter of the second word has been misread.[98] In fact, in spite of the detective's attempt to interpret this almost illegible note, his only very limited success can therefore be seen to represent the somewhat passive course that his investigation takes. He never successfully 'reads' the note, and never really reconstructs the story of the crime himself; rather, it is the criminal Kriukovskaia who, whilst not herself the actual author of the note, reveals its contents in much the same way that she provides a full account of her crime and its background in her extensive letter of confession.

Sokolova's *The Song Has Been Sung* ascribes a similar degree of importance to a ripped piece of paper that is found, not during the first examination of the tutor Bazhlanov's body *in situ*, but by the narrator-detective when he goes to inspect it a little later. The narrator is informed by the local policeman that the piece of paper in question fell out of Bazhlanov's pocket when his body was moved and that the piece of lace that was also discovered had previously been in his hand. The investigator is outraged to learn that his investigative task is complicated by the fact that Count Osinskii, upon whose estate the crime has occurred, has removed other pieces of paper, as well as other physical evidence, from the crime scene without his knowledge. The narrator-investigator explicitly states that this piece of paper (as well as the lace) constitutes the most important clue in the case and attempts to decipher both its provenance and its contents. However, in contrast to the Shkliarevskii story, the paper has been ripped into so many tiny pieces that putting them back together is impossible. Nevertheless, the detective is able to surmise that the pieces come from a letter that was hastily written, both in ink and pencil: the ink marks are firmer and rounder, whilst those in pencil, although indecipherable, reveal the hand of a woman. He further notes that the paper itself has a smell of patchouli, Bazhlanov's favourite scent. The letter, though illegible, functions nevertheless as a legible clue of a possible motive, that is a love affair, for the murder of the tutor.

There are myriad other instances in early Russian detective fiction where the criminal investigator is represented as a reader. In Panov's *The Harvest Gathering*, for example, the narrator describes the lodgings of the investigator, Ivan Gerasimovich, as a place where books occupy a prominent position. In his *Murder in Medveditsa Village*, the judicial investigator reads the local policeman's initial report into the death of Grosheva and criticizes it for being wrongly focused: it goes to the trouble of detailing the dimensions of her hut and the various livestock there, but does not give much information about the victim herself. His subsequent re-examination of the murder scene becomes, therefore, not just a new start for the criminal investigation but a corrective reading of this first deficient account. In Shkliarevskii's 'The Tale of a Judicial Investigator', during his search for the provenance of the belt that has been used to strangle Pyl'neva, the narrator-investigator recalls how he has recently read an English novel in which the crime is solved by finding a scrap of paper that contains a tallow candle. He declares his hope that the belt in the current case might play a similar role. And in Zarin's *In Search of a Murderer*, one of the policemen, Prokhorov, is described as lying in bed reading the works of the famous jurist A. F. Koni, another actual historical figure.[99] Whatever the specificities of these various instances, however, it is obvious that what they all offer is a degree of metatextual reflection upon the various acts of reading and interpretation that constitute not only a criminal investigation, but also a literary fiction that describes a criminal investigation. The detective unmistakeably functions as an intradiegetic figuration of the extratextual reader, thereby associating the act of interpretation that the latter executes beyond the boundaries of the text with the investigation conducted by the former in the fictional world. However, as criticism of crime fiction has previously shown, in the hall of mirrors that is metatextuality in the genre, the figure of the detective features almost as frequently in the guise of a writer as he does in that of a reader.

## Detectives as Authors and the Power of the Written Word

What works of detective fiction also clearly reveal is the central importance of acts of writing to their fictionalized presentation of the judicial process. Although the judicial reforms in Russia in the early 1860s replaced secret written procedures with oral proceedings in the context of the trial, public and official acts of writing continued to play a highly significant role in criminal investigations. As such, Russian crime fiction furnishes the reader with numerous examples of detectives engaged in acts of writing, acts that metatextually suggest this figure as a double of the extradiegetic author of the literary text. In so doing, these works provide an implicit reflection on the status and potential of written language not only in the context of a criminal investigation but also in that of the literary work. Specifically, in illustrating the extent to which judicial investigations in this era rely upon the written word for their execution, Russian detective fiction demonstrates the potential of the word to direct action in the extratextual world and, most crucially, to serve as an instrument of truth and justice. This illustration invites the reader to consider the status of the written word in the literary context and its ability to mediate perception of both the intradiegetic and extradiegetic worlds and to provide a version of the 'truth'. Moreover, in the examples it provides of the limitations of the written word, detective fiction provides implicit warnings about the reliability of logocentric worlds and of man's unending desire to invest belief in the notions of truth and justice. Whilst Russian detective fiction is replete with examples of the significance attached to the written word and to acts of writing, this section of the chapter will focus its attention primarily on Panov's novella *Murder in Medveditsa Village*.

As outlined elsewhere, Panov's novella illustrates the essential role played not just by written communication but also by oral speech in the course of the criminal investigation.[100] Indeed, such is the centrality of the concept of language here that *Murder in Medveditsa Village* appears to provide an early validation of Hutter's assertion that, 'detective fiction is the peculiarly modern distillation of a general literary experience that makes central the subtle interaction with, and interpretation of, language'.[101] In a work where the most significant action (the murder of Grosheva) has taken place before the beginning of the narrative proper, it is the various acts of receiving, reading, preparing, signing and sending innumerable written documents that can be seen to take centre stage. The written word is thus highlighted as being of critical importance to the investigation and as enjoying a privileged relationship to authority and justice. Moreover, it is language, and especially the written word, that plays the decisive role in structuring the various networks of authority operating in and around the fictional world. To some extent, the spotlight that Panov shines on the relationship between language, power and truth can be considered to root his story in the historical fact of 1860s Russia. However, as the analysis below demonstrates, in its interrogation of the various functions of, and possibilities inherent in, language, *Murder in Medveditsa Village* reveals a greater preoccupation with the self-reflexive potential of detective fiction than with purely mimetic representation.

Chapter 1 above has noted how Foucault argues that the nineteenth century witnessed the birth of a new conception of the criminal in which this figure became the object of a whole series of examinations. Drawing on Foucault, Herzog explains that this 'examination':

> leaves behind it a whole meticulous archive constituted in terms of bodies and days. The examination that places individuals in a field of surveillance also situates them in a network of writing; it engages them in a whole mass of documents that capture and fix them. The procedures of examination were accompanied (...) by a system of intense registration and of documentary accumulation. A 'power of writing' was constituted as an essential part in the mechanisms of discipline.[102]

Although Foucault's examples of such 'examinations' do not specifically include the criminal investigation, it is plainly a procedure that is equally concerned with constructing systems of disciplining documentation and in which the act of writing is granted considerable power.[103] *Murder in Medveditsa Village* makes this preoccupation and symbolic significance abundantly clear in a number of different ways: it associates an understanding of the written word with a respect for the law; employs literacy as the fundamental indicator of social difference and professional competence; records the preparation and reception of a countless number of documents; foregrounds the detective as the most authoritative writer and characterizes his writing as a performative act; associates report-taking with scientific objectivity; and exploits writing in its various forms as the determiner of hierarchical relationships between figures involved in the narrative contract of the literary text.

The central significance assigned to acts of writing in Panov's novella, particularly those by the investigator, is foreshadowed by the fact that the written word lies at the heart of almost all of its opening action. The first act described in the text is not the discovery of the murder of Grosheva, but the attempt made by another woman to deliver a 'грамотка' ('official document') to the judicial investigator.[104] She rings at the gates of a large house in the town of N., but when she fails to gain entry, the local deacon, who is sitting in his window opposite, calls her over to inquire about her business. She tells him that she has come from Medveditsa with the document but that she does not know to whom to deliver it. The deacon takes it from her, reads the address on the envelope and informs her that it is intended for the judicial investigator who is currently playing cards opposite in the home of the local police inspector. The notion that the written word is of the greatest significance in this story is promoted by having the following seventeen pages of the narrative dedicated to a description of how these official papers are delivered, read and discussed. The woman walks over to the police inspector's house and informs him that she has an official document for him; he takes the envelope from her, reads the address on it and goes into the other room to announce that a package has arrived for Andrei Petrovich. The judicial investigator then reads the recipient details on the envelope out loud to the other card players before digesting the contents inside silently. Having done so, he announces that he needs to leave immediately before handing the package to a young man beside him because 'это и до вас касается' ('it concerns you too').[105] This unidentified character duly proceeds to read it out loud to the other guests, and the description of this act of reading occupies three full pages in the text. Furthermore, because this official document contains two 'протоколы' ('statements'), one of which announces the fact of the murder, it functions as the trigger for all of the subsequent action described in *Murder in Medveditsa Village*. Without this written documentation, which presents the official request for the detective to undertake an investigation into the crime, there would be no search for the culprit and no attendant narrative. As such, it constitutes the first example of the use of 'performative' writing (where language directly executes an action) that will be discussed in greater detail below. Not only that, but the other statement, in its detailing of the preliminary search of the crime scene conducted by the local policeman mentioned above, and of the testimony of local peasants that they do not know the culprit's identity, represents a written substitute for a more direct description of the first stages of the investigation. It would have been possible for the novella to have opened with a description of the discovery of Grosheva's body and the policeman's subsequent search given from the point of view of one of the peasants, for example. However, Panov chooses to insert an additional layer of mediation such that these actions are not described directly in the narrative but via written reports which are subsequently read aloud by fictional characters. This choice of presentation implicitly ascribes dominance to written documents that report actions over the mere description of physical events within the diegesis because the reader is made primarily dependent upon the former for his/her information.

Although the first appearance of Andrei Petrovich in *Murder in Medveditsa Village* sees him cast as a reader of the official document that is delivered, the remainder of the work depicts him primarily as a *writer* whose most reliable and favourite tool in his investigation is the written word. The novella is replete with numerous instances when he authors official documents that include: statements of searches undertaken ('протокол осмотра'); orders for searches to be carried out; a document ('акт') about the transportation of the victim's body for autopsy; requests for the supply of census information from the local priest; orders for various witnesses to present themselves in Medveditsa; numerous witness depositions ('показание'); records of interrogations; a notification to the local criminal tribunal of the main suspect Grishanin's attempt to kill him; a written decision ('постановление') to place the suspect under house arrest; accounts of Grishanin's attempts to deny his own earlier accusations; and numerous reports about how events in the investigation unfold. Barely an action takes place in the diegesis that is not translated into written form by Andrei Petrovich and the judicial investigator's method is largely informed by the desire to leave a complete documentary record (or 'archive', to borrow Herzog's term) of his work. Writing is the action that this detective performs more frequently than any other and the progress of his inquiry into the murder can be charted in terms of the production and reception of written evidence. In the centrality of the position that the act of authorship occupies in *Murder in Medveditsa Village*, therefore, it initially appears to conform to, although ultimately proves to disrupt, profoundly, Sita A. Schütt's view that writing functions 'as antidote to criminality'.[106]

This notion of the written word as a potential remedy for crime should come as no surprise given the degree to which the exercise of the law is dependent upon the power of language. In *Force de loi*, Jacques Derrida makes clear the close inter-relationship between the law, language and power when he states:

> Au commencement de la justice, il y aura eu le *logos*, le langage ou la langue, mais cela n'est pas nécessairement contradictoire avec un autre *incipit* qui dirait: «Au commencement il y aura eu la force.»[107]

> [At the beginning of justice there will have been *logos*, speech or language, but this is not necessarily in contradiction with another *incipit*, which would say: 'In the beginning there will have been force.']

There is no law without force or power; language possesses an inherent power; the law makes use of the power possessed by language. In certain respects, the law has no existence outside of language and, in the journey towards modernity, the force of the law has become increasingly logocentric as it is embodied in written statutes. The actions of Panov's judicial investigator leave the reader in no doubt about his firm belief in this (legal) power of the written word as the best form of evidence. Time and again, Andrei Petrovich is at pains to convert, with a minimum of delay, actions he has undertaken or events that he has witnessed into written documents. His sense of urgency is at its most acute when it is a question of translating oral testimony into written form. There is not a single occasion in the novella when the description of Andrei Petrovich's verbal interrogation of a witness or the main suspect is not immediately followed by at least one line that notes the writing up of this testimony. The judicial investigator's conduct in this regard is an enactment of the notion that the written word is 'more stable' than its spoken equivalent.[108] His perspicacity in ensuring that there is a written record of almost every event that occurs in the course of his investigation can be seen to go beyond the call of duty and to reveal the necessity he feels to 'fix the past' by means of writing.[109] The perceived 'volatility'[110] of oral language that this need betrays is rendered most obvious in the conduct of the main suspect, Grishanin. He is a character whose spoken words, right from the outset, are shown to be acutely unstable, as he constantly denies having uttered, or blatantly contradicts, an earlier statement he has made. In the description of one of his various interrogations, for example, during which Grishanin needlessly lies about having spoken to the victim's neighbour on the eve of the murder, a special emphasis is placed on variations of the verb 'to say': its repetition on six occasions in only eleven lines of text emphasizes the untrustworthiness inherent in his words precisely because they are 'spoken'.[111] Consequently, when, at a later stage in the story, Grishanin concedes for the first time that a previous accusation he has made is false, Andrei Petrovich rushes to find the means to convert these words into written form. The detective's methodology repeatedly privileges the written word as having a closer relationship to 'truth'. Grishanin's oral speech is characterized by his impulse to lie constantly; however, in his repeated acts of transcribing this speech, Andrei Petrovich endeavours to arrive at and capture the 'truth' that exists behind them. And this promotion of the association between the written word and truth provides metatextual commentary upon the status of the literary text.

*Murder in Medveditsa Village* also establishes an association between the exercise of judicial authority and the written word by means of its illustration of the 'performative'[112] nature of much of Andrei Petrovich's writing. The law is a sphere of human activity that makes particular use of this potential for some language to 'do things' as suspects are placed 'under arrest' and criminals are judged to be 'guilty' simply by means of words that are uttered. Although much of the theory devoted to performatives makes reference to the act of speech, it is nevertheless applicable, as Panov's novella makes clear, to the written form of language. Andrei Petrovich's status as a 'figure of social authority'[113] is conferred, at least in part, by the executive force implied by his writing of legally binding, actionable documents. For instance, in his authorship of a written decision to place Grishanin under house arrest, the judicial investigator produces an utterance which performs an illocutionary act (the issue of a command that must be followed):[114] he ensures by means of this declaration that the suspect is taken into custody. Without the written document, the round-the-clock presence of guards would not be put in place, nor would it be legally sanctioned.[115] Others of his written documents can be considered to possess a more indirect illocutionary force. When he inscribes orders into a written document, for example, he obliges others to obey his words and to become subservient to him: information must be delivered to him by the local priest; witnesses summoned must turn up in person to answer his questions; searches of premises must be conducted. It is also specifically the performative force of Andrei Petrovich's written word that makes the illiterate peasants in the village so mistrustful of it: they are afraid to 'sign' the written records of their testimony that he prepares because they fear the consequences that these documents might enact upon them.[116] And because of his judicial status, his words possess a higher degree of such performative authority than those uttered by another character, such as the doctor. Whilst it is obviously the case that the judicial investigator's oral speech carries the same weight of authority, his decision to issue the vast majority of his orders through written documents promotes the written form as being of most consequence.

Moreover, in the combination of the performative force of many of Andrei Petrovich's acts of authorship and his position of legal and social authority, it becomes possible to talk about the depiction of a certain 'ritualization', or even 'fetishization', of writing in *Murder in Medveditsa Village*. In both cases, the act of writing is elevated to a position of special importance in the diegesis that also imbues it with metatextual potential. Catherine Bell explains that 'ritualization involves the differentiation and privileging of particular activities' and she identifies 'restricted codes of communication to heighten the formality of movement and speech; distinct and specialized personnel' as two tendencies which distinguish this practice.[117] By the mere fact of his literacy, Andrei Petrovich is differentiated from the majority of the other characters in the diegesis and his writing is privileged not only by himself, but also by the peasants and by the dominant position it occupies in the narrative. As the representative of the law charged with solving the murder, Andrei Petrovich is himself an example of 'specialized personnel'. Although the reader witnesses him authoring a never-ending stream of written documents, these are both restricted in their variety (they all pertain to the conduct of his criminal investigation) and are always highly formal (requiring the inclusion of certain prescribed information and validating signatures). Whilst the simple possession of literacy informs the construction of social hierarchies in Panov's novella, it is by means of the importance and authority attributed to his writing, through its 'ritualization', that Andrei Petrovich establishes a position of even greater power for himself. As Bell states, 'ritualization is first and foremost a strategy for the construction of certain types of power relationships'.[118] The judicial investigator's command and deployment of the written word in this ritualistic form effectively makes him 'a monitoring and disciplining agency'[119] who exercises his authority over those around him, particularly the suspect Grishanin. However, the degree to which the central importance attached to the written word is actually undermined or perverted by its 'fetishization' might also be considered. The exaggerated repetition of these acts of writing suggests not merely the execution of professional duty but the enactment of a more personal obsession. Moreover, it begins to empty the written word of some of its sense such that Andrei Petrovich's production of documents begins to appear automated and non-individualized. In this sense, the 'fetishization' implicitly poses a threat to the status of the written word in *Murder in Medveditsa Village*, a threat that is substantiated by the role played by oral speech and non-verbal language elsewhere in the novella.

In fact, Russian detective fiction more generally demonstrates that it is well aware of the limitations of the written word as a guarantor of truth and justice. In *Murder in Medveditsa Village*, as noted above, Panov acknowledges this situation by having the all-important confession from Grishanin come in reaction to the frightened crying of his victim's young daughter who is not yet old enough to speak, let alone write. In Shkliarevskii's 'The Tale of a Judicial Investigator', the shortcomings of the written word are illustrated rather more directly. Shkliarevskii's story is another work that attaches considerable significance to acts of writing: in considering the various suspects in the murder of Nastasia Pyl'neva, the narrator-investigator notes that one reason to suspect her husband is that he is in possession of several letters written to her by the student Garnitskii who is thought to be her lover. However, it is primarily in the climax of the story that the role of the written word comes to the fore. Having decided that neither the love nor the jealousy of a male suitor is the likely motive for the murder, the investigator is struck by the probability that the crime has been committed by somebody for whom Pyl'neva's existence is an inconvenience. At first, as he explains his reasoning for this new belief, the narrator does not name the suspect that he has in mind, but then he writes a letter to Aleksandra Lastova, and notes that he has carefully considered every word in it so as not to arouse her suspicion. The significance of the letter is demonstrated by the fact that it is included directly in the text in its entirety: it states that his investigation is now complete; that he is indebted to her more than anyone else for revealing the true details of the case; thanks her for entrusting him with it; and asks her to come to his office as soon as possible.[120] Given the investigator's subsequent admission that Lastova is in fact the main suspect in the murder, it is evident that the letter is intended to be read in two ways: by Lastova as an expression of gratitude for her help in the investigation; but by the more informed reader as an accusation of her as the murderer. At this stage, it appears as if the narrator's investigative prowess, expressed in part by means of this letter, will pay dividends as a means of bringing Lastova to justice. Similarly, as Lastova seemingly admits defeat by the narrator when she confesses all of the details of her motives for, and execution of, the murder of her sister, he not only listens but also writes down her testimony, in an act intended, like those of Panov's protagonist, to make it more secure.

Ultimately, however, these two acts of writing prove to be utterly inadequate, and in the case of the letter, ironically serve to incriminate the narrator-investigator himself. The narrator himself acknowledges, in a relatively conventional gesture, the inability of his written record to do justice to the emotional nature of Lastova's verbal confession. The shortcomings of the written word go further, however: in the face of the disappearance of the material evidence of the signet ring that Lastova cunningly swallows, and of her insistence that she is an innocent bystander, this entirely coherent and persuasive written record of the crime and her testimony counts for absolutely nothing. The narrator's description of how, at this utter repudiation of her earlier confession of guilt, 'бумага чуть не выпала у меня из рук' ('the paper almost fell out of my hands'),[121] is symbolic of the defeat of his investigative efforts. Furthermore, the narrator notes in the coda to the story that these two written documents (his letter and report) are subsequently used against him when he is removed from the investigation. He is accused of transcribing her confession as a means of blackmailing her and his composition of the letter is similarly explained as an attempt to trap her into ceding to his amorous intentions. Whilst the reader recognizes such accusations as false and recognizes the written documents as encapsulating the actual truth of the case, both the act of writing and the concept of truth are deprived of their power and significance at the conclusion of Shkliarevskii's story. Such interrogation of the written word and the complication of its relationship to the issue of truth is obviously metatextual. Just as the narrator-investigator's construction of a (correct) version of events is destroyed by Lastova's retraction of her confession and counter-accusation of the investigator, so the successful construction of fictional worlds by the written word in the literary act is interrogated and undermined. Such destruction cautions the reader against an unquestioning belief in the existence of truth and justice, whether it be in the diegetic world constructed entirely out of the written word, or in the extradiegetic world where the written word still has such significance ascribed to it.

## Conclusion

The examination of instances of intertextuality and metatextuality in early Russian crime fiction in this chapter has provided ample evidence of the range of intention and execution in the genre during this period. In terms of intertextuality, at the more earnest end of the spectrum, authors of crime fiction demonstrate not only a keen knowledge of more canonical literary forebears, but a desire to weave reference to these works into their own in quite subtle and complex ways. Simultaneously, this device allows Russian crime fiction to inscribe itself into a light-hearted and playful relationship with its predecessors in the genre and to associate itself with its foreign cousins. Moreover, by means of these various references, Russian crime fiction implicitly rewards readers for their devotion to the genre and further delineates the image of the ideal reader. With regard to the status of newspapers as popular intertexts in crime fiction, there is undoubtedly more work to be done on this topic. The relationship is intriguing in both socio-historical and narratological terms, because of the ways in which the literary-fictional text repeatedly invokes and represents a source text that has a supposedly closer relationship to factual experience. It is, though, in the discussion of metatextual practice in Russian crime fiction that the true riches of the genre reveal themselves most strikingly. Whilst recognition of the detective as both figural reader and writer is nothing new in criticism of the genre, early Russian crime fiction offers examples of this symbolic representation being enacted in original and meaningful ways. Again, there are at one and the same time socio-historical and narratological interpretations that can be made in such representation. Writing as an authoritative act *par excellence* in late Imperial Russia is not to be underestimated for its political power; however, the invitation that the depiction of acts of writing in these narratives extends to a critical evaluation of the intersection between the written word, truth, power and literature proves to be highly stimulating.

## Notes to Chapter 5

1. David Gascoigne, *The Games of Fiction: Georges Perec and Modern French Ludic Narrative* (Oxford and Berlin: Peter Lang, 2006), p. 16.
2. Dove, 'The Detection Formula and the Act of Reading', p. 25.
3. Kathleen Belin Owen, '"The Game's Afoot": Predecessors and Pursuits of a Postmodern Detective Novel', in *Theory and Practice of Classic Detective Fiction*, ed. by Jerome Delamater and Ruth Prigozy (Westport, CT: Greenwood, 1997), pp. 73–84; Patricia Merivale and Susan E. Sweeney, '"The Game's Afoot": On the Trail of the Metaphysical Detective Story', in *Detecting Texts: The Metaphysical Detective Story from Poe to Postmodernism*, ed. by Patricia Merivale and Susan E. Sweeney (Philadelphia, PA: University of Pennsylvania Press, 1999), pp. 1–24. The original phrase appears on p. 214 of volume 19 of *The Complete Works of Arthur Conan Doyle*, ed. by Neil McCaw (Newcastle: Cambridge Scholars Publishing, 2009).
4. R. Gordon Kelly, *Mystery Fiction and Modern Life* (Jackson, MS: University Press of Mississippi, 1998), p. 163.
5. Gascoigne, *The Games of Fiction*, p. 17.
6. Sweeney, 'Locked Rooms', p. 2. In *Detection and its Designs*, Peter Thoms makes a similar claim, arguing that: 'nineteenth-century detective fiction is an inherently self-reflexive form' (p. 1). Whether they explicitly term the genre 'self-reflexive' or not, there are many other critics who express similar views, including Roger Caillois, Peter Brooks and Joan Copjec. See Peter Brooks, *Reading for the Plot: Design and Intention in Narrative* (New York, NY: Vintage, 1985) and Joan Copjec, 'The Phenomenal Nonphenomenal: Private Space in Film Noir', in *Shades of Noir: A Reader*, ed. by Joan Copjec (London and New York, NY: Verso, 1993), pp. 167–97
7. Sweeney, 'Locked Rooms', pp. 2–3. Sweeney returns to this same topic a year later in an article entitled 'Purloined Letters: Poe, Doyle, Nabokov' and provides another useful elaboration of how she conceives of the genre's self-reflexivity: 'Every detective story is profoundly concerned with storytelling itself. Those properties of detective fiction that make it an archetypal narrative form — its structure (the story of a crime, which is gradually recovered by the story of an investigation); its thematic focus on reading; and its dramatization of the relationship between reader and writer — all indicate its inherent self-reflexivity.' (Sweeney, 'Purloined Letters: Poe, Doyle, Nabokov', *Russian Literature Triquarterly*, 24 (1991), 213–37 (p. 213))
8. Thoms, *Detection and its Designs*, p. 1. Thoms identifies an ultimately subversive intention behind the self-reflexivity of detective fiction when he claims that: 'the very form that emphasizes the piecing together of narrative pattern also incorporates a contradictory impulse that subverts that story-making process. Even as early works of detection plant the evidence their fictional investigators discover and structure into solutions, they also disperse additional clues to complicate that first reading.' (p. 145) He attributes this impulse not only to a general distrust of the law, but also to an anxiety on the part of the authors regarding their own authority as storytellers. Such distrust and anxiety is not, however, especially evident in Russian works of detective fiction of the late Imperial period.
9. Poe's interest in 'mutilated language' is discussed by Shawn James Rosenheim in *The Cryptographic Imagination: Secret Writing from Edgar Poe to the Internet* (Baltimore, MD and London: The Johns Hopkins University Press, 1997), pp. 69–70.
10. For further discussion of this novel's self-reflexivity, see Gale MacLachlan, 'Detectives and Criminals as Players in "Le Théâtre du crime": A Reading of Émile Gaboriau's *Le Crime d'Orcival*', in *Telling Performances: Essays on Gender, Narrative, and Performance*, ed. by Brian Nelson, Anne Freadman and Philip Anderson (Newark, NJ: University of Delaware Press, 2001), pp. 39–54.
11. Thoms, *Detection and its Designs*, p. 99. Janice MacDonald claims that 'Betteredge himself believes in the power and veracity of literature. He shows that a novel can be as powerful as scripture by discovering truths in rereadings and consultations with his well-worn copy of *Robinson Crusoe*' (Janice MacDonald, 'Parody and Detective Fiction', in *Theory and Practice of Classic Detective Fiction*, , ed. by Delamater and Prigozy, pp. 61–72 (p. 66)).
12. Claire Whitehead, 'The Temptation of the Reader: The Search for Meaning in Boris Akunin's *Pelagia Trilogy*', *Slavonic and East European Review*, 94.1 (2016), 29–56.

13. In 'How People Die', Shkliarevskii's narrator expresses his reluctance to take on the investigation into the petty thief, Krapivkin, because he knows that, if found guilty, the punishment will be too severe for such a trifling theft. See *Sochineniia A. Shkliarevskogo*, p. 111. The narrator in Panov's *Three Courts* records his frustration at having interviewed so many potential witnesses to the murder of Elena Vladimirovna, and of having received so little useful information (p. 28). The narrator-investigator in Sokolova's novella voices his sense of responsibility at arriving in the town of K*** as a newly instituted judicial investigator, of whom so much is expected given the recent changes in the law. See *Spetaia pesnia*, pp. 3–4.

14. This justification has been quoted at some length in Chapter 1 above on p. 39.

15. Timofeev, *Zapiski sledovatelia*, pp. 11–12. The narrator shows a similar preoccupation with retaining the reader's interest when he justifies his decision to report Marianna Bodresova's first account of her life story in his words rather than hers by saying: 'Рассказ Бодресовой передаю своими словами, чтобы не повредить интересу ее историю, потому что не берусь со всею пунктуальностью выразить его словами самой Марианны' ('I will provide Bodresova's story in my own words so as not to damage its interest because I cannot undertake to tell it in all its precision in the words of Marianna herself') (Timofeev, *Zapiski sledovatelia*, p. 48).

16. Timofeev, *Zapiski sledovatelia*, p. 23.

17. See Ansgar Nünning, 'On Metanarrative: Towards a Definition, a Typology and an Outline of the Functions of Metanarrative Commentary', in *The Dynamics of Narrative Form: Studies in Anglo-American Narratology*, ed. by John Pier (Berlin and New York, NY: de Gruyter, 2004), pp. 11–57 (p. 18). As illustrated in Chapter 4 above, in Timofeev's 'The Married Woman', the narrator upbraids himself for having spoken proleptically about possible conclusions in the case and says that it is important for the case to be allowed to 'tell itself'; see *Iz vospominanii sudebnogo sledovatelia*, p. 95.

18. Timofeev, *Zapiski sledovatelia*, p. 226.

19. Ibid., p. 281.

20. Sokolovskii, *Ostrog i zhizn'*, p. 10.

21. Nünning, 'On Metanarrative', p. 17.

22. Ibid., p. 34.

23. Shkliarevskii, *Povesti i rasskazy*, p. 107. Because it refers explicitly to the fictionality (or not) of the narrated text, this comment is metafictional rather than metanarrative.

24. Akhsharumov, *Kontsy v vodu*, p. 115.

25. R. L. Antropov, *Genii russkogo syska I. D. Putilin: rasskazy o ego pokhozheniiakh*, <http://www.royallib.com/read/dobriy_roman/geniy_russkogo_siska_id_putilin.html#475> [accessed, 6 June 16]. This 'Predislovie avtora' does not appear in either the *Taina Sukharevoi bashni* or *Shef sysknoi politsii Sankt-Peterburga Ivan Dmitrievich Putilin* collections.

26. Ibid.

27. Fludernik, *An Introduction to Narratology*, p. 61.

28. Ibid.

29. Julia Kristeva, 'Word, Dialogue, and Novel', in *Desire in Language: A Semiotic Approach to Literature and Art* (New York, NY: Columbia University Press, 1980), p. 65.

30. María Jesús Martínez Alfaro, 'Intertextuality: Origins and Development of the Concept', *Atlantis*, 18.1–2 (1996), 268–85 (p. 268).

31. Emma Bielecki uses this term to refer to the detective fiction of Maurice Leblanc in her chapter 'Arsène Lupin: Rewriting History', p. 48.

32. Hanna Charney, *The Detective Novel of Manners: Hedonism, Morality, and the Life of Reason* (London and Toronto: Associated University Press, 1981), p. 1.

33. Edgar Allan Poe, *Selected Tales*, ed. by David Van Leer (Oxford: Oxford University Press, 2008), p. 116.

34. Ibid., p. 105.

35. Wilkie Collins, *The Moonstone*, ed. by John Sutherland (Oxford: Oxford University Press, 1999; first published 1868), p. 434.

36. Linda Hutcheon, *A Theory of Parody: The Teachings of Twentieth-century Art Forms* (New York and London: Methuen, 1985), pp. 40–41.

37. Sokolovskii, *Ostrog i zhizn'*, p. 117; N. V. Gogol, *Sobranie sochinenii v shesti tomakh*, III (Moscow: Khudozhestvennaia literatura, 1952), p. 131.

38. Ibid., p. 124.

39. Shkliarevskii, *Rasskazy i povesti*, p. 120.

40. Ibid., p. 121.

41. Ibid., p. 131. Elsewhere in Shkliarevskii, references are made to the work of the poet Nikolai Nekrasov and to Charles Dickens's *Oliver Twist* in the story 'Semeinoe neschastie' ('Family Misfortune'), as well as to V. V. Krestovskii, whose 1864 social novel *Peterburgskie trushchoby* is considered to be an important precursor to the development of crime fiction in Russia.

42. Judith Still and Michael Worton, 'Introduction', in Michael Worton and Judith Still, *Intertextuality: Theories and Practices* (Manchester: Manchester University Press, 1990), pp. 1–44 (p. 13).

43. Lermontov produced various versions of the poem between 1829 and 1839. The composer, Anton Rubenshtein, adapted the poem into a hugely successful opera, written in 1871.

44. Zarin, *V poiskakh ubiitsy*, pp. 232–33.

45. Akhsharumov, *Kontsy v vodu*, p. 144.

46. Panov, *Tri suda*, p. 143.

47. A. P. Chekhov, 'Shvedskaia spichka: ugolovnyi rasskaz', in *Polnoe sobranie sochinenii i pisem v tridtsati tomakh*, II (Moscow: Nauka, 1975), p. 202. A similarly inappropriate reference to Pushkin is made implicitly in the preface to Chekhov's *The Shooting Party* when Kamyshev borrows his term 'звук[и] сладк[ие]' ('sweet sounds') to characterize his own writing which, as the voice of the editor makes clear, has absolutely nothing in common with that of Russia's national poet. See *Polnoe sobranie sochinenii i pisem*, III (Moscow: Nauka, 1975), p. 243.

48. See Whitehead, 'Playing at Detectives: Parody in *The Swedish Match*', *Essays in Poetics*, 30 (2005), pp. 229–46 (p. 240).

49. MacLachlan, 'Detectives and Criminals as Players', pp. 52–53.

50. Arthur Conan Doyle, *A Study in Scarlet*, in *The Complete Works of Arthur Conan Doyle*, ed. by Neil McCaw (Newcastle: Cambridge Scholars, 2009), p. 14.

51. It is notable that works in the Russian genre do not make mention of Poe's Dupin to the same extent as do French or British works. References in Russian works tend to be restricted to Monsieur Lecoq and Sherlock Holmes, as well as to the interesting hybrid figure of Ivan Dmitrievich Putilin, who has been mentioned above but who will be discussed in more detail below. As Joan Delaney Grossman has shown, the history of Poe's translation and reception into Russian in the nineteenth century was quite distinct from that in France, with his detective stories being translated much later in Russia. See Joan Delaney Grossman, *Edgar Allan Poe in Russia: A Study in Legend and Literary Influence* (Wurzburg: JAL-Verlag, 1973). Conan Doyle's novels were hugely successful in Russia: he was first translated into Russian in the 1890s, and in the early part of the twentieth century, according to Reitblat, ranked as the ninth most popular foreign writer in Russia in terms of circulation, one place ahead of William Shakespeare (see Reitblat, *Ot Bovy k Bal'montu*, p. 282).

52. A. I. Sokolova, *Bez sleda: ugolovnyi roman*, in *Rodina*, 1 (1890), pp. 60–61.

53. Akhsharumov, *Kontsy v vodu*, p. 127.

54. Zarin, *V poiskakh ubiitsy*, p. 393.

55. Panov, *Pomoch'*, p. 333.

56. A.P. Chekhov, *Sobraniie sochinenii*, III, p. 244. The translation is taken from *The Shooting Party*, trans. by Ronald Wilks (London: Penguin, 2004), p. 6.

57. Zarin, *V poiskakh ubiitsy*, p. 205.

58. Ibid.

59. Ibid.

60. Ibid., p. 242.

61. Ibid., p. 363.

62. M. V. Shevliakov, *Iz oblasti prikliuchenii: po rasskazam byvshego nachal'nika Sankt-Peterburgskoi sysknoi politsii* (St Petersburg: Demakov, 1898). In fact, it is commonly accepted that Shevliakov had previously been a ghostwriter for the actual Putilin when he had written his memoirs.

63. Putilin continues to figure in more contemporary detective fiction: he is the protagonist in Leonid Yuzefovich's trilogy of novels that begins with *Kostium Arlekvina*, and which have all been made into television serials, as well as in works by Igor Moskvin which present investigations into real crimes.

64. Antropov published *Genii russkogo syska I. D. Putilin: rasskazy o ego pokhozhdeniiakh* in 1908 and *Russkii syshchik I. D. Putilin: prestupleniia, raskrytye nachal'nikom Sankt-Peterburgskoi sysknoi politsii I. D. Putilinym* in two volumes between 1907 and 1917.

65. P. Orlovets, *Prikliucheniia Sherloka Kholmsa protiv Nata Pinkertona v Rossii* (Salamandra P.V.V., 2011), p. 33. See <http://www.salamandrapvv.blogspot.co.uk>.

66. Stephen Rachman proposes a number of interpretations for the intertextual references to newspapers in Poe's work, including: the impulse to straddle the fact/fiction boundary; the expression of a critique of the representation of reality as presented in the city daily newspapers; and a recognition of the competition that existed in the nineteenth century between newspapers and literary fiction in the representation of crime. See Rachman, 'Poe and the Origins of Detective Fiction'.

67. See McReynolds, *Murder Most Russian*, p. 124.

68. McReynolds has persuasively demonstrated that there are numerous instances when Russian crime fiction takes its inspiration from articles on crime that appeared in newspapers. In turn, these fictional works were serialized, particularly in the boulevard press, in the latter part of the nineteenth century. See Chapter 4 of *Murder Most Russian*, especially pp. 118–40.

69. Zarin, *V poiskakh ubiitsy*, p. 357. It is worth noting here that this first chapter of 'Chetvertyi' places a particular emphasis on written documents. In addition to these references to the newspaper, Vera is described as receiving another letter that she reads attentively before breathing a sigh of relief. The dénouement of the story reveals this letter to have come from Sanin, informing her that the letters being used to blackmail her have been retrieved.

70. Ibid., p. 358.

71. Ibid.

72. Shkliarevskii, 'Rasskaz sudebnogo sledovatelia', in *Chto pobudilo k ubiistvu?*, p. 84.

73. Shkliarevskii, 'Utro posle bala: rasskaz prisiazhnogo poverennogo' in *Utro posle bala*, p. 39 and p. 116. For an account of the history of jury trials in Russia, and the institution's role as a form of entertainment, see Chapter 3 in McReynolds's *Murder Most Russian* (pp. 79–112).

74. Panov, *Tri suda*, p. 62.

75. Poe, *Selected Tales*, p. 117.

76. Rachman, 'Poe and the Origins of Detective Fiction', p. 20.

77. Panov, *Tri suda*, p. 63.

78. Simon Kemp, 'The Many-Layered Palimpsest: Metafiction, Genre Fiction and Georges Perec's *53 Jours*', in *Rewriting Wrongs: French Crime Fiction and the Palimpsest*, ed. by Angela Kimyongür and Amy Wigelsworth (Newcastle: Cambridge Scholars, 2014), pp. 163–73 (p. 163).

79. The definition is taken from Alfaro, 'Intertextuality', p. 274. The original notion is outlined in Mikhail Bakhtin, *The Dialogic Imagination*, trans. by Caryl Emerson and Michael Holquist (Austin, TX: University of Texas Press, 1981), pp. 412–13.

80. Shkliarevskii, *Rasskazy i povesti*, p. 123.

81. Ibid., pp. 126. The narrator specifically cites the reading of works by Paul de Coq, Paul Feval and Honoré de Balzac at this point.

82. Ibid., p. 148.

83. Ibid., p. 165.

84. Ibid., p. 173.

85. Shkliarevskii, *Povesti i rasskazy*, p. 73.

86. Panov, *Tri suda*, p. 137.

87. Zarin, *V poiskakh ubiitsy*, p. 211.

88. Ibid.

89. Sweeney, 'Locked Rooms', p. 8.

90. Poe, *Selected Tales*, p. 95.

91. Timofeev, *Zapiski sledovatelia*, pp. 8–9.

92. One case is entitled 'О повесившейся как бы будто бы крестьянке' ('Some sort of, as it were, hanged peasant woman') whilst another is labelled: 'О намерении крестьянина В-ского, произвести из ревности обезображение на лице и животе девицы С-кой' ('On the intention of a V___ district peasant to disfigure out of jealousy the face and stomach of a young girl from S___ district') (*Zapiski sledovatelia*, p. 36).

93. Dostoevskii, *Prestuplenie i nakazanie*, p. 267/p. 308.

94. Ibid., p. 268/p. 309.

95. Ibid., p. 276/p. 318.

96. Ibid., p. 270/p. 312.

97. Shkliarevskii, 'Sekretnoe sledstvie' in *Chto pubudilo k ublistru?*, p. 183.

98. Ibid., p. 213.

99. Zarin, *V poiskakh ubiitsy*, p. 301.

100. See my article, 'The Letter of the Law: Literacy and Orality in S. A. Panov's *Murder in Medveditsa Village*', *Slavonic and East European Review*, 89.1 (2011), 1–28, for a fuller discussion of the role of language in Panov's novella.

101. Hutter, 'Dreams, Transformations, and Literature', p. 234.

102. Herzog, 'Crime Stories', p. 37.

103. Foucault's examples of 'examinations' are those conducted in the military, prisons, hospitals and schools.

104. Panov, *Ubiistvo v derevne Medveditse*, p. 7.

105. Ibid., p. 11.

106. Schütt, 'French Crime Fiction', p. 67. Schütt makes her claim in respect of Émile Gaboriau's 1876 work *Le Petit Vieux des Batignolles* (*The Little Old Man of Batignolles*). The disruption in Panov's work stems from the fact that, in spite of the investigator's manifold acts of writing, it is in fact an act of non-verbal speech (crying) from the victim's young daughter that prompts the all-important confession from Grishanin.

107. Jacques Derrida, *Force de loi* (Paris: Galilée, 1994), p. 26. The translation is taken from Derrida, *Acts of Religion*, ed. by Gil Anidjar (London: Routledge, 2002), p. 238.

108. Eckart Voigts-Virchow, *Introduction to Media Studies* (Stuttgart: Klett Sprachen, 2005), p. 117.

109. Ibid.

110. Ibid.

111. Panov, *Ubiistvo v derevne Medveditse*, pp. 163–64. The frequency with which these verbs related to 'saying' appear here is not a constant feature of the novella but rather a marked difference in these descriptions of the oral interrogation of Grishanin. This scene serves as an interesting counterpoint to the discussion in Chapter 3 above of the drama and immediacy associated with passages of direct dialogue.

112. The term 'performative' was introduced by John L. Austin in *How to do Things with Words* (Cambridge, MA: Harvard University Press, 1962).

113. Thomas, 'The Fingerprint of the Foreigner', p. 656.

114. The terms employed here are taken from John R. Searle, 'How Performatives Work', *Linguistics and Philosophy*, 12 (1989), 535–58.

115. The narrator-investigator in Sokolovskii's story 'Unpleasant Moments' also reflects on the performative power of his writing when he outlines the process of remanding someone to prison. He talks during this passage of how the investigator produces a written record that is then read out loud to the accused:

> в постановлении прописываются все улики и доказательства, из которых, как из логического построения, вытекает финал: заключение подсудимого. Это постановление прочитывается вслух следователем подсудимому, который и расписывается внизу постановления: «такой-то слушал о том-то». (*Ostrog i zhizn'*, pp. 14–15)

> [in this written decision are included all of the clues and proof, from which, as if from a logical construction, flows the finale: the incarceration of the accused. This written document is read aloud by the investigator to the accused who has to write underneath it: 'X has listened to the account of Y'.]

116. Being illiterate, the peasants depicted here and in other works of crime fiction are not able to sign their names on such documents, but simply make the mark of three crosses and have the local scribe add their name.

117. Catherine Bell, *Ritual Theory, Ritual Practice* (Oxford: Oxford University Press, 1992), pp. 204–05.

118. Ibid., p. 197.

119. Thomas, 'The Fingerprint of the Foreigner', p. 656.

120. Shkliarevskii, 'Rasskaz sudebnogo sledovatelia', in *Chto pobudilo k ubiistvu?*, p. 124.

121. Ibid., p. 132.

# CHAPTER 6

# Bending the Rules of the Game:
# Parody in Russian Detective Fiction

The previous chapter has established that self-consciousness, whether it is expressed in the form of intertextuality or metatextuality, is a notable characteristic of Russian detective fiction from its earliest incarnations. Whereas that chapter has concentrated on the works' awareness of themselves primarily as literary texts, this concluding chapter is dedicated to works that betray this same self-consciousness, but with especial regard to the generic conventions at work in detective fiction. Specifically, the works to be discussed here showcase self-consciousness through the exercise of parody, which, as Linda Hutcheon has claimed, 'is one of the major forms of modern self-reflexivity'.[1] Hutcheon defines parody as 'a form of imitation, but imitation characterized by ironic inversion [...] [it] is, in another formulation, repetition with critical distance, which marks difference rather than similarity'.[2] The various acts of imitation, inversion and repetition performed by a given text all imply an awareness of the previous text or texts that are being manipulated, and particularly of their characteristic structures and conventions. In his essay 'Dostoevskii i Gogol': (k teorii parodii)' ('Dostoevskii and Gogol: (Towards a Theory of Parody)') from 1921, the Russian Formalist Iurii Tynianov explains the textual doubling present in parody by means of a comparison:

> Стилизация близка к пародии. И та и другая живут двойною жизнью: за планом произведения стоит другой план, стилизуемый или пародируемый. Но в пародии обязательна невязка обоих планов, смещение их [...].[3]

> [Stylization is close to parody. Both live a double life: behind the plane of the work there stands another plane, that which is stylized or parodied. But in parody there has to be a disharmony or parallax between the two planes [...].]

Although Tynianov cites playfulness as a defining factor only of stylization, Hutcheon extends this interpretation when she says that 'this ironic *playing* with multiple conventions, this extended repetition with critical difference, is what I mean by modern parody' (emphasis added).[4]

It is Hutcheon also who, whilst acknowledging the contribution made by Formalist critics to the study of parody, makes the crucial insertion of the figure of the reader into this model. She characterizes her approach to parody as both formal and pragmatic and is keen to emphasize that 'texts do not generate anything —

until they are perceived and interpreted'.[5] In stressing the skills required for parody to function, she underscores the role played not only by the author but also by the reader:

> When we speak of parody, we do not just mean two texts that interrelate in a certain way. We also imply an intention to parody another work (or set of conventions) and both a recognition of that intent and an ability to find and interpret the backgrounded text in its relation to the parody. [...] parody is a sophisticated genre in the demands it makes on its practitioners and its interpreters. The encoder, then the decoder, must effect a structural superimposition of texts that incorporates the old into the new.[6]

Although the recognition of parodic intent is not necessarily always straightforward, the highly conventional nature of detective fiction is considered by some critics to simplify its relationship to the practice. For example, Janice MacDonald argues that:

> [...] detective fiction creates the context necessary for audience recognition of parody. Readers of detective fiction often read widely within the genre, and 'addicted' readers are likely to have read (and recognize allusions to) the original of any given parody. This preknowledge is necessary to the appreciation of parody.[7]

As is well known, if the reader does not recognize the fact that ironic allusions are being made in parody, then the work in question fails in that regard and creates a quite different effect upon the reader.[8] However, MacDonald and others, who consider popular literature to be particularly formulaic, consider failure in these genres to be less likely. In their discussion of the potential for parody in detective fiction, Lizabeth Paravisini and Carlos Yorio highlight the question of generic evolution, which was raised by Formalist critics, as well as the role of formula:

> From its beginning as a genre, detective fiction contained within it the seed of its own metamorphosis: it was a genre which adhered rigidly to a formula, offering a familiar combination of characters and settings, and prototypical detective figures.[9]

To counter any temptation to consider that such 'addiction' to the genre, and consequent familiarity with conventions, is a phenomenon unique to the twentieth-century context, MacDonald cites the example of Fergus W. Hume, whose *The Mystery of a Hansom Cab* (1886) at one time outsold Conan Doyle's Sherlock Holmes stories. In a preface written for an edition of the novel ten years after its original publication, Hume claimed to have identified the style in which he would write simply by asking a Melbourne bookseller which books he sold most of. The reply cited the popularity of Émile Gaboriau, so Hume wrote a detective novel. MacDonald contends persuasively that this anecdote demonstrates that 'even as early as 1886, the detective novel had reached such a stage of formula that any reasonably intelligent wordsmith could manufacture one, given an accurate recipe'.[10] This argument is borne out in the Russian context by the fact that one of the authors to be discussed in the present chapter, Chekhov, appears to have the prevalence of such formulaic practice in his sights when he explicitly characterizes his new work as a parody in a letter to his editor, Nikolai Leikin. Writing in September 1883, Chekhov explains the circumstances surrounding his submission of a story to the journal *Al'manakh strekozy* (*The Dragonfly*), rather than to Leikin's journal, *Oskolki* (*Fragments*), which had been his publishing home up until that point in his career:

> Недавно я искусился. Получил я приглашение от Буквы написать что-нибудь в «Альманах Стрекозы»... Я искусился и написал огромнейший рассказ в печатный лист. Рассказ пойдет. Название его «Шведская спичка», а суть — пародия на уголовные рассказы. Вышел смешной рассказ. Мне нравится премии «Стрекозы».[11]

> [Recently I gave in to temptation. I received an invitation from Bukva to write something for *The Dragonfly*... I was tempted and wrote my longest story to date. The story will do. It is called 'The Safety Match', and in essence it is a parody of detective stories. It has turned out humorous. I like *The Dragonfly*'s rates of pay.]

Chekhov's admission clearly suggests that, by the time of his composition of 'The Swedish Match' in 1883, the genre of the 'уголовный роман/рассказ' ('crime novel/story') was sufficiently well established in Russia to become the subject of ironic and parodic attention.[12] However, as the discussion to come makes clear, Chekhov's detective story departs from the usual 'recipe' for the genre and far exceeds what 'any reasonably intelligent wordsmith' might produce.

It is fitting for a monograph devoted to the poetics of Russian detective fiction that the final chapter should concentrate on works that, by means of parody, show a keen awareness of the conventions operating in the genre. The previous chapters have served to construct the figure of a competent reader who is sufficiently well versed in the genre's conventions to recognize when they are being deployed with ironic inversion, imitation and/or critical distance. This closing chapter, which is dedicated to an analysis of two parodies, therefore invites that reader to refer back to certain of the poetic structures that have been identified previously in order to appreciate how they are reconfigured. On the basis that parody is likely to target the most recognizable or characteristic features in a genre, discussion of these works helps to underscore which devices or structures have become the most clearly established and, consequently, the most appropriate targets for irony. The two works to be considered are Semyon Panov's novella *From the Life of a Provincial Town*, which was first published in 1876, and Chekhov's 'The Swedish Match'. Panov's work features a judicial investigator, Vadim Vadimovich Polumordin, who confounds the reader's generic expectations by persecuting two innocent people, the town scrivener, Isaak Onufrievich Kantalovich, and a woman named only as Ampleeva, in the case of an abandoned child who has died. Chekhov's 'The Swedish Match' recounts the story of the investigation conducted by two detective figures, the judicial investigator Nikolai Yermolaich Chubikov and his younger assistant and secretary Diukovskii, into the apparent death of Mark Ivanych Kliauzov who, in the dénouement, turns out in fact to still be alive.

What these two works make abundantly clear is that, as Tynianov and Hutcheon both contend, parody can take a variety of forms and can have a range of intent.[13]

*From the Life of a Provincial Town* and 'The Swedish Match' are parodies that operate in distinct fashions and prompt quite different reading experiences. The first half of the chapter below is dedicated to a discussion of Panov's novella and to the various ways in which it departs from generic convention. It focuses on elements of poetics that have been analysed in previous chapters, including: the impact of the title and subtitle; the profile and performance of the narrator, including the exploitation of omniscience and shifting perspectives; and the depiction of the character and authority of the investigator figure. It also considers the part played in the parody by the horizon of expectations created by Panov's other works, as well as the characterization of other figures in the fictional world, particularly the way in which the narrative voice modulates the reader's reaction to them. Finally, it highlights how the notions of truth and justice, that are so central to the genre of crime fiction, prove to be fallible and corruptible in the wrong hands. The second half of the chapter switches its attention to Chekhov's rather subtler parody, 'The Swedish Match'. The impact of the narrative voice is again examined, especially its use of official-sounding judicial language, as well as the role played by direct dialogue in the story. The characterization of the investigating figures is also central to the analysis, notably the way in which the reader's reaction to their performances is regulated over the course of Chekhov's work. This section of the chapter also addresses the question of whether the seemingly parodic ending of the story actually does debunk the genre's conventions. This is followed by a consideration of how the story ironizes other conventional patterns encountered within detective fiction before a conclusion that addresses whether either of these works can be considered to initiate a process of generic metamorphosis, as Paravisini and Yorio suggest parody does.

## Parody in Panov's *From the Life of a Provincial Town*: The Horizon of Expectations and Unpredictable Narrator Performance

At least some of the effect created by *From the Life of a Provincial Town* can be traced to the fact that, at the time of its publication, Panov was already known for penning 'straight' works of detective fiction. Readers familiar with his two works from 1872, *The Harvest Gathering* and *Murder in Medveditsa Village*, and with *Three Courts*, which appears as the first work in the same collected volume, are likely to approach the 1876 novella with expectations of a similar and generically conventional work. However, its particular combination of title, subtitle and epigraph could reasonably be interpreted as early paratextual clues to the work's ambiguous nature. The main title, *From the Life of a Provincial Town*, recalls Panov's earlier *The Harvest Gathering* in opting not to signal explicitly the criminal-investigative content of the work and its association with the crime fiction genre.[14] In fact, this title implicitly suggests a rather closer identification with the popular nineteenth-century Russian genre of the society tale. Nevertheless, the subtitle 'Iz zapisok sudebnogo sledovatelia' ('From the Notes of a Judicial Investigator') clearly links the story not only with the genre in general but, in the use of the specific term 'notes' that has been discussed in the opening chapter of this monograph, with the earliest examples published in Russia. Although the early works styled as 'notes' have been shown to straddle generic borders, they can in no way be considered parodies; so Panov's use of 'notes' arguably suggests that his work will be generically 'straight'.[15] It is, however, the presence of the Anglo-Norman maxim 'Honni soit qui mal y pense' as an epigraph on the title page that, albeit in hindsight, gives the clearest indication as to the work's parodic intent.[16] For the ideal reader that this epigraph envisages, the fact that the saying 'shame on him who thinks evil of it' is frequently used ironically to insinuate the presence of hidden agendas or conflicts of interests indicates the likelihood that the novella's plot will not be conventional. That said, there are likely to be many readers for whom the implications of this maxim will be unclear and where the presence of a phrase in a non-Cyrillic, foreign language merely serves to characterize the extrafictional voice as educated and authoritative.[17]

It is not only the author's name and the combination of titles and subtitles that provides the reader with a sense of familiarity with regards to *From the Life of a Provincial Town*. The opening line identifies the geographical location of the novella's action as the town of N., which is used in all but one of Panov's other works. It is the general setting for the action in *The Harvest Gathering*, where the opening sentence describes the first-person narrator travelling along a country road in the N. district before deciding to visit his friend the investigator in the village of Gridin. And the town itself is the location of the judicial investigator's main office in both *Murder in Medveditsa Village* and *Murder in Mukhtolovaia Grove*. This coincidence of location therefore functions as an implicit invitation to the informed reader to anticipate that *From the Life of a Provincial Town* will develop in much the same way as these other works. However, the stance of critical distance adopted by this particular text is implicitly indicated by the fact that its opening pages are quite distinct from those in Panov's other work. What *From the Life of a Provincial Town* does is to exaggerate ironically the generic formula of having a social gathering interrupted by the summoning of the detective to investigate a crime. Unlike *Murder in Medveditsa Village* and *The Harvest Gathering*, in which the description of social encounters between friends is cut short during the opening chapter, and the myriad other works in the genre where the announcement of the crime also happens at a very early stage, this novella is extremely slow to get started. Although the informed reader will recognize the narrator's description of the lack of activity in N. in the evening, the fact that no mention of a criminal case is made until well into the third chapter is unusual. Indeed, it initially appears that the main title of the work is the most fitting, as the opening chapters provide an extended description of the mundane activities and petty personalities of N.'s inhabitants. The unconventional nature of the work is further signalled by having the announcement of the crime come not from a representative of the judicial system, but from malicious gossip amongst the gathered company. Moreover, even after the case of the death of the abandoned child is mentioned, the criminal investigation still does not begin, and the apparent reluctance of the detective figure to take on the case confounds the generic expectations of the reader. Such examples make clear that *From the Life of a*

*Provincial Town* succeeds in simultaneously embodying characteristics that encourage the reader to expect a straight work of detective fiction whilst also hinting at more unusual practice.

Earlier sections of this monograph have demonstrated how aspects of the narrator's performance construct authority and generate suspense by controlling the reader's access to information. For the purposes of the present discussion, the most significant elements of this performance are privilege and the presentation by the narrative voice of direct dialogue. Chapter 2 has provided examples of works in which the autodiegetic narrators 'overstep' the limits of their privilege in order to earn the type of authority usually accorded to heterodiegetic voices. Whereas such instances have been viewed as acceptable deviations from the norm arising out of the desire for epistemic authority, Panov's *From the Life of a Provincial Town* provides an example of far more unpredictable, and thus parodic, narrator performance. Crucially, what Panov's novella does is that it takes various conventional aspects of the narrative voice that are used to generate suspense in other works and exaggerates the manner in which they are deployed to a point where they are clearly ironized. In so doing, it shines a light on the extent to which the reader is manipulated by such devices in even the 'straightest' examples of the genre.

*From the Life of a Provincial Town* is narrated by a heterodiegetic voice that does not belong to a character in the fictional world. An early indication of the critical distance that Panov's work adopts vis-à-vis earlier examples in the genre stems from the uncertainty surrounding how the status of this narrative voice is to be reconciled with the term 'notes' used in its subtitle. The works by Sokolovskii, Stepanov and Timofeev that have styled themselves in this same way have each featured the autodiegetic voice of the investigator as both narrator and central protagonist. At no point in Panov's novella, however, is mention made of an act of memoir-writing taking place. The only official investigator in the diegesis is Vadim Vadimovich Polumordin and the reader is never informed that he commits an account of the case to paper; nor is there a frame narrative that suggests the presence of an alternative note-taking figure. The use of the term 'notes' in the subtitle comes, therefore, to seem like something of an empty generic moniker that brings with it none of the usual assurances of a narrative legitimized by direct and authentic lived experience.

In a similar fashion, much of the parodic effect of *From the Life of a Provincial Town* can be traced to the fact that the initial impression that the reader is encouraged to form about the competence and reliability of this heterodiegetic narrative voice proves to be misleading. In fact, the situation is not even as straightforward as the narrative voice ultimately showing itself to be unreliable when the reader has been encouraged to think the opposite; it is rather that the reader can never be sure whether the narrator s/he is dealing with is reliable or unreliable. At the outset of the novella, and particularly in the opening description of the evening scene in N., the narrative voice appears to be as informative and objective as its heterodiegetic stance suggests it should be. The narrator immediately provides a time and date for the action, and the picture of the closed shutters and sounds of singing emanating from various houses is indicative of a birds-eye, seemingly omnipresent perspective. Focusing on one house in particular, the narrator gives full rank and name details for Lieutenant Porfirii Matveevich Tselyi, before informing the reader that he is waiting for guests who are coming to play whist. During the course of this opening chapter, the narrative voice employs a relatively mobile point of view that attaches itself temporarily to various different characters in order to build up a full picture of events. The reader observes what takes place at the Tselyi household from the host's perspective, but also from positions located closer to his servant, Anton, Tseyli's wife, Varvara Aleksandrovna, the investigator, Polumordin, as well as the doctor, Nikolai Nikolaevich Antonov. The sense here is that the narrator is keen to provide a complete and informative picture of events that take place in the fictional world.

The impression created by this use of perspective is reinforced by the narrator's exploitation of omniscient privilege at various stages throughout the novella. This voice's possession of a superhuman degree of privilege is demonstrated in original fashion during a description early in the second chapter. During an account of the scene in a different part of the town of N. earlier on the same evening, the narrator notes how a dog begins to bark and gives the following explanation as to why:

> В конце улицы у перекрестка показалась фигура человека, шагавшего по направлению к трактиру. Хотя человеческий глаз не различил бы никак что кто-то идет, однако чуткость собаки взяла свое.[18]

> [At the end of the street by a crossroads appeared the figure of a man walking in the direction of the tavern. Although a human eye would never have been able to make out that someone was moving, the dog's senses were keen enough to do so.]

In providing information that, it is claimed, a human being would not be able to discern, the narrator is clearly signalling his own omniscient privilege. Although the somewhat unusual style of this claim might be taken to foreshadow implicitly the ultimately disruptive nature of the exploitation of this privilege, *From the Life of a Provincial Town* features plenty of other examples where it is used straightforwardly. Amongst the many descriptions informed by a purely external perspective, the narrator also proves capable of informing the reader how the scrivener, Isaak Onufrievich Kantalovich, feels when he is cornered by a group of boisterous pigs on his way to the tavern in the second chapter. Later in the same chapter, the narrator provides insight into the mind of this same character in order to inform the reader how Kantalovich feels after his meeting with his only friend in the town, Kalikst Kalikstovich Zentokovskii, and how he also wishes to go out and see Ampleeva. The narrator's omniscience does not extend solely to the figure of Kantalovich; there are also numerous instances of it providing insight into the thoughts and feelings of Polumordin as his persecution of the scrivener and Ampleeva develops.

The sense of confidence in the narrative voice that is encouraged by such demonstrations of omniscient privilege is deepened by its repeated displays of self-consciousness, albeit expressed in stylized fashion. The heterodiegetic narrator appears keen to establish a sense of intimacy and shared experience between himself and the reader by means of remarks intended to draw the latter into the diegesis. So, for example, in the opening chapter, when the narrator describes how Tselyi goes into the drawing room, the narrator adds: 'куда и мы за ним последуем' ('where we will follow him').[19] Similarly, this chapter closes with the statement, 'Но оставим их, и перенесемся на время в другую часть города' ('But let us leave them and move to another part of town for a while'),[20] which provides further proof of the narrative voice's omnipresence. Although the reader recognizes such suggestions of a simultaneity between *fabula* and *siuzhet* as nothing more than a literary convention, they remain effective as a means of establishing a degree of trust between this figure and the narrator. The narrative voice also attempts to garner the reader's trust by means of nods to its consciousness of the storytelling role. At various points, the narrator flags up his diegetic authority by reminding the reader of, particularly, characters who have been encountered at prior moments. In the second chapter, for example, the narrator introduces the unnamed midwife as one of the new arrivals at Tselyi's house by saying: 'с которою мы отчасти познакомились в первой главе' ('whom we partly met in the first chapter').[21] Such indications of the storytelling competence of the narrator have been encountered elsewhere in Russian detective fiction, and have a similar effect of encouraging the reader to have confidence in the abilities of this voice.

The key area, however, in which the narrator cultivates an — ultimately disingenuous — image of himself as a reliable and informative voice is the provision of explicit commentary or judgement upon the diegetic characters and their actions. As will be discussed in greater detail below, a considerable degree of the parody in Panov's novella stems from the generically unconventional depiction of a corrupt and conniving judicial investigator. There are various instances in *From the Life of a Provincial Town* when the heterodiegetic narrator proves willing to characterize this central protagonist in explicitly negative terms. In the third chapter, for example, the narrator describes the detective thus: 'Полумордин же, уездный франт, в полном смысле этого слова, глупый, легкомысленный, ветреный неуч, щекотал свое самолюбие тем, что про него говорили, что он за Целой ухаживает' ('Polumordin, after all, was the town dandy, in the full sense of the word; a silly, flippant, frivolous ignoramus whose vanity was tickled by the fact that people said he was keen on [Varvara Aleksandrovna] Tselaia').[22] Although there are numerous other occasions when the narrator chooses not to condemn the judicial investigator so openly, this characterization proves to the reader that he is capable of doing so. Similarly, in a novella where malicious untruths spoken about certain characters lie at the heart of the action, it is significant that the heterodiegetic narrator does at times explicitly point out such behaviour to the reader. In the third chapter, following a claim made in direct speech by the apothecary Shindovskii about Kantalovich wanting to take his arm, the narrator says: 'аптекарь, как мы видели, врал: он сам, первый подал Огрызке руку, но он это сделал только в тайне, как и Зентоковский' ('the apothecary, as we have seen, was lying: he had himself offered his arm to Ogryzko [Kantalovich] first, but only in secret, just like Zentokovskii'). The narrator presses home his point when he remarks: 'он, как и все в городе Н., примыкал к большинству и своего мнения не имел' ('just like everyone in the town of N., he sided with the majority and did not have his own opinion').[23] There are plenty of other times, however, when the narrator allows even more duplicitous statements and actions to go entirely uncommented.

The examples above make clear the degree of authority and privilege that the heterodiegetic voice possesses in *From the Life of a Provincial Town*. However, a key strand of the novella's parody of generic conventions stems from the fact that these abilities are exploited in an entirely unpredictable fashion. The narrative voice frequently opts not to function as an informative or helpful guide to the reader, leaving him/her with little more than the unreliable voices in the diegetic world upon which to base interpretation. Initially, the inconsistencies in the narrator's performance appear inconsequential; however, as the novella progresses, their effect becomes increasingly disruptive. In the opening chapter, for example, the narrator aligns the visual point of view with Polumordin as he talks to Varvara Aleksandrovna, and then describes an event that frightens them both: 'Но в это время кто-то стукнул с улицы в ставни, и она и он встали, невольно испуганные, и отошли от окна' ('But at that moment someone knocked on the shutters from the street and they both stood up, frightened unwittingly, and moved away from the window').[24] Any further reaction to the incident is initially delayed by a passage of direct dialogue as the doctor, Antonov, belatedly arrives at the whist evening. Although the narrator records how Varvara Aleksandrovna explains what has just happened, and how Polumordin is still listening at the window and how he claims, in direct speech, that it was the scrivener, Kantalovich, who knocked, he does not provide any more explanation. This lack of interpretive commentary means that the reader struggles to understand why Polumordin is so annoyed by such a seemingly trivial event and why he is so insistent, in spite of the reasonable objections voiced by other characters, that it was Kantalovich who knocked. Shifts in point of view so as to generate suspense by obscuring information are standard fare in detective fiction; however, in relation to such an inconsequential incident, the use of limited point of view, unsupplemented by the narrative voice, is an unnecessary distraction for the reader here.[25]

The narrator employs limited perspective and privilege to more generically conventional ends in an example from the latter stages of the third chapter of *From the Life of a Provincial Town*. This chapter has shifted the focus back from Kantalovich and Zentokovskii to the party at Tselyi's house and has seen the first suggestions of the involvement of the former and Ampleeva in the case of the death of the abandoned child. At one stage the narrator describes how Varvara Aleksandrovna, the midwife and Polumordin go off together into another room laughing about the case, whereupon the investigator swears to have his enemies exiled to Siberia. A few pages later, the narrator describes how Polumordin again leads these two women off into another room, but then reports: 'О чем там разговаривали они, сказать трудно!' ('It's difficult to say what they talked about there!').[26] He goes on to report that, on the basis of the occasional word that emanates from the other room, it is possible to conclude that they are forming a plan of attack 'против злодеев' ('against the evil-doers').[27] On the one hand, such a switch to limited perspective and privilege can be read as generically conventional: it inspires a sense of curiosity in the reader to find out what precisely it is that the characters have been talking about and what they are plotting against Kantalovich and Ampleeva. On the other, the obviously constructed nature of the switch exaggerates conventional practice and, coming so close on the heels of the use of omniscient privilege, seems rather forced.[28] Moreover, the appearance of the term 'evil-doers' in the narrator's speech suggests the presence of free indirect discourse that blurs the line between the voice of the narrator and those of the intradiegetic characters. It is the narrator's frequent failure to function as a distinct and informative voice during the remainder of the novella that disrupts normal generic practice so parodically.

Combined with the repeated use of a limited perspective, the narrator's reticence to judge characters explicitly leaves the reader on even shakier epistemic and interpretive ground than is the generic norm. As the novella progresses, it becomes increasingly difficult for the reader to keep in mind that Kantalovich and Ampleeva are not the parents of the abandoned child because the case against them is constructed by so many of the characters, all of whom appear blind to the falsity of their accusations. Crucially, the narrative voice fails to function as an objective and reliable voice to counter this conspiracy. One key method in this regard is the use of numerous passages of direct dialogue between characters that go largely uncommented by the heterodiegetic voice. In the fifth chapter, for example, the narrator reports a conversation between Tselyi, Polumordin and, later, Troiantsev, the local police inspector, who has only been introduced in the preceding chapter, but is another key motivator in the conspiracy. Tselyi tells Polumordin that he has heard from Troiantsev that this latter knows 'из верного источника' ('from a reliable source')[29] that Kantalovich and Ampleeva are involved in the case of the abandoned child. Although the reader suspects that this is not the truth because Polumordin has earlier asked Troiantsev for help in substantiating the accusation against Kantalovich by any means, the narrator opts not to step in to point out the falsity of the inspector's claim. After Troiantsev joins the conversation, Polumordin gives more details of the state of his investigation: he states with utter conviction that the child belongs to Kantalovich and Ampleeva; that someone took it to the Roshchinskii house on their orders; that Ampleeva sewing clothes for it is proof of her relationship to the child; and that Kantalovich is proven to be the father by the fact that he went with Ampleeva to see the deceased child lying in its coffin. Although the reader knows that these accusations are based on nothing more than gossip and hears the trio agree to work together to get written testimony that implicates Kantalovich, the narrative voice again remains silent throughout the conversation. It does no more than provide the most peremptory tags on the dialogue and offers no explicit commentary whatsoever on the speciousness of what is being said and the corrupt nature of the plan being hatched. This is a technique that is used again and again in Panov's novella to permit the narrative voice not to expand on the characters' behaviour and speech.

Even outside the specific context of direct dialogue, however, the narrative voice repeatedly adopts a deliberately unhelpful position. The starkest example of the narrator's failure to comment on the actions of the intradiegetic characters comes in the closing chapter of the novella. At Kantalovich's suggestion, Ampleeva requests to undergo a medical examination to prove that she cannot be the mother of the abandoned child. Even though the narrator has previously informed the reader that, amongst all the various characters who have contributed to the conspiracy against the pair, only the doctor remains convinced of Ampleeva's guilt at this point, the generically informed reader still expects the medical examination to exonerate her. However, the narrator reports:

> По окончании осмотра, доктор написал акт, который и прочел вслух. В нем значилось, что: по внешним признакам, им усмотренным, он приходил к заключению, что Амплеева дней четырнадцать тому назад разрешилась от бремени.[30]

> [At the end of his examination, the doctor wrote out an official document that he then read aloud. In it he said that, on the basis of the external evidence that he had examined, he had come to the conclusion that Ampleeva had given birth approximately fourteen days previously.]

The reader schooled in earlier examples of Russian detective fiction is accustomed to doctors collaborating with judicial investigators on their cases and to the use of official written documents attesting to the facts of their examinations. However, Panov's novella provides the only example of this collaboration being corrupted and of the doctor's statement apparently comprising a lie. Yet, the reader can only surmise that the doctor is lying here: the narrative voice opts not to intervene actively at this point, or even later when Polumordin asks the doctor if he is sure of what he has found, in order to state categorically that the doctor's conclusions are false. This silence means that the reader can do no more than assume, based on the earlier characterization of the doctor and the circumstances of the case, that he has fabricated his report; however, a considerable degree of doubt is allowed to persist. This uncertainty is shown to extend at this point to Polumordin himself as the narrator describes how the detective begins to wonder whether Ampleeva might not, after all, be the mother of the abandoned child when he knows that the initial accusation was entirely fabricated. Although a lack of full disclosure from the narrative voice is a staple of detective fiction, the exploitation of this device in *From the Life of a Provincial Town* is exaggerated to a degree that is clearly parodic.

The novella's most extreme point of deviation from the generic norm is one that should be attributed not only to the heterodiegetic narrative voice but also to the extrafictional voice responsible for the overall construction of the work. Just as the opening of *From the Life of a Provincial Town* has suggested that the work might not fulfil conventional expectations, so its ending parodically frustrates the reader's wishes. Even though the reader recognizes that the collective persecution of Kantalovich and Ampleeva distinguishes Panov's work from usual detective fiction practice, the desire for a clear resolution of events persists. However, the novella's dénouement completely undermines the convention that states that works in the genre are 'end-oriented'. *From the Life of a Provincial Town* closes as it has opened: with a description of the group of friends playing whist at Tselyi's house. The narrator observes that there is only one topic of conversation that evening, and that is the case involving Kantalovich and Ampleeva. With the exception of one remark from the doctor (about not being able to help in proving Kantalovich's guilt, which perhaps suggests the dishonesty of his examination of Ampleeva), no new information is revealed and no judgement is passed by the narrator either on the characters or on the case they have constructed. In fact, the narrator abdicates any responsibility for providing satisfactory concluding information for the novella: there is no information about whether Kantalovich and Ampleeva are actually arrested, brought to trial or punished. It is as if the curtain is brought down on the novella before the events have played out to their end; and the decision to do so shines an ironic spotlight on the genre's conventional need for a definite conclusion. The parodic misdirection of the reader is made absolutely evident by the fact that the work's final paragraph sees the narrator describe how Polumordin revels in the handkerchief that he has been given by Varvara Aleksandrovna as a memento. The reader remains unsure about the true nature of the relationship between these two characters: is it romantic or not? However, this intrigue is as of nothing compared to the principal interest that s/he has invested in the story of the fabricated case against Kantalovich and Ampleeva and which is left entirely unresolved.

## Generic Inversion in the Characterization of the Judicial Investigator

Chapter 2 above has focused attention upon the various ways in which Russian crime fiction constructs the investigator as a figure of social and diegetic authority. In the immediate post-reform period of the 1860s and 1870s, the judicial investigator functioned as an expression of the hope placed in the revised legal system and the genre portrayed him in a positive light. The authority and power attributed to this figure arises not only out of his personal qualities but also out of a description of him as *more* educated or insightful or professional than certain other members of society. Nevertheless, as the discussion of the detectives in both Panov's *The Harvest Gathering* and Shkliarevskii's 'The Tale of a Judicial Investigator' has shown, there are exceptions to the model of the skilled and successful criminal investigator. In particular, the example of Ivan Gerasimovich in Panov's earlier novella functions as a precursor to the characterization of Polumordin in *From the Life of a Provincial Town*. Although Gerasimovich is depicted as educated and dedicated to his profession, his investigative skill and judgement are rather overshadowed by those of his friend, the narrator. Similarly, the judicial investigator in Panov's *Three Courts* initially draws an incorrect conclusion about the culprit in the murder of Elena Ruslanova and is forced to reopen the investigation when Anna Bobrova confesses her guilt. In spite of such weaknesses or missteps, these two detectives can still be classed as conventional models in the genre. In the characterization of Polumordin, however, the generic norm is almost completely inverted in a move that is unmistakeably parodic. In fact, Panov's depiction of this judicial investigator can be read as an ironic deconstruction of almost all of the conventionally positive traits usually ascribed by Russian crime fiction to this figure.

One of the earliest indications of the unconventional characterization of Polumordin in *From the Life of a Provincial Town* is the fact that, although he repeatedly refers to himself as 'московский студент',[31] this description is left without any meaningful elaboration. Rather than underscoring his legal qualifications, his bookishness or his ability to speak or understand other languages, as happens elsewhere in the genre, the repetitive nature of this claim actually empties it of any significance, making it sound hollow and thereby undermining Polumordin's standing. As the reader notes elsewhere in the work, Polumordin is keen to observe the effect that his words have on other people, without giving much consideration to their actual significance. His repeated invocation of his supposed education appears to be in the same vein. As demonstrated above, the heterodiegetic narrator is not blind to the shortcomings of the central protagonist and is able to pass explicit negative judgement on him. So, for example, during the description of the first evening of whist-playing at Tselyi's residence, the narrator describes Polumordin as 'молодой человек, в котором честолюбие играло первую роль' ('a young man motivated primarily by ambition').[32] The development of the novella makes the veracity of this statement shockingly clear: the investigator is so determined to gain promotion out of the town of N. that he is prepared to pervert the course of justice entirely. He is happy to put his animosity towards the police supervisor, Troiantsev, to one side in order to pursue his persecution of Kantalovich, someone he hates even more. He also displays no qualms in attempting to prosecute Ampleeva, who appears to be a character entirely beyond reproach.

The judicial investigators discussed in the genre up to this point have all been depicted as men who possess a good knowledge of the law and demonstrate exemplary professionalism. Polumordin defies the expectations created by these generic models in almost every way imaginable, although this does not mean that he is characterized in an unremittingly negative light.[33] First, during an early discussion at Tseyli's soirée about the case of the abandoned child, Panov's protagonist demonstrates a lesser degree of legal knowledge than informed readers are accustomed to. When Tselyi suggests that the punishment for this crime of abandonment must be imprisonment, Polumordin interrupts to suggest it is actually the harsher sentence of 'каторжная работа' ('hard labour').[34] However, when the doctor counters by asking whether the abandonment actually represents a crime in the legal, rather than merely the moral, sense, Polumordin hesitates and the narrator notes that he realizes 'неосторожность, с которою он изобличил свое шаткое знание законов' ('the carelessness with which he has revealed his shaky knowledge of the law').[35] Polumordin then has to admit to Tselyi that, whilst hard labour is the harshest sentence imposable in such cases, it is also possible that the culprits will incur nothing more than a fine. Moreover, Polumordin repeatedly appears to be relatively uninterested in the pursuit of criminal cases and the ends of justice. When he first mentions to Tselyi that he has heard of the death of the abandoned child that evening, he does nothing more than say that it is another case to be dealt with. It is the doctor, Antonov, who then brings the subject up again as he says that he has just examined the child's corpse and goes on to provide a few additional details.

Polumordin does not immediately join this conversation and, when he does, it is to complain about how busy he is and how this case will just add to his workload. This is hardly the reaction that the reader of detective fiction is primed to expect. Polumordin only begins to show a degree more interest in getting involved when Varvara Aleksandrovna expresses her outrage at the 'ужасное преступление' ('horrific crime')[36] and doubts his ability to solve it. He only pledges to unravel the mystery when he bets Tselyi a case of champagne that he can be successful. He does not appear to be interested in solving the case for its own sake or in the interests of justice, but only as a means of impressing Varvara Aleksandrovna and not losing face amongst his friends. Indeed, at no point during the novella does Polumordin express sympathy for the plight of the dead child, nor does he waver in his persecution of two people whom he knows to be innocent. Such behaviour is starkly different from that exemplified by the humane, empathetic and professionally responsible investigators encountered in most Russian crime fiction.

Polumordin's lack of interest in undertaking the case of the dead child is indicative of his unprofessional attitude to his job more broadly. Other investigators in works of Russian detective fiction have voiced their dissatisfaction with certain aspects of their job, particularly their relative isolation, the workload and the relatively slow pace of justice. However, Polumordin's complaints are again much more self-interested: in the opening chapter he voices his unhappiness at how much running around he has to do on different cases 'за какие-нибудь медные гроши, которые называют жалованием' ('for a few measly pennies that are called a salary').[37] Later on, the reader is told that Polumordin's primary reason for undertaking criminal cases in the countryside around the town of N. is financial. He frequently loses a large part of his salary gambling in the early part of the month and so then leaves town, ostensibly on business, but also because it is cheaper to live in the countryside.[38] Early Russian crime fiction, in particular, portrays many urban investigators facing challenging situations when at work in rural communities; however, unlike Polumordin, they are shown to be doing their jobs for the right reasons and with the appropriate degree of skill. Not so Polumordin, who once again seems to be abdicating his professional responsibilities in sole pursuit of his own welfare and comfort. It is indicative of the inversion of usual generic practice in *From the Life of a Provincial Town* that it is not until well over halfway through that Polumordin is seen engaged in proper judicial work. Even on those occasions where he is doing something other than playing cards or endeavouring to construct the spurious case against Kantalovich and Ampleeva, he is shown in an unflattering light. So, for example, in the fifth chapter, the narrator describes how the investigator never gets to bed at a decent hour and then has to be woken up at 11 o'clock each morning by one of his colleagues in order to begin work. When he is then in his office, it is his scribe who is shown to be far more professionally responsible: he reminds Polumordin that if the title given to cases by police is altered, as Polumordin suggests it should be, it will be impossible to find the documents again once they are refiled. It is again this scribe who corrects Polumordin when he gets the details of cases and of his investigative duties wrong.

However, perhaps the most damning indictment of Polumordin is that he appears to be entirely oblivious to the manner in which he fails in his professional duties and abuses his authority. During a conversation with Varvara Aleksandrovna in the fifth chapter, he explains not only his commitment to the case against Kantalovich, but also his supposed talents as an investigator:

> Если нужно раскрыть преступление, я его раскрою, если есть малейшая возможность. Я обязан это делать, в силу принятой мною служебной присяги [...] У меня есть особый инстинкт, который руководит мною. Мне иногда стоит взглянуть в лицо, и я угадываю преступника. Я вполне убежден, что Огрызко и Амплеева никто иные, как родители этого ребенка; поэтому я нравственно и формально обязан произвести следствие, доказать их преступление.[39]

> [If there is a crime to uncover, I will do so, even if there is but the remotest possibility. I am obliged to do that on the basis of the professional oath I have sworn [...] I have a particular instinct that guides me. Sometimes it is enough for me to look at someone's face in order to identify that he is a criminal. I am completely convinced that Ogryzko [Kantalovich] and Ampleeva are none other than the parents of this child. As such, I am morally and formally obliged to conduct an investigation in order to prove their crime.]

Although Polumordin displays not a hint of self-awareness here, his claims are judged by the reader to be not just completely misguided, but also deeply ironic. This is an investigator who demonstrates none of the conventional skill or dedication expected by the reader; at no point does he betray any intuition as a detective such as has been seen elsewhere. He appears to have lost sight entirely of the fact that he is not tracking a criminal in Kantalovich, but attempting to destroy an innocent man for the simple reason that he finds him annoying. For the reader it is obvious that what guides Polumordin is not a respect for justice or the law, but a wholly misguided sense of responsibility towards Varvara Aleksandrovna, and a huge dose of arrogance. Whilst some of Polumordin's shortcomings strike the reader as humorous, as the novella progresses, his unconventional abdication of his professional obligations comes to seem increasingly shocking. So much so, in fact, that the reader finds himself/herself in the unusual, generically inverted position of desiring the failure of the judicial investigator's efforts. In provoking this sense of anger and frustration at the detective's non-conformist conduct, *From the Life of a Provincial Town* lays bare to the reader, perhaps more plainly than non-parodic works are able to do, the degree of emotional investment s/he makes in the 'just' resolution of the crime. And it is this investment that makes the non-ending of the novella so frustrating: the reader sees neither the prosecution of Kantalovich and Ampleeva, nor the comeuppance s/he desires for Polumordin.

## An Almost Entirely Corrupted Fictional World

The far-reaching nature of Panov's parody in *From the Life of a Provincial Town* means that Polumordin is far from alone in being characterized negatively. With the exception of Ampleeva, all of the other characters in the fictional world have little to recommend them, a fact that leaves the reader with a sense of a town that, in an implicit nod to the setting of NN in Nikolai Gogol's *Dead Souls*, is utterly corrupt, both morally and legally. Panov's approach in this respect can be considered to be parodic because it disrupts the reader's expectation that there will be some distinction drawn between right and wrong, good and evil. The reader's view of Polumordin's persecution of Kantalovich is complicated by the fact that the victim himself is hardly described in glowing terms. Crucially, the scrivener is first introduced to the reader from the perspective of Polumordin who, as we have seen, accuses him of having knocked at the shutters: the investigator's reaction to this trivial incident speaks to the animosity between them. Thereafter, the more detailed picture given of him in the second chapter is prefaced with a description of his comically tumble-down house, in which he and Zentokovskii have to keep changing rooms because they are so ridiculously small and the floors so uneven. The narrator then describes him thus:

> Н-ский стряпчий был человек пятидесяти пяти, среднего роста, худощавый, рыжий, грязный. Фигура его была вполне отталкивающая. Он был постоянно одет грязно, за что и подвергался всеобщему осмеянию, даже нечистоплотных мещан города Н. [...] Характер у него был строптивый, мстительный.[40]

> [N.'s scrivener was a man of about fifty-five, of medium height, thin, red-headed and dirty. His face was completely repulsive. He was always dressed in dirty clothes such that he was always the target of everyone's ridicule, even that of the not exactly cleanly merchants of N. [...] He had an obstinate and vengeful personality.]

This characterization hardly humanizes Kantalovich for the reader, a fact that means that he initially appears to be a potentially legitimate target for Polumordin's ire. He has fallen out with almost everybody in the town, gets invited only rarely to social gatherings and appears, at the outset, to revel perversely in his position as social outcast.

The reader also recognizes the irony of having Kantalovich and Polumordin share certain personality traits, especially their inflated sense of self and ego. Echoing Polumordin's desire to have everyone in the town speculating about his relationship with Varvara Aleksandrovna, Kantalovich informs Zentokovskii that 'без меня Н. провалился бы давно! Должны мне, скоты, целовать руки, что я у них служу. Без меня сколько бы поиздохло несчастных в полиции' ('without me the town of N. would have fallen long ago! These brutes should be kissing my hands to thank me for serving them. Without me, how many of these unfortunates would have found themselves in the hands of the police').[41] The scrivener seems oblivious to the contradiction that exists between this claim and his repeated threat to take all of his enemies to court for various perceived misdemeanours. The reader's opinion of Kantalovich is also negatively influenced by the description that is given of how he interrogates Zentokovskii about a recent picnic in the town. Polumordin, Varvara Aleksandrovna, the doctor Antonov and the midwife were all present and Kantalovich desires the information so that he can draw a caricature of the gathering. The narrator describes how he takes a piece of paper and sketches out the various elements of the scene, but then this voice adds: 'Но так как рисовать он был не мастер, то карикатура вышла очень плохая. По этому [sic] он недурно сделал, что снизу подписал «пикник, в котором участвовали такие-то»' ('But given that he was not very good at drawing, the caricature turned out really badly. Because of that he wisely wrote underneath: 'a picnic, at which the following were present').[42] Further irony is directed at Kantalovich by the fact that he depicts himself in his sketch as a rook, sitting on a branch above the scene, as if he sincerely believes that he occupies a position of omniscient power in the town of N.[43] As with the incident with the shutters in the previous chapter, the fact of the composition of this caricature appears to be relatively insignificant. However, the development of the novella demonstrates that it serves, in fact, as the primary catalyst for the spurious case that Polumordin builds against Kantalovich and Ampleeva. In a genre where the conventional trigger for a judicial investigation is a serious crime, the choice of the shutter-knocking and the caricature is clearly intended as parodic debasement. Moreover, the unsympathetic portrait painted of Kantalovich as the ostensible victim in the case complicates the usual dichotomy of good/evil that underpins the genre.

One of the great strengths of *From the Life of a Provincial Town* is the manner in which the narrative voice is able continually to modulate the reader's sense of positive disposition towards various characters. Kantalovich is a case in point. Having somewhat legitimized Polumordin's persecution of the scrivener by painting an initially unfavourable picture of him, the novella then complicates the reader's reaction by pointing out certain more favourable characteristics. Kantalovich's early declaration that he is disliked by others in the town because 'я правду люблю и не позволю никому поступать против закона' ('I love the truth and will not allow anyone to transgress the law') simultaneously speaks to his arrogance, while also revealing something of his true nature. Although he is guilty of too frequently threatening others with legal proceedings, he is actually shown to have a much firmer knowledge of the law and a greater desire to see it upheld than does Polumordin. Moreover, he is capable of a degree of empathy that is never witnessed in the judicial investigator. When, at the opening of Chapter 6, both Kantalovich and Ampleeva receive official summonses from Polumordin, the reader experiences genuine sympathy for the scrivener and sees how he spends a considerable amount of time advising Ampleeva about how to put a stop to the case. His suggestions appear reasonable and are only unsuccessful because of the determination and corruption of Polumordin and the doctor. Yet, at the same time as he is being shown in a more positive light, Kantalovich is also providing reminders of his less wholesome side: he spreads malicious gossip about Varvara Aleksandrovna and implicates different innocent people in the case of the abandoned child. What *From the Life of a Provincial Town* thereby demonstrates is the extent to which the reader's reactions can be manipulated and controlled over the course of the novella. The reader never feels on solid ground about how to respond to particular characters at a given moment, and this hesitation significantly complicates the negotiation of a moral and emotional response to the diegesis that is conventionally expected by crime fiction.

The disruption that Panov's novella presents to the usual practice in the genre is sustained in the fact that so many of the other characters in the fictional world are similarly described in negative terms. So, for instance, Kantalovich's interlocutor during much of Chapter 2, Zentokovskii, is described as being a cheerful gasbag and a man who acts like a newspaper in carrying information from one house to another, embellishing his stories on the way. The tenuous relationship to the notion of truth that this description suggests is reinforced by the revelation that he was exiled to the town of N. some four years previously, although the narrator does not say what for. Although, unlike Kantalovich, Zentokovskii is on friendly terms with almost everyone in town, the narrator still characterizes him as 'никому не нужное существование' ('a creature who was not necessary to anyone').[44] Like so many of the other characters, Zentokovskii also demonstrates precious little self-awareness: his nickname 'elephant' stems from the annoying way in which he plays cards, and yet he thinks of himself as a great player. The doctor, Antonov, in spite of initially appearing to be a voice of some reason as he attempts to appease Polumordin after the shutter-knocking incident, actually transpires to be the most corrupt figure in the fictional world. It might be argued that the support he lends the investigator in the case against Kantalovich and Ampleeva is consistent with previous generic practice where doctors and detectives have been shown to cooperate. However, the fact that Antonov's persecution of Ampleeva is so extreme and misogynistic, and that he loses sight entirely of the spurious nature of the case, undermines any sense of conventionality. Nor are the female characters spared. Varvara Aleksandrovna demonstrates her self-centredness both in her need for male suitors to fawn over her and in the fact that her only concern about the fire that rages in the town is that, if N. is destroyed, her husband will lose his job. Moreover, she is a key initiating figure of the action against Kantalovich, saying that it presents an opportunity 'освободи[ть]ся от этого негодяя' ('to free ourselves from that wretch').[45] And the midwife, whilst unnamed, stands at the centre of much of the malicious gossip that is spread about the case of the abandoned child and that is used to persecute Kantalovich and Ampleeva.

## The Ironization of Notions of Truth and Justice and the Judicial System

Other works of Russian crime fiction discussed in this monograph have expressed a degree of dissatisfaction with the way in which the legal system functions. Sokolovskii's narrator in *Prison and Life* makes clear, for instance, how difficult he personally finds his new responsibility of depriving people of their freedom. The judicial investigator in Panov's *Murder in Medveditsa Village* complains about the sheer number of cases he is supposed to deal with and the length of time that it takes these cases to progress to a conclusion. However, as the discussion of the characterization of Polumordin has intimated, there is no work that comes close to *From the Life of a Provincial Town* in terms of undermining the reader's faith in the judicial system. Significantly, not only is the status of the judicial apparatus targeted, but the broader concepts of truth and justice, which implicitly underpin all work in the genre, are also debunked and devalued in Panov's parody. The ironic attitude displayed towards these concepts highlights to the reader in an instructive manner the extent to which responses to them in the genre are informed by something akin to a blind faith in their ultimate victory.

Even before Polumordin has hijacked the judicial system to further his own corrupt agenda against Kantalovich and Ampleeva, its standing in the town of N. is ridiculed by the description of the location of the law courts above a tavern. There is no more eloquent expression of the manner in which the judicial system and the rule of law are (frequently drunkenly) disrespected by the inhabitants of the town of N. than the physical proximity of these two establishments. Kantalovich makes himself unpopular by attempting to get this tavern closed down; however, he does so not because its location is inappropriate from a legal standpoint, but because he dislikes being disturbed by the noise of its patrons in his home opposite. Panov's novella also exaggerates the depiction found elsewhere in the genre of instances when the law is implemented either unprofessionally or ineffectually. So, for example, works such as Timofeev's *Notes of an Investigator* have demonstrated how less well-educated figures in the legal system can produce unsatisfactory written documents that the judicial investigator has to supplement or correct. Panov again enacts this convention more extremely. The second chapter of *From the Life of a Provincial Town* sees Zentokovskii read out one of the official letters that has just been delivered to Kantalovich and that the scrivener needs to work on. Following generic convention, the text of this letter is reproduced in the narrative in full, but it is shown to be utterly meaningless in its recitation of hollow numerical statutes. The letter has no real content and, as such, the judicial system itself must be seen to be denuded of any real meaning or application. On the very next page a second letter is reproduced and this one makes even starker the irony being directed at the law. It charges Kantalovich with finding out the convictions of a peasant from Astrakhan who is temporarily staying in the town; however, the dispatch fails to include the name of the peasant and so is rendered utterly useless. The value of the law and the judicial system is also implicitly questioned by an argument that takes place between Polumordin and Kantalovich in the penultimate chapter. Polumordin informs the scrivener that he has been summoned in order that he can be questioned about his knowledge of Ampleeva's involvement in the abandonment of the deceased child. When Kantalovich challenges Polumordin's right to conduct this investigation, the narrator informs the reader that an argument ensues:

> Стряпчий приводил свои статьи закона; следователь цитировал свои законоположения. Кончилось тем, что они, перелистав, так сказать, весь свод законов, остались каждый при своем, и к единогласию не пришли.[46]

> [The scrivener introduced his legal statutes; the investigator cited his own. The conclusion was that, having leafed through, so to speak, the entire legal code, they each remained convinced that they were right and came to no agreement.]

Clearly, part of the cause of this argument is the simple fact of the antagonism that exists between the two men; however, the law itself does not emerge unscathed from this exchange. What the quarrel suggests is that the legal code is susceptible to being appropriated to support mutually antagonistic positions, without definitively providing proof of the truth of either one or the other. Whilst both Polumordin and Kantalovich have been shown to have a not infallible grasp of the law, the legal code is here implicitly accused of being potentially suspect in the support it provides to contradictory positions. The law, it is suggested here, does not possess an objective, immutable existence in the world that unfailingly serves the ends of justice and good. Rather, in the references here to the 'citation' and 'leafing through' of statutes, Kantalovich and Polumordin's confrontation reminds the reader that the law is embodied in linguistic structures which, just like the literary text itself, are open to interpretation. As such, the law becomes a more subjective and fallible concept that can be manipulated for individual, contradictory and, sometimes, unjust ends.

In the town of N., notions of truth and justice appear to have been entirely debased and corrupted. In the hands of various of the figures in the fictional world of *From the Life of a Provincial Town*, the law becomes an instrument that can be used to persecute innocent people. The case against Ampleeva (and Kantalovich) is initiated after Varvara Aleksandrovna suggests 'while laughing': 'уж не она ли подкинула ребенка?' ('maybe it was actually her [Ampleeva] who abandoned the child?').[47] Tselyi's wife knows this suggestion not to be true, but within a few minutes she presents it as 'most probable', and at no subsequent point does she intervene to put an end to the investigation that it triggers. The law here is not viewed as a fundamental social structure that is pursued diligently and professionally; it is no different from any other item that might be the subject of gossip around a card table. The fate of Kantalovich, such as it is depicted, also gives the lie to the widespread belief in the extrafictional world that justice will prevail. Kantalovich is a man, as noted above, who declares that he 'loves the truth' and he firmly believes that, if people understand the law faithfully, all will turn out well. However, *From the Life of a Provincial Town* demonstrates the naivety of that view. Moreover, the experience of Kantalovich is that, as has been demonstrated in Chapter 5, there are occasions on which the power of the written word with regard to the law is also limited. Like other legal representatives before him, Kantalovich places great stock in the written statutes that his law book contains: he is shown to author very many written documents and to copy out others in his professional duty. However, none of these actually get him anywhere or do anything to counter the malicious plot being constructed against himself and Ampleeva. Rather, they give him an unhelpful and false sense of security and trust in a legal system that is actually being deployed against him by Polumordin and others. In the latter stages of the novella, Kantalovich is described as writing a long and verbose report to the gubernatorial procurator that details the various activities of the judicial investigator. However, the reader now suspects that documents such as this one will have no positive effect in counteracting the machinations of Polumordin and his friends, such is the widespread disregard demonstrated for the law and the truth. *From the Life of a Provincial Town* makes clear that the law is little safeguard against human evil if enough of the system has been corrupted. Society law, as enacted in the town of N., where gossip and personal relationships count for everything, holds sway over legal statute. In the context of this corrupted and venal provincial society, the law, as embodied in the written word, becomes utterly undermined and offers no protection to its citizens.

### 'The Swedish Match': Chekhov's Approach to Parody

If Panov's novella enacts its parody primarily through a process of ironic inversion of generic convention, then Chekhov's story, 'The Swedish Match', creates its effects through a skilful process of repetition and imitation, yet with crucial points of difference. Chekhov's story produces a parodic reconfiguring of detective fiction that is rather subtler in its processes than is Panov's work. For a relatively greater part of its length, 'The Swedish Match' adheres more closely to conventional generic practice before revealing the sting in its tail. The fact that the apparent murder victim, Mark Ivanych Kliauzov, is found at the end of the story not to be dead, just dead drunk and hidden in the bathhouse of his lover, makes obvious the parodic status of the work. Elsewhere, I have claimed that this discovery 'turns the entire story on its head', a comment that demonstrates the fact that this revelation of Kliauzov's non-murder comes as a complete surprise to the reader.[48] The fact that it produces this effect shows how well Chekhov has mastered the conventions of the detective story genre. On a first reading, the story probably seems, even to an informed reader, as though it could function as a straight, non-parodic text. However, the discovery of the non-murder obliges the reader to reassess the assumptions that have been made up until this point and to look, by means of re-reading, for clues that have been placed at earlier stages as to this unexpected outcome. It then becomes fascinating to consider how Chekhov has planted the evidence of this parody throughout and how the genre's conventions have been manipulated to indicate to the reader, albeit in relatively subtle ways, that this is a text that does not conform to expectations or to the usual generic formula.

After Dostoevskii, Chekhov is the best known of the authors included in this study of Russian crime fiction. Nevertheless, 'The Swedish Match' is a story that has received relatively little attention compared to others in Chekhov's oeuvre. In the West, the story is omitted entirely from a number of surveys of Chekhov's work and is given only the most peremptory treatment in others.[49] This appears to be as much the case in Russia, where the 1954 film adaptation of the story is arguably better known than its literary inspiration. Among those commentators who do make reference to 'The Swedish Match', many content themselves with repeating Chekhov's claim that the story is a parody, pastiche or satire on the detective story without delving very much deeper. The aim of this analysis, therefore, is to offer a more sustained and detailed discussion of how Chekhov effects his parody, and what it might have to say about the conventions of detective fiction and their limitations. It addresses many of the same aspects of poetics as the previous discussion of Panov's *From the Life of a Provincial Town*, including: the impact of the title and subtitle; the characteristics and performance of the narrative voice; and the characterization of the detective figures. It also demonstrates how, particularly in hindsight, Chekhov parodies a number of conventional detective fiction patterns or motifs in a manner that foreshadows the unconventional ending. The discussion concludes with a consideration of what the exercise of parody does to the notion of re-reading in the context of the detective genre and how Chekhov's story manages subtly but productively to complicate the exercise of parody.

## Setting the Reader Up and the Performance of the Narrative Voice

In his theory of an aesthetic of reception, H. R. Jauss argues that a literary work:

> awakens memories of that which was already read, [...] and with its beginning arouses expectations for the 'middle and end', which can then be maintained intact or altered, reoriented, or even fulfilled ironically in the course of the reading according to specific rules of the genre or type of text. [...] The new text evokes for the reader (listener) the horizon of expectations and rules familiar from earlier texts, which are then varied, corrected, altered, or even just reproduced.[50]

The key element in the success of Chekhov's parody in 'The Swedish Match' is its ability to 'awaken memories' of, and to create expectations for, a 'straight' work of detective fiction. The first evidence of the desire to misdirect the reader comes with the story's subtitle, 'уголовный рассказ' ('a crime story'). By means of this subtitle, Chekhov associates his story with those works that have used the same or similar formulations and that have showcased non-parodic practice in the genre. For example, D. A. Linev's 1877 novel is entitled *Ispoved' prestupnika: ugolovnyi roman* (*Confession of a Criminal: A Crime Novel*) and was one of the most read publications of that year.[51] Other authors, including Timofeev and P. I. Telepnev on one occasion each, as well as Shkliarevskii repeatedly, use the title or subtitle 'из уголовной хроники' or 'из уголовной летописи' ('from the judicial chronicle') as a means of earning quasi-documentary status for their works in the 1870s and early 1880s.[52] In none of these cases is the execution of the work of detective fiction anything other than generically conventional, a fact that ensures that Chekhov's reader is not primed to expect a parody in 'The Swedish Match'. Moreover, in the light of the subtitle, the story's main title is likely also to be read conventionally: the 'safety match' appears to be the type of insignificant object that so often in the genre turns out to be a significant clue to the mystery. The role of this item in the enactment of the parody will be discussed in more detail below.

Chekhov's story conforms to straight generic practice in a further important regard by including the announcement of the death of Mark Ivanych Kliauzov at an early stage, in the very first sentence in fact.[53] As Chapter 4 has shown, there exist different generic models when it comes to the timing of the announcement of the crime that initiates the detective's investigation. However, arguably the most common set-up encountered is the early revelation of the crime, usually within the first page or so, which then propels the remainder of the narrative. In

Chekhov's story, the reader is thus primed to expect that the narrative that follows this declaration will recount the (eventually successful) search for the victim's body and the identity of the culprit. The description of the appearance of the character who announces Kliauzov's death also conforms to the reader's expectations: s/he is told that a well-dressed young man enters the police superintendent's office and that he is 'бледен и крайне взволнован' ('pale and extremely agitated').[54] There is nothing in this description to make the reader question the legitimacy of the crime being reported, because the demeanour of the informant, Psekov, Kliauzov's steward, is entirely in keeping with his own belief that Mark Ivanych is dead. Psekov's appearance is reminiscent of that of various other characters in Russian crime fiction at similar moments: Marianna Bodresova in Timofeev's 'Murder and Suicide' is said to be 'pale, thin and exhausted' when she is arrested after her suicide attempt, whilst Pyl'neva's neighbours in Shkliarevskii's 'The Tale of a Judicial Investigator' are described as screaming for the district police officer in alarm at the discovery of her body.

'The Swedish Match' further encourages the reader to take the announcement of Kliauzov's murder at face value by negatively characterizing the victim at an early stage. Although not without sympathy, the *stanovoi* (local police officer), Evgraf Kuzmich, laments the end that Kliauzov has met by saying: 'Говорил я тебе, что ты плохим кончишь! Говорил я тебе сердяге, — не слушался. Распутство не доводит до добра!' ('I told you that you'd come to a bad end. I told you, my dear, and you wouldn't listen. Debauchery never ends well').[55] He expands slightly on this comment later in the same conversation when he describes Kliauzov thus: 'Умный малый, образованный, добрый такой [...] Но распутник, царствие ему небесное! Я всего ожидал!' ('He was an intelligent and educated man, and kind [...] But a libertine, may God have mercy on his soul. I expected all of this to happen').[56] The mention here of Kliauzov's less-than-laudable behaviour is presented precisely as a possible explanation for his death and the reader is undoubtedly influenced by it. As will be discussed in greater detail below, the narrative voice does not intervene here to point out the error of the police officer's suppositions about Kliauzov's fate and so the reader has no reason not to invest trust in this version of events.

Just as in Panov's *From the Life of a Provincial Town*, much of the responsibility for the successful effect of Chekhov's parody in 'The Swedish Match' is obviously borne by the narrative voice. As in the earlier parody, the strategy is one of encouraging the reader to place trust initially in the authority and abilities of the narrator only for that voice then to studiously avoid providing overt clues to the non-conventional nature of the story. It is telling that both of these parodic works feature narrators that are not actors in the story world, and who therefore provide an account of the action from a primarily external perspective. In an echo of the situation in Panov's work, the heterodiegetic voice in 'The Swedish Match' provides early indications of its seemingly informative and reliable nature. For instance, the reader is immediately given the exact date and an (almost) exact location for the action and is provided with full details of Psekov's name, rank and appearance. The posterior temporal perspective of this voice on the story world also encourages reader confidence because the recounting of the *suizhet* only begins once all of the action in the *fabula* has elapsed. One justification for the characterization of Chekhov's story as a subtler parody is the fact that aspects of the narrator's performance here differ somewhat from those encountered in *From the Life of a Provincial Town*. In contrast to Panov's novella, the narrative voice in 'The Swedish Match' does not provide any evidence of its omniscient privilege. Whilst the opening lines of the story are informative, they reveal the almost exclusively external perspective of the voice that is maintained throughout the remainder of the narrative. On only one occasion, at a very late stage, does the narrator offer access to the inner thoughts of a character.

Much of the trust that the reader places in the performance of Chekhov's narrator stems from the relatively detailed descriptions that this voice provides about the actions of characters and the layout of certain scenes. Many of these observations owe their level of detail to the narrator aligning his point of view very closely, but still externally, with one of the intradiegetic characters. So, for example, when the two investigators enter Kliauzov's room for the first time with the local police officer, the narrator describes the appearance first of the door and then of the room from a position located close to Chubikov's perspective. When the search moves outside Kliauzov's hut, the point of view during the inspection of the surrounding area is most closely aligned with Diukovskii's visual perspective and the detailed observation is explained by the fact that he is desperately looking for clues. Similarly, when suspicion falls on Psekov the steward and he is brought in for questioning, the reader encounters comprehensive descriptions of his physical appearance and, most especially, what he is wearing. These descriptions are informed by a visual perspective first aligned with Diukovskii and then with Chubikov as they both note that his trousers match the colour of the scrap of material found outside Kliauzov's hut. This strict maintenance of an external perspective has two principal consequences that are pertinent to this discussion: the first is that the narrator's later failures to provide full information or to pass explicit judgement go rather less noticed than has been the case in *From the Life of a Provincial Town*; secondly, a re-reading of Chekhov's story suggests that this emphasis on external observation rather than internal analysis or reflection proves to be misleadingly reassuring. The reader thinks s/he is being given a full and detailed picture of events and situations in the story world when, in actuality, significant elements of the pertinent information (such as the fact that there is no body and Kliauzov is not actually dead) are omitted.

The uninvolved, and supposedly objective, position of the narrator finds exaggerated expression in the use at times of the officialese typical of police reports. This style is particularly to the fore in the opening pages of 'The Swedish Match' when the initial details of the murder and the supposed scene of the crime are laid out for the reader. Not only are the descriptions again quite detailed at these points (the reader is informed that 'дверь оказалась сосновою, выкрашенной в желтую краску и неповрежденной' ('the door turned out to be made of pine, painted yellow and not to have been tampered with')),[57] they are punctuated by the type of agentless dynamic passives ('приступлено было ко взлому' ('they proceeded to break open the door')) and reflexive passives ('их глазам представилось следующее зрелище' ('the following spectacle met their eyes')) that are identified by Martina Björklund as being characteristic of police reports.[58] Such constructions are intended to convey a sense of unmediated report where the facts remain undistorted by the subjective consciousness of a narrating voice: they seem to present themselves while the narrator plays only the most minimal role. The almost mechanistic impression created by such constructions is reinforced by the use of defamiliarizing descriptions, themselves also a staple of police language. For example, describing the crowd that gathers to watch the initial investigation, the narrator records, 'Кое-где попадались бледные, заплаканные физиономии' ('here and there pale and tearful physiognomies were to be seen') where the noun suggests a degree of alienation.[59] A little later on, describing the objects found in Kliauzov's room, the reader is informed that 'на столике [...] лежала серебряная монета двадцатикопеечного достоинства' ('on a little table lay a silver coin of twenty kopeks' value').[60] This is clearly reminiscent of the type of police speak that succeeds in dehumanizing so much of what is recorded. However, on a re-reading of the story, it strikes the reader that this use of officialese is rather exaggerated, and not simply because no crime has actually been committed. It serves implicitly to create a (misleading) impression of the serious attitude adopted by the various investigative figures. However, it simultaneously jars with the type of more emotional response that has been displayed and voiced by these same men upon hearing of Kliauzov's demise. Similar remarks can be made with regard to the narrator's choice of expression in his description of Diukovskii's initial examination of Kliauzov's hut and its environs. The narrative voice uses the same formulation 'Дюковскому удалось...' ('Diukovskii succeeded in...') to describe first how the young assistant finds broken branches on a bush outside the hut and then finds a trace of dried blood in the grass. The exact repetition of the same phrase, as well as the narrator's comment that the search turned up 'много полезных указаний' ('many useful leads'),[61] appears on a first reading to encourage the reader to believe that Diukovskii's discoveries are of significance to the progress of the investigation. However, in hindsight, it appears to be unnecessarily emphatic of the assistant's success and, perhaps therefore, to foreshadow the ultimate irrelevance of these supposed clues.

Given the significant role assigned to direct speech in crime fiction, it is appropriate that this aspect of the story, and in particular the narrator's relationship to it, proves to be a key element in the execution of parody in 'The Swedish Match'. As is generically conventional, Chekhov's story is constituted, to a considerable extent, from acts of direct speech between characters in the fictional world. Dialogue is introduced at an early point in the story, appearing immediately after the introductory paragraph of orientation, and remains thereafter a notable feature throughout. One key contribution that it makes to the parodic nature of 'The Swedish Match' is that it repeatedly allows the heterodiegetic narrator unobtrusively not to comment in any substantive manner on misleading statements about the 'crime'. So, for example, on the opening page, Psekov advances an idea about how the crime might have been committed that constitutes a red herring for the entire subsequent investigation: 'злодеи пробрались к нему через окно' ('the criminals got into his room through the window').[62] The narrator provides only the most peremptory tag upon this allegation from Psekov, and does not interject to point out the erroneous identification of 'criminals'. During the same conversation, the local policeman repeats the claim that Kliauzov has been murdered and the narrative voice provides no commentary here that might indicate that this statement is supposition rather than fact. Upon a second reading of the story, it also becomes obvious that certain other key information has also been presented in acts of direct speech and that, again, the narrator has not intervened to provide additional commentary. Two typical examples occur at an early stage of the narrative when the investigator Chubikov and his assistant, Diukovskii, first arrive at Kliauzov's estate. As Chubikov shakes hands with those present he reprises the accusation of murder in the form of repeated interrogatives ('Неужели? Марка Иваныча? Убили?' ('Really? Mark Ivanych? Murdered?')) and then ends his first act of speech with 'Нет, это невозможно! Не-воз-мож-но!' ('No, it's impossible! Im-poss-ible!').[63] At first, this exclamation can be read as an appropriately shocked reaction to the news of Kliauzov's murder and Chubikov's sense of regret at the death. However, in the light of the story's unconventional dénouement, the investigator's words actually serve to presage the discovery that Kliauzov has not in fact been murdered — his murder is indeed 'impossible'. However, by allowing Chubikov's words to stand uncommented, the narrator ensures that their true significance cannot be comprehended and the misdirection of the investigation continues. Diukovskii's quiet question later on the same page, 'А где же Марк Иваныч?' ('But where is Mark Ivanych then?'),[64] functions in a very similar fashion. This query, prompted by the absence of Kliauzov's body from the supposed crime scene, works in retrospect as an ironic revelation of the key to the mystery: the fact that there is no body is proof that there has been no murder. Of course, Diukovskii himself does not realize at this stage the premonitionary value of his question. However, the narrator's temporal stance means that he could hint at it, but he chooses not to.

In anticipation of remarks to be made below in the section dealing with characterization, it is also important to observe that, in an echo of Panov's novella, the presence of untagged direct dialogue permits the narrator to sidestep overt commentary on unconventional elements in the investigators' performance. As the investigation into Kliauzov's murder progresses, Diukovskii gives voice to increasingly outlandish theories about how the crime might have been committed and seemingly accuses almost everyone he comes across. The fact that most of these theories and accusations are made in direct speech ensures that potential intimations of their unreliability are included but not commented on by the narrator. Diukovskii's acts of direct speech in the middle section of the story, where he outlines the reasons why Nikolashka the valet should be considered a suspect and where he argues that Kliauzov has been murdered by someone who was jealous of his relationship with the maid Akul'ka, are punctuated with repeated instances of ellipsis.[65] These punctuation marks implicitly indicate the tenuous, unsubstantiated and spontaneous nature of the theories being concocted by Diukovskii and invite the reader to doubt their veracity. Again, however, the narrator chooses not to step in and comment overtly on the direct speech to guide the reader more actively to a particular conclusion about the reliability of Diukovskii's behaviour. Rather more seriously, a couple of pages later, the reader is presented with a long passage of direct speech by Chubikov in which he 'tells' Psekov the story of his, Psekov's, involvement in Kliauzov's murder. This version of events is presented as fact to the suspect by the investigator, in spite of being riddled with holes as represented by more ellipsis and, once again, it receives no commentary from the narrator. Subsequently, of course, the reader's initial suspicions as to the erroneous nature of this accusation are confirmed by the discovery of Kliauzov alive and well in the bathhouse; however, the narrator does nothing at this stage to help the reader anticipate this revelation. The narrator's silence here strikes the reader as a more egregious abdication of his duty given that he has previously described the very negative effect that imprisonment has already had on the innocent Psekov. The sole justification for Psekov's false arrest rests on the erroneous theories proposed by Diukovskii and Chubikov, so the narrator's decision not to comment explicitly on their consolidation of the attack against him seems to be an important, and morally dubious, omission.

One final remark to be made concerning the role that the narrator's relative silence plays in the parody in 'The Swedish Match' is based on the evidence supplied by the closing lines of the story. As if to underline the important contribution that dialogue makes to the effect of the story, it closes with an exchange between the local police officer and his wife about the outcome of the investigation. The very final words of the story belong to the local policeman and are: 'Говорил я тебе, что распутство не доводит до добра! Говорил я тебе, — не слушался!' ('I told you that debauchery never ends well! I told you, but you wouldn't listen!').[66] The alert reader will notice of course that this closing exclamation is an almost exact repetition of the same character's earlier lament upon the discovery of the crime. The reappearance of these words to close the story functions as a humorous implicit commentary upon the elliptical and parodic nature of the work. However, as on so many previous occasions, the narrator opts not to indicate directly the ironic status of these words, leaving the reader to do the interpretive work alone. In fact, this consistent lack of interpretive commentary on direct dialogue is representative of the narrator's performance throughout 'The Swedish Match', where the inappropriate or unprofessional behaviour of the investigators is not directly indicated by the narrative voice.

## Playing Games with Characterization

Albeit not to the same extreme degree as has been noted in Panov's *From the Life of a Provincial Town*, certain elements of the characterization in Chekhov's story suggest the presence of ironic inversion or exaggeration. 'The Swedish Match' initially encourages the reader's conventional expectations by introducing at an early stage a local police officer, Evgraf Kuzmich, who, in his relative ineffectuality, conforms to generic type. He prepares the ground for the subsequent introduction of Chubikov and Diukovskii by seeming from the outset to be largely incompetent even before the alleged victim is found in the bathhouse at *his* property and in the amorous company of *his* wife. He is characterized by a passivity that is given effective expression by the repeated description of him 'sighing' whenever he speaks. Indeed, the only contribution that Kuzmich actually makes to the case is to summon other guardians of the law before retiring to Psekov's house to drink tea. In rather more unconventional, although not entirely unseen, fashion for the genre of crime fiction, the doctor in Chekhov's story, Tiutiuev, fails to contribute anything meaningful to the investigation of the 'crime'.[67] Although by no means as corrupt as the figure of Antonov in Panov's novella, Tiutiuev is another passive figure who seems uninterested either in Kliauzov's disappearance or in the course of the criminal investigation. When he arrives at Kuzmich's office, he is described as looking unhealthy and of failing to greet any of the other people present. He then makes a comment about the Serbs and Austria (in reference to the Bulgarian Crisis of 1885–88) that is of no relevance to the investigation. His lack of interest and laziness are given ironically eloquent expression when, after Diukovskii finds a trail of blood on the grass leading away from Kliauzov's hut, the doctor says nothing more than: 'Да, кровь' ('Yes, blood').[68] Such concision clearly exaggerates the convention of having doctors function as mouthpieces of factual, scientific interpretations of material evidence.

Earlier works in the genre, such as Panov's *The Harvest Gathering*, have depicted fictional worlds in which criminal investigations are hampered by the inebriated state of many of the witnesses. However, 'The Swedish Match' appears to interpret this aspect of the genre with some irony as the unreliability of witnesses is overstated. Four of the five people who are interviewed about events on the night of Kliauzov's disappearance (Psekov, Nikolashka, Danilka and the maid, Akul'ka) are unable to provide any useful information because they say that they were too drunk. In the case of the first two, this inability to recall their whereabouts or activities leaves them vulnerable to accusations that lead to their temporary incarceration. Even Kliauzov's sister, although not incapable because of inebriation, provides Chubikov and Diukovskii with no useful information when they question her. Maria Ivanovna's one act of speech is characterized by what seems to be, particularly in retrospect, an exaggerated use of negatives: 'Ах, не спрашивайте меня! Ничего я не могу вам сказать! Ничего! Умоляю вас! Я ничего... Что я могу? Ах, нет, нет... ни слова про брата!' ('Ah, please don't ask me! I can't tell you anything! Nothing! I beg you! Nothing... what can I tell you? Ah, no no... not a word about my brother').[69] Diukovskii chooses to interpret Maria's insistence that she knows nothing as a sign that she is hiding something; however, there is another way to look at her insistent repetition of the word 'nothing'. It is tempting, in the context of Chekhov's story, to read the absence of information at the heart of the investigation that results from Maria's interrogation, as well as those of the other characters, as an ironic hint at the lack of an actual crime. It is not just that these characters know nothing or pretend to know nothing; it is that, because of the lack of a murder, there is not actually much to know.

However, it is by means of the characterization of the two investigator figures, Chubikov and Diukovskii, that Chekhov's 'The Swedish Match' most skilfully enacts its parodic exploitation of generic conventions. The earlier discussion of the figure of Polumordin in *From the Life of a Provincial Town* has demonstrated how he departs at almost every turn from the reader's expectations of how a judicial investigator should behave. Chekhov's parody does not function, in this respect, so much as an inversion of usual practice, but as an adept repetition, with critical distance, of previous examples. And it is one in which the reader's relationship to the investigative figures is constantly being adjusted and played with. The key to Chekhov's parody here is the unfamiliarly unstable and seemingly ever-shifting ground that the reader finds him/herself on with regard to an evaluation of the detectives' performance. Things get off to a relatively conventional start. The initial introduction of the ineffectual local police officer sets the scene for the entry of more competent investigators in the shape of Nikolai Ermolaevich Chubikov and his ever-present assistant, Diukovskii. This early comparison automatically earns them both the greater degree of authority that has been constructed for judicial investigators in a similar fashion in numerous previous works. Moreover, the standing of Chubikov is initially promoted by the narrator's description of him as:

высокий, плотный старик лет шестидесяти, подвизается на своем поприще уже четверть столетия. Известен всему уезду как человек честный, умный, энергичный и любящий свое дело.

[a tall, thick-set old man of about sixty who has been in his line of work for twenty-five years. He was known to the whole district as an honest, intelligent, energetic man, who was devoted to his work.][70]

This characterization appears to be relatively straightforward and certainly encourages the reader to place trust in his ability. The trope of a pair of investigators working as a team is also, by the early 1880s, a recognizable generic feature of Russian crime fiction. Panov's *The Harvest Gathering* has seen the autodiegetic narrator act as a secretary to his investigator friend and prove to be more adept at forcing a confession; there is also the example of the investigator in Stepanov's 'They Wanted to Betray the Court and God's Will' who works in concert with a *syshchik* (detective), Kunitsyn, to uncover the truth behind the unsolved death of the peasant, Zadornyi. However, the unconventional exploitation of this feature in Chekhov's story derives from the fact that the reader is repeatedly prompted to reassess his opinion of the relative abilities and reliability of the two investigator figures as the story progresses.

In spite of the positive characterization attached to Chubikov at the outset, it is initially the conduct of Diukovskii that garners a more sympathetic reaction from the reader. It is the younger man who appears to be more energetic and proactive in his investigation of Kliauzov's hut and its immediate surroundings; and yet his efforts are met with repeated dismissals from Chubikov who keeps telling him to be quiet, as if Diukovskii were a young child rather than an assistant. When Diukovskii asks where Kliauzov is, he is told 'rudely' by Chubikov not to interfere and is directed to inspect the floor instead. Diukovskii obediently follows orders and reports the results of his examination: he has found no stains or scratches but has found the safety match of the title. Reasoning that Kliauzov did not use such matches, the young man deduces that it should be considered a clue. However, Chubikov merely laughs at him and advises him that his time would be better spent doing something else: 'чем спички искать, вы бы лучше постель осмотрели' ('rather than looking for matches, you would do better to examine the bed').[71] In fact, Chubikov repeatedly employs this condescending formulation ('you would do better to...') to redirect Diukovskii's attention away from what he considers to be irrelevant aspects of the crime scene. By contrast, Chubikov is somewhat undermined in the reader's eyes by aligning himself with the ineffectual police officer, Kuzmich. Crucially, he confides to Kuzmich that the Kliauzov case is undoubtedly similar to that of the merchant Portretov that he investigated in 1870; affirming Psekov's earlier allegation, Chubikov reveals that Portretov was also murdered and dragged out of a window. Although the narrator's introduction of Chubikov has stressed his experience and reputation, even on a first reading his attitude to the investigation seems overly passive and reliant on pre-convictions. A re-reading of the story only strengthens the initial impression of Diukovskii as an energetic and dedicated would-be investigator, and Chubikov as the rather dismissive and passive authority figure. What the dénouement of 'The Swedish Match' makes clear is not only that Chubikov's reference to the earlier investigation constitutes a serious misreading of the circumstances pertaining to Kliauzov's case, but also that Diukovskii's early declaration of the importance to the case of the match is absolutely correct. The challenge for the reader is that this initial attribution of greater sympathy and reliability to Diukovskii is playfully manipulated and destabilized on numerous occasions throughout the remainder of the text.

In the early stages of the story, various elements argue against Chubikov's dismissal of Diukovskii as an interfering and unhelpful presence in the investigation. The young secretary's explanation of the safety match as a clue (it is not of the type used by the local peasants and indicates some outside, higher-class involvement) appears to be rationally logical.[72] In line with practice seen elsewhere in the genre, Diukovskii's speech positively differentiates him from the local peasants implicated in the crime: whilst the valet, Nikolashka's, speech is inflected with dialectical markers ('я был выпимши'), the secretary uses both the term 'alibi' and the Latin 'non dubitandum est'.[73] Moreover, in line with the role he assigns himself of reporting observations and drawing conclusions, Diukovskii's speech in the first half of the story earns him authority in the eyes of the reader because it is self-assured, emotionally neutral and complete: it includes no partial sentences or lacunae in the form of elliptical points. Again, these features distinguish him favourably not only from those under suspicion who frequently falter in their speech but also from his own, rather more hesitant performance in the middle section of for the reader, however, is that this initially positive characterization of Diukovskii is not consistently maintained throughout the length of the story, and the narrative voice repeatedly opts not to intervene to provide orienting commentary. For example, the young secretary's practice of enunciating his findings aloud during the initial examination of Kliauzov's hut becomes exaggerated as he continually verbalizes his various, and ever more outlandish, theories of how the crime has been committed. Diukovskii's status as a rational, analysing deducer of truth begins to be undermined most clearly after the first visit that he and Chubikov make to Kliauzov's sister. As noted above, Maria Ivanovna offers very little in the way of information regarding her brother's death; however, this proves to be no barrier to Diukovskii's desire to hypothesize and to accuse. He suddenly exclaims 'чертова баба' ('a devil of a woman') in the type of emotional outburst atypical of the calm rationalist the initiated reader is used to meeting in detective stories. He goes on: 'по-видимому, что-то знает и скрывает. И у горничной что-то на лице написано...' ('apparently she knows something and is hiding it. And there is something peculiar in the maid's expression ...').[74] Diukovskii is undermined here by his use of the epistemic modal adverb ('apparently') and the indefinite pronouns: these indicate a shift away from rational deduction towards emotional inference based on physical appearance or attitude.[75]

These syntactic clues to the parodic undermining of the figure of the detective are swiftly multiplied over the course of the subsequent passages. Once returned from Maria Ivanovna's, Diukovskii assails Chubikov with his theories about Psekov's undoubted involvement in the crime:

Дело, батенька, не в бабе. Дело в подленьком, гаденьком, скверненьком чувстве... Скромному молодому человеку не понравилось, видите ли, что не он верх взял. Самолюбие, видите ли... Мстить захотелось... Потом-с... Толстые губы его сильно говорят о чувственности. Помните, как он губами причмокивал, когда Акульку с Наной сравнивал?[76]

[The old woman is not the point, my good sir. The point is the nasty, disgusting, mean feeling... The discreet young man did not like to be cut out, do you see. Vanity, do you see... He longed to be revenged... Then... His thick lips are a strong indication of sensuality. Do you remember how he smacked his lips when he compared Akul'ka to Nana?]

But these lines and those that follow portray none of the attributes either expected of detectives in this genre or that have been displayed previously by Diukovskii. His speech is peppered with five instances of ellipsis here; he poses four rhetorical questions as though seeking Chubikov's approval and twice repeats the phrase 'do you see' for the same effect. Gone are his earlier confidence and emotional detachment and in their place is something quite different. These syntactic clues to changes being wrought in Diukovskii can be explained by the content of his outburst. He alleges that Psekov was 'burning with passion', that he was suffering wounded vanity and unrequited passion, emotions attested to by the way he 'smacked his lips'. Diukovskii's observations and accusations seem to snowball, in which detectives are conventionally expected to proceed. In Shkliarevskii's 'The Tale of a Judicial Investigator', for instance, the autodiegetic narrator does not, as we have seen, overtly reveal his suspicions about Aleksandra Lastova until a relatively late stage; whilst in Panov's *The Harvest Gathering*, details about the 'coup d'état' are not elaborated for the reader in advance. Chubikov voices the doubts that begin to arise about Diukovskii's behaviour at this stage when he asks him if he is feeling well or whether, perhaps, he has a headache. Indeed, this question forms part of a somewhat broader move to undermine the reliability of Diukovskii. Whilst not overtly commented on by the narrator, this shift in attitude is seemingly implied by the rather Gothically-inflected description of how Diukovskii's 'eyes shone brightly' as he spoke. No longer then does Diukovskii appear to be a representative of reasonable thought; rather he is characterized now as a man prone to moments of over-enthusiasm and unreason.

The sense of exaggeration is reinforced during the description that is given of Diukovskii's behaviour when he returns from his individual search for clues that he has begged Chubikov to be allowed to undertake at the opening of the second part of the story. His use here of the Latin phrase 'veni, vidi, vici' as he arrives back cannot fail to sound an ironic note. He follows it up with the overly arrogant declaration: 'клянусь вам честью, я начинаю веровать в свою гениальность' ('I respectfully declare that I am beginning to believe in my own genius').[77] Although detectives in Russian crime fiction frequently demonstrate self-confidence and a belief in their own abilities, it is rarely expressed in such strident terms. Furthermore, the sense of excess persists as Diukovskii claims that, during his search for the source of the safety match in the various shops and taverns in the local area, he lost hope of success some twenty times. The attentive reader realizes that his search has only taken a few hours that day and so Diukovskii's expression of his despondency is ironically undermined by this over-embellishment. Diukovskii's standing is further compromised when Chubikov dismisses him as a madman when he claims that they need to go and question Kuzmich's wife, Olga Petrovna, immediately about the safety match. The secretary's efforts to entreat Chubikov to cede to his request also appear to be parodically exaggerated. Diukovskii begins by insulting Chubikov for his reluctance before changing tack and pleading: 'Прошу вас! Прошу не для себя, а в интересах правосудия' ('I beg you! I beg you not for my own sake but in the interests of justice'),[78] and falling to his knees in supplication. He then tries to appeal to Chubikov's sense of vanity by suggesting that solving this crime will make the investigator famous all over Russia and will lead to him being put in charge of important cases. With the best will in the world, the resolution of the mystery surrounding the disappearance of a debauched local landowner is unlikely to lead to such professional elevation. Similarly, Diukovskii's repetition of the phrase 'именем закона' ('in the name of the law') when they do eventually arrive at Olga Petrovna's house and demand to see Kliauzov seems overly officious and self-aggrandizing. However, although Chubikov repeatedly belittles Diukovskii's efforts in a manner consistent with his performance throughout the story, the narrator

Diukovskii's efforts as either laudable or laughable and thus leaves the reader to his/ her own devices in terms of assessing the authority and reliability that should be accorded to his version of events and plan of action. Having initially encouraged the reader, albeit implicitly, to view Diukovskii's attitude and abilities positively, much of the main body of 'The Swedish Match', up to the point of the discovery of Kliauzov in the bathhouse, therefore, seems intended to undermine him in the reader's eyes. The revelation of the sting in the story's tail, and the non-murder of Kliauzov, only complicates things further.

### Unconventional Parody, and Irony Directed at Detective Fiction Patterns

For many critics, the simple fact of the revelation that Kliauzov has not been murdered is sufficient to justify categorizing 'The Swedish Match' as a parody.[79] It is undoubtedly the case that the construction of the narrative is designed to ensure that the revelation of this outcome makes a significant impact upon the reader. In addition to Chubikov's conviction that Diukovskii is making a fool of them both by insisting on the visit to Olga Petrovna, the exploitation of temporal structures is intended to emphasize the shock value of the discovery. The pace of the narrative is slowed right down at this point and the suspense is drawn out in exemplary fashion as Chubikov repeatedly stutters when he tries to excuse their visit by claiming that they have only called in because their carriage has broken down. All the while, he has Diukovskii offering advice in his ear about physically 'overwhelming' Olga Petrovna rather than allowing her to guess the intention behind their call. There is even the confrontation with the necessary obstructive witness, in the person of Olga Petrovna herself, who conveniently fails to reveal everything she knows about Kliauzov's state when the investigators accuse her of his murder. Rather than voice the obvious objection to their charge that her lover is still alive, she claims not to understand what is happening, asks how the detectives have found out and, finally, inquires what they want with Kliauzov. All of these manoeuvres retard the eventual revelation that the body in her bathhouse is not dead, but snoring inebriatedly, and that it does indeed belong to Kliauzov. There is surely no more assured way of debunking and parodying the conventions of the detective genre than by having the supposed murder victim turn up alive and well. As Donald Rayfield puts it, '[when] the detective finds the victim alive and unharmed, a Russian Lecoq is nipped in the bud'.[80]

However, this statement represents an oversimplification. The fact that Kliauzov is found not to have been murdered should not be the grounds upon which to undermine Diukovskii's status as an investigator. It is far more productive to consider whether or not this revelation actually constitutes a straightforwardly parodic inversion of crime fiction's usual pattern. The highly adept manner in which Chekhov plays not only with the conventions of crime fiction but with the notion of parody is demonstrated by the fact that the discovery of Kliauzov is not the end of the story. The final two pages that follow this revelation provide the opportunity complicated in a manner that enriches the story even further. Diukovskii himself appears disappointed at having found Kliauzov alive rather than dead and repeatedly calls it 'непостижимо' ('incomprehensible');[81] and the discovery prompts Chubikov into more of the condescending dismissals of his secretary that have been a feature of the opening sections of the story. However, the act of discovering Kliauzov alive does not, in actuality, make Diukovskii a failure as an investigator. Rather, it is precisely his powers of detection and deduction in certain aspects of his search that have led him and his boss to Olga Petrovna's bathhouse. The account of events given by Kliauzov about the circumstances of his disappearance reveals to the two investigators where their hypotheses have been correct, and where they have been wide of the mark. So, for instance, Kliauzov confirms that Olga Petrovna did enter his hut via the window and also dragged him back out of it, as had been surmised. He did not lose his boot during this struggle, however; rather he threw it out of the window at Olga Petrovna to try to get her to leave him alone. Olga Petrovna has beaten him up a little bit for being drunk, but Diukovskii's theories about how Kliauzov was held down by two people, suffocated by a third before being stabbed and dragged along by the river are all shown to be utter nonsense.

However, the suspicion that the safety match represents a significant clue is proven to be accurate and the manner in which Diukovskii rationally traces its provenance is laudable: he describes how he visited all the shops and inns in the district in order to identify the only person to have bought such matches, Olga Petrovna. Although Chubikov's anger at his sidekick as they return from her house might be justifiable in terms of the perceived embarrassment of having found the murder victim alive, the threats he makes to Diukovskii when this latter insists upon the legitimacy of his method in following the match are less excusable. The failure of the investigation is not proven by the fact that Kliauzov has not been killed; its roots go much further back to the very start of the story and the willingness to believe in the fact of a murder despite the absence of a body. For this false premise, Chubikov is as much to blame as is Diukovskii. Indeed, the realization that the initial announcement of the murder of Kliauzov has got the entire story off on the wrong, and generically inverted, foot provides the most persuasive illustration of the consequences of the narrator's lack of commentary. The catalyst for the entirety of the narrative of 'The Swedish Match' is the description in the opening paragraph of how a well-dressed young man appears in the police office and 'заявил, что его хозяин, отставной гвардии корнет Марк Иванович Кляузов, убит' ('announced that his landowner, the retired guards' cornet, Mark Ivanovich Kliauzov, had been murdered').[82] Crucially, unlike the repetition of this accusation on the following page, this opening declaration comes not in the direct speech of an intradiegetic character, but in a section of indirectly reported speech provided by the narrative voice. For the reader, the involvement of the supposedly authoritative narrator in the revelation of this information implicitly validates it as a reliable and trustworthy claim. There appears to be no grounds upon which to question, on a first reading, the commencement of a murder investigation aimed at finding Kliauzov's body. Ultimately, however, it is the narrator's silence with regard to the true nature of

Kliauzov's disappearance that allows the narrative to progress and the parody to be constructed. Such a performance thus comes to represent an instance when Chekhov's story takes the omission of vital information by the narrative voice that is conventional in crime fiction to an extreme degree. It is not just that the narrator fails to provide important orienting information here, but that he has enacted a misdirection that underpins the entirety of the narrative. Whilst subtly executed, therefore, such a gap comes to seem almost more extreme than any of the oversights enacted by the narrator in Panov's *From the Life of a Provincial Town*.

What the revelation of Kliauzov's non-murder also makes clear is the degree to which Chekhov's 'The Swedish Match' operates by parodically disrupting certain of the patterns upon which crime fiction conventionally relies. First, as seen above, the dénouement of the story makes clear that the entire plot has been a red herring given that, in the absence of a crime, there was never a need for detection in the first place. As has been noted in Chapter 4, Porter contends that detective fiction is a genre committed to an act of recovery, narrating plots that set out to close logico-temporal gaps between the present discovery of an act and its past causes.[83] What Chekhov's story does, however, is to disrupt fundamentally this basic linear pattern by ultimately revealing that no 'recovery' was necessary, no gap needed to be closed, because there was no act to account for. Or perhaps it would be more accurate to say that the 'gap' that exists is one that is inappropriate as a subject for crime fiction: it is a drunken disappearance rather than a murder. Whatever the case, the sense that 'The Swedish Match' is a work that exposes the fallacy of the generic notion of a line of progression from A to B, such as is implied in Porter's argument, is one that is reinforced in other ways. Most significantly, the story is marked by a circularity and self-generation of plot that must be considered as a parodic take on conventional generic practice. For instance, numerous other works in the genre, including Shkliarevskii's 'The Tale of a Judicial Investigator' and Panov's *The Harvest Gathering*, have employed the trope of multiple suspects coming under suspicion at various points before the eventual culprit is unmasked. However, Diukovskii's approach appears ironically to target this practice by lining up a series of at least four suspects, all of whom he believes to be somehow simultaneously implicated in the crime. Moreover, the basis of his suspicions against the three male suspects (Nikolashka, Psekov and Danilka) is their involvement with the same woman, Akul'ka, and the possibility that they are prompted to murder Kliauzov because of their jealousy of his relationship with her. However, what the narrative makes clear is that virtually every male character in the story, including both Diukovskii and Chubikov, has had intimate relations with Akul'ka at some point and, in the terms of the investigator's rationale, might therefore be considered to be a suspect. Émile Gaboriau favoured the inclusion of lurid hints of personal scandal in his detective novels and it is true that such elements can play an important role in providing impediments to the successful resolution of criminal investigations. However, the involvement of so many men in this network of intimacy with Akul'ka comes to seem exaggerated and to undermine such lines of relation as a realistic basis for suspicion.

Not only that, but the sense of redundant circularity rather than linear progression is reinforced during the description of the interrogation of Nikolashka during which he repeats the assertion that Kliauzov has been murdered. When Chubikov asks him where his master's body is at present, the answer that comes is: 'Сказывают, в окно вытащили и в саду закопали' ('It's said that he was dragged out of the window and buried in the garden').[84] However, as the investigator realizes, all that Nikolashka is doing here is repeating the theory about Kliauzov that has been elaborated by Diukovskii at a slightly earlier stage. The investigation here is not making progress along a line of A to B, but operating in a more elliptical fashion in which hypotheses become the basis upon which further, factual-sounding claims for the fate of Kliauzov are made. As such, Diukovskii's subsequent spiralling journey around the inns and taverns of the area in search of the safety match function as an eloquent metaphor for the entirety of this generically unconventional criminal investigation.

This sense of a self-generating mystery and a self-referential investigation is also promoted by Chekhov's brief invocation of the pattern of the locked-door mystery.[85] During the first examination of the crime scene, the investigators pay particular attention to the door into Kliauzov's hut and find it to be intact, whereupon they are informed that it was found locked from the inside. Consequently, much attention is then directed to the window as the point of ingress and egress and, as has been noted, it is this fact that prompts Chubikov to make his mistaken connection to the previous case of the murder of Portretov. However, the locked-door mystery, with all of its metatextual potential, is a generic pattern that Chekhov's story flirts with briefly but ultimately does not develop in any meaningful way. Indeed, the choice to invoke this model but then not pursue it arguably functions as another implicit clue to the parodic exercise enacted by the narrative. The link to Poe, and the ironic exploitation of the generic framework provided by his detective stories, is a key facet of the parody constructed in 'The Swedish Match'. Crucially, a considerable degree of the trust initially placed in the character of Diukovskii, as has been seen, stems from his practice of detailed visual observation and rational deduction during his early examination of Kliauzov's hut. Whilst Chubikov is more passive and intent on dismissing Diukovskii's efforts, the young secretary earns a degree of authority by his active approach and attention to detail. However, given that the story turns out to be a parody of a tale of ratiocination, it is important to look at the terms in which this exercise of apparent reason is communicated.

Most notably, the opening acts of speech in Diukovskii's report of what he observes in Kliauzov's hut are, unconventionally but significantly, dominated by negative expressions or accounts of what he does *not* find. He says, for instance, 'на полу ничего особенного не заметно [...] ни пятен, ни царапин [...] ни кровяных, ни каких-либо других пятен... Свежих разрывов также нет' ('there was nothing particularly of note on the floor [...] no stains or scratches [...] neither blood stains nor any other stains... There were also no fresh rips').[86] The fact that negatives or absences outweigh positive observations or discoveries at this early stage of the report functions as an implicit indication of the eventual parodic outcome of the investigation. The lack of so many evidential clues foreshadows the absence of a murder or crime in the story. This pattern is quite distinct from that encountered in the vast majority of detective works studied here, where the investigations proceed on the basis of positive clues. Further disruption to the model of rational deduction is to be found in the increasingly outlandish 'logical' leaps that Diukovskii makes in his investigative reasoning in the middle section of 'The Swedish Match'. The secretary's various theories to account for the involvement of Nikolashka, Psekov and Danilka, and especially the victim's sister, Maria Ivanovna, have little in common with the more sober and considered rationalization expected in the genre. What the exaggeration here demonstrates, potentially, is that all of the various deductive leaps performed in the genre are actually artificially constructed and highly unlikely, but that the reader is usually prepared to forgive them as part of the game. What Chekhov's story ultimately does, therefore, is to invoke a number of the patterns that underpin the functioning of conventional crime fiction, but then to lay them bare through a process of exaggeration. In so doing, 'The Swedish Match' makes the reader more acutely aware of the artifice and the effect of these leaps. Throughout Chekhov's story the non-parodic patterns of the genre are visible behind the exaggerated and ironized forms that they take here, a shadowing effect that allows the reader to appreciate more clearly the way in which both the parodic and non-parodic elements function and affect the reading experience.

## Conclusion

Ultimately, then, what the parodies in *From the Life of a Provincial Town* and 'The Swedish Match' both achieve is an eloquent reinforcement of the generic conventions in crime fiction. These conventions do not need to be adhered to in order for them to be underscored. Each work succeeds in making the informed reader more aware of the 'formula' of crime fiction and of the horizon of expectations that s/he brings to the genre. They lay bare, whether by means of inversion, perversion or exaggeration, the ways in which the reader is manipulated in his/her epistemic search by the devices and structures that are typically encountered in the genre. Although they are quite distinct in their effect, the two works resemble each other to the extent that they make a number of the same poetic devices and generic conventions the target of their ironic practice. In both, the status and performance of the detective as an active, moral and reliable pursuer of truth and justice is constructed in unusual ways. The two works exploit the generically privileged standing accorded to acts of direct speech in order to generate information gaps that are quite original in nature. Crucially, though, what Panov and Chekhov underline most starkly is the degree to which, in all forms of detective fiction, as well as in literary texts more broadly, the reader is heavily dependent upon the narrative voice for interpretive guidance. In *From the Life of a Provincial Town*, much of the parody derives from the fact that, far from being reliable and authoritative, the narrator proves to be unpredictable and uneven in his performance. In both works, but especially in 'The Swedish Match', the reader is made to realize the degree to which all works in the genre employ narrator silence as the key device to promote curiosity and suspense. Although the investigators in the works do not necessarily conform to the impeccable professional standards established by those depicted in the earliest examples of the genre in Russia, that is not the most essential element of the parody. The most crucial ingredient required for the parody to succeed is that the narrative voice must exaggerate its unconstructive, and possibly unreliable, role in mediating the diegesis.

This distinction reveals another key aspect of the parodies written by Panov and Chekhov. Whilst there might be a degree of social criticism implied by their depiction of corrupt or ineffectual investigators, and the venality, viciousness, or simply drunkenness, of members of provincial Russian society, both of these works are far more preoccupied with the intertextual and the metatextual than the extratextual. They are focused on practice and generic conventions in the texts on both planes of parody: that of the pre-existing text that acts as a backdrop and that of the original text that interrogates convention. In spite of the reference to literary-historical development that is implied here, and that has frequently appeared in other discussions of the nature of parody, it is neither desirable nor possible to claim that these two parodies of Russian detective fiction usher in a period of renewal or regeneration in the genre. The practice of Russian detective fiction does not become radically different after the publication of either the Panov novella in 1876 or the Chekhov story seven years later. It is not possible to trace the influence of these works in future iterations of the genre. They are neither destructive of what had come before nor specifically generative of what came afterwards. Both works stand, nevertheless, as informative windows onto the poetic devices and structures that exert such an influence over the reader of crime fiction.

## Notes to Chapter 6

1. Linda Hutcheon, *A Theory of Parody: The Teachings of Twentieth-century Art Forms* (New York and London: Methuen, 1985), p. 2.
2. Ibid., p. 6.
3. Iu. N. Tynianov, *Poetika, istoriia literatury, kino* (Moscow: Nauka, 1977), p. 201. The translation is taken from J. Douglas Clayton, 'Soviet Views of Parody: Tynianov and Morozov', *Canadian-American Slavic Studies*, 7.4 (1973), 485–93 (p. 486).
4. Hutcheon, *A Theory of Parody*, p. 7.
5. Ibid., p. 23.
6. Ibid., p. 22 and p. 33.
7. MacDonald, 'Parody and Detective Fiction', p. 63. MacDonald's 'addicted readers' probably resemble closely the concept of the ideal or informed reader referred to elsewhere in this monograph.
8. As Hutcheon explains in *A Theory of Parody*: 'It is true that, if the decoder does not notice, or cannot identify, an intended allusion or quotation, he or she will merely naturalize it, adapting it to the context of the work as a whole. In the more extended form of parody which we have been considering, such naturalization would eliminate a significant part of both the form and content of the text.' (p. 34)
9. Lizabeth Paravisini and Carlos Yorio, 'Is It Or Isn't It? The Duality of Parodic Detective Fiction', in *Comic Crime*, ed. by Earl Bargainnier (Bowling Green, OH: Bowling Green Popular Press, 1987), pp. 181–93 (p. 183). Formalist critics, such as Tynianov, considered parody to be part of a process of literary-historical transformation over time.

10. MacDonald, 'Parody and Detective Fiction', p. 68.
11. A. P. Chekhov, *Polnoe sobranie sochinenii i pisem v tridsati tomakh, Pis'ma*, 1 (Moscow: Nauka, 1974), p. 86.
12. As noted in the previous chapter, in *The Shooting Party*, published the following year, Chekhov's frame narrator makes clear potential targets of parody by telling Kamyshev that people are fed up with Gaboriau and Shkliarevskii.
13. Tynianov, *Poetika*, p. 284; Hutcheon, *A Theory of Parody*, p. 15.
14. It should also be remembered that the subtitle of *The Harvest Gathering* is 'A Sketch from Rural Life', which creates a greater degree of resemblance between the nature of the two titles.
15. The relationship between the text of Panov's novella and this notion of an investigator's notes will be discussed in greater detail below.
16. In the Russian context, Aleksandr Pushkin's works provide myriad examples of the potential inherent in epigraphs as ironic or ludic spaces.
17. The impact of the use of Latin phrases, in particular, with reference to the authority of the detective figure has been discussed above in Chapter 2. Panov uses a similar combination of title, subtitle and epigraph in *Murder in Mukhtolovaia Grove*, also from 1876, where the Latin epigraph reads 'errare humanum est'.
18. Panov, *Iz zhizni uezdnogo gorodka*, p. 216.
19. Ibid., p. 198.
20. Ibid., p. 213.
21. Ibid., p. 244.
22. Ibid., p. 255. The detective's surname, Polumordin, which literally means 'one with half a face', unmistakeably implies a negative characterization.
23. Ibid., p. 251.
24. Ibid., p. 205.
25. The same could be said about the extended passage at the start of the second chapter during which the narrative voice chooses not to identify any of the characters by name, preferring instead to use unnecessarily oblique references such as 'рыжая голова' ('redhead'). The narrator's playful self-consciousness is in evidence when he brings this passage to a close by asking 'Но кто же были они таковы?...' ('But who exactly were these people?...') (p. 223), revealing their names and then shifting to a position of providing a very detailed picture of Zentokovskii's house.
26. Ibid., p. 262.
27. Ibid., p. 263.
28. Panov's novella provides other examples of the use of limited perspective to provoke the reader's curiosity. In Chapter 5, the reader is not immediately informed of the contents of a letter that Polumordin receives that makes his face 'light up' (p. 296). In the following chapter, Kantalovich makes a passing reference to Zentokovskii having spoken to him about the gossip at the card evening about the case of the abandoned child; however, the limited perspective of the intradiegetic character is not supplemented by the narrator to inform the reader of what exactly the scrivener has been told (p. 311).
29. Ibid., p. 306.
30. Ibid., p. 346.
31. Ibid., pp. 199 and 201.
32. Ibid., p. 199.
33. Polumordin does offer the occasional glimpse of more positive behaviour and standards. For instance, the narrator informs the reader that he refuses to dine every day at the Tselyi household (even though he is invited) in order to maintain some professional objectivity. Moreover, in the opening chapter his concerned questioning to Varvara Aleksandrovna about why her husband does not seek treatment for his anxiety-induced head-shaking appears to be motivated by genuine concern (pp. 204–05).
34. Ibid., p. 209.
35. Ibid., pp. 209–10.
36. Ibid., p. 208.
37. Ibid., p. 207.

38. It is generically unconventional to see a judicial investigator depicted as a bad gambler: an over-indulgence in games of chance, especially when losing impacts upon professional conduct, is seen as being incommensurate with the obligations of the post.

39. Panov, *Iz zhizni uezdnogo gorodka*, p. 304.

40. Ibid., pp. 225–26.

41. Ibid., p. 230.

42. Ibid., p. 237.

43. There are notable similarities between Panov's depiction of this caricature-drawing episode and that which Anton Chekhov includes in his much later story 'Chelovek v futliare' ('Man in a Case') from 1898. In the Chekhov story, which describes life in a similarly dull provincial town, it is the drawing of a caricature entitled 'The Lovesick Anthropos', depicting Belikov riding a bicycle with Varvara Kovalenko, that prompts the downfall and death of the protagonist who cannot bear the thought of other people in the town laughing at him. It is not known whether Chekhov had read *From the Life of a Provincial Town*, but the similarities are striking.

44. Panov, *Iz zhizni uezdnogo gorodka*, p. 223.

45. Ibid., p. 252.

46. Ibid., p. 333.

47. Ibid., p. 250.

48. See Whitehead, 'Playing at Detectives'.

49. The story is not discussed in Peter M. Bitsilli's *Chekhov's Art: A Stylistic Analysis*, trans. by Toby W. Clyman and Edwina Jannie Cruise (Ann Arbor, MI: Ardis, 1983). Donald Rayfield does, however, briefly discuss the story in his *Understanding Chekhov* (London: Bristol Classical Press, 1999) and argues that it represents Chekhov's most successful pastiche of detective stories.

50. H. R. Jauss, *Towards an Aesthetic of Reception*, trans. by Timothy Bahti (Minneapolis, MN: University of Minnesota Press, 1982), p. 23.

51. See Reitblat, *Ot Bovy k Bal'montu*, p. 199.

52. See Timofeev's *Iz ugolovnoi khroniki* (*From the Judicial Chronicle*) from 1879, Telepnev's *Ubiistvo v Puzyrevskie baniakh: rasskaz iz ugolovnoi letopisi* (*Murder in the Puzyrevskie Baths: A Tale from the Judicial Chronicle*) (Saratov: Ishchenko, 1879) and various of Shkliarevskii's works, including *Ubiistvo bez sledov: rasskaz iz ugolovnoi khroniki* (*Murder Without Clues: A Tale from the Judicial Chronicle*) (St Petersburg: Obolenskii, 1878) and *Russkii Tichborn: iz ugolovnoi khroniki* (*Russian Tichborne: From the Judicial Chronicle*) (first publication unknown; St Petersburg: Suvorin, 1903).

53. The specific context of the announcement will be discussed in greater detail below.

54. A. P. Chekhov, 'Shvedskaia spichka', in *Polnoe sobranie sochinenii i pisem v tridtsati tomakh*, II (Moscow: Nauka, 1975), p. 201.

55. Ibid., p. 202.

56. Ibid.

57. Ibid.

58. Martina Björklund, 'On the Russian Agentive Passive', *Glossos*, 4 (2003), 1–18 (p. 8).

59. Chekhov, 'Shvedskaia spichka', p. 201.

60. Ibid., p. 203.

61. Ibid., p. 205.

62. Ibid., p. 201.

63. Ibid., p. 203.

64. Ibid.

65. Ibid., p. 211.

66. Ibid., p. 221.

67. The names of both the doctor and the district police officer who arrives with him, Artsybashev-Svistakovskii, implicitly suggest that they will be of no use to the investigation. 'Tiutiu' is colloquial Russian for 'gone very quickly' as is 'prosvistel', where the root 'svist' appears in the policeman's name.

68. Ibid., p. 205.

69. Ibid., p. 210.

70. Ibid., p. 202.

71. Ibid., p. 204.
72. The literal translation of the story's title is 'The Swedish Match', and indicates what, at the time of the story's publication, was a new development in smoking technology. As such, it would not, as Diukovskii surmises, have been the most common means of lighting a cigarette used in the rural setting of Chekhov's story.
73. Chekhov, 'Shvedskaia spichka', p. 210.
74. Ibid.
75. In *Language, Ideology and Point of View* (London: Routledge, 1993), Paul Simpson argues that epistemic modal adverbs are a key element in the system of modality in a language and that 'the epistemic system is possibly the most important regarding the analysis of point of view in fiction [because it] is concerned with the speaker's confidence or lack of confidence in the truth of a proposition expressed' (p. 48).
76. Chekhov, 'Shvedskaia spichka', p. 211.
77. Ibid., p. 215.
78. Ibid., p. 216.
79. See, for instance, Donald Rayfield, *Understanding Chekhov*.
80. Ibid., p. 19.
81. Chekhov, 'Shvedskaia spichka', p. 219.
82. Ibid., p. 201.
83. Porter, *The Pursuit of Crime*, p. 29.
84. Chekhov, 'Shvedskaia spichka', p. 208.
85. Locked-door mysteries are closely associated with the work of Edgar Allan Poe, especially 'The Murders in the Rue Morgue'.
86. Chekhov, 'Shvedskaia spichka', p. 204.

# CONCLUSION

The study has demonstrated that, from the earliest years of its existence in the 1860s, Russian crime fiction boasted a wealth of original and entertaining writing; and this previously little-known chapter in Russian literary history has generously repaid the interest shown in it. The analysis conducted here of *Crime and Punishment* and 'The Swedish Match' has provided further confirmation of the talents of Dostoevskii and Chekhov respectively. However, arguably the more important contribution to scholarship made by this research is the attention that has been devoted to the various other, relatively obscure authors who contributed to the genre in innovative ways and who deserve to have their reputations in contemporary literary studies enhanced. The stories by Timofeev and Shkliarevskii, and the novellas written by Panov, in particular, stand out for their enduring quality and for the scope they have offered for a productive narratological analysis. Timofeev's story 'Murder and Suicide' has sustained much discussion during this book, but others of his narratives, notably 'A Crime of Superstition' with its striking depiction of violence that inspires a sense of the abject, deserve to be discussed at greater length. Each of Panov's five works from the 1870s, but most especially *Murder in Medveditsa Village* and *Three Courts*, offer scope for further interrogation, not least from the point of view of gender studies and notions of performance and performativity as these relate to the criminal investigation. With respect to gender, although her *The Song Has Been Sung* has been discussed here, A. I. Sokolova wrote many other works of crime fiction that warrant further research. As was acknowledged at the outset, this examination of late Imperial-era Russian crime fiction had necessarily to be somewhat selective in the authors that it considered. There are other writers and other works of crime fiction, such as P. I. Telepnev's *Ubiistvo v Puzyrevskie baniakh: rasskaz iz ugolovnoi letopisi* (*Murder in the Puzyrevskie Baths: A Tale from the Criminal Chronicle*) (1879) and Ivan Ponomarev's *Peterburgskie pauki* (*Petersburg Spiders*) (1888) that have not been discussed here because of space constraints. It is hoped that this book will serve as an inspiration to other literary scholars to devote time to the analysis and popularization of works of crime fiction from this pre-revolutionary period.

With an eye to future work, it is abundantly evident from the works studied here that examples of Russian crime fiction from this early period would happily lend themselves to examination from a variety of other angles. For instance, whilst primarily focused on a narratological consideration of the devices employed in Russian detective fiction, this discussion has occasionally indicated the socio-historical significance that can be read into them; but a great deal more could be said in this regard. In its analysis of the construction of the authority of the detective in these early works, reference has been made to this figure as a surrogate priest. Substantially more work could be undertaken in the future on the intersections, for example, between early Russian crime fiction and the institution of the Church and the role of religion that are depicted in these texts. Similarly, the issue of the presentation of gender roles in crime fiction is one that, whilst potentially highly productive, has not been addressed here. The link between notions of masculinity and the figure of the detective as ideal imago is an area that would warrant further consideration, whilst the role of women as either statistically more frequent victims of crime or as instigators of the criminal transgression would undoubtedly prove to be a stimulating topic of discussion. As more and more of the primary texts from this period become more readily available thanks to reissue either in print or online, there is cause for optimism that the present book, like that of Louise McReynolds relatively recently, will act as a catalyst for other scholarly studies of the genre at this time.

It is important, however, not to lose sight of the significant results that have been achieved thanks to the narratologically focused reading of early Russian crime fiction conducted here. A consideration of the ways in which the very earliest works in the genre actively seek to blur the lines between fiction and non-fiction has not only allowed key devices associated with each mode of writing to be identified but has underscored points of resemblance between crime fiction and other related genres. The focus on the construction of authority in the opening chapter, but most particularly in Chapter 2, has provided further persuasive evidence about the centrally important role played by notions and images of power in the genre. Authority is not simply a function of characterization, either individual or relative, but is determined to a significant degree by the status and privilege of the narrative voice that is employed in works of crime fiction. Indeed, it comes as no surprise to understand that the role of the narrative voice, and the decisions pertaining to its performance that are made by the implied author, lies at the root of much of the effect that works of crime fiction create upon the reader. The second part of this study has highlighted, by means of its focus upon the effects of curiosity and suspense, how poetic devices can be harnessed in order to modulate the reader's access to knowledge. Simply put, what every reader of crime fiction wants when they begin to read a narrative and confront the mystery that is presented, is to uncover the missing information that will allow them (and the detective) to reconstruct a full and unambiguous story of the crime and its various circumstances. The various techniques related to multiple voice and temporal presentation (as well as to the manipulation of point of view) that have been discussed in Chapters 3 and 4, have clearly illustrated the contribution that these elements of construction make, on the one hand, to the fragmentation in the *siuzhet* of the truth of the crime in the *fabula*, and on the other, to the process of reconstruction that takes place over the course of the story. Not only does the discussion here use primary texts never previously discussed in such detail, but it also extends the analysis of these devices beyond the point where earlier critical analysis of crime fiction has ventured. There has been something of a tendency in crime fiction criticism since the 1980s to view the presence of elements of metatextuality and parody in the genre as features primarily associated with postmodern iterations of the genre. However, the third part of this book has clearly given the lie to that belief. Russian crime fiction from the late Imperial era clearly demonstrates a very keen awareness of its ludic potential, whilst often still associating the inclusion of intertextual and metatextual touches with the question of authority and legitimacy. Finally, although it is difficult to see them either as regenerative or as destructive, as theorists of the practice often seem to desire, the parodies produced by Panov and Chekhov have provided entertaining proof that those practising crime fiction in Russia in the nineteenth century were full aware of, and fully prepared to challenge, the conventions operating in the genre at an early stage.

The focus directed throughout this book upon the effect of particular poetic devices upon the experience of the reader has been intended to extend the reach of its conclusions beyond the boundaries of crime fiction. Although issues of authority and the provocation of curiosity and suspense can be seen to be acutely relevant to this genre, they are by no means uniquely so. Consider, for instance, the degree to which crime fiction throws into sharp focus the extent to which the question of authority and reliability is at the heart of almost everything that we read, as well as of various other cultural consumables. In the current post-truth age of fake news, the issue of authority and its negotiation is surely becoming more, rather than less, significant. The belief that reference to factual, lived experience proffers a greater legitimacy and authority to the text is also one that informs very many other literary genres and cultural media outside crime fiction. The examination of authority undertaken here has demonstrated the natural inclination readers feel towards hierarchizing the various voices encountered in the literary text and the extent to which the text responds or plays up to this desire. Moreover, we have seen how works of crime fiction have much to teach us about the nature of our expectations as readers in terms of what constitutes a properly plotted and satisfactorily resolved literary narrative. Whatever the fragmentation or obfuscation that is presented at the outset of a literary text, and whatever lessons postmodernism is supposed to have taught us about the fallacy of teleology, readers still overwhelmingly seek wholeness and clarity by the end of the narrative. A close examination of the various temporal structures employed in crime fiction makes clear the degree to which so many of a reader's judgements about characters and events in the fictional world are a consequence of the order, frequency and pace in, or at, which a narrative is constructed. However, none of these devices is unique to this genre: in every literary work, temporal anachronies can be employed to complicate and enrich the narrative experience of the reader. Equally, crime fiction is no different from any other literary genre with respect to the way in which it demonstrates an awareness of itself as a literary artefact constructed more than anything else by means of reference to similar literary artefacts. It is not even a feature exclusive to works of so-called popular literature that they feel the need to legitimize themselves by means of reference to supposedly more canonical forebears or by self-consciously interrogating the status of literature vis-à-vis other cultural forms. A careful study of crime fiction, arguably from any national tradition and any historical period, has an important contribution to make to the appreciation of the construction of any and all literary texts.

Even though this study has not had a chronological or teleological analysis of early Russian crime fiction as its main focus, it is nevertheless worth considering the historical legacy that the genre from this period bequeathed. Crucially, the significance of the narrative structures identified and discussed in this book is proven by the fact that notable commonalities of practice exist between the genre in this late Imperial era and in subsequent periods. So, for instance, although crime fiction was largely repressed during the early Soviet period under Stalin, with various publishing houses and journals closed down, and various works of so-called 'boulevard' literature removed from public libraries, the genre blossomed again during the relative liberalization of the Thaw period. During this time, the detective novel reappeared in Russia with the works of authors such as Iulian Semenov, Arkadii Adamov and the Vainer brothers proving to be hugely popular both in print and in various television adaptations. In spite of the obvious political and ideological differences between the Soviet period and the late nineteenth century, certain of the generic features developed in the earliest years of crime fiction in Russia remain in play in these later works. To take just one example, Semenov's short novel, *Petrovka 38*, first published in 1965, is devoted to a realistic depiction of the everyday life and intimacies of various 'ordinary' people, whether criminals or police detectives, and their various confrontations with a range of forms of authority as embodied in judicial institutions. In much the same way as in works from the 1860s and 1870s, there is implied discussion within Semenov's novel on the question of whether criminal activity should be considered to be an expression of individual free will or a phenomenon that is more collectively and socially determined. Members of the investigative team express their desire to combine professionalism with a healthy dose of empathy and humanity on various occasions, but especially with regard to the young perpetrator, Lionka, who has got himself drunkenly caught up in a crime. The work's story line is fragmented and refracted by means of the presentation of a number of different points of view and narrative voices that complicate the recounting of both the criminal and the investigative *fabula*. Much of its effect and stylization can be traced to the degree to which it represents the speech of the various characters directly in the text. *Petrovka 38* also proves to be a striking example of the ends to which the manipulation of temporal structures can be employed. Whilst the pace at the outset is rather sedate, in keeping with the preparation of the first murder, the latter stages of the novella are characterized by a sustained use of a much more frenetic rhythm as the cat-and-mouse game between criminals and detectives reaches its peak. Finally, Semenov's work expresses a notable degree of self-consciousness about the continual dialogue between literary presentations of popular fiction and other cultural forms, most especially in the case of *Petrovka 38* of Western fashion and film.

Moving even closer to the present day, it is apposite to note the debt that the work of Boris Akunin in the post-Soviet period owes to the development of crime fiction in its earliest years. More than any other writer of crime fiction in the post-1991 age, Akunin overtly references Russia's pre-twentieth-century history, not least by temporally locating the action of many of his novels in the relatively distant past. His Erast Fandorin novels span the late Imperial era, whilst his Sister Pelagiia trilogy is set in the final years of the nineteenth century; and this temporal location has prompted critics to talk of Akunin as referring back to a 'golden age' of Russian history. However, the links between Akunin's work and those actually produced in the late nineteenth century run much deeper. Most notably, his novels distinguish themselves in the contemporary literary scene by being steeped in both intertextual and metatextual references, used not only to legitimize but also to complicate the reader's access to knowledge. In the Sister Pelagiia novels in particular, Akunin adroitly combines questions of 'truth' and knowledge with the role of religion as elements within the Russian Orthodox Church are depicted as the wrongdoers at the same time as the protagonist nun struggles with doubts around her own faith. The choice of a nun as heroine not only reimagines and reconfigures many of the conventional gender roles developed over the earlier history of the genre, but also looks back to the time in the late Imperial era when much of the authority invested in the detective figure derived from his status as a surrogate priest. From a more purely socio-historical perspective, the institution of the Church is illustrated as being as corrupt and corrupting a phenomenon as the existence of serfdom and feudal rule in the late nineteenth century. In Akunin's trilogy, the use of multiple, and intersecting, timelines needs to be viewed not only as an instance of postmodern interrogation of teleological historical interpretation, but also, perhaps more simply, as a key tool in the modulation of curiosity and suspense, as has been demonstrated more than a century earlier by the work of Akhsharumov and Shkliarevskii. There can be no question that, given Akunin's novels' myriad references to works by Dostoevskii and Chekhov, most especially in the Pelagiia trilogy, this present-day master of the genre is fully aware of his status as a successor to these 'greats' in the realm not just of Russian literature, but of Russian crime fiction. However, what his novels very clearly prove is that the poetic devices employed by a whole raft of early Russian crime writers, not just the better known, continue to be relevant and effective tools in the creation of a mystery up to the present day.

# BIBLIOGRAPHY

## Primary Texts

AKHSHARUMOV, N. D. *Kontsy v vodu* (Moscow: Sovremennik, 1996; first published in *Otechestvennye zapiski*, X–XII, 1872)

ANTROPOV, R. L./DOBRYI, ROMAN, *Taina Sukharevoi bashni: detektivnye rasskazy* (Tashkent: Adolat, 1992), including: 'Potselui bronzovoi devy'

—— *Shef sysknoi politsii Sankt-Peterburga Ivan Dmitrievich Putilin (Sochineniia v dvukh tomakh)* (Moscow: Olma, 2003), including: 'Belye golubi i sizye gorlitsy', 'Ognennyi krest'

—— *Genii russkogo syska I. D. Putilin: rasskazy o ego pokhozhdeniiakh* (<http://www.royallib.com/read/dobriy_roman/geniy_russkogo_siska_id_putilin.html#o>)

A. P. CHEKHOV, *Polnoe sobranie sochinenii i pisem v tridsati tomakh, Pis'ma*, I (Moscow: Nauka, 1974)

—— *Pis'ma*, in *Polnoe sobranie sochinenii i pisem v tridsati tomakh,* I (Moscow: Nauka, 1974)

—— 'Shvedskaia spichka: ugolovnyi rasskaz', in *Polnoe sobranie sochinenii i pisem v tridtsati tomakh,* II (Moscow: Nauka, 1975; first published 1883)

—— *Drama na okhote: istinnoe proisshestvie*, in *Polnoe sobranie sochinenii i pisem v tridtsati tomakh,* III (Moscow: Nauka, 1975; first published 1884–85)

—— *The Shooting Party*, trans. by Ronald Wilks (London: Penguin, 2004)

COLLINS, WILKIE, *The Woman in White*, ed. by Matthew Sweet (London: Penguin, 2003; first published 1859)

—— *The Moonstone*, ed. by John Sutherland (Oxford: Oxford University Press, 1999; first published 1868)

CONAN DOYLE, ARTHUR, *The Complete Works of Arthur Conan Doyle*, ed. by Neil McCaw (Newcastle: Cambridge Scholars, 2009)

DOSTOEVSKII, F. M., *Zapiski iz mertvogo doma* (first published in *Vremia*, 2 (1860))

—— 'Protsess Lasenera', *Vremia*, 2 (1861)

—— 'Madam Lakost'', *Vremia*, 5 (1861)

—— 'Tainstvennoe ubiistvo: iz ugolovnykh del Frantsii 1840 goda', *Vremia*, 1 (1862)

—— 'Ubiitsy Peshara: Frantsuzskoe ugolovnoe delo 1857–58 g.', *Vremia*, 2 (1862)

—— *Prestuplenie i nakazanie*, in *Sobranie sochinenii v desiati tomakh*, V (Moscow: Khudozhestvennaia literatura, 1958; first published 1866)

—— *Crime and Punishment*, trans. by Oliver Ready (London: Penguin, 2014)

—— 'Sreda', in *Dnevnik pisatelia* (St Petersburg: Lenizdat, 1999; first published 1873)

—— *A Writer's Diary, Volume 1 1873–1876*, trans. by Kenneth Lantz (Evanston, IL: Northwestern University Press, 1997)

—— *Brat'ia Karamazovy*, in *Sobranie sochinenii v desiati tomakh*, IX (Moscow: Khudozhestvennaia literatura, 1958; first published 1880)

—— *The Brothers Karamazov*, trans. by David Magarshack (London: Penguin, 1982)

GABORIAU, ÉMILE, *L'Affaire Lerouge* (Paris: Dentu, 1880; first published 1865)

—— *Le Crime d'Orcival* (Paris: Les Editions français réunis, 1963; first published 1866–67)

GASPEY, THOMAS, *Richmond: or, Scenes in the Life of a Bow Street Officer, Drawn Up from His Private Memoranda* (London: Colburn, 1827)

GOGOL, N. V., *Sobranie sochinenii v shesti tomakh*, III (Moscow: Khudozhestvennaia literatura, 1952)

LACENAIRE, PIERRE FRANÇOIS, *Mémoires, poèmes et lettres* (Paris, Albin Michel: 1968; first published 1836)

ORLOVETS, P., *Prikliucheniia Sherloka Kholmsa protiv Nata Pinkertona v Rossii* (Salamandra P.V.V., 2011; originally published Moscow: Vilde, 1909), including: 'Taina Fontanki'

PANOV, S. A., *Ubiistvo v derevne Medveditse: iuridicheskaia povest'* (St Petersburg: Bazunov, 1872)

——*Pomoch': ocherk iz sel'skoi zhizni* (St Petersburg: Bazunov, 1872)

——*Ubiistvo v Mukhtolovoi roshche: rasskaz sudebnogo sledovatelia* (St Petersburg: Sokolov, 1876)

——*Tri suda, ili ubiistvo vo vremia bala: rasskaz sudebnogo sledovatelia v dvukh chastiakh* (St Petersburg: Skariatin, 1876)

——*Iz zhizni uezdnogo gorodka: iz zapisok sudebnogo sledovatelia* (St Petersburg: Skariatin, 1876)

POE, EDGAR ALLAN, *Selected Tales*, ed. by David Van Leer (Oxford: Oxford University Press, 2008), including: 'The Murders in the Rue Morgue' (first published 1841); 'The Mystery of Marie Rogêt' (first published 1842); 'The Purloined Letter' (first published 1844)

POPOV, K., *Vinovatye i pravye: rasskazy sudebnogo sledovatelia* (Salamandra P.V.V., 2013, <http://www.salamandrapvv.blogspot.co.uk/p/blog-page_87.html>; originally published Moscow: Mamontov, 1871), including: 'Konchina greshnitsy'

SHEVLIAKOV, M. V., *Iz oblasti prikliuchenii: po rasskazam byvshego nachal'nika Sankt-Peterburgskoi sysknoi politsii* (St Petersburg: Demakov, 1898)

SHKLIAREVSKII, A. A., *Povesti i rasskazy* (Moscow: Bakhmetev, 1872), including: 'Liudskoe uchastie'; 'Otchego on ubil ikh?: rasskaz sledovatelia'

——*Sochineniia A. Shkliarevskogo: Rasskazy sledovatelia* (St Petersburg: Trub, 1872), including: 'Kak liudi pogibaiut: rasskaz sledovatelia'; 'Rasskaz sudebnogo sledovatelia'

——*Rasskazy sudebnogo sledovatelia* (Moscow: Kudriavtsevaia, 1878); including: 'Semeinoe neschastie'

——*Utro posle bala & Neraskrytoe prestuplenie: rasskazy iz ugolovnoi khroniki* (Moscow: Kudriavtsevaia, 1878), including: 'Utro posle bala: rasskaz prisiazhnogo poverennogo'; 'Neraskrytoe prestuplenie: rasskaz sudebnogo sledovatelia'

——*Ubiistvo bez sledov: rasskaz iz ugolovnoi khroniki* (St. Petersburg: Obolenskii, 1878)

——*Novye rasskazy* (Moscow: Khlebnikov, 1880), including: 'Rokovaia sud'ba: rasskaz sledovatelia'

——*Russkii Tichborn: iz ugolovnoi khroniki* (first publication unknown; St Petersburg: Suvorin, 1903)

——*Chto pobudilo k ubiistvu? Rasskazy sledovatelia* (Moscow: Khudozhestvennaia literatura, 1993), including: 'Chto pobudilo k ubiistvu?: rasskaz sledovatelia'; 'Rasskaz sudebnogo sledovatelia'; 'Sekretnoe sledstvie'; 'Samoubiitsa li ona?'

SOKOLOVA, A. I., *Bez sleda: ugolovnyi roman*, Rodina, I (1890), pp. 1–148

——*Spetaia pesnia: iz zapisok starogo sledovatelia* (Moscow: Prosin, 1892)

SOKOLOVSKII, N. M., *Ostrog i zhizn': iz zapisok sledovatelia* (St Petersburg: Ovsiannikov, 1866), including: 'Skvernye minuty'; 'Myl'nye puzyri'; 'Nabolevshie'; 'Posledniaia stranitsa'; 'Diadia Foma'; 'Samoubiitsa'; 'Chapurin'; 'Trushkov'; 'Shamsheev'

STEPANOV, P. I., *Pravye i vinovatye: zapiski sledovatelia sorokovykh godov* (St Petersburg: Genkel', 1869), including: 'Uzdechka konokrada'; 'Podnevol'nyi brak'; 'Khoteli predat' sudu i vole Bozhiei'

TELEPNEV, P. I., *Ubiistvo v Puzyrevskykh baniakh: rasskaz iz ugolovnoi letopisi* (Saratov: Ishchenko, 1879)

TIMOFEEV, N. P., *Zapiski sledovatelia* (St Petersburg: Plotnikov, 1872), including: 'Pervye vpechatleniia'; 'Ubiistvo i samoubiistvo'; 'Podzhigateli'; 'Tiuremnyi mir'; 'Grabitel'skaia shaika'; 'Prestuplenie sueveriia'; 'Prostitutka'

——*Iz vospominanii sudebnogo sledovatelia: ocherki i rasskazy* (Moscow: Ioganson, 1878), including: 'Tri zhizni: rasskaz iz vospominanii sudebnogo sledovatelia'; 'Muzhniaia zhena: bytovoi ocherk iz vospominanii sudebnogo sledovatelia'; 'Katorga dushi: rasskaz iz vospominanii sudebnogo sledovatelia'; 'Nezakonnarozhdennaia: rasskaz iz vospominanii sudebnogo sledovatelia'

——*Iz ugolovnoi khroniki* (Moscow: Lavrov, 1879)

——*V pogone: na poiskakh za pokhishchennym rebenkom* (Moscow: Smirnov, 1880)

——*Otchego poezda kuvyrkaiutsia: zheleznodorozhnyi roman* (Moscow: Martynov, 1881)

——*Po nabliudeniiam v ugolovnom sude* (Moscow: Mamontov, 1881)

——*Sud prisiazhnykh v Rossii: sudebnye ocherki* (Moscow: Mamontov, 1881)

VIDOCQ, E.-F., *Mémoires de Vidocq, Chef de la Police de Sûreté, jusqu'en 1827, aujourd'hui propriétaire et fabricant de papiers à Saint-Mandé* (1828)

WATERS (Russell, William), *Recollections of a Police-Officer* (London: 1856; first published in *Chambers's Edinburgh Journal*, 1849–53)

ZARIN, A. E., *V poiskakh ubiitsy: romany, rasskazy* (Moscow: Sovremennik, 1995; first published 1915), contains: *V poiskakh ubiitsy* (1915); 'Chetvertyi: istoriia odnogo syska' (1909); 'Propavshii artel'shchik' (1909); 'Poteria chesti: tragicheskaia istoriia' (1909)

## Secondary Criticism

ALFARO, MARÍA JESÚS MARTÍNEZ, 'Intertextuality: Origins and Development of the Concept', *Atlantis*, 18.1–2 (1996), 268–85

AUSTIN, JOHN L., *How to do Things with Words* (Cambridge, MA: Harvard University Press, 1962)

AYDELOTTE, WILLIAM O., 'The Detective Story as a Historical Source', in *The Mystery Writer's Art*, ed. by Francis M. Nevins (Bowling Green, OH: Bowling Green University Popular Press, 1971), pp. 306–25

BAKHTIN, MIKHAIL, *The Dialogic Imagination*, trans. by Caryl Emerson and Michael Holquist (Austin, TX: University of Texas Press, 1981)

——*Problems of Dostoevsky's Poetics*, trans. by Caryl Emerson (Minneapolis, MN: University of Minnesota Press, 1984)

BAL, MIEKE, *Narratologie: Les instances du récit* (Paris: Klincksieck, 1977)

BELINSKII, VISSARION G., *Selected Philosophical Works* (Moscow: Foreign Languages Publishing House, 1948)

BELL, CATHERINE, *Ritual Theory, Ritual Practice* (Oxford: Oxford University Press, 1992)

BELSEY, CATHERINE, *Critical Practice* (London: Methuen, 1980)

BENNETT, DONNA, 'The Detective Story: Towards a Definition of Genre', *PTL: A Journal for Descriptive Poetics and the Theory of Literature*, 4 (1979), 233–66

BENSTOCK, SHARI, 'At the Margin of the Discourse: Footnotes in the Fictional Text', *PMLA*, 98.2 (1983), 204–25

BIELECKI, EMMA, 'Arsene Lupin: Rewriting History', in *Rewriting Wrongs: French Crime Fiction and the Palimpsest*, ed. by Angela Kimyongür and Amy Wigelsworth (Newcastle: Cambridge Scholars Publishing, 2014), pp. 47–61

BITSILLI, PETER M., *Chekhov's Art: A Stylistic Analysis*, trans. by Toby W. Clyman and Edwina Jannie Cruise (Ann Arbor, MI: Ardis, 1983)

BJÖRKLUND, MARTINA, 'On the Russian Agentive Passive', *Glossos*, 4 (2003), 1–18

BOOTH, WAYNE *The Rhetoric of Fiction* (Chicago, IL: University of Chicago Press, 1971)

BRIDGEMAN, TERESA, 'Time and Space', in *The Cambridge Companion to Narrative*, ed. by David Herman (Cambridge: Cambridge University Press), pp. 52–65

BROOKS, JEFFREY *When Russia Learned to Read: Literacy and Popular Literature, 1861–1917* (Evanston, IL: Northwestern University Press, 2003)

BROOKS, PETER, *Reading for the Plot: Design and Intention in Narrative* (New York, NY: Vintage, 1985)

BURNHAM, WILLIAM, 'The Legal Context and Contributions of Dostoevsky's *Crime and Punishment*', *Michigan Law Review*, 100.6 (2002), pp. 1227–48

BURRY, ALEXANDER, *Multi-Mediated Dostoevsky: Transposing Novels into Opera, Film, and Drama* (Evanston, IL: Northwestern University Press, 2011)

BURTON, STACY, 'Bakhtin, Temporality and Modern Narrative: Writing "The Whole Triumphant Murderous Unstoppable Chute"', *Comparative Literature*, 48.1 (1996), 39–62

CHARNEY, HANNA, *The Detective Novel of Manners: Hedonism, Morality, and the Life of Reason* (London and Toronto: Associated University Press, 1981)

CLAYTON, J. DOUGLAS, 'Soviet Views of Parody: Tynianov and Morozov', *Canadian-American Slavic Studies*, 7.4 (1973), 485–93

COHN, DORRIT, *The Distinction of Fiction* (Baltimore, MD: The Johns Hopkins University Press, 1999)

COPJEC, JOAN, 'The Phenomenal Nonphenomenal: Private Space in Film Noir', in *Shades of Noir: A Reader*, ed. by Joan Copjec (London & New York, NY: Verso, 1993), pp. 167–97

CORNWELL, NEIL, ed., *Reference Guide to Russian Literature* (London: Fitzroy Dearborn, 1998)

DAVIS, LENNARD J., *Factual Fictions: The Origins of the English Novel* (New York, NY: Columbia University Press, 1983)

DERRIDA, JACQUES, *Force de loi* (Paris: Galilée, 1994)

——*Acts of Religion*, ed. by Gil Anidjar (London: Routledge, 2002)

DOVE, GEORGE N., 'The Detection Formula and the Act of Reading', in *The Cunning Craft: Original Essays on Detective Fiction and Literary Theory*, ed. by Ronald G. Walker and June M. Frazer (Macomb, IL: Western Illinois University Press, 1990), pp. 25–37

DRALYUK, BORIS, *Western Crime Fiction Goes East: The Russian Pinkerton Craze, 1907–1934* (Leiden: Brill, 2012)

FANGER, DONALD, 'Dostoevsky's Early Feuilletons: Approaches to a Myth of the City', *Slavic Review*, 22:3 (1963), 469–82

FISH, STANLEY, 'Literature in the Reader: Affective Stylistics', in *Reader Response Criticism: From Formalism to Post Structuralism*, ed. by Jane P. Tompkins (Baltimore, MD: The John Hopkins University Press, 1980), pp. 70–100

FLUDERNIK, MONIKA, *An Introduction to Narratology* (London: Routledge, 2009)

FOGEL, AARON, *Coercion to Speak: Conrad's Poetics of Dialogue* (Cambridge, MA: Harvard University Press, 1985)

FOINITSKII, I. IA., 'Russkaia karatel'naia sistema', in *Sbornik gosudarstvennykh znanii*, ed. by V. P. Bezobrazov, 1 (St Petersburg, Kozanchikov: 1874)

FOLEY, BARBARA, *Telling the Truth: The Theory and Practice of Documentary Fiction* (Ithaca, NY: Cornell University Press, 1986)

FOUCAULT, MICHEL, *Discipline and Punish: The Birth of the Prison* (London: Penguin, 1991)

FRANK, JOSEPH, *Dostoevsky: The Stir of Liberation, 1860–1865* (Princeton, NJ: Princeton University Press, 1986)

FRANK, STEPHEN P., *Crime, Cultural Conflict and Justice in Rural Russia, 1856–1914* (Berkeley, CA: University of California Press, 1999)

GASCOIGNE, DAVID, *The Games of Fiction: Georges Perec and Modern French Ludic Narrative* (Oxford and Berlin: Peter Lang, 2006)

GENETTE, GÉRARD, *Figures III* (Paris: Seuil, 1972)
——*Narrative Discourse: An Essay in Method*, trans. by Jane E. Lewin (Ithaca, NY: Cornell University Press, 1980)
——*Palimpsests: Literature in the Second Degree*, trans. by C. Newman and C. Doubinsky (Lincoln, NE: University of Nebraska Press, 1997)
GINZBURG, LYDIA, *On Psychological Prose*, trans. and ed. by Judson Rosengrant (Princeton, NJ: Princeton University Press, 1991)
GROSSMAN, JOAN DELANEY, *Edgar Allan Poe in Russia: A Study in Legend and Literary Influence* (Wurzburg: JAL-Verlag, 1973)
HAYMAN, DAVID and ERIC RABKIN, *Form in Fiction: An Introduction to the Analysis of Narrative Prose* (New York, NY: St. Martin's Press, 1974)
HERMAN, DAVID, 'Dialogue in a Discourse Context: Scenes of Talk in Fictional Narrative', *Narrative Inquiry*, 16.1 (2006), 75–84
HERZOG, TODD, 'Crime Stories: Criminal, Society and the Modernist Case History', *Representations*, 80 (2002), 34–61
HOLMGREN, BETH, ed., *The Russian Memoir: History and Literature* (Evanston, IL: Northwestern University Press, 2003)
HÜHN, PETER, 'The Detective as Reader: Narrativity and Reading Concepts in Detective Fiction', *Modern Fiction Studies*, 33.3 (1987), 451–66
HUTCHEON, LINDA, *A Theory of Parody: The Teachings of Twentieth-century Art Forms* (New York and London: Methuen, 1985)
HUTTER, ALBERT D., 'Dreams, Transformations, and Literature: The Implications of Detective Fiction', in *The Poetics of Murder: Detective Fiction and Literary Theory*, ed. by Glenn W. Most and William M. Stowe (New York, NY: Harcourt Brace Jovanovich, 1983), pp. 230–51 [Originally published in *Victorian Studies*, 19.2 (1975), 181–209]
JAUSS, H. R., *Towards an Aesthetic of Reception*, trans. by Timothy Bahti (Minneapolis, MN: University of Minnesota Press, 1982)
JOHAE, ANTONY, 'Towards an Iconography of "Crime and Punishment"', in *Fyodor Dostoevsky's Crime and Punishment*, ed. by Harold Bloom (Philadelphia, PA: Chelsea House, 2003), pp. 243–56
KANEVSKAIA, MARIA, 'Struktura detektivnogo siuzheta v "Brat'ia Karamazovykh"', *Russkaia literatura deviatnadtsatogo veka*, 1 (2002), 46–63
KAYMAN, MARTIN A., 'The Short Story from Poe to Chesterton', in *The Cambridge Companion to Crime Fiction*, ed. by Martin Priestman (Cambridge: Cambridge University Press, 2003), pp. 41–58
KEILY, DAVID, '*The Brothers Karamazov* and the Fate of Russian Truth: Shifts in the Construction and Interpretation of Narrative after the Judicial Reform of 1864', unpublished PhD thesis, Harvard University, 1996
KELLY, R. GORDON, *Mystery Fiction and Modern Life* (Jackson, MS: University Press of Mississippi, 1998)
KEMP, SIMON, 'The Many-Layered Palimpsest: Metafiction, Genre Fiction and Georges Perec's *53 Jours*', in *Rewriting Wrongs: French Crime Fiction and the Palimpsest*, ed. by Angela Kimyongür and Amy Wigelsworth (Newcastle: Cambridge Scholars, 2014), pp. 163–73
KLIOUTCHKINE, KONSTANTINE, 'The Rise of *Crime and Punishment* from the Air of the Media', *Slavic Review*, 61.1 (2002), 88–108
KRISTEVA, JULIA, 'Word, Dialogue, and Novel', in *Desire in Language: A Semiotic Approach to Literature and Art* (New York, NY: Columbia University Press, 1980), pp. 64–91
KUTSCHEROFF, SAMUEL 'Administration of Justice under Nicholas I of Russia', *American Slavic and East European Review*, 7.2 (1948), 125–38
LANSER, SUSAN, *The Narrative Act* (Princeton, NJ: Princeton University Press, 1981)

——*Fictions of Authority: Women Writers and Narrative Voice* (Ithaca, NY: Cornell University Press, 1992)

LITS, MARC, *Le Roman policier: introduction à la théorie et à l'histoire d'un genre littéraire* (Liège: Editions du CÉFAL, 1993)

LOKHVITSKII, A., 'Sudebnye sledovateli', *Russkoe slovo*, 9 (1860), 1–21

LOVELL, STEPHEN, 'Looking at Listening in Late Imperial Russia', *The Russian Review*, 72.4 (2013), 551–55

LOVITT, CARL R., 'Controlling Discourse in Detective Fiction, or Caring Very Much Who Killed Roger Ackroyd', in *The Cunning Craft*, ed. by Walker and Frazer (Macomb, IL.: Western Illinois University Press, 1990), pp. 68–85

MACDONALD, JANICE, 'Parody and Detective Fiction', in *Theory and Practice of Classic Detective Fiction*, ed. by Jerome Delamater and Ruth Prigozy (Westport, CT; Greenwood, 1997), pp. 61–72

MACLACHLAN, GALE, 'Detectives and Criminals as Players in "Le Théâtre du crime": A Reading of Émile Gaboriau's *Le Crime d'Orcival*', in *Telling Performances: Essays on Gender, Narrative, and Performance*, ed. by Brian Nelson, Anne Freadman and Philip Anderson (Newark, NJ: University of Delaware Press, 2001), pp. 39–54

MALMGREN, CARL D., 'Anatomy of Murder: Mystery, Detective and Crime Fiction', *Journal of Popular Culture*, 30.4 (1997), 115–35

MARCUS, LAURA, 'Detection and Literary Fiction', in *The Cambridge Companion to Crime Fiction*, ed. by Martin Priestman (Cambridge: Cambridge University Press, 2003), pp. 245–67

MARTIN, ANDREW, 'Top 10: The Best Dialogue in Crime Fiction', <http://www.theguardian.com/books/2015/nov/25/top-10-crime-fiction-dialogue-agatha-christie-chandler-amis>[accessed 15 December 16.]

MCREYNOLDS, LOUISE, *Murder Most Russian: True Crime and Punishment in Late Imperial Russia* (Ithaca, NY: Cornell University Press, 2013)

——'"Who Cares who Killed Ivan Ivanovich?": The Literary Detective in Tsarist Russia', *Russian History*, 36 (2009), 391–406

MERIVALE, PATRICIA and SUSAN E. SWEENEY, eds, *Detecting Texts: The Metaphysical Detective Story from Poe to Postmodernism* (Philadelphia: University of Pennsylvania Press, 1999)

MESSAC, RÉGIS, *Le Detective-Novel et l'influence de la pensée scientifique* (Paris: Slatkine Reprints, 1975)

MORSON, GARY SAUL, *The Boundaries of Genre: Dostoevsky's Diary of a Writer and the Traditions of Literary Utopia* (Evanston, IL: Northwestern University Press, 1988)

——*Narrative and Freedom: The Shadows of Time* (New Haven, CT: Yale University Press, 1994)

MURAV, HARRIET, *Russia's Legal Fictions* (Ann Arbor, MI: University of Michigan Press, 1998)

NÜNNING, ANSGAR, 'On Metanarrative: Towards a Definition, a Typology and an Outline of the Functions of Metanarrative Commentary', in *The Dynamics of Narrative Form: Studies in Anglo-American Narratology*, ed. by John Pier (Berlin and New York, NY: de Gruyter, 2004), pp. 11–57

OELER, KARLA, 'The Dead Wives in the Dead House: Narrative Inconsistency and Genre Confusion in Dostoevskii's Autobiographical Prison Novel', *Slavic Review*, 61.3 (2002), 519–34

OLCOTT, ANTONY *Russian Pulp: The Detektiv and the Russian Way of Crime* (New York and Oxford: Rowman & Littlefield, 2001)

OUSBY, IAN, *Bloodhounds of Heaven: The Detective in English Fiction From Godwin to Doyle* (Cambridge, MA: Harvard University Press, 1976)

OWEN, KATHLEEN BELIN, '"The Game's Afoot": Predecessors and Pursuits of a Postmodern Detective Novel', in *Theory and Practice of Classic Detective Fiction*, ed. by Jerome Delamater and Ruth Prigozy (Westport, CT; Greenwood, 1997), pp. 73–84

PARAVISINI, LIZABETH and CARLOS YORIO, 'Is It Or Isn't It? The Duality of Parodic Detective Fiction', in *Comic Crime*, ed. by Earl Bargainnier (Bowling Green, OH: Bowling Green Popular Press, 1987), pp. 181–93

PARRETT, AARON, 'The Medical Detective and the Victorian Fear of Degeneration', in *Formal Investigations: Aesthetic Style in Late-Victorian and Edwardian Detective Fiction*, ed. by Paul Fox and Koray Melikoğlu (Stuttgart: ibidem, 2007), pp. 97–114

PORTER, DENNIS, *The Pursuit of Crime: Art and Ideology in Detective Fiction* (New Haven, CT: Yale University Press, 1981)

PRCHAL, TIMOTHY R., 'An Ideal Helpmate: The Detective Character as (Fictional) Object and Ideal Imago', in *Theory and Practice of Classic Detective Fiction*, ed. by Jerome Delamater and Ruth Prigozy (Westport, CT: Greenwood, 1997), pp. 29–37

PRIESTMAN, MARTIN, *Detective Fiction and Literature: The Figure in the Carpet* (Basingstoke: Macmillan, 1990)

PRIESTMAN, MARTIN, ed., *The Cambridge Companion to Crime Fiction* (Cambridge: Cambridge University Press, 2003)

RACHMAN, STEPHEN, 'Poe and the Origins of Detective Fiction', in *The Cambridge Companion to American Crime Fiction*, ed. by Catherine Ross Nickerson (Cambridge: Cambridge University Press, 2010), pp. 17–28

RAYFIELD, DONALD, *Understanding Chekhov* (London: Bristol Classical Press, 1999)

REITBLAT, A. I., '«Russkii Gaboriau» ili uchenik Dostoevskogo?', in *Chto pobudilo k ubiistvu?: Rasskazy sledovatelia*, ed. by A. I. Reitblat (Moscow: Khudozhestvennaia literatura, 1993), pp. 5–13

—— 'Detektivnaia literatura i russkii chitatel', in *Knizhnoe delo v Rossii vo vtoroi polovine XIX–nachale XX veka*, no. 7 (1994), 126–40

—— *Ot Bovy k Bal'montu i drugie raboty po istoricheskoi sotsiologii russkoi literatury* (Moscow: Novoe literaturnoe obozrenie, 2009)

RONNER, AMY, *Dostoevsky and the Law* (Durham, NC: Carolina Academic Press, 2015)

ROSENHEIM, SHAWN JAMES, *The Cryptographic Imagination: Secret Writing from Edgar Poe to the Internet* (Baltimore, MD and London: The Johns Hopkins University Press, 1997)

ROTH, MARTY *Foul and Fair Play: Reading Genre in Classic Detective Fiction* (Athens, GA: University of Georgia Press, 1995)

SALZANI, CARLO, 'The City as Crime Scene: Walter Benjamin and the Traces of the Detective', *New German Critique*, 100, Vol.34:1 (2007), 165–87

SCHOLES, ROBERT and ROBERT KELLOGG, *The Nature of Narrative* (New York, NY: Oxford University Press, 1966)

SCHUR, ANNA, 'The Limits of Listening: Particularity, Compassion and Dostoevsky's "Bookish Humaneness"', *The Russian Review*, 72.4 (2013), 573–89

SCHÜTT, SITA A., 'French Crime Fiction', in *The Cambridge Companion to Crime Fiction*, ed. by Martin Priestman (Cambridge: Cambridge University Press, 2003), pp. 59–76

SEARLE, JOHN R., 'How Performatives Work', *Linguistics and Philosophy*, 12 (1989), 535–58

SEGAL, EYAL, 'Closure in Detective Fiction', *Poetics Today*, 31.2 (2010), 153–215

SHKLOVSKII, VIKTOR, *Theory of Prose*, trans. by Benjamin Sher (Normal, IL: Dalkey Archive Press, 1991)

SHPAYER-MAKOV, HAIA, 'Explaining the Rise and Success of Detective Memoirs in Britain', in *Police Detectives in History, 1750–1950*, ed. by Clive Emsley and Haia Shpayer-Makov (Aldershot: Ashgate, 2006), pp. 103–33

SHUVALOVA, V. A., 'O sushchnosti sudebnoi reformy 1864g. v Rossii', *Sovetskoe gosurdarstvo i pravo*, 10 (1964), 121–27

SIMPSON, PAUL, *Language, Ideology and Point of View* (London: Routledge, 1993)

SOBOLEV, OLGA 'Boris Akunin and the Rise of the Russian Detective Genre', *Australian Slavonic and East European Studies*, 18.1–2 (2004), 63–85

STERNBERG, MEIR, *Expositional Modes and Temporal Ordering in Fiction* (Baltimore, MD: The Johns Hopkins University Press, 1978)

——'Telling in Time (II): Chronology, Teleology, Narrativity', *Poetics Today*, 13.3 (1992), 463–541

STILL, JUDITH and MICHAEL WORTON, 'Introduction', in Still and Worton, *Intertextuality: Theories and Practices* (Manchester: Manchester University Press, 1990), pp. 1–44

SWEENEY, S. E., 'Locked Rooms: Detective Fiction, Narrative Theory, and Self-Reflexivity', in *The Cunning Craft: Original Essays on Detective Fiction and Literary Theory*, ed. by Ronald G. Walker and June M. Frazer (Macomb, IL: Western Illinois University Press, 1990), pp. 1–14

——'Purloined Letters: Poe, Doyle, Nabokov', *Russian Literature Triquarterly*, 24 (1991), 213–37

SYMONS, JULIAN, *Bloody Murder: from the detective story to the crime novel: a history* (London: Pan Books, 1994; first published 1972)

TERRAS, VICTOR (ed.), *Handbook of Russian Literature* (New Haven, CT: Yale University Press, 1985)

THOMAS, BRONWEN, 'Dialogue', in *The Cambridge Companion to Narrative*, ed. by David Herman (Cambridge: Cambridge University Press, 2007), pp. 80–93

——*Fictional Dialogue: Speech and Conversation in the Modern and Postmodern Novel* (Lincoln, NE: University of Nebraska Press, 2012)

THOMAS, RONALD R., 'The Fingerprint of the Foreigner: Colonizing the Criminal Body in 1890s Detective Fiction and Criminal Anthropology', *English Literary History*, 61.3 (1994), 655–83

THOMPSON, DIANE OENNING, *The Brothers Karamazov and the Poetics of Memory* (Cambridge: Cambridge University Press, 1991)

THOMS, PETER, *Detection and its Designs: Narrative and Power in Nineteenth-Century Detective Fiction* (Athens, OH: Ohio University Press, 1998)

TODOROV, TZVETAN, *Poétique de la prose* (Paris: Seuil, 1971)

——*The Poetics of Prose*, trans. by Richard Howard (Ithaca, NY: Cornell University Press, 1977)

TYNIANOV, IU. N., *Poetika, istoriia literatury, kino* (Moscow: Nauka, 1977)

VASSENA, RAFFAELLA, *Reawakening National Identity: Dostoevskii's Diary of a Writer and its Impact on Russian Society* (Bern: Peter Lang, 2007)

VOIGTS-VIRCHOW, ECKART, *Introduction to Media Studies* (Stuttgart: Klett Sprachen, 2005)

WEISBERG, RICHARD, *The Failure of the Word: The Protagonist as Lawyer in Modern Fiction* (New Haven, CT: Yale University Press, 1984)

WHITEHEAD, CLAIRE, 'Playing at Detectives: Parody in *The Swedish Match*', *Essays in Poetics*, 30 (2005), 229–46

——'The Letter of the Law: Literacy and Orality in S. A. Panov's *Murder in Medveditsa Village*', *Slavonic and East European Review*, 89.1 (2011), 1–28

——'Debating Detectives: The Influence of *publitsistika* on Nineteenth-Century Russian Crime Fiction', *Modern Language Review*, 107.1 (2012), 230–58

——'Shkliarevskii and Russian Detective Fiction: The Influence of Dostoevskii', in *Dostoevskii: Influence, Comparison and Transposition*, ed. by Joe Andrew and Robert Reid (Amsterdam: Rodopi, 2013), pp. 101–21

——'The Temptation of the Reader: The Search for Meaning in Boris Akunin's *Pelagia* Trilogy', *Slavonic and East European Review*, 94.1 (2016), 29–56

WORTMAN, RICHARD, *The Development of a Russian Legal Consciousness* (Chicago, IL: Chicago University Press, 1976)

WORTON, MICHAEL and JUDITH STILL, *Intertextuality: Theories and Practices* (Manchester: Manchester University Press, 1990)

YOUNG, SARAH J., 'Fyodor Dostoevsky (1821–1881): "Fantastic Realism"', in *The Cambridge Companion to European Novelists*, ed. by Michael Bell (Cambridge: Cambridge University Press, 2012), pp. 259–76

# INDEX

Lightning Source UK Ltd.
Milton Keynes UK
UKHW031833100121
376733UK00005B/358

9 781781 886885